Inside the *Apparat*

Inside the *Apparat*

Perspectives on the Soviet System
From Former Functionaries

Edited by

Uri Ra'anan

Igor Lukes

Lexington Books
D.C. Heath and Company/Lexington, Massachusetts/Toronto

Library of Congress Cataloging-in-Publication Data

Ra'anan, Uri, 1926–
   Inside the apparat : perspectives on the Soviet system from former functionaries / Uri Ra'anan, Igor Lukes.
     p.   cm.
   Includes bibliographical references.
   ISBN 0–669–21985–1 (alk. paper), — ISBN 0–669–24226–8 (pbk. : alk. paper)
     1.   Soviet Union—Politics and government—1917– —Decision making.
   2.   Soviet Union—Foreign relations—1917– —Decision making.
   3.   Kommunisticheskaia partiia Sovetskogo Soiuza—Decision making.
   4.   Defectors—Soviet Union—Interviews. I.   Lukes, Igor.
   II. Title.
   JN6529.D4R33   1990
   354.4707'25—dc20   89–13451
                                                 CIP

Grateful acknowledgment is made to the International Security Studies Program, Fletcher School of Law & Diplomacy, Tufts University, for permission to draw upon its copyrighted Oral History depository.

Published simultaneously in Canada
Printed in the United States of America
Casebound International Standard Book Number: 0–669–21985–1
Paperbound International Standard Book Number: 0–669–24226–8
Library of Congress Catalog Card Number: 89–13451

The paper used in this publication meets
the minimum requirements of American National Standard
for Information Sciences—Permanence of Paper
for Printed Library Materials, ANSI Z39.48–1948. ∞™

Year and printing of this book.

90 91 92 8 7 6 5 4 3 2 1

Contents

Abbreviations

AAPSO	Afro-Asian People's Solidarity Organization
ABM	Anti-Ballistic Missile (Treaty), signed by the US and USSR in May 1972
ANC	African National Congress; formed in 1912 as a black nationalist movement within South Africa
BBC	British Broadcasting Corporation
BOR	Office of the Protection of the Government in Poland
CC	Central Committee of the Communist Party
CI	Counterintelligence
CIA	Central Intelligence Agency
COPWE	Commission of the Progressive Workers of Ethiopia
CP	Communist Party
CPSU	Communist Party of the Soviet Union
DAO	Department of Administrative Organs, CC CPSU
DCA	Department of Cadres Abroad, CC CPSU
DGI	General Directorate of Security, the Cuban state security apparatus
DOE	Cuban Department of Special Operations
DPEP	Department of Propaganda and Political Education; Sandinista internal propaganda agency
DS	*Darzhavna Sigurnost;* Bulgarian State Security
ETA	Basque Homeland and Liberty; a Basque terrorist organization
FMLN	Farabundo Marti National Liberation Front, the umbrella organization containing the five Salvadoran guerilla factions
FNLA	Angolan National Liberation Front
FRELIMO	Front for the Liberation of Mozambique, a Marxist-Leninist movement, the vanguard ruling party in Mozambique

FRG   Federal Republic of Germany

FSLN   The Sandinista National Liberation Front, the governing party of Nicaragua

GKS   State Committee for Foreign Economic Relations, USSR Council of Ministers

GPP   Prolonged Popular War, one of the three Sandinista factions

GRU   *Glavnoye Razvedatelnoye Upravlenie;* Soviet Military Intelligence

IA   Institute of Africa, USSR Academy of Sciences

ID   International Department, CC CPSU

IID   International Information Department, CC CPSU; no longer in existence

ILA   Institute of Latin America, USSR Academy of Sciences

IMEiMO   Institute of World Economics and International Relations, USSR Academy of Sciences

IOJ   International Organization of Journalists

IOS   Institute of Oriental Studies, USSR Academy of Sciences

IRA   Irish Republican Army, terrorist organization

IUSA   Institute for the Study of the USA; after 1974, Institute for the Study of the USA and Canada, USSR Academy of Sciences

KGB   *Komitet Gosudarstvennoy Oborony;* Soviet Committee of State Security

KOK   *Komitet Obrony Kraju;* the Polish State Defense Council

KSC   *Komunisticka Strana Ceskoslovenska;* the Czechoslovak Communist Party

MFA   Ministry of Foreign Affairs, USSR Council of Ministers

MGB   USSR Ministry of State Security, predecessor of present-day KGB

MPLA   Popular Movement for the Liberation of Angola. Victorious Soviet- and Cuban-supported faction in the three-way struggle for power in Angola led by Agostinho Neto; renamed MPLA-Party of Labor (MPLA-PT); currently led by José Eduardo dos Santos

MVD   Soviet Ministry of Internal Affairs

NATO   North Atlantic Treaty Organization

NKVD   The Soviet People's Commissariat for Internal Affairs; after 1946, the Ministry of Internal Affairs (MVD)

NKGB   The former Soviet People's Commissariat of State Security, the present-day KGB

OGPU	Former name of the KGB
OPEROD	The Operations Department of the Soviet Guards Directorate. Officially an offshoot of the OGPU, its function was to guard party and government leaders. Its main duty was to guard Stalin
PAIGC	African Party for the Independence of Guinea-Bissau and Cape Verde, national liberation movement turned Marxist-Leninist. Ruling party in Guinea-Bissau and Cape Verde
PCC	Party Control Commission of the CPSU
PDPA	People's Democratic Party of Afghanistan, the ruling pro-Soviet organization
PLO	Palestinian Liberation Organization; umbrella organization of Palestinian factions; formed in 1964; the main governing body is the Palestine National Council; chaired by Yasser Arafat
PRC	People's Republic of China
PUWP	Polish United Workers' Party
PVO	Soviet anti-air defense
PZPR	*Polska Zjednoczona Partia Robotnicza;* see PUWP
RSFSR	Russian Soviet Federated Socialist Republic, one of the 15 Union Republics of the USSR
SALT	Strategic Arms Limitation Talks
SAM	Surface-to-Air Missiles
SDC	Soviet State Defense Committee, GKO (*Gosudarstvennoy Komitet Oborony*)
SMERSH	*Smert Shpionam,* Soviet military counterespionage organization
StB	*Statni Bezpecnost;* Czechoslovak state security
SWAPO	South-West African People's Organization; formed in 1960 and one of the forty-five political parties in Namibia
UJ	Union of Journalists, Soviet component of the IOJ
VOA	Voice of America, U.S. government broadcasting service
VPK	Military-Industrial Commission, USSR Council of Ministers
WPC	World Peace Council; a Soviet-sponsored organization which has in the past taken a leading role in many "front" programs and activities
WPE	Ruling party of Ethiopia
WSW	Polish military counter-intelligence service
ZANU	Zimbabwe African National Union, formerly Chinese-backed, led by Robert Mugabe

ZAPU   Zimbabwe African Peoples Union. Soviet-backed national
            liberation movement led by Joshua Nkomo; lost in Rhodesian
            power struggle to ZANU

Z-2   *Zarzad-2;* Polish military intelligence, the Second Bureau

ZS   *Zpravodajska sprava;* Czechoslovak military intelligence

Preface

Perhaps never, and certainly not since the early days of Khrushchev's ascendancy, has there been such a spate of developments in the USSR and Eastern Europe as during the last four years. Almost all of the analyses and appraisals, by the media and by governments, have attempted to assess the degree of change in Soviet decision making and to question whether that process is irreversible. To arrive at a meaningful evaluation, however, a firm foundation of knowledge is required of the nature of the *apparat* during the pre-Gorbachev period, the manner in which it functioned, and whether, in fact, current developments have affected it.

Even then, comparisons would be difficult to make, if only because structural changes have not been unilinear, but rather of an improvisatory nature, including successive edicts that are often mutually incompatible or create entities with identical or overlapping jurisdictions. Moreover, correlations are particularly hard to establish when one is dealing with two independent variables. Not only are current developments opaque, but surprisingly little knowledge has been extracted about the modus operandi of the *apparat* during the preceding years.

One reason for this failure has to do with inadequate utilization of the sources of knowledge that are available. While the traditional tools of Sovietology have been employed with greater or lesser success, far too little advantage has been taken of the human resources at our disposal. The reference, of course, is to the availability of former senior officials from the USSR, and its allied and client states. The fact that most of them predate the advent of the Gorbachev period does not constitute a serious drawback. Collectively, they are capable of providing detailed insights into the various portions of the *apparat* in which they served. Their utilization can result in a multidimensional picture of the decision-making machinery in a closed society.

Such insights are essential not merely for comparative purposes, but because there is every reason to believe that, to a major extent, the *apparat* continues to function along the lines described by former Soviet and East European officials—Gorbachev's dramatic gestures notwithstanding. The revelations derived from oral history tapings of interviews with such officials demonstrate the deep roots taken by the Soviet bureaucracy and give insight into its particular manner of handling affairs of state. In analyzing the nature of the *apparat,* it becomes apparent why its radical transformation or even a significant weakening of its pervasive presence has to be considered unrealistic. Indeed, four years into Gorbachev's administration, his failure to make a serious dent in the armor of bureaucracy is evident.

Consequently, a work based on oral history interviews with "defectors" and senior émigrés, albeit most of them left the USSR before 1985, portrays not merely the past, but a phenomenon that continues to be with us to this very moment and is likely to persist.

Moreover, the depiction in the book of individual career patterns, including promotion and demotion, concerns persons who make up the core of the Soviet bureaucracy right now, since many of them were just beginning to ascend the professional ladder precisely at the time on which many of the interviews focus.

In attempting to shed light upon the Soviet bureaucracy's decision-making process, with particular emphasis on foreign affairs and defense, this book, as a product of the oral history project, may provide a solid foundation for assessing the events of the Gorbachev period, and for revealing the modus operandi of an *apparat* that does not appear to have changed its way to any meaningful extent. An understanding of this phenomenon is essential, particularly because, as a result of widespread fascination with Gorbachev personally, so many publications have focused primarily upon him, thereby failing to produce a truly three-dimensional picture of the manner in which the system functions.

Acknowledgments

The oral history project that provides the basis for this book was implemented over a six-year period by the Fletcher School's International Security Studies Program (ISSP). The interviews were conducted by Professors Richard H. Shultz and Robert L. Pfaltzgraff, Jr., by the authors/editors (hereafter referred to as editors) of this volume, and by a team of outstanding graduates, ably led by Mr. Steven Adragna. The documentary material that resulted from the project is now on deposit at the Fletcher School, which has copyright, and is available to the scholarly community. The permission given by Fletcher's ISSP to draw upon that material for publication in this work is gratefully acknowledged.

The oral history project was made possible by two triennial grants from the J. Howard Pew Freedom Trust to Fletcher's International Security Studies Program. Of necessity, this book contains but a small percentage of the material accumulated in the course of the project. Consequently, the editors faced difficult choices with regard to the selection of appropriate excerpts; moreover, given substantial overlap of substance both between interviews and within interviews, the organization of material proved to be a Herculean task. To provide perspective, however, it should be realized that following publication of this book and a companion volume on decision making in Western societies—edited by Professors Robert L. Pfaltzgraff, Jr. and Richard H. Shultz, as well as by Dr. Jacquelyn K. Davis, with the assistance of Mr. Steven Adragna—all the oral history material will be stored on microfilm for the convenience of future researchers.

In addition to these colleagues, the editors wish to express their appreciation to the following contributors:

Kate Martin, who rode herd upon editors whose discipline did not always live up to her standards and who managed the whole team with a smile. James Shannon Robbins, for the many hours spent patiently compiling sets of material, only to find that much of this work had to be redone—sometimes even four or five times—as the editors kept refining the product. Also the other members of the team: Jeffrey Miller, a member of a generation that can control computers rather than being controlled by them; Yesim Cilesiz, who dealt with pressure in her customary courteous and competent manner; and Sandra Medeiros, whose enthusiasm is infectious. The editors appreciate also the work done by Ruth Shaver in coping with the voluminous manuscript.

Above all, the editors and the team as a whole wish to express their gratitude to the leadership of Boston University, which chartered the Institute for the Study of Conflict, Ideology & Policy, and to whose ever-present support and generosity the Institute's faculty owes this and so many other products of its labor. The unfailing assistance provided by the Sarah Scaife Foundation, Inc., has fueled the Institute's ongoing activities and been a source of constant encouragement; a challenge grant from the Arthur Vining Davis Foundations has proven to be a catalyst for other awards as well as a significant source of funds; and the Earhart Foundation has enabled the Institute to bring research fellows on board. The members of the Institute deeply appreciate the magnanimous support they have received.

Introduction

In preclassical civilizations, memory was preserved and passed on to future generations by means of oral history. Direct participants shared their impressions and knowledge of important events with their contemporaries and heirs. It may be presumed that the purpose of such communication was twofold: to remember and to learn. Gradually, historians began employing considerably more sophisticated and multifaceted tools of historical description, and oral history became but one of many approaches.

In the contemporary period, open societies reveal enormous amounts of information about themselves. Archives and libraries are constantly expanding to store all the data becoming available to the public and to professional historians who wish to study almost any aspect of public life in the West, not to mention material made accessible under the Freedom of Information Act. By definition, this is not the case with closed societies, such as the Soviet Union, its allies, and clients. Despite recent developments, it remains unlikely that their archives will be opened completely to Western researchers wishing to analyze primary sources concerning the Central Committee of the CPSU (Communist Party of the Soviet Union) or the Czechoslovak Foreign Ministry. Therefore, the editors of this volume decided to view the modus operandi of the Soviet (and Soviet-style) *apparat* through the prism of oral history.

Why add oral history to other, time-honored methods of analysis of the Soviet and Soviet-style political systems? Notwithstanding recent dramatic initiatives by Mikhail Gorbachev which have unleashed a veritable flood of information to Moscow-watchers, the Soviet Union continues to be a state controlled by a large, bureaucratic *apparat* under the command of a small number of men working in the Kremlin. Exactly how this group operates, how it is structured, and who has the power to make what decisions are topics on which little light has been shed under *glasnost;* correspondingly, these subjects have not been studied adequately in the West.

An additional reason for the absence of appropriate Western analysis, is that decision-making at the apex of the Soviet power pyramid must be viewed as a process which remains complex and is in a constant state of flux. The structure is complex primarily because there is a large degree of overlapping, some of it intentional, between various institutional jurisdictions with ill-defined boundaries. Indeed, there are areas of the system which fall simultaneously under the (often conflicting) competences of two or more powerful institutions.

The Main Political Administration (MPA) of the Soviet armed forces comes to mind as an example of this phenomenon: officially under the Soviet Ministry of Defense, it is actually a Department of the CPSU Central Committee, with the KGB, in addition to the GRU (Soviet military intelligence) actively seeking to influence its work. In East European countries, such as Poland and Czechoslovakia, the MPA's position in the *apparat* is defined even less clearly because, in addition to the domestic structures of governance, there are also official and unofficial communication links with the Soviet party, government, military, and intelligence organs which exercise control through these transmission belts. The resulting web of power interests is complex and significantly at variance with the formal decision-making system the structure of which can be found in official Soviet and East European handbooks on government.

Moreover, the Soviet power structure continues to change kaleidoscopically. This is mainly due to the fact that personalities seem to matter more than institutional affiliations and loyalties. The interviewees quoted in this book asserted repeatedly that the degree to which an individual can raise the importance of his office within the *apparat* is incomparably greater than is the case in open societies. Consequently, there is a gap between the formal institutional structure and the actual, de facto, decision-making hierarchy.

Given such limitations, it is hardly surprising that so far relatively few scholarly studies of the Soviet Union have penetrated its façade and revealed aspects of the ongoing contest for power. Of course, there are exceptions. The outstanding works by Merle Fainsod, Robert Conquest, Leonard Schapiro, and Michel Tatu, to name a few, in various ways demonstrated to the Sovietological community how much could be ascertained by determined and sophisticated analysts, relying primarily upon sources in the public domain.

The present work belongs to a different category, attempting to examine the functioning of the decision-making *apparat* in the USSR and its clients, as revealed by former high-ranking officials from the party, governmental, military and security sectors in the Soviet Union, Eastern Europe, Cuba, Ethiopia, Nicaragua and Afghanistan. In interviewing these personalities, answers were sought to questions surprisingly ignored by the international relations and defense community, perhaps because certain aspects of the Soviet system have been taken for granted. What is the real focus of power in the Soviet Union? Just how do the Politburo, the Central Committee Secretariat, the Council of Ministers, and the State Defense Council function and interact? Who determines their agendas? Is the general secretary in an unchallenging position to monopolize certain aspects of the decision-making process? What role belongs to the CPSU Central Committee *apparat,* that is, the "non-elected" Secretariat, with its departments and sections? What standing do the personal chanceries of individual Politburo members have? How do the arms of the Soviet power system communicate internally? What are the transmission belts that enable Soviet military and political influence to play its role in the capitals of the USSR's East European allies and Third World clients?

While engaged in this project, the editors were only conscious of the hidden shoals and consequent problems menacing the unwary in any endeavor based exclusively on an oral-history approach. This method in vacuo cannot hope to elicit the complexities of the Soviet system. Consequently, the editors and their colleagues conducted interviews only after (or in the context of) painstaking and disciplined textual analysis of Soviet publications and pictorial evidence, detailed examination of biographical data, and (wherever relevant) study of statistical trends, and material in the public domain obtained through national technical means. The editors realize that the oral history approach must be applied in combination with these basic features of Sovietology. Together they can help to refute the pessimistic assumption that Soviet-style closed societies are, ipso facto, unknowable. At the same time, they also help to refute the optimistic belief that mirror imaging, based upon the familiar aspects of open societies, can produce meaningful results.

The editors believe that the quantity and quality of information presented in this book can make a meaningful contribution even when viewed in isolation. It becomes all the more valuable when integrated with the other, more conventional dimensions of Sovietology.

The editors had to accept certain limitations inherent in the oral-history approach. Presentation of the Soviet system as viewed through the eyes of its former officials necessarily invites the question whether the statements quoted are verifiable, or even whether deliberate misinformation can be ruled out. The editors sought to address these pitfalls through exhaustive research before each interview, by cross-referencing responses, and by interviewing a significant number of respondents.

This project, nevertheless, was subject to very human limitations. Interviewees, deliberately or unwittingly, may exaggerate the number of topics on which they can speak with authority. Old-time rivalries, of a personal or institutional nature, may surface. Former military, diplomatic, or intelligence officials each tend to ascribe possibly disproportionate influence to their respective branches of the Soviet (or East European) pyramid of power. Stressing the importance of one's own influence on the course of history is an understandable facet of human frailty. The biographical profiles which follow this introduction are intended to provide readers with background concerning the interviewees before their testimonies are presented.

Other limitations of the oral-history approach to the study of closed societies should be mentioned. Because of the compartmentalization of the Soviet system, and the strict enforcement of the "need-to-know" rule, most of the interviewees spent their official careers within a single institution. Some were diplomats, some party officials, others were from the intelligence branches, yet others were in the military or in the academic institutes. Very few were able to combine the perspectives of several institutions of the *apparat*. The resulting picture conveyed by any one interviewee, as the editors are aware, may be subject to some degree of distortion.

In the case of interviewees from open societies, these imperfections can be redressed by reference to the documentary record. This can be done only rarely where interviewees from closed societies are concerned. Therefore, the frailty of human memory assumes a greater role. Nevertheless, except in the most obvious cases of error, the editors chose not to correct the interviewees. The policy throughout the project was to let the interviewees speak for themselves as freely and naturally as possible.

The present work provides the reader, whether a Soviet specialist or an interested generalist, with glimpses of living history. It also casts unexpected light on the workings of political systems of the Soviet type. No effort was made to minimize discrepancies in the information provided by the former officials interviewed. The editors do not endorse any specific opinion expressed; the views presented are those of the interviewees. The main objective has been to convey to the reader what has been ascertained as well as some of the excitement which accompanied the discovery of previously known aspects of the manner in which the Soviet system functions.

Subsumed frequently under the unfortunate name of "defectors," an implicit pejorative for persons who literally have risked their lives to come across, our interviewees and their invaluable strategic knowledge (concerning the manner in which the system as a whole functions) have not always been fully utilized. What they have to offer, moreover, in many instances is supplemented by the insights of émigrés, whose positions may have been less lofty but whose number are considerable larger.[1]

At this point, it may be objected that, whatever the merits of the sources mentioned, the era of *glasnost* linked to the name of Gorbachev is producing so many revelations that the interpretation of more arcane material may be outdated and, perhaps, altogether unnecessary. However, this objection

---

[1] The introduction includes material excerpted from a statement by Prof. Uri Ra'anan on "The Potential Role of Oral History Projects Concerning Former Senior Officials and Émigrés from the USSR, its Allies, and Client States," *Hearings Before the Permanent Subcommittee on Investigations of the Committee on Governmental Affairs of the U.S. Senate on* "The Federal Government's Handling of Soviet and Communist Bloc Defectors," Oct. 8–9, 1987, pp. 720–776.

overlooks two problems: The present situation in the USSR is giving rise to a large volume of "background noise," which serves as much to confuse as to reveal the character of Soviet developments (unless one has a reliable methodological compass to guide one's selection of the real as opposed to the apparent factors at play); and this period in Soviet history may well prove to be evanescent, and it is conceivable that some years from now analysts of the USSR may have to rely once more primarily on the more esoteric tools of their trade. (With regard to the first of these points, historians may recall that on the eve of Operation Overlord the Allies had to decide whether to impose a total news blackout or, on the contrary, to emit as much deliberate background noise as possible to confuse the enemy. They chose the latter with eminently satisfactory results. This is not to say that *glasnost* is meant necessarily to constitute deliberate deception, but the overall effect may be analogous.)

Defectors and émigrés bring with them insights that provide flavor, texture, and color that could not be distilled from the interpretation of other material, however sensitive and penetrating. In effect, these personalities present a unique source of oral history obtained through in-depth, thoroughly prepared interviews.

To be sure, there are several myths related to this particular source of information. One concerns the presumed inaccessibility of such personalities, another takes it for granted that, in official debriefings, and in their subsequent publication of articles and books, these ex-officials have provided the international affairs and security community with all or most of the knowledge at their disposal. None of these assumptions is necessarily well founded:

It is true that quite a few of these potential interviewees still are—or are believed to be—high on the hit list of the Soviet security agencies (or their clients), and are compelled, therefore, to take appropriate precautions. However, they are eager to be utilized as a resource. Once they discover that they are dealing with responsible, knowledgeable, and serious scholars, they are likely to cooperate.

The agencies involved in the original debriefings of such former officials tend to be preoccupied with the search for tactical information, required urgently, such as the names and locations of the adversary's agents, the modus operandi of hostile networks, specific military data, etc. Strategic information of much longer-term significance, revealing, as it were, the *Gestalt* of the closed society (the functioning of the system as a whole, particularly the decision-making process, how information reaches the top, precisely where ultimate authority rests in terms of institutions and individuals, how decisions are translated into policy implementation and by whom, etc.) is viewed, understandably, as being of less urgency.

Many of these former Soviet officials soon find themselves in financial straits and attempt to rectify the situation by means of a successful book or two. Publishers, however, generally are interested in colorful and dramatic material, dealing with danger and escape, or providing portraits of leaders encountered by the authors during their careers. Consequently, it should not be surprising that significant information of a wider, longer-term, strategic nature can still be retained by the interviewees in our sample, previous debriefings and publications notwithstanding. (Among the reasons for this phenomenon is the culture barrier between open and closed societies.)

Such information requires patient, laborious, and time-consuming preparatory and follow-up work, if an optimal product is to be obtained. Thus, all of the relevant information relating to the interviewee's work and career has to be distilled carefully from the open literature and reinforced with data available from the more conventional Sovietological methodologies. A long, detailed, and carefully annotated protocol (i.e., questionnaire) follows, and the subject has to be taken, step by step, through this list of questions. The tape obtained as a result has to be transcribed, conscientiously edited, and annotated, to be sent to the interviewee for final touches and confirmation. Obviously, the larger the number of personalities interviewed, the more cross-referencing is required throughout this process.

In most instances, the results obtained offer data of an intimate nature that more conventional approaches cannot be expected to reveal. This may include conversations between the interviewees and important personalities on the Soviet scene, the treatment of sensitive issues at the highest levels of the state and party, of which, for one reason or another, the interviewee's work provided glimpses, and fortuitous nuggets not anticipated during the preparatory stage and not necessarily viewed as significant by the former official.

Parenthetically, it should be noted that this particular form of oral history also plays a socially useful role. The interviewees often have lost all hope of contact with their families, their lives frequently are endangered, they are isolated, and feel in many cases that they "have been squeezed out like lemons and flung away." The result can be prolonged bouts of depression, sometimes leading to suicide or redefection (which may amount to the same thing). Their involvement in a project of this type demonstrates that their usefulness to society has not been exhausted but that, on the contrary, they have a very significant role to play in enlightening both the academic and the policy-making communities.

It should be pointed out also that oral history need not be confined to former high officials who have come in from the cold. Émigrés who at one stage or another of their lives were involved in work likely to have attracted attention higher up, particularly in science and technology, may have become aware of aspects of the decision-making process, sometimes as "objects," and occasionally as participants or onlookers in that system. Individuals may have been situated, however long ago, at an especially crucial location in a project of great sensitivity and importance (all the more if it had military implications at the time). They may have been affected directly by decisions concerning the direction of further progress and/or additional resource allocation for that particular project.

Oral history information is likely to be significant even when viewed in isolation, but is incomparably more so when integrated with the three other, more conventional dimensions of Sovietology mentioned earlier—textual analysis, examination of biographical information, and integration of concrete data (obtained through national technical means or derived from statistical information).

Collectively, the interviewees could provide reasonably detailed information about different components or aspects of the topics investigated, viewed from various points in time. Given their respective locations on many intersections of the vertical and horizontal lines of the "grid" which has resulted from the multiplicity of experiences contributed by these personalities—in terms of institutions, levels of responsibility, and periods—information and insights gathered allowed investigators to begin fitting together different parts of the Soviet jigsaw puzzle.

Personalities who held positions in the operational arms of the *apparat* of the USSR (or of its allies, clients, or surrogates) that function in the international arena were likely to have come into contact with aspects of policy formation and implementation, as well as leadership perceptions of success and failure. They were situated appropriately to comprehend Soviet operational patterns, coordinated of surrogate elements, and the assets and liabilities of the apparatus. Thus, it became more feasible to develop and test hypotheses concerning Soviet doctrine, strategy, policy, and operations. Examples of questions examined include: Has there been any continuity in Soviet strategy during the period under investigation? Has this been an evolving policy with an upward escalatory trend or has it been marked by stops and starts and a lack of continuity?

After years of this work, our assessment indicates that the interviewees constitute a highly useful and sophisticated source of information. The Soviet Union appears to share this view, since it regards defections as very damaging substantively (that is, not merely propagandistically).

Defectors from the USSR and other Communist countries may be divided into the following categories: scholars and intellectuals; personnel in science and technology; diplomats and security officers; military personnel; seamen and fishermen; athletes; and performing artists. From an analytical perspective, reasons for defection might be categorized as follows: ideological–political; ethical–religious; personal–familial; and circumstantial (danger, threat to status, etc.). The number of defectors from communist countries is not large, numbering only in the hundreds.[2]

The most knowledgeable former Soviet officials, with the more perceptive

---

[2] Vladislav Krasnov, *Soviet Defectors: The KGB Wanted List* (Stanford, CA: Hoover Institution Press, 1986).

insights, can help specialists, on a long-term basis, to assess Soviet policy and activities concerning specific issues. Of course, it is not feasible to shed light upon every problem area in this manner, but it is instructive to note what long-term value the knowledge and experience even of defectors from the 1950s and 1960s can have.

A major aspect that can be illuminated with the aid of such material relates to broader Soviet strategy and policy. Perceptive debriefing can provide a window into activities that parallel the defector's own area of responsibility and, while usually second-hand (derived from associates, extrapolation from personal experience, and scuttlebutt), can be highly significant.

Given the glacial nature of change in the Soviet Union, oral history can utilize debriefing of individuals who came to the West over remarkably long periods of time. Thus, another benefit of a project that integrates multiple interviews is to demonstrate the elements both of continuity and of inconsistency in Soviet strategy and policy implementation (including organization) with regard to international and security affairs during the whole post-World War II period.[3]

The work of the oral history project already has produced highly significant insights which, viewed in concert with the other sources of information discussed above, make it possible to discuss critical issues which have preoccupied Soviet decision-makers.

It is not our intention to preempt the substantive information which emerged from the interviews. Suffice it so say that the traditionally accepted picture of the manner in which the Soviet system functions should be questioned in several very significant aspects, not least among them the concept that the Politburo normally serves as the forum in which major decisions are seriously debated or decided simply by a majority of votes. On this particular question, the material gathered from the interviews reinforces earlier doubts that had arisen when comparing the total hours devoted to normal sessions of the Politburo with the huge number of issues before its members. In this context, moreover, it has to be remembered that the leadership of the CPSU is expected to deal with matters considered trivial (or at least outside the normal area of concern) by traditional governments, such as permitting a particular novel to be published or a movie to be made. However, the editors feel that the interviewees should be permitted to speak for themselves and that the book has little to gain from intrusive editorializing.

---

[3] The methodological and substantive aspects of oral history work are discussed more extensively by Prof. Uri Ra'anan in "Alternate Methodologies for the Assessment of Soviet Strategic Defense Capabilities," *Emerging Doctrines and Technologies* (Lexington: Lexington Books, 1988) and "Oral History: A Neglected Dimension of Sovietology," *Strategic Review* XV, no. 2 (1987), both with the participation of Prof. Richard H. Shultz.

Biographical Profiles of Interviewees

"Mehmet Aziz," a former major general of the Afghan army who served as chief of operations and chief of personnel, Aziz observed Soviet penetration of the Afghan officer corps over a long period. He agreed to be interviewed under a pseudonym.

Juan Benemelis, a former senior Cuban Foreign Ministry official, served in various posts in Africa and the Arabian Peninsula.

Miguel Bolaños-Hunter, a former senior counterintelligence officer in the state security apparatus of the Nicaraguan Sandinista regime, was trained in Cuba by DGI (Cuban intelligence). He was responsible for overseeing Western media representatives and embassies.

Michael Checinski is currently a professor of economics at the U.S. Army Russian Institute in the Federal Republic of Germany. After years in German concentration camps, including Auschwitz, he became an officer in Polish military counterintelligence in 1947. Subsequently, he became a lecturer at the Military-Political Academy in Warsaw and a researcher at the Institute of War Economy. Mr. Checinski has published a large number of studies concerning East European military and economic issues.

Peter Deriabin is a native of Siberia, who served with distinction as a Soviet army officer in World War II, receiving six medals and three citations. In 1944, he was selected to join Soviet military counterintelligence, SMERSH. He graduated from the Higher Counterintelligence School and the University of Marxism-Leninism in Moscow. Subsequently, he became a major in the Kremlin's Bodyguard Administration. In 1954, Mr. Deriabin left his post as a Soviet counterintelligence officer in Austria and requested political asylum in the United States. He is the author and editor of several well-known books.

Anatoly Fedoseyev, a former Soviet scientist and senior military designer, was sent to Germany in May 1945 to collect scientifically relevant information. Later, he established himself as a successful designer of components of powerful Soviet land-based and sea-based radars. Fedoseyev has insight into decision-making concerning Soviet research and development. He is a Lenin Prize winner and was awarded the title of Hero of Socialist Labor. He now lives in the West.

"George Gregory," who agreed to be interviewed on the condition that he remain anonymous, was a Soviet intelligence officer for 35 years before leaving the Soviet Union. He served in both the first and second directorates of the KGB and specialized in "active measures."

"Jan Hus," before deciding to seek political asylum in the United States, had been an official of the Czechoslovak ministry of foreign affairs. He held a senior position in the International Department of the Czechoslovak Communist Party's Central Committee; at one time he worked with the Soviet Institute for the Study of the USA and Canada (ISShAK). He asked to remain anonymous.

Karel Kaplan, author and historian, currently resides in the Federal Republic of Germany. After a brief career in the Czechoslovak Communist Party *apparat,* Mr. Kaplan was sent to several party schools. He promptly advanced and established himself as one of the top historians working with the Czechoslovak Communist Party's Central Committee. Mr. Kaplan was among the few historians who worked on the 1963 and 1968 commissions investigating the so-called Slansky trial. He gained access to hitherto unavailable evidence regarding the Communist putsch of 1948, the Stalinist period in Czechoslovakia, and relations between Moscow and Prague. He is among the most prolific writers on power-World War II Czechoslovakia; his books have appeared in all major European languages and in the United States.

Vladimir Kostov, formerly a senior Bulgarian official who worked in propaganda and communications, has special insights into the activities of Bulgarian intelligence and the behavior patterns of the Bulgarian leadership. He survived one of the notorious "Bulgarian umbrella assassination" attempts and now lives in Munich.

Tadeusz Kucharski, having graduated from the Foreign Trade Department of the Main School of Planning and Statistics in Warsaw, was selected to join the International Commission for Supervision and Control which operated in North and South Vietnam under the Geneva agreements. Later, he witnessed the final stages of the Vietnam war as a member of the International Commission for Control and Supervision under the Paris agreement. Mr. Kucharski served in a variety of responsible positions as a Polish foreign ministry official, including work in the Polish Embassy in Angola as a trade specialist. He left the Embassy to seek political asylum in the United States after the Jaruzelski take-over in December 1981.

Stanislav Levchenko was born shortly after the German invasion of the Soviet Union in 1941, and grew up in Stalinist and post-Stalin Russia. In 1958, he became a student at the Institute of Oriental Languages at Moscow University, specializing in Japanese studies. Originally employed at the Institute of Oceanography and Fisheries, Stanislav Levchenko was gradually drawn into the world of Soviet intelligence. After a brief involvement with the military intelligence, he became a KGB intelligence officer. Mr. Levchenko worked with various front organizations, under the direction of the International Department of the CPSU Central Committee. In 1979, while posted in Japan and under the cover of Soviet journalist, KGB Major Levchenko decided to request political asylum in the United States. He has authored numerous publications dealing with Soviet use of "active measures."

Jose Luis Llovio joined the anti-Batista movement in Cuba as a young student. In 1957, he became a member of the 26th July Movement at Havana University and became involved in a variety of revolutionary actions. In the late 1950s, he studied medicine in Paris, and carried out public relations campaigns on behalf of the movement. After his return to Cuba, Mr. Llovio's life fluctuated between periods of imprisonment in Fidel Castro's jails and official appointments, specifically as a capital investment expert. From 1972 to 1977, he held a responsible position in the Cuban sugar industry complex. In December 1981, Mr. Llovio and his wife escaped from Castro's jurisdiction while changing planes in Canada. In October 1984, Jose Llovio was granted political asylum in the United States.

Zdenek Mlynar was educated as a lawyer in the Soviet Union, where he came to know Mikhail Gorbachev as a classmate. He established himself as one of Czechoslovakia's principal legal scholars in the 1950s and 1960s, and during the 1968 Prague Spring, he served as a member of the Czechoslovak Communist Party Politburo and a secretary of the central committee. On the night of the Soviet-led invasion in August 1968, Mr. Mlynar personally drafted the all-important official resolution denouncing the occupation of Czechoslovakia. In the postinvasion days, he emerged as one of the most cool-headed and decisive Czech politicians joining the Dubček team in its fateful negotiations with Brezhnev and his colleagues in Moscow. Expelled from all responsible positions after 1969, Mr. Mlynar chose exile and resides now in Austria.

Gallina Orionova is a former research fellow at the Institute for the Study of the United States and Canada of the USSR Academy of Sciences. Ms. Orionova now lives in England.

Eden Pastora Gomez, a senior military official of the Sandinista government of Nicaragua, was known by the pen name of "Commander Zero" and served as commander of the Sandinista guerrilla forces that defeated the National Guard of the former Somoza government. He served as vice-minister of defense, supervising the Sandinista Popular Militias, before his resignation in the fall of 1981. After 1982, he led one of the anti-Sandinista guerrilla groups.

Jiri Pelikan advanced rapidly to positions of influence and power, as a young communist in post–World War II Czechoslovakia. After becoming associated with the International Union of Students, a front organization with headquarters in Prague, he became one of the most influential political and cultural personalities in Czechoslovakia. During 1968, Mr. Pelikan was the director general of Czechoslovak television, an institution which greatly contributed to the emergence and direction of the Prague Spring. After the Soviet invasion in August 1968, Mr. Pelikan was dismissed from his post and sent to Rome as a Czechoslovak diplomat. Shortly thereafter, he severed his links with the post-invasion regime of Gustav Husak and became one of the major figures in the Czech socialist emigration. Now a citizen of Italy, he represents his new country as a deputy in the European Parliament.

A. Piatigorsky is a former research fellow at the Institute of Oriental Studies of the USSR Academy of Sciences. He now lives in England.

Zdzislaw Rurarz spent "thirty-six years, three months, and three days" of his life as a Polish communist in a variety of responsible positions. In 1956, he became an officer of the Polish military intelligence service, the Z-2. He advanced to become an advisor to Polish party chief Gierek and regularly attended meetings of the Politburo. Between 1977 and 1979, he was a member of two Soviet-led think tanks and gained access to high-level geopolitical planning by the Warsaw Pact. During the Solidarity period, Dr. Rurarz served as Polish ambassador to Japan. He resigned from this position in protest against Gen. Wojciech Jaruzelski's imposition of martial law in December 1981. The Polish government sentenced him to death. Dr. Rurarz has been granted political asylum in the United States.

Jan Sejna, the product of a Czech peasant environment, was a Communist Party member since his youth. Mr. Sejna's career proceeded at a spectacular pace. A colonel by the age of twenty-seven, he began accumulating one important position after another. From 1956 to 1968, he served near the top of

Czechoslovakia's politico-military elite, as chief of staff to the minister of defense, secretary of the military committee of the Communist Party's Central Committee, first secretary of the Main Party Committee at the Defense Ministry and member of the Military Section of the Central Committee's Administration Department. In addition, Mr. Sejna was a personal friend of the Czechoslovak president and first secretary of the Communist Party, Antonin Novotny. General Sejna's escape to the West on 25 February 1968, shocked the Czechoslovak and Soviet party, intelligence, and military circles and accelerated the fall of Novotny's regime in Prague.

Arkady Shevchenko, one of the best-known personalities among Soviet defectors, is now a successful author and public speaker. His long career inside the Soviet *apparat* exposed him to important decision makers in Moscow. Consequently, he is able to draw accurate portraits of such personalities as former Soviet Foreign Minister Andrei Gromyko—whom he served as adviser—and the former Soviet ambassador in Washington, Anatoly Dobrynin. Dr. Shevchenko's long and successful career in the Soviet foreign service culminated in his appointment as United Nations under secretary general. During the late 1970s, he agreed to provide the U.S. government with important information on Soviet diplomatic and intelligence activities in the United States. In April 1978, Dr. Shevchenko severed his ties with the Soviet government and subsequently became a U.S. citizen.

Ota Sik is at present a professor of economics at St. Gallen, Switzerland. Mr. Sik joined the Czechoslovak Communist Youth Organization prior to the Second World War. After involvement in the anti-German underground movement, he spent four years in a concentration camp. Having joined the Czechoslovak Communist Party *apparat* after the war, and having completed his education, Dr. Sik rose quickly to important politico-economic positions in Novotny's Czechoslovakia. During the 1968 Prague Spring period, which he had helped to bring about, he was a Deputy Prime Minister in the Czechoslovak government and one of the fathers of the reformist platform. Professor Sik has authored a score of books on current problems, mostly developing his original economic theories.

"William Stiller" is a former Soviet official with a background in intelligence and foreign affairs. Stiller, who wishes to remain anonymous, now resides in the United States.

Stefan Svirdlev is a former high-ranking Bulgarian intelligence officer, now working at Radio Free Europe in Munich.

Michael Voslensky graduated from Moscow State University as a specialist in modern Western history. Having completed his graduate studies, Dr. Voslensky in 1946 became a member of the Soviet team working on the Nuremberg trials. After Stalin's death, he worked briefly at the Soviet Academy of Sciences, becoming involved in the activities of the World Peace Council, first in Vienna and later in Prague. On his return to the Soviet Union, Dr. Voslensky worked in a variety of positions within the Soviet *apparat*. He became a secretary of the Commission on Scientific Aspects of Disarmament of the USSR Academy of Sciences and professor at the Patrice Lumumba University where he held a chair in world history. In 1972, Dr. Voslensky was selected to go to West Germany as a visiting professor. Deprived of his Soviet citizenship in 1977, he is now director of the Institute of Contemporary Soviet Research in Munich.

Goshu Wolde, originally trained as a lawyer and educated in Great Britain, joined the forces which brought about the revolution in Ethiopia. As a major of the Ethiopian army, Mr. Wolde observed the rapid rise and fall of Generals Aman and Teferi Banti as well as the spectacular career of one of his colleagues, another army officer, Chairman Mengistu. In 1977, he was selected to attend a nine-month course at the Frunze Military Academy in the Soviet Union. After a career in the Ministry of Education, Mr. Wolde became the foreign minister of Ethiopia. Having observed the gradual radicalization of the Ethiopian political life, he resigned from his post and obtained political asylum in the United States.

1

Careers, Appointments, Promotions, Dismissals, and Alignments: The Personal Factor

The interviewees confirm that the Leninist summary of politics as "Who—Whom"[1] continues to be relevant in analyzing the present-day Soviet system. Therefore, linkages that are revealed by biographies of individual players in the Soviet arena provide a key for decoding the nature and meaning of politics as practiced in communist states. The personal element, of course, plays a role in every society. However, given communist elites whose place and prerogatives are legitimized by their supposed function as interpreters of a single, objective, revealed truth, leaving no constitutional room for associations based primarily upon different worldviews and policy platforms, groupings inevitably come to be based on feudal relationships between barons who offer protection, privileges and promotion, and retainers who reciprocate through service and loyalty. The public careers of Soviet officials, from entry point to culmination, reflect this fundamental factor, of which nepotism is only one element. In a society in which privilege is the result primarily of political power and influence, it is understandable that those who have reached the top would try to secure power and privilege for their children and other relations. As the bureaucracy has expanded, a network of barter trade, in influence, complete with standard bribery prices, has solidified within each socialist system. The top layer of the Soviet elite does not constitute a very large community?[2] Therefore, it is not difficult for a member of that stratum to have personal relationships with

---

[1]Malcolm Muggeridge, then a British correspondent stationed briefly in the Soviet Union, once asked M. Oumansky, head of the Kremlin's Press Department and later Soviet ambassador in Washington, "Who—whom?" Oumansky replied only when Muggeridge was leaving the country, but did so with frankness. His whispered reply was "I—they." See *Chronicles of Wasted Time: Chronicle I, The Green Stick* (NY: William Morrow and Co., Inc., 1973), pp. 205–276, especially 264–5.

[2]For an interesting effort to arrive at a quantitative assessment of the Soviet elite, see Michael Voslensky, *Nomenklatura: The Soviet Ruling Class, An Insider's Report* (Garden City, NJ: Doubleday and Company, Inc., 1984), pp. 92–96.

many other elite comrades, or to have indirect channels of communication with them through family, friends, coworkers, and dependents.

Career Beginnings: Nepotism

Most of the interviewees mentioned nepotism at one point or another. Stanislav Levchenko, a former senior member of the Soviet disinformation apparatus, was particularly outspoken on the subject. According to him, nepotism begins at the lowest level of career placement and continues directly up to the Central Committee, which he describes as the upper nobility, that is, feudal magnates whose holdings consist not of manors but of their modern equivalent—access to power.

> In the university department where I was a student . . . almost one hundred percent of the students entered . . . through nepotism and corruption. . . . [The student's] choice does not matter at all, unless [one's] father is a high ranking KGB,[3] International Department, or MFA[4] official. If he wants [his child] to specialize in the Middle East and [to be assigned] to a Soviet embassy in the region, he will push [him] into this career path. It is a very rare case when the student is interested in [the topic] he applies to study. . . . [The students'] main concern is their career and privileges. . . .
>
> Most of the children of influential [personalities] go to the Institute of International Relations. . . . [About one-third attempt to go on] to the Ministry of Foreign Affairs or the Ministry of Foreign Trade. . . . [T]he parents of the graduate will approach their friends to secure their child a job, through a VIP who can make a telephone call to arrange for a transfer. In my time most of these cases were favorably resolved. I do not remember anybody [from my class] walking the Moscow streets without a job.

Levchenko goes on to describe how the personal influence approach affects the way in which posts are filled before graduation:

> The head of the Middle Eastern Department . . . of the Ministry of Foreign Affairs . . . has two to four deputies. By the time the graduation period comes at the Institute of Foreign Relations and at Moscow University (usually June), the director and his deputies [will have spent] a considerable amount of time with the families of the graduates. Before the graduation exams are over, the pie has already been cut up and the best places filled. Sometimes [graduates of universities, as opposed to institutes] were not

---

[3] *Komitet Gosudarstvennoy Bezopasnosti,* Soviet Committee of State Security.
[4] Ministry of Foreign Affairs, USSR Council of Ministers.

placed because they were not that close to the authorities. . . . In my time, the fathers who served in the KGB, in the Ministry of Foreign Affairs, or Foreign Trade preferred to send their children to specialized schools, like the Institute of International Relations, but not to the university. Today the university operates in the same way as any other Soviet school specializing in international relations.

Stanislav Levchenko proceeds to demonstrate the effects of the mutual accommodation system at the highest level of Soviet politics:

The Central Committee is actually the cream of the . . . Soviet bureaucracy. [Its members] have achieved their positions through nepotism. At the same time they are the "knights" of the Soviet system. . . . They do not change Politburos, but they do influence who will be there. That is why it [may seem] naive [but is true, just the same, when it is said] that a Soviet leader has achieved the top position, [but] that he does not feel comfortable enough, because he does not have a consensus. . . . Gorbachev got himself in position, and even if he does not now have a consensus, sooner or later he will. He will outsmart his opponents and outlive them. All of them want to improve their positions, so he will get them in, in return for their support. Otherwise, they will all get tired of waiting for promotions. The number one person wants to win their support sooner rather than later. At any rate, Voslensky describes this process well in *Nomenklatura*. . . . The Central Committee and the people around it . . . are the people who govern the country. That is, they are the nobles of the Soviet social revolution. This process will continue as they use nepotism to get high positions for their children.

Jan Hus, a former Czechoslovak official who had studied in the Soviet Union, found that nepotism played a key role not so much in the educational process but rather in assignments after graduation. The ablest of the students might obtain access to higher education even if they are unrelated to persons in power:

The Czechoslovak students [until October 1968] were not typical. Almost all the rest of the foreign students [in the USSR] at that time were children of important party people in their respective countries. It was the same with about half of the Soviet students. However, the other half of Soviet students were army veterans or children with a good communist [that is, proletarian] background. The Soviet system was fairer than the Eastern European systems, except for the Czechoslovak system, in that it also allowed people of simple backgrounds to attend the Institute. When these other students graduated, however, they had difficulty competing with the *nomenklatura's* children for careers. The very successful and bright ones could compete, but they were a very small percentage of the class.

Hus notes that this process of refreshing the pool of elites can be hampered by major crises, such as the Prague Spring or the Solidarity period. The Party *apparat* becomes adamant about keeping out all those it does not know and cannot trust. However, resourceful individuals can find their way around.

> In Central Europe, after events such as 1968 in Czechoslovakia and Solidarity in Poland, the Party has become much more involved in the selection process. People who once would have been tolerated are not now. . . . There is no longer a chance for anyone outside to influence policy. . . . At present, much tighter party control is weakened, however, by a system of bribes and nepotism leading to . . . advancement. If a butcher knows a leading party official and bribes him, he could get his antiparty son into school, while a communist might not be able to get his son in, unless he, too, knows someone or is [himself] important. The system is rotten and should be analyzed in this light.

Juan Benemelis notes that a similar situation prevails in Cuba. However, given the generally poor standard of living and unmistakable economic gap between the elite and the broad masses, the consequences of failure are severe. The "need" for nepotism consequently is greater:

> When one is a member of the *nomenklatura,* his children receive outrageously preferential treatment, even more than in the USSR, because the economic situation is worse in Cuba. The differentiation is more apparent. The children of the *nomenklatura* receive a very different education. Some of them came out in Mariel.[5]

Although the system controlling access to privileges and appointments is generally influenced by nepotism and corruption, some interviewees report that there are at least elements of meritocracy and also of chance. For instance, Tadeusz Kucharski's impression of the postgraduation employment assignments in Warsaw was that, aside from the obvious plums offered to the favored sons and daughters, there was no discernible pattern of appointments among those without influential relatives of friends:

> I do not specifically know why I was selected for the Foreign Service with [another student]. Maybe our graduating professor, Libera, decided that we had the qualifications to enter the Foreign Service. There are no objective reasons. Either someone likes you or not.

A. Piatigorsky notes that for the academics, the golden rule of American universities, that is, publish or perish, had no meaning at all. Where influence is the key, the professional wisdom was "advise and rise," as he explains:

---

[5] The one-time mass exodus of Cubans, including some criminals, allowed by Castro.

The more times one is responsible for that particular task [briefing higher-ups], the more chances of promotion there are, regardless of how much he publishes. For instance, during my period at the Institute, I published three books and something like eighty or ninety articles. I was not promoted, but I was never offended because I knew perfectly well that it had nothing to do with the real focus of our activity, the real purpose of the Institute.

No system can function successfully if the most important positions are filled entirely through influence, rather than merit. Some areas require skills without which the apparatus would fall apart. Not surprisingly, Levchenko notes that the KGB is one of the institutions less affected by nepotism than the rest.

Speaking of parents, the KGB is not free of nepotism, but it is less visible than in other parts of the system. The KGB must be more practical for the survival of the intelligence system. If the sons and daughters of Soviet bureaucrats enter the KGB, they never work, . . . For instance, for a while I worked with a person whose father was chief of the flower supply department of the Moscow Soviet, which makes him close not only to funerals and wedding parties, but also to top officials. He can supply them with all sorts of out-of-season flowers. His son was in the KGB and was taken care of. In Japan, it was very strange. He was not allowed to take part in any risk operations where he could get caught red-handed and sent home. This occurred to the point where people did not like him very much. So the KGB does have the problems of nepotism and corruption, but not overwhelmingly.

However, even the well connected cannot rely on nepotism forever, nor need it always be the only explanation for an official's rise within the party. Yuri Andropov's[6] son, for example, profited handsomely from his father's position. However, we are told, he demonstrated that he could make do on his own:

He [Andropov's son] is not an outstanding thinker like Trofimenko,[7] but he is quite intelligent and deserved the positions he has achieved. Certainly his father's name helped him, but he was still brighter than many of the Soviet ambassadors I met. He was clever enough to establish his own reputation. He has done much on his own to establish his position, so that he could maintain it on the basis of his own merit after his father died. Normally, the son will not last politically after his father's death. He rarely talked about his father, whom I never met, but I had the feeling that his father preferred for him not to establish his position on the basis of the family name. They

---

[6] Yuri V. Andropov, former general secretary, Central Committee, Communist Party of the Soviet Union (CC CPSU); chairman, USSR Committee for State Security (KGB); deceased.

[7] Genrikh Trofimenko, senior analyst at the United States of America and Canada Institute of the USSR Academy of Sciences.

had a good relationship, but the older Andropov would not have liked it if he always had to rescue his son from trouble as other important fathers have had to do.

Peter Deriabin concurs with Levchenko that, especially in the KGB, other factors than nepotism or connections come into play.

I only got into the Guards Directorate through an accident. I did have an impeccable record and that made me very eligible. I had nine government awards for bravery in the war, six medals, and three orders; I was a party member since 1940; I was a Komsomol secretary in naval SMERSH,[8] and also did Komsomol work at the regiment and battalion levels.

During [the postwar] period of turmoil, the Soviet leaders were looking for the most trusted people to send abroad; loyalty was more important than training. If it were today, with my broken German I would not even be sent abroad. Because of the shortage of trained personnel, people without good language skills were posted abroad; today all officers going abroad know at least one foreign language.

Career advancement derives also from elements of chance. Jan Sejna notes:

At that time [post-1948 Czechoslovakia], promotions came very fast. Mine were not so fast. . . . I was lucky. [A new defense minister, General Lomsky, was appointed; I was] called to the Politburo and [told] that he did not have any political experience. . . . I was told, "You will be his chief of staff and practically the watchdog from the party's point of view."

Even when one is associated with a member of the elite who is in a favorable position to influence appointments, there are certain barriers to advancement—usually competing candidates supported by other members of the elite. The process can become messy:

At the higher levels . . . one must spend up to fifty percent of [one's] time playing the game. Otherwise someone else is guaranteed to be promoted ahead of [one]. An official must do his best to establish the best possible relations with the important people in the Administrative Organs Department, in the party Organs Department, or whatever department is most closely connected with his career. . . .

The single most important role in this process is played by the party Organs Department. However, Politburo members prefer to keep these decisions in their own hands. . . , Once [decisions] go to the Politburo, they have to deal with the first secretary and the other members. Each member will

---

[8] *Smert Shpionam,* Soviet military counterespionage in World War II.

try to advance his own protégés, keeping . . . reserve lists ready if needed. Very often the Ministry of Interior will be asked to supply information on party members and although [it is] not supposed to do so, [it] will go ahead and check on these people. Naturally things can be concealed, or blown out of proportion, depending on who is running the check. And it is [the Ministry of the Interior that prepares] the recommendations for the first secretary, the Politburo, or the Secretariat.

Hus believes that ability is beginning to matter at the highest levels of the party today, and that Gorbachev is mostly responsible:

Chernayev[9] is an example of how more people are now being selected on the basis of knowledge than before. He was regarded as an able person. . . . [Zagladin][10] was seen as being too doctrinaire and too close to Ponomarev.[11] Gorbachev did not want someone who was too doctrinaire.

Party Membership

Party membership and advancement are assured if one can exploit the connections mentioned earlier. On the lower levels, however, workers and peasants find party membership a nuisance as much as a benefit. Since they do not constitute competition for the elite, and merely lend an aura of legitimacy to the "workers' party," gaining membership in the party is an easy task for genuine proletarians.

In Czechoslovakia, shortly after the Communist Party took power in February 1948, the need for reliable cadres of working class or peasant origin was obvious. Jan Sejna's rise within the party demonstrates that such individuals could advance quickly toward the upper levels of the pyramid of power. His career shows that one could exploit one's youth and humble background to gain quick access to channels of power:

[B]ecause one of my father's brothers had been a communist from the beginning, because we were so poor, and because I was a little bit more educated than others, I was selected by the party professionals from the first. I was eighteen and already secretary of the Regional Party Committee in charge of agriculture in the region of West Bohemia. . . . It does not matter if the Communist Party in a given country is very small. It is the party's strategy and tactics, as well as how they use young people, which are important.

---

[9] Personal assistant to Gorbachev and head of his private chancery.

[10] Vadim V. Zagladin, member of the CC CPSU; former first deputy chief of the International Department, CC CPSU.

[11] Boris N. Ponomarev, former secretary, CC CPSU, former candidate member of Politburo and chief of the International Department.

[When] I was twenty-seven . . . they called me and said that I would be elected to the Central Committee; I said, "how so?" They said the Politburo had already decided. I was naive, because I was from the village. What did I know about this big game? Nothing. In November, they told me that I had already been elected to Parliament in the summer. The Politburo had already decided and I was of course elected by 99.9 percent.

In the USSR, while workers and peasant have little trouble being admitted to the communist party, the intelligentsia has to compete for a relatively limited proportion of party memberships. This poses particular problems for the staff of research institutes, as described by Gallina Orionova:

It is very easy for workers and peasants to join the Party, but not for the intelligentsia and especially not in the institutes because [individuals compete for this advantage]. I was never a party member. It was suggested that I join, but I did not do it. If you want to join the party, you should really have very good elbows. . . . Sometimes in a year there are only two or three vacancies for party membership in an institute of over four hundred people, so you must completely abandon your academic work and go out and campaign. As an offshoot it may mean that you will slip on the ladder of promotion because you must neglect your work. . . .

At least one-third [of the institute staff are party members]. [Those] older than thirty-five who intend to stay in the Soviet Union . . . try to become party members because it's a safe ticket. You can go abroad, you can get better positions. [Those] who really want to make a career of it will join the party. . . . Among young people, it is very difficult to [enter the party]; it is a sort of . . . club.

According to Tadeusz Kucharski, the party gains legitimacy not only by bringing in workers but also by promoting a few who remain outside the party itself, but join a related organization, for example, the Komsomol and its East European counterparts. Those fortunate few are not at liberty to follow their own paths, however:

It is possible for some people who are not party members, but were members of the Socialist Youth, to be promoted. This serves as an example that not everyone has to be in the party. However, they must follow the party line and its instructions.

On the other hand, Kucharski notes that even those within the party have little or no influence if they are merely members of the primary party organizations; policy decisions are made well above this level:

The opinion of the party cell does not matter at all in determining promotions. It is very weak and without any real power. It is only designed to hold meetings about general party policy and collect membership dues. In determining who should be the new director of an enterprise, people within that enterprise would not be contacted; only internal security would be contacted by the Central Committee.

While in the developed socialist states there is fierce competition for entry into the upper-echelons of the party among those wishing to gain access to privileges and power, the situation is reversed in developing countries under communist rule. Such regimes must quickly establish a loyal class of party professionals to govern the state. Lack of success in this regard can have serious consequences: an important reason for the failure of the Soviet Union to secure a stable, pro-Soviet Afghanistan was the inability of the PDPA[12] to attract members. In Ethiopia, according to Goshu Wolde, the membership drive is meeting with more success.

> At the time of its creation, there were about forty thousand people in the WPE [the ruling party of Ethiopia]. There has been a very powerful recruitment drive over the last two and a half years, and because of this, the figure has jumped to about eighty or one hundred thousand; perhaps it could even be more if you consider the candidate members. Before you become a full member, you have to pass through a phase in which you have no voting rights. You simply belong, but don't yet have a regular membership card. These come from across the length and width of the country, and many are members of the armed forces, the police and security forces. Many also are from the civilian sector, perhaps teachers, recruited workers and peasants, representatives of the women's and youth associations, and so on. It is difficult for me to characterize the percentages now, but when the party was created, the vast majority were from the armed forces and the security forces.

The advantages of higher party membership have been well described in Voslensky's *Nomenklatura* and elsewhere—access to power, information, Western goods, luxury food, fine living quarters and cars, better medical facilities. Focusing on Kaganovich[13] after his dismissal, George Gregory demonstrates that the privilege game can continue even after an *apparatchik* has been forced to resign. This confirms Voslensky's contention that, excepting the period of Stalin's rule, once a member of the elite, always a member of the elite.

> Kaganovich was seen in Moscow. He was shopping and there was a line. People urged him to go to the front but he refused and said he was just an

---

[12] People's Democratic Party of Afghanistan.

[13] Lazar M. Kaganovich, former First Deputy Chairman, USSR Council of Ministers, and member of the Politburo, CC CPSU: removed from the Central Committe in 1957.

ordinary person. The CC later decided this was a provocation. They told him it was bad to go to the regular shops; they gave him access to the special shops. Not because they liked him but because they were afraid of further "provocations" against the Soviet state.

Appointments and Promotions at the Top

At the highest levels, the promotion game is most intense and influence becomes crucial. Arkady Shevchenko explains that mechanisms for deciding who obtains these higher-level positions officially do not exist. Rather, the final decision is a product of the interplay of the desires of a variety of important personalities who control appointments:

> [Appointment struggles are handled] by behind-the-scenes lobbying. Gromyko,[14] for example, was always lobbying for all these appointments. How did he do it? It was done through . . . conversations with Brezhnev[15] and with other members of the Politburo. It's never done in a way where somebody makes a proposal, and somebody else makes a counterproposal. I've never heard of such a thing.
>
> Whatever personnel appointments go up for approval by the Politburo, or by the Secretariat of the party, or for approval by the foreign minister, who has a whole department for this, all appointments to the Central Committee's departments, all proposals that deal with personnel have to be screened by the KGB. They are sent automatically to the KGB. This includes high-level appointments. If . . . Grechko[16] himself, as in my time, or even Ustinov[17] proposed to appoint some of his generals or to transfer some of the generals (even in case of the highest appointments), they sent the [candidate's] name to the KGB. On everybody who belongs to the *nomenklatura,* there is another file which is never seen [outside the KGB]. What is in there, you can only guess. Then the KGB gives its view to the agency that is dealing with this [candidate for top-level appointment].
>
> If we're talking about a party appointment, it goes to the [party Organization] Department of the Central Committee which handles the party apparatus. . . . Then, [the] party Organization Department would ask the KGB for its opinion. This doesn't mean that in 100 percent of the cases where the KGB considers that this man should not be appointed, . . . he will not be appointed. KGB can be overruled. I know of specific cases.

---

[14] Andrey A. Gromyko, former member of the Politburo, CC CPSU; former chairman, Presidium, Supreme Soviet; former Soviet minister of foreign affairs.

[15] Leonid I. Brezhnev, former general secretary, CC CPSU; deceased.

[16] Andrey A. Grechko, former Soviet minister of defense; former member, Politburo, CC CPSU; deceased.

[17] Dmitri F. Ustinov, former Soviet minister of defense; former member of Politburo, CC CPSU; marshal of the Soviet Union; deceased.

The importance of personal contacts can hardly be overestimated in any political system, open or closed. But the top Soviet elite seems to rely on connections between itself and new candidates more than most political systems in modern history. In response to the question how Politburo appointments are decided, Shevchenko responded:

> This is an absolutely personal thing, in which the key role is played by the general secretary and in which you want to be his closest associate in the Politburo. This is the only way such things can be decided. There is no formal procedure. . . . [Persons] who might potentially become members of the Politburo are put on some kind of register. This register exists, either in the head of the general secretary or the person who deals with the appointments, like Ligachev[18] or his predecessors in charge of the [party Organization] Department. . . . If it comes through the Foreign Ministry it's the "Cadres Abroad" Department. . . . The same thing applies to all echelons, to all appointments, even the most important.
>
> In the Foreign Ministry, for example, . . . the American Department would never suggest to Gromyko whom to appoint for ambassador to the United States. The First European Department would never suggest whom to appoint as the ambassador to France. No department of the Central Committee will suggest whom to appoint to all the key positions. I'm talking about the key positions. This is the case with all the full members of the Politburo, the candidate members, the secretaries of the Party, and, to a substantial degree, the chiefs of the Central Committee Departments.
>
> This doesn't mean that this is entirely the decision of the general secretary. The role of the other secretaries of the party and the other influential members of the Politburo comes into play here. This also doesn't exclude the possibility that someone can become a member of the Politburo at the suggestion of some of the people who are close to the general secretary. There are no rules . . . and there is no seniority.

In most Eastern European countries there is, of course, another essential factor governing advancement, namely one's relationship with personalities in Moscow. Sejna emphasizes that in Czechoslovakia, having Soviet connections, professional or personal, constituted a considerable advantage:

> In the military, for example, from the level of division commander on up, one must have graduated from the [Soviet] Academy of the General Staff. That is true throughout the Warsaw Pact, except for Romania probably. This produced real dissent among Czechoslovak officers. . . . Yet the fact is that if one received training in the Soviet Union, and particularly if one also took a Soviet wife, his career would go very well.

---

[18] Yegor K. Ligachev, member of the Politburo and secretary of the CC CPSU; chairman of the Central Committee's Agriculture Commission.

However, the Soviet overseers had special requirements that were not always predictable. For instance, in their eyes, a candidate with a less than perfect character or record may be preferable since he may be controlled more easily. In the case of the Czechoslovak defense minister, General Lomsky, there was something in his background that Soviet advisers in Prague could use against him:

> The Soviets always preferred people that were in some way compromised over pure communists. That is why they permitted [General Lomsky] to be minister of defense. One reason why they killed so many of the volunteers who fought in Spain was because these people were [pure] communists, who could turn around to the Soviet advisers and say, "Hey, where were you while I was fighting in Spain?"

The extent of Soviet influence on the careers of the average Eastern European *apparatchik* is difficult to estimate. It is reasonable to assume that the higher one climbs in the government, the more important the role of the Soviet Union becomes. Direct Soviet involvement in promotion processes of the Polish military reaches down to the level of colonels, as Michael Checinski relates:

> I was responsible for moving all high-ranking officers. By "moving" I mean that, for example, anyone who wanted to become a colonel would have to receive my OK. . . . An example: I received a request from the Cadres Department which asked whether I could accept such and such a person to be promoted to a colonel. I would answer yes or no. No explanation. The explanation was only for my superior, a Soviet. In my report to him I would say that my opinion is yes or no, and I would have to explain—he is a drunkard, he is corrupt. [This applied] [e]ven if he was our secret agent (it was a principle that secret agents had to be promoted).
>
> I was also responsible for people within the organization, within the party structure, the General Staff. . . . People had no idea how this worked. They all feared the counterintelligence officers. The cadres within the political administration [of the army] were dependent upon my opinion. Everything was in one section [counterintelligence]. Sometimes I had telephone calls on a special line.

A few notes on early retirement are in order. In the dark past, of course, many career paths ended with the bullet or behind barbed wire. The post-Stalin *apparatchik,* on the other hand, usually has been allowed to retire with a pension. It is no longer viewed as risky to allow persons to retire when their careers have been terminated. The days of executing a man because he knew about certain excesses in the system have ended. Levchenko describes a situation in which an aging KGB official was moved out of the way into a comfortable pasture:

When Brezhnev was still alive, [he asked, at a Politburo meeting, who the head of the KGB First Directorate was, and upon receiving the KGB chairman's response, went on to ask] "What is his age?" "Seventy-something." "We are going through an important time. I would like to fire that old son of a bitch, and get ourselves a new, efficient one, who is not a professional KGB-oriented person, but a person who will keep in mind Politburo directives, decisions, and aspirations." [The man in question] was fired and became one of "the councillors of the chairman of the KGB, which is a nice job. There is nothing to do. They do not let the [head of the KGB First Directorate] die without pay. They need to keep [such persons] happy, so they get their fat salaries. They can stay at home and live another twenty years.

Then [Brezhnev would] say to the KGB chairman, Gromyko, and Ponomarev: "Let's think whom we can put into that position. It is very important. [It] must be an entirely trustworthy person, without adventurism." These three people think and come up with five or six different candidates. Finally, Ponomarev wins out with . . . [the] chief of some sector in the International Department, [who] knows a foreign language, and was directly involved in sensitive types of Soviet policy [decisions], and so he became [head] of the First [chief] Directorate. It is an entirely different thing to be the chief of a section in the International Department, where there are twenty people, [or head] of the largest intelligence service in the history of civilization.

Before considering the dynamics of the career system in more detail, a profile of the successful person in the socialist system should be provided. As in other political systems, smoothness, intelligence, boldness, and the ability to adapt to new directions matter enormously. In the Soviet case, loyalty to the party and connections with security organs play an additional, and powerful, role, as illustrated by Michael Voslensky:

The chief of the Soviet delegation [to the WPC],[19] Gulyaev, was just from the Comintern. . . . He never told me, but other people who came from the Comintern told me that he had come from the NKVD.[20] And in the Comintern, he was the chief of the Cadres Department . . . the department of personnel. Gulyaev was a master of intrigue, very smooth, polite, friendly, but at the same time maneuvering. He tried and was successful in outmaneuvering his deputy. He organized intrigues against different people in the Council. His main objective was that he be number one. The general secretary, a French communist named Jean Lafite, was his marionette and [Gulyaev] wanted to be the absolute leader of the WPC, while not appearing to be so. He wanted everyone to suspect that he was indeed in complete con-

---

[19] World Peace Council, a Soviet-sponsored organization which has, in the past, taken a leading role in many front programs and activities.

[20] The People's Commissariat for Internal Affairs; after 1946, the Ministry of International Affairs (MVD).

trol. You could never believe him, never trust him. He was the type of person who could climb up in the party structure. He came from the NKVD and said officially that he was an engineer.

Factions

Formation and Operation

A particularly significant facet of the convoluted power structure of closed societies is factionalism. Because only one political party exists, associations cannot be formed officially in the furtherance of different policies. Therefore, of necessity, the political process is channeled into power contests between groups based primarily upon personal allegiances and linkages. Such factions, to be sure, can manipulate specific issues in an effort to delegitimate one another. When one faction defeats another, the outcome guarantees only that the members of the prevailing group will obtain job security (at least temporarily). It does *not* mean necessarily that whatever issue had been in contention will be implemented along the lines which had been advocated by the winning faction before the struggle was decided. The power contest between Malenkov[21] and Beria,[22] on one side, and Zhdanov,[23] on the other, over the treatment of the Soviet zone of Eastern Europe after World War II constitutes a prime example of this: Zhdanov lost the power struggle but several of his concepts were implemented after his demise.[24] Factions play a major role in the (party and state) political process in closed societies, as our witnesses testify.

Marx claimed that the cause of human alienation was private property and division of labor. The destruction of capitalism would eliminate alienation. Communism, argued Marx, is accomplished humanism. However, "Hus" presents a less optimistic view. Communism is almost synonymous with permanent power struggles. Even citizens outside the party elite are drawn into the cycle of conflict:

> Once communism is introduced . . . [i]t creates long-term animosities and a desire for revenge. If someone is put into prison, then someone in his family will try to find a way to [retaliate] many years later. . . . Under communism everything is a power struggle.

---

[21] George M. Malenkov, former chairman, USSR Council of Ministers; briefly first party secretary of the CC CPSU; Politburo member; deceased.

[22] Lavrenty P. Beria, former chief of the NKVD; Plitburo member; executed after Stalin's death.

[23] Andrey A. Zhdanov, former CPSU chief in Leningrad; Politburo member; deceased.

[24] See Gavriel D. Ra'anan, *International Policy Formation in the USSR: Factional Debates' during the Zhdanovshchina* (Hamden, Ct: Archon Books, 1983), passim.

The phenomenon of factionalism is not confined to the Politburo. Analysts tend to focus on this level because it is here that factional struggles are most visible. However, one should not assume that factions exist only at the very highest level; they extend to middle-level bureaucrats and local administrators. As Voslensky says, factions are such a feature of Soviet life that they do not even require central coordination:

> [All political institutions have] these factions, and . . . [e]ach faction has its people everywhere in the apparatus . . . [members] of the *nomenklatura* . . . know whom they have to propose [for particular posts]; . . . this is their job. They must know.

Sejna tells of the ease with which factions operate. One member advances and does his best to bring his trusted associates along:

> When I was in Prague, I routinely promoted my friends, people who had been with me when I was a *politruk*[25] of a brigade in Litomerice or wherever. But for me, these men would never have made it to Prague because they were not being reserved for anything.

Orionova indicates one does not remain necessarily in the same faction throughout one's career. Some groups succeed, others fail, and when a faction is eclipsed one abandons it as rapidly as possible to avoid being associated too closely with the unsuccessful. Even friendship is a fleeting factor:

> Well, there is nepotism, yes. But . . . the emphasis is much more on your current position, so you constantly attach yourself to new strata, to new groups. You do not stick with an old group which is not successful. If they are not succesful, you [abandon] them immediately. It is the psychological, political climate which very often defines your friends.

In response to the question whether *protektsia* carries over when one moves from one institute to another, that is, whether influence that helped one in one location would be lost when one left that position, she responded:

> You don't quite lose it. It is a very inflexible, static system. This was true in my case. There was no chance that I could leave the IUSA,[26] which was considered to be the ultimate goal by most people, to go to another institute or to the publishing house Nauka because I was fed up with the people I was

---

[25] A political commissar. For an outstanding analysis of this function, see Timothy J. Colton, *Commissars, Commanders, and Civilian Authority: The Structure of Soviet Military Politics* (Cambridge, MA: Harvard University Press, 1979).

[26] Institute for the Study of the USA; after 1974, Institute for the Study of the USA and Canada.

working with or because I felt too confined by the subject I was studying. It would be taken as a sort of betrayal. There are cases when one can sometimes swap jobs. Trofimenko, for example, was head of section at IMRD (Institute of the International Workers' Movement), but that is second-rate compared to IUSA, and he got much more at IUSA than he could have had he stayed at IMRD. So it was alright for him to move to IUSA. But it is very unusual since he has lost all his contacts at IMRD. . . . On the other hand, when Skorov [head of IUSA Second Department, which studies the U.S. economy] came from IMEiMO[27] and became deputy director, it was a promotion since he had not been deputy director before. So presumably he [retained] contacts with his old institute. But this was so because it was a promotion, not a demotion. When Trofimenko married a chief of section at the Institute, it was decided that this sort of family tie was inappropriate, so she was moved to IMEiMO. . . . It is thought to be much better to spread family connections over two different institutes.

The success of faction depends primarily on its leader. If the chief prospers, all below who are associated with him will do well also. As Sejna points out, the leader needs able persons in his faction to further his quest for power. Similarly, capable individuals are interested in staying with an ambitious leader to further their own interests:

At the same time, the most influential [personalities] in the party try to push forward their own people . . . whom they feel they can count on. Meanwhile the [persons] being promoted . . . seek the support of whoever will help them go higher still. It may not be enough to be friends with the first secretary either. If the head of the Administrative Organs Department is against someone, [that person] can expect problems.

One should be alert, Sejna cautions:

[Persons are] in trouble if their superior is demoted. It is said that one must have a good sense of which way the wind is blowing if [one is] to survive in this business.

William Stiller elaborates on the tactics of survival in political systems plagued by factional struggles and stresses the need for constant vigilance:

One of the favorite pastimes was to pick up rumors about what was going on, and which way it was going. I remember two diplomatic couriers coming in April of 1971, and they told me that there was a problem going

---

[27] Institute of World Economics and Interntional Relations; formerly the Institute of World Economics and World Politics.

on between Podgorny[28] and Brezhnev, and that Podgorny might go. I am absolutely sure they told the ambassador and everyone else on a confidential basis. We all talked about it among ourselves as well. We learned to do this at the Institute.

Victor Kudryavtsev was very popular; when his father was dismissed from Cuba he was not too popular [any longer]. Dmitrii Tarabrin was very popular, but when we learned that something had happened to his father, he was ostracized. The same thing happened with Nosenko's[29] brother. We learned very early in life that you have to have a feel for what's going on at the top at all times, with your higher-up friends, with your relatives; one had to know which way the wind is blowing. Each faction has an interest in spreading rumors that it is doing well, and also to give visible signs. These things are carefully watched by people in the bureaucracy, and they react accordingly. I think it's a way of building a power base throughout the society.

In Mengistu's[30] Ethiopia, Wolde had a particularly harsh experience, in which the downfall of his patron almost cost him his life:

I lived a very difficult life immediately after the execution of [General] Aman, [my protector]. I did not know whether or not I would be executed because I was too close to Aman, as a second lieutenant in the Third Division in Harar. I was his aide-de-camp there. . . . We were very close. Our families were very close as well. . . . [T]here were many people who were expecting me also to be called one day and to be executed for being very close to him. But it's just good fortune, I think, that I was not killed. But perhaps it may be because I knew Mengistu also during his days in Harar and at that time he also used to respect General Aman. And my relation with Aman was a professional one. He selected me for the job and I had no personal interest in him. He was from the northern part of Ethiopia, from Eritrea. I am not. Because our relationship was very professional, they thought I had nothing to do with him. The minister of public security, who happens to be my personal friend, told me later that there were people in the Dergue who pointed their fingers at me. But Mengistu and some of the others, I think, thought that was no reason to execute me, and so I was saved.

In the Soviet Foreign Ministry, predictably, one's relationship with Gromyko was the key to a successful career.

---

[28] Nikolay V. Podgorny, former member of the Politburo; former secretary of the CC CPSU; former chairman of the Presidium of the USSR Supreme Soviet.

[29] Yuriy Nosenko, a Soviet defector who claimed to have had access to the KGB file on Lee Harvey Oswald.

[30] Mengistu Haile Mariam, current leader of Ethiopia.

Semyonov[31] was held in rather high regard by employees of the Ministry of Foreign Affairs. Gromyko, on the other hand, was not—particularly by young people. Gromyko basically stood for the prevention of career development if one was not connected [to him]. Gromyko's people just skyrocketed in their careers. We were absolutely positive that the only way you could get ahead in the Ministry of Foreign Affairs was by virtue of your [familial] relationships . . . and how they related to Gromyko [personally]. For ordinary mortal people, you had to be satisfied that, by the time you were sixty years old, you might work up to ambassador [or] you might not.

Levchenko, in responding to the question how an "unofficial" body, like the general secretary's personal chancery, is staffed, and whether it is true that leading members of Brezhnev's chancery were chosen by Gromyko, states:

[There is] the possibility that [Gromyko went] directly to Brezhnev and [said]: "I know you have a place which will be vacant and I have an excellent person." Undoubtedly there is a lot of mutual suspicion in the Politburo, but in [matters] like that they have no other way out but to trust each other. Otherwise they really will not be able to work.

Polyanskiy[32] [provided an example of the way the system functions]. He had in his mind thousands of names of people who started as low-ranking party bureaucrats and were gradually climbing up. His mind is like a computer. Otherwise, he is a very silly person, and really not creative or capable. Even in Japan, he would get *Pravda* and *Izvestia,* which would get there three days late and are not much of newspapers anyway. He would read all the information in every article, come across the name of a minor official from some out-of-the-way place, and know everything about him. It was just unbelievable, scary really. I was already quite upset will all kinds of other things, fed up. Where is the guarantee that other members of the Politburo are not as stupid as he is and are just sitting around doing the same thing? Sure, the answer is not everyone, but he was not just fired because of stupidity.

Factional divisions manifest themselves differently at different levels of the hierarchy. Zdzislaw Rurarz explains that in Poland, personal connections are not as important at the lower levels:

[I]n Poland, personal ties may be less important in staffing [lower] levels, but at higher levels personal ties still play a large role.

Sejna believes that promotion at the top depends primarily on connections—whom one knows and whom one supports. Responding to the

---

[31] Vladimir S. Semyonov, former deputy foreign minister and soviet ambassador to the Federal Republic of Germany.

[32] Dimitriy Stepanovich Polyanskiy, one-time member of the Politburo, later USSR ambassador to Japan.

question whether reserves [two slightly lower appointees kept as potential replacements for a higher-level official] move up automatically if an official is demoted or replaced, he said:

> No, it is not automatic. At the lower levels it is automatic, but not at the top levels. You cannot tell me that Ligachev, who was first secretary in [an *oblast*], was reserved for the Politburo of the CPSU, for example. Nobody had ever even considered him. It was just that Andropov or Gorbachev knew him, and when someone suggested [another candidate] for the post, [Gorbachev] insisted on Ligachev since he knew him. There might be ten thousand people in the Soviet Union more qualified than Ligachev, but Gorbachev knows Ligachev and that is all that really matters. Or it was the same thing between Ogarkov[33] and Malinovsky.[34] If someone rises to the top whom you know, you are lucky.

Promotions are not the only objects of contention in factional struggles. At the top of the pyramid, one competes with other factional leaders for influence over decision making, and the result of that contest may determine the thrust of the policy in the USSR and Eastern Europe, according to Hus.

> [To some extent policy decisions reflected the correlation of forces in] the power struggle in Moscow. If Ponomarev, in his relations with Brezhnev, had the upper hand over Gromyko, then he [Ponomarev] could [substitute] his agenda [for] Gromyko's more cautious [approach over decolonization of Africa]. Gromyko needed to take other factors, such as relations with Portugal or the U.S. into account. These complicated the simple issue of gaining independence. For Ponomarev to [have his] directive [implemented meant] that he had gained Brezhnev's approval and was in a stronger position than Gromyko, who was responsible for the Soviet Union's overall foreign policy. . . .
>   Ponomarev did not really coordinate his position [with his colleagues], because it was basically ideological. . . . He believed in conquering the world with communism. If he needed information or help from Andropov, Andropov would give him that assistance without a doubt. . . . I do know that Suslov[35] was a strong backer of Ponomarev.

In a similar vein, Kucharski observed that policy "debates" among the Soviet elite are settled not so much on the objective merits of the competing views, as in accordance with the relative power of the personalities involved:

---

[33] Nikolay V. Ogarkov, former Soviet chief of staff; marshal of the Soviet Union.

[34] Rodion Y. Malinovsky, former marshal of the Soviet Union; USSR minister of defense; commander in chief, Far East troops; deceased.

[35] Mikhail A. Suslov, former member of the Soviet Politburo and secretary, CC CPSU; deceased.

In a dispute [between] different personalities at the Politburo or Secretariat level, it is always clear who is right: It is whoever holds the more important position. Whatever Arbatov[36] or someone else would say is totally irrelevant, unless he is asked by someone who wishes to use his views. It is said that Arbatov is a protégé of Yakovlev.[37] In this respect it is possible that Arbatov would be asked about his views. Those officials who do not know Arbatov could care less. Also Foreign Ministry officials who are authorized to communicate with the Politburo will not be overruled by Arbatov. Therefore, Arbatov does not hold a formal role in this system; rather, it depends on his personal relationships with [persons at the top] level.

"Extended Family"

In the establishment of factions within the leadership, nepotism rears its head, no less than among more humble personalities at the outset of their careers, as discussed earlier in this book. Historically, the extended family, enhanced by marital links, was the basis of the earlier form of factionalism. This phenomenon continues to characterize contemporary closed societies. Moreover, to keep a promising career on track, one must not antagonize those who have helped along the way—especially extended family connections. Gregory refers to the feudal analogy:

> Zhivkov[38] [in Bulgaria] is very careful on this subject. He is supporting the careers of the children of his associates—a feudal system [of benefices] for all so they [may] not [become] unhappy.

Orionova explains that a member of the sub-elite can exploit family ties for his own benefit, creating a mutual support system:

> By taking on . . . children of the elite, Arbatov was trying to build up his own connections and reputation. The Institute [of the United States and Canada] was staffed, therefore, with such persons. There are not many places in Moscow where a graduate can go, and one wouldn't send one's child to a provincial city to live. The only place to live in Russia is Moscow, and so one tries to stay in the city. If someone, even the deputy director of IMEiMO, calls Arbatov and says, "we'll help your son (who is at IMEiMO), but I need your help with my daughter (who graduated from the Institute of Foreign Affairs)," she would come to the institute as a typist or as clerical staff and advance from there.

---

[36] Georgy A. Arbatov, director of the Soviet Institute for the Study of the USA and Canada; member of the CC CPSU; member of the Soviet Committee for the Defense of Peace.

[37] Aleksandr N. Yakovlev, Chairman, International Commission, and Secretary, CC CPSU; Politburo member.

[38] Todor Zhivkov, former Chief of the Bulgarian Communist Party.

Nepotism based on family connections can on occasion turn into a double-edged sword. If one's protector loses this position he becomes, sometimes overnight, a millstone around one's neck, and one's career invariably takes a sudden dive. This happened to Khrushchev's family; subsequently, members of Brezhnev's clan experienced a similar fate, demonstrating the continued validity of an old adage,[39] mentioned here by Sejna:

> Once someone is on the "black list," all his family and friends are in trouble too.

Voslensky stresses that intermarriage and personal relationships play an important role in the creation of factional alignments, as was the case in the Middle Ages. At the same time, he cautions against applying biographical data too mechanically:

> *Q:* So without knowing the familial relationships we lack an important ingredient in trying to evaluate the situation. When they don't print who the wives are, they are really depriving us of an important input.
>
> *Voslensky:* Sure. . . . [I]t's very important who the wives are, who the good friends are.
>
> *Q:* That is why biography is so important?
>
> *Voslensky:* Yes, yes. [However], very often this principle is considered . . . a bit formalistically. "They worked together in the same party committee. Aha!" But maybe they were enemies.

Voslensky also maintains that being promoted by a certain person is insufficient by itself as a criterion for establishing factional affiliation. For instance: Ligachev, Ryzhkov, Vorotnikov, and Solomentsev[40] all came from the *apparat* of the RSFSR [Russian Soviet Federated Socialist Republic] and they had at one time or another been promoted by Kirilenko.[41] However,

> Kirilenko was an organizational secretary. . . . So if everybody has been promoted by Kirilenko, it does not mean that all of them had been picked up by Kirilenko personally. . . . There are perhaps some members of the Secretariat or the Politburo who would say, "I know that guy. He is a good man,

---

[39] See Anthony D'Agostino, *Soviet Succession Struggles; Kremlinology and the Russian Question from Lenin to Gorbachev* (Boston: Allen and Unwin, 1988), pp. 210–215.

[40] Nikolay I. Ryzhkov, member of the Politburo of the CC CPSU and chairman of the Soviet Council of Ministers; Vitaly I. Vorotnikov, CC CPSU Politburo member, former chairman of the RSFSR Council of Ministers, currently chairman of the Presidium of the RSFSR Supreme Soviet; Mikhail S. Solomentsev, former chairman of the party Control Commission, and former member of the CC CPSU Politburo.

[41] Andrey P. Kirilenko, former secretary of the CC CPSU, and former member of the Politburo.

and he would not be bad for this job." And [if] Kirilenko has no feelings about him one way or the other, he will be appointed.

Shevchenko suggests that the factional situation is fluid because members of the elite have been known to change allegiance:

> It's not always the case that [individuals] suffer, who have been closely associated with someone who . . . has been pushed out. It very much depends. Kirilenko could appoint someone, or could promote someone, but you should not think that if someone is promoted by [a leading personality who subsequently is ousted or dies, he necessarily carries] a stigma for the rest of his life, that he is [always] considered Kirilenko's man, or Andropov's man, or Chernenko's man.

Ethnicity also plays a role in the growth of factions, as Orionova points out:

> All the elites from the republics go to Russian schools and are Russian-educated. Everyone knows that the only way to get to the top, even in the republics, is to stay close to the Russians . . . close to the Russian elite. Every representative of any ethnic group prefers to live in Moscow.

Power Struggles

The way Moscow and its Eastern European clients handle promotions, demotions, and succession struggles provides students of the Soviet Union with a useful window on the most characteristic mechanisms of a closed political system.[42] Our interviewees, for instance Jiri Pelikan, stress that Soviet-style systems operate on the principle of unified leadership. Nevertheless, he and virtually all of our interviewees affirm that political circles in Moscow and in Eastern European capitals are aware of serious differences within the Soviet Politburo. How does one obtain promotion to important positions, including the Politburo? Voslensky intimates that when it comes to having two candidates for one post, each with his own factional backing, the swords are sharpened for conflict:

> *Q:* Let's take a very specific [albeit] hypothetical case—[promotion to] first secretary in [some *oblast*]. Who proposes, who has to ratify this appointment . . . [which carries with it] membership in the Central Committee? . . . [I]s that ratified at the level of the Politburo?
>
> *Voslensky:* No, certainly not. It will be decided . . . with regard to [*oblast* level posts] . . . at the Regional Committee by the Secretariat of the Party

---

[42] For a study of this topic, see D'Agostino, *Soviet Succession Struggles,* passim.

Central Committee, but the Politburo will be informed previously. If there is no veto from the Politburo, it will be decided by the Secretariat. . . . There is no concrete [scenario for dealing with rival condidates, supported by opposing factions; consequently] there are all these intrigues in the apparatus. . . . The secretaries will be involved and some members of the Politburo, then the decision will be ripe. There will be a compromise if compromise is necessary. There [may be the] victory of one clan. [The contest may involve smears of a candidate's reputation.] It's intrigue, it's gossip. It's pressure. . . . [I]t is necessary to find the weakness in [an opposing candidate's] position. Maybe [they have] something [on] him, or [on] his parents or his daughter or his son or his wife.

Such promotions are not "rammed through," Voslensky suggests. The general secretary does not, at least now, have dictatorial control over the Politburo and the Secretariat. He must reach a consensus to promote his protégés, otherwise he will be confronted by opposition. When the decision is made to elevate someone to the position even of candidate member, and certainly of a full member of the Politburo, who is involved in this decision.

The Politburo itself. . . . Practically, [candidates are] co-opted. Theoretically, it will be done by the Central Committee meeting in plenary session, but practically they are co-opted. . . . Gorbachev alone can do many things but he is limited to [lower-level] appointments.

Similarly, according to Sejna, candidates will not be ousted solely at the whim of the general secretary. This is especially the case, states Sejna, with regard to the Secretariat of the party Central Committee:

How can a party secretary be ousted? That is a more difficult problem than promoting or demoting a member of the Politburo. Grishin[43] and Shevardnadze[44] [did] not attend the meetings of the Secretariat when this small group [sat] down and decided whom to move up and whom to oust. One day Podgorny goes off to Africa on a visit, and the next day he is thrown out. That is how it works. Or, somebody on the Secretariat [wanted] to oust Gromyko, so he [was] kicked upstairs. Or Gromyko may have had Gorbachev on his side, as he may have backed Gorbachev against Romanov.[45] In all likelihood it [was] one of these party secretaries who informed Gromyko of the change. . . .

It is more important that Gorbachev have the secretaries on his side than the members of the Politburo. Members of the Politburo can be removed much more readily than secretaries. If Gorbachev were to go before

---

[43] Viktor V. Grishin, former member of the CC CPSU Politburo and former Moscow party chief.

[44] Eduard A. Shevardnadze, Soviet foreign minister, Politburo member.

[45] Grigory V. Romanov, former secretary, CC CPSU; former Politburo member.

the meeting of the party secretaries and say that [one of the secretaries] should step aside for the good of the party, [if this proposal were] opposed by a majority of the secretaries, he would be compelled to withdraw his request.

Sejna reports that the situation is similar in Czechoslovakia:

At the meetings of the [Czechoslovak] Central Committee, such changes are always the last item on the agenda. The members of the Central Committee come back from their coffee break and find before them a piece of paper stating that the following changes have been recommended by the Politburo. The members are then asked whether they have any objections. They never do.

To be removed from the Secretariat is far harder. The other secretaries have to organize completely behind the back of the one to be removed. Furthermore, the first secretary must also agree and that is not easy. They are all top bosses and are likely to fight.

Once the decision is made to remove a high official, it is implemented quickly. Several interviewees confirm that sometimes it is done in a very straightforward manner, while on other occasions the victim returns from a trip to find his situation dramatically altered. Vladimir Kostov, speaking about Bulgarian political reality, stresses the importance of consulting with the local Soviet embassy before a major change in the composition of the top elite is implemented:

It is not an accident the best contacts that [the Bulgarian communist leader] Zhivkov has are the minister of interior and the minister of defense. We know from history the example of [Anton Yugov[46]]. He was the prime minister, a member of the Politburo, yet his case was never an issue before the Politburo. Shortly before the party Congress, a few state security officers appeared at his home and told him that he had nothing to do at the conference. What happened is that the day before, Zhivkov was in Moscow and got the OK for this. So there is nothing to discuss. . . . At the same Congress, a few delegates attacked [Yugov] very sharply. He could not defend himself. This is possible chiefly because of the role in Bulgaria of the Soviet embassy and Soviet agents. Bulgarian leaders are afraid to have contacts among themselves. . . . It is always possible for the first secretary to organize the group against somebody from the Politburo. As far as I know this is how they attacked Vulko Chervenkov[47] in 1957. But it is not typical. It depends on the view of the first secretary.

---

[46] Anton Yugov, former Bulgarian communist prime minister; former minister of the interior.
[47] Vulko Chervenkov, Bulgaria's "Little Stalin," purged from the party by Todor Zhivkov.

Shevchenko discusses the mechanisms available in the Soviet system for ousting members of the top political elite, just below the Politburo level:

> In the case of someone being dismissed . . . it could be done, from what I know, in one of two ways. One, you could come to your office one day and find on your desk a decision of the Politburo. You can call anyone, any number you like, if your phone has not been disconnected by this time—because it would be very quickly disconnected. And if you try to call your friends in the Politburo, you can't—because it will just be a normal telephone again. Two, if someone still retains power or influence, I think it's done in such a way that the secretary-general just tells you the reasons, in an open way.

Rurarz, the former Polish ambassador in Tokyo who resigned from his post in protest over the military takeover by General Jaruzelski, provides a nugget of information. He describes how Gierek[48] dismissed General Moczar, a "hard-liner" and a man of Moscow, from the Politburo:

> By accident, I witnessed the end of the career of General Mieczyslaw Moczar, former chief of the Ministry of Internal Affairs, a member of the "old Politburo." About a week before the opening of the sixth PUWP[49] Party Congress, in December 1971, I was waiting to see Gierek, when one of his two secretaries, beautiful girls from the Ministry of the Interior, told me that I would have to wait longer, as Moczar was on his way to see Gierek. Just before Moczar came, I saw Babiuch and Kania[50] enter Gierek's office. Then Moczar arrived, shook hands with me, and began nervously walking the corridor in front of the Politburo meeting room (Gierek's office adjoined the room where Politburo meetings were held). But there was no meeting of the Politburo that day; Moczar was just waiting for the verdict. I didn't want to speak to him, because I smelled that something was wrong. Later I learned from Waszczuk that at that very meeting Moczar was dropped from the Politburo. The consensus of those three officials—Gierek, Kania, and Babiuch—was sufficient to dismiss him. The official announcement, of course, was made only at the party congress. . . .
>
> The main cause of Moczar's dismissal was the rebellion he organized against Gierek, which Szlachcic, at that time minister of internal affairs, discovered. They kept him in the Politburo long afterwards, but only because he was Moscow's man; once they'd cleared it with the Soviets, Moczar was dropped. He had never been a Polish nationalist; in fact, he was Ukrainian, only a tool of Moscow.

---

[48] Edward Gierek, former leader of the Polish Communist Party (PZPR); his fall in 1980 was followed by the emergence of the Solidarity movement.

[49] Polish United Workers' Party.

[50] Stanislaw Kania, briefly leader of the Polish Communist Party, replaced by General Wojciech Jaruzelski.

So under Gierek, dismissals were not discussed in full sessions of the Politburo; the decision was confined to a few people. Bierut or Gomulka,[51] on the other hand, would abruptly fire whomever they wanted. But Gierek had to have the support of at least Kania and Babiuch.

The fate of the staff members of the political elite in Moscow often mirrors that of their ex-employer. In this example from the early 1950s, Deriabin tells of a group of unfortunates who did not even have time to clean out their desks:

In late April or early May 1952, General Vlasik[52] left the Guards Directorate to run a concentration camp near Sverdlovsk. . . . When [the members of] Vlasik's secretariat returned from the train station after saying good-bye, the Personnel Directorate told them that their jobs were filled, their passes were taken away, and they were told that they no longer worked for the Guards. There were other people doing their jobs by the time they got back from the train station.

Historical examples of power struggles among the leadership include the maneuvers of the ill-fated "Leningrad group," including Andrei Zhdanov. Deriabin elaborates:

In 1946, during a victory celebration, in May or June I believe, all the marshals, generals, CPSU secretaries, *obkom* officials, etc., came to congratulate Stalin on the victory in World War II. They asked him what his next victory would be and he replied that he thought it was time for him to slow down and retire (he did not use the word retire but "*mne pora na pokoy*" [it's time for me to rest]). Through 1947 and into 1948, there was much talk about how to relieve the work burden of comrade Stalin in order to preserve his health. I started in the Guards Directorate in 1947, so I do not know about Stalin's health before that time. The suggestion to relieve Stalin's work load allegedly came from Zhdanov but I cannot directly confirm that.

In any event the idea was to move the capital of the Russian republic to Leningrad, leaving Moscow as only the federal capital. Zhdanov was . . . going to be . . . the number two man to Stalin. [A.A.] Kuznetsov was to be the boss [of the new capital of the RSFSR], Rodionov,[53] the chairman of the Council of Ministers of the Russian republic, and M.V. Basov [then chairman of the RSFSR Gosplan], chairman of the Presidium of the Russian republic. Basov was not arrested during the affair but was sent by Stalin to [an academic post] in 1949. I saw him myself when I attended lectures there during that time.

[51] Boleslaw Beirut, former president of Poland; deceased; Wladyslaw Gomulka, former general secretary of the PZPR; deceased.

[52] General Nikolay Vlasik, Stalin's first and most enduring bodyguard; deceased.

[53] Mikhail I. Rodionov, former chairman of the RSFSR Council of Ministers; purged in the "Leningrad affair."

Voznesensky[54] was also involved in the projected reorganization—he was supposed to become the chairman of the Council of Ministers of the USSR: I did not see it at the time but I can see in retrospect that other members of the Leningrad organization, notably Popkov[55] and Danilov, also played important roles.

Later in this book, material will be presented concerning the jostling for position between Beria and Abakumov,[56] a battle that Beria eventually won. In the following excerpt, Gregory explains how Beria's subsequent liquidation was accomplished:

Beria was the most powerful man and his downfall was the product of the internal struggle between Malenkov, Kaganovich, and Khrushchev. . . . Three or four months [subsequently], we had a long meeting and a protocol was read detailing the "crimes" of Beria. I had no sympathy for Beria—he had perpetrated many horrible crimes against Georgians and many others—but the list of crimes took five hours to read. I remember that the first accusation was that he loved young girls. Second, that he used his position to have sex with the wives of KGB officers. Third, that he was the agent of the UK intelligence services from 1919. Fourth, that he was an agent of international imperialism. Fifth, and most important, when Stalin was dying, the Politburo members were crying and beginning to mourn, but Beria was already planning for the new government. This meant that Beria did not like our "dear father" Stalin.[57] This is ironic because Beria was Stalin's closest friend. . . .

The first reason for Beria's execution was fear of his power. Beria had the KGB, the guards, etc., and if he gave an order to arrest Khrushchev, Malenkov, or Bulganin,[58] it would be done. The others only realized after his arrest that Beria had bugged their phones. They were afraid of him. It is possible that Khrushchev had informers that told him Beria was planning something. In any case, they decided that if Beria was around he could author a coup with the KGB and the palace guard.

Maybe Khrushchev wanted to take power immediately, kill Beria, etc., but it took time. He had to wait for a suitable time to fulfill his intentions. Beria was close to Malenkov, and Khrushchev realized it was impossible to destroy these two strong men at the same time. They often stayed together. . . . After Stalin died, Khrushchev and others saw that the main

---

[54] Nikolay A. Voznesensky, former Politburo member, executed in 1950 for alleged part in the "Leningrad affair."

[55] Pyotr S. Popkov, Leningrad CPSU member, executed in 1949 for alleged participation in the "Leningrad affair."

[56] Viktor S. Abakumov, former Soviet minister of state security; deceased.

[57] It may be noted that in his oration at Stalin's funeral, Beria went out of his way to praise and cite Lenin, rather than the deceased whose memory was supposed to be honored.

[58] Nikolay A. Bulganin, former chairman, USSR Council of Ministers (COM); former member of the Politburo of the CC; former marshal of the USSR.

contenders for power were Beria and Malenkov. So they first destroyed Beria, and then Malenkov.

Malenkov was the next to fall to his opponents. The speed of his removal and subsequent drift to obscurity has earned Malenkov the title "the forgotten first secretary," and the announcement of his death in the summer of 1988 took many analysts of the USSR by surprise. It had been assumed that he had been dead for many years. Gregory continues:

> The reason [for Malenkov's fall] was . . . Malenkov's desire to reduce military industry. He actually did this for a time; many factories were shifted to producing high-quality consumer goods. For example, I bought a baby carriage made by a former airplane factory. I have never since seen as good a quality carriage as that one. Malenkov was a clever man. He realized that the standard of living had to be increased. He felt that there were enough nuclear weapons for deterrence and that it was not necessary to think that the U.S. would attack; if we were attacked, we had enough to retaliate.
>
> The minister of defense was later unhappy with Malenkov for cutting warships—this was another reason for his dismissal. Malenkov also stated that the Soviet Union would shift from arms production to consumer goods. He was later accused of making this speech without Politburo approval, but this is a lie. It was approved; this was only used to discredit him later. Malenkov's policy was opposed by Khrushchev and others who wanted to build up Soviet military power. They also personally disliked Malenkov. He was younger and also very close to Stalin. Stalin made many appointments after discussion with Malenkov, and Khrushchev remembered this. Also, when he was first secretary of the Moscow Communist Party, Malenkov was sent to the Ukraine [where Khrushchev was installed at the time]. When he returned, he told Stalin that things could be run better and Khrushchev remembered this as well. Khrushchev was waiting for an opportunity and it came after Malenkov's speech. Khrushchev, Bulganin, and Kaganovich (who hated Malenkov) were all very ambitious men.
>
> In the Politburo, if several members are against you, you can be dismissed if you have made any mistake. The official accusation was that he made an unauthorized speech. Malenkov lost the . . . chairman of the Council of Ministers position but he was not dismissed from the Politburo.

Khrushchev rose to power once Beria and Malenkov were removed, and he, of course, was to be overthrown in turn. In 1957, an unsuccessful attempt to oust Khrushchev took place, and in 1964, a second attempt swept Khrushchev into the netherworld of retirement. A comparison of the two events indicates the correlation of forces necessary to achieve the removal of a leader. Gregory stresses the crucial role of Serov, whose ties with Khrushchev went back to the pre–World War II period. At the same time, Gregory is skeptical about the theory that Khrushchev, during the first challenge to his rule, was rescued in part by Marshal Zhukov:

I have read much about the anti-party group and the events of [1957]. It has been stated that Zhukov supported Khrushchev in the call for assembling the members of the CC. This is not true. Serov[59] did this, not Zhukov. . . . Serov sent messages to the KGB to make sure that all CC members would be in Moscow the following day. The CC members were accompanied like prisoners—not by mere officers but by regional heads or deputy heads of the KGB. I knew some CC members from Georgia and they told me they were afraid—they thought they were under arrest. They received no explanation. When Serov told Khrushchev they were assembled in Moscow, Khrushchev faced the anti-party group and said, "You are against me but I am the leader of the people. We must ask the members of the CC. Do they want me as leader or you? It is not my decision but it must be the decision of the CC of the CPSU." When the members arrived, they were told by the KGB of a disagreement and that they had to support Khrushchev.

Q: So the Red Army was not involved?

Gregory: No. This is a confusion of what happened, absolutely untrue. Zhukov was not involved. It was Serov.

Q: Why did the others not arrest Khrushchev when he returned from Finland?

Gregory: Because Serov was behind Khrushchev and without the KGB you cannot arrest anyone.

Q: But when Malenkov, Kaganovich, and the others decided to remove Khrushchev from power in his absence, they must have had some reason to believe they could succeed.

Gregory: They decided Khrushchev had to go but this was impossible if the KGB was not on their side. Khrushchev was able to dismiss Zhukov because the KGB was in the hands of Khrushchev. At that time, Khrushchev was popular among the Soviet people. To give an example, when he was dismissed in 1964, it was the result of a Politburo meeting. Brezhnev said that Khrushchev wanted to take his case to the Soviet people but he was not allowed. The KGB guard prevented him from leaving. Kharlamov, head of Moscow radio and TV was dismissed because he was close to Khrushchev. The new leadership was afraid that a media message about Khrushchev being dismissed by an opposition group would be broadcast.

Q: In 1957, [Khrushchev's opponents] failed because they did not have KGB support. In 1964, they succeeded because they had KGB support. What led to this change?

Gregory: Khrushchev's authority declined severely after the Cuban missile crisis. The KGB, the Red Army, even the Soviet people believed he was a strong leader. No one knew about his theatrics at the UN—we only

---

[59] Ivan A. Serov, former chairman of the KGB and chief of Soviet military intelligence (GRU); responsible, inter alia, for mass deportations before and during World War II; dismissed in connection with the Penkovskiy case; deceased.

heard he made a strong presentation. We did not like what Khrushchev wanted to do in Cuba. When the Soviet soldiers were sent to Odessa for shipment to Cuba, many deserted. They did not want to go. They were scared to be so far from the Motherland and they did not want to go and die in Cuba in the event something happened. It was a big mistake on Khrushchev's part to agree to remove the missiles. The people felt such a great country should not have to make concessions like that, especially after all of Khrushchev's rhetoric.

Another factor was all the stories about Krushchev. Everybody had an anecdote—taxi drivers, everyone. This information was collected by the KGB and Brezhnev and the others knew about this. Also, Khrushchev was seventy years old. When his retirement was discussed earlier, he promised the Politburo he would lead until he was seventy-one. I know this because I had a friend who was an assistant for Khrushchev—Leonid Zavgarodni. He was also from the 2nd Chief Directorate of the KGB. He said Khrushchev cried and asked for two or three more months from the Politburo and then he would retire. Then Adzhubey[60] went into the meeting and Brezhnev sent him out under guard.

Q: Did Adzhubey, a man with no official standing, actually attend Politburo meetings?

Gregory: He was Krushchev's son-in-law and had attended all the past meetings. The guards took Adzhubey out and he immediately telephoned Kharlamov but Kharlamov was dismissed at that time. Khrushchev had lost his authority, was the butt of many jokes and we realized he was a peasant who became [leader of the USSR]. In 1964, I was in Gagra on vacation with my wife and Khrushchev was in Pitzunda, very close by. We waited for Adzhubey—Chkhikvishvili called me and told me to meet him as a [fellow] Georgian. He was head of a section of the CC and is now deputy head of a state committee for publishing affairs. Adzhubey never came but Mikoyan[61] arrived and told Khrushchev to come to a meeting in Moscow. Khrushchev did not want to interrupt his vacation but Mikoyan told him it was very urgent. Khrushchev had no suspicion that he was to be dismissed—he believed in Mikoyan. Khrushchev had saved Mikoyan's life in the "anti-party" period. They left the same night by plane and the next morning Khrushchev was dismissed. Mikoyan's role was very dirty. Brezhnev knew that Mikoyan would do it in spite of his relationship to Khrushchev. Mikoyan was buried near Khrushchev but not in the Kremlin Wall.

It was possible to oust Khrushchev because he lost his authority among Soviet officials.

---

[60] Aleksei Ivanovich Adzhubey, born 1912, Khrushchev's son-in-law and chief editor of *Izvestia,* 1959–1964, removed from the Central Committee and all other official posts after Khrushchev's fall in 1964.
[61] Anastas I. Mikoyan, former chairman of the Presidium of the USSR Supreme Soviet and Politburo member; deceased.

Finally, an example from Poland shows the additional dynamic of Soviet influence in power struggles outside the USSR, especially in Eastern Europe. The removal of Gomulka by Gierek occurred with tacit Kremlin approval. When Gierek himself, however, chose to assert some of his power against Moscow, Soviet influence was direct and uncompromising, as told by Rurarz:

> The Soviets were interested in ousting Gierek on the pretext of the strikes. He went to the Crimea on 27 July as the strikes had subsided, but [were] still going in Gdansk—even increasing in intensity. Two weeks later, the Gdansk shipyard went on strike. Gierek was in the Crimea until the 17th of August, and it was rumored that he was unaware that the strikes even were still going on. Apparently the Soviets were not letting news pass to him.
>
> To make a digression, during the Eighth PUWP Congress in February 1980, Premier Jaroszewicz and Politburo member and secretary for economic affairs Stefan Olszowski were unexpectedly removed from the Politburo. Apparently, Moscow had not been consulted, because Suslov, who was present at the [Polish] Party congress, jumped up, shouting *Myatezh!* which means "rebellion," and left. Jaroszewicz and Olszowski were of course the Soviet men in the Politburo. A few months later there were food price hikes, but the reaction of the regime to the triggered-off strikes was so strange that the regime's true motives were an open question. As far as I know, Gierek never officially resigned but was simply arrested by General Jaruzelski and put to the Szaserow Street military hospital in Praga, part of Warsaw. It was then again Jaruzelski who convened the Politburo and proposed Kania as Gierek's successor. . . . Solidarity didn't know [this] and [it] is still not understood in the West.

Vignettes I. USSR

The interviewees provide detailed illustrations of the personal element as a critical factor in power struggles. Deriabin explains the (increasingly hostile) interactions between Beria and Abakumov, prior to Stalin's death, in shaping the role of the security apparatus:

> **Beria and Abakumov.** At one time they were fairly close; Beria promoted Abakumov and they seemed to work well from 1938 to 1943. This changed because Abakumov got closer to Stalin and did not need to rely on Beria. Abakumov impressed Stalin through his work in two areas. First, Abakumov managed successful disinformation campaigns, specifically during the Rostov and North Caucasus operations and during the operations around Kursk. Second, Abakumov was responsible for the second echelon of Stalin's personal guard, the SMERSH officers. In this capacity, he uncovered a German plot in 1944 to assassinate Stalin. A former Soviet officer who had been captured by the Germans was sent to kill Stalin on Arbat Street, on Stalin's way to the Kremlin. Abakumov discovered the plan

through a source of his in the *Abwehr* (German military intelligence), and the man was captured after he parachuted in near Moscow and shot. This of course greatly increased Abakumov's standing in the eyes of Stalin and Abakumov accordingly drifted further and further from Beria and Merkulov.

By 1945, Stalin had begun to mistrust Beria. Stalin made Beria a . . . marshal in July 1945, and a Politburo member in December, but by mid-January 1946, he dismissed Beria as the people's commissar of the NKVD.[62] Stalin appointed Kruglov, not Merkulov,[63] to replace Beria. At that time *Pravda* published a photograph of Kruglov [as heading] what was then called MVD with Merkulov [as heading] the NKGB. But the day after the photograph was published, the NKGB became the MGB with Abakumov as its head. So Merkulov was never really the minister of state security for more than a day. Beria selected Merkulov to become the chief of Soviet property abroad, among other things, under the Council of Ministers of the USSR. This body later became something like the Under Ministry for Foreign Trade. Merkulov also was responsible for certain economic areas in East Germany. . . .

Beria . . . played an important role in Abakumov's removal. Between 1947 and 1951, Beria tried in vain to get control of the security apparatus. As I mentioned before, Abakumov, with Poskrebyshev's[64] and therefore Stalin's approval, kept certain reports away from Beria. Beria was upset and could see his power slipping away and probably felt he was being set up by Stalin to be blamed for internal problems in the future.

Abakumov had worked under Beria before, but by the end of 1947, Abakumov had drifted completely away from Beria. Abakumov replaced virtually all the people who had worked for Beria; the only exceptions [concerned] administrative personnel such as an old major general in charge of file registration. The personnel chief, Major General Babkin, was a Beria man and he was replaced immediately and sent to Novosibirsk when Abakumov took over.

An old NKVD man, Svinelupov, took his place; even though he had worked for Beria, Abakumov thought he could trust him. Abakumov tried to get Lieutenant General Vradiy into this position and as his personal deputy but it was not approved by the CPSU Central Committee. Positions from department chief and higher had to be approved by *Otdel Karatelnykh Organov* [Department of Punitive Organs] of the CPSU, now known as the Department of Administrative Organs. They did not approve of Vradiy because of his role fighting the *basmachi* [Moslem resistance] in Central Asia when he killed many innocent people. During World War II, Vradiy worked

---

[62] In 1946, the People's Commissariat for internal affairs (NKVD) became the Ministry of Internal Affairs (MVD), while the People's Commissariat for State Security (NKGB) became the Ministry of State Security (MGB).

[63] In subsequent years, it was to turn out that Merkulov was Beria's loyal deputy, whereas Kruglov betrayed him.

[64] Aleksandr N. Proskrebyshev headed Stalin's personal chancery.

for Abakumov as chief of personnel in SMERSH and had a questionable past in that role as well so he was not approved. The best that Abakumov could do was appoint Vradiy deputy chief of the Personnel Directorate of the MGB under Svinelupov.

Khrushchev, the Red Army, and the KGB. Like Deriabin, Sejna stresses the personal element, but pays attention no less to institutional rivalries. Speaking about the Khrushchev era, Sejna describes divergent policy concepts, as they appeared to a visiting Czechoslovak army delegation:

> In 1963, when he [Khrushchev] told us that we had to play a greater role in gathering intelligence and acquiring Western technology, we began to see the growing problem Khrushchev was having with the Soviet military. Marshal Malinovsky turned to Khrushchev and said, "Comrade Khrushchev, I believe that socialism will survive only in those countries in which Soviet tanks are sitting." (We had been discussing Western Europe.) These military people are very realistic. Then Khrushchev said, "Rodion Rodionovich, I agree with you, but there is a small difference between us. Where you want to see our tanks in such a country yesterday, I am content to wait for tomorrow." We knew there was a problem there. Khrushchev's statement showed at the same time his philosophy of peaceful coexistence. We can wait, but after fifteen years, watch out.

Gradually, the party leadership and the KGB turned against the general secretary. Sejna continues:

> One would have thought that no one could touch Khrushchev, the general secretary of the CPSU, but in the ongoing game that these bureaucrats play, the party apparatus ended up combining with the KGB against the general secretary. By demoting top officers, cutting the size of the military and ousting Zhukov, Khrushchev lost the support of the armed forces. There was no one left to stand by him. Still, it can take time for these new coalitions to form. Previously, the KGB had convinced Khrushchev that Zhukov was his enemy and so [the latter] came back from Yugoslavia to find that he had lost his position, although everyone was afraid to be the one to tell him.

Gorbachev. According to the interviewees, the same elements of power struggle manifest themselves whenever a member of the top elite seeks to gain and maintain power; Shevchenko addresses the initial stages of the Gorbachev era, but integrates some new elements:

> I strongly believe that the period of personal dictatorship in the Soviet Union is gone forever. Khrushchev was the last person who tried to do something with this power. It's not propaganda when they say "collective leader-

ship". . . . As they say, Gorbachev is first among equals but he is not the new czar. . . .

Who are really Gorbachev's teachers? One would assume logically and automatically that he is a product of the party apparatus. He is a man of the party and so, like Brezhnev, he has solid ground. But don't forget that even Brezhnev never tried to remove all his opposition. That's why all his old advisers perpetuated their positions. That's why he had enormous support of the party apparatus. He relied entirely on the party apparatus and he could deal with the KGB and the army, often in the way he wanted.

Gorbachev is really a product of the party. What happened is that he has the support of some elements of the party which are strong. It's true that they are younger people coming up in the party apparatus, more energetic people. They [represent a segment] of the apparatus which supports him. But in doing all that [drive against corruption], he is removing a lot of people. By having this drive . . . he is definitely antagonizing other sectors in the Party apparatus. We cannot say that the whole apparatus is behind Gorbachev. He has split it. He has created antagonism, which is always dangerous in the Soviet Union. . . .

I'm not surprised that he is relying so much on the KGB. There is only one strong force in the Soviet Union that will gain substantially from what Gorbachev is doing. The essence of the Gorbachev policy—and I'm not talking about the economy—is a restoration of the strict work discipline, fighting against autonomism and trying to revive patriotic feelings in the Soviet Union and a sense of responsibility. . . . Moreover, if we look at the efforts of Gorbachev to introduce the missing stage of development, [with the introduction of computers, etc., we must ask] who will watch how these computers will be used? And the Soviets will only have 25,000 personal computers, not 25 million as we have. Who will watch in the new data processing revolution the intellectuals' [access to] video, the possibility of [their access to] direct television? Who will control . . . these economic changes? . . . Who will do this job? It will be the KGB.

They have a chance not only to become a stronger power, but also to increase their personnel and increase their influence. That is what is going on. Moreover, Gorbachev is very acceptable to them because Gorbachev has no intention of changing the political system in the Soviet Union.

Wolde views Gorbachev's career as following a classical CPSU pattern:

He [Gorbachev] kept a very low profile, always on the sidelines and deferring to the decisions of his seniors, like Gromyko and so on. He was very much a man of the system, a team player, and later on I came to realize that this person must have really positioned himself in such a way that throughout his whole life he was very loyal to the party system, to the decision makers, to the boss, be it the party leader or the senior leadership. When he came out of the shadows, as it were, he exuded a lot of self-confidence and a great deal of authority that shows he is in command. He did give me that impression [when] I saw him with Brezhnev and Chernenko.

Vignettes II: Poland

Zdzislaw Rurarz describes factional struggles in Poland from the 1950s to the early 1970s. There is, however, a variable in the Polish case—the presence of low-profile groups controlled by unseen actors. It is interesting to note that in Poland political factions often take on labels associating them with a geographic location. The tendency to focus on an accidental feature, such as the name of Warsaw's suburb, rather than on the group's political agenda, may be an attempt by the group to divert attention from its true character before it is strong enough to act decisively. Rurarz here speaks of the 1950s, describing three competing factions:

> I think that there was a major anti-Soviet plot in the time between Bierut's death and October 1956. The Natolin[65] was actually not as [completely] pro-Soviet as many would think, and they were not very unified: some of them were unhappy with many Soviet practices, while others were very much pro-Soviet. On the other hand, the Pulawska group was openly anti-Soviet and had penetrated the armed forces, through General Komar (Internal Security Corps), General Frey-Bielecki, and Admiral Studzinski. One can only speculate [that the Polish army's aversion to the USSR was caused by the fact that] many Polish officers [had been] executed during Stalin's era, and many others were threatened with death. This led to extensive anti-Sovietism in the military. To what extent [Marshal] Rokossovsky[66] was unaware of that or was just closing his eyes to it, we shall probably never know. . . .
>
> Gomulka [constituting a third group] had two close collaborators in Zenon Kliszko (who was a broken man) and Loga-Sowinski. Spychalski was less important, [even] though [he was] marshal and minister of defense,[67] because he was pretty much a clown (as was Loga-Sowinski), but what Gomulka didn't know, and many of us knew, was that Spychalski was an active undercover NKVD agent in Poland, [and remained so] even when arrested. Gomulka made a big mistake in trusting him. Spychalski was not at all a specialist in military affairs, but provided "fifth column" penetration of the Polish armed forces for the Soviets. . . . Gomulka was not a specialist in military affairs either. By trusting in Spychalski [he] simply lost the Polish army again. . . .
>
> [Spychalski eventually] lost control completely and was ridiculed. Nobody paid any attention to him. When Jaruzelski became chief of general

---

[65] The Natolinists, so-named after the Braniki palace at Natolin, where they held their meetings. Headed by a Polish Stalinist, Zenon Nowak, they fought against the group formed around Wladyslaw Gomulka.

[66] Konstantin K. Rokossovsky was a GULAG prisoner whom Stalin released in 1941 to fight the Germans. Stalin promoted Rokossovsky to the rank of marshal. After the Red Army ousted the Germans from Poland, Stalin imposed him on the Poles as that country's minister of defense, 1949–1956.

[67] 1956–1968; he succeeded Rokossovsky.

staff in 1965 he was already, in fact, head of the Polish army. In April 1968, he officially replaced Spychalski. That was the end. Gomulka had only Kliszko and Loga-Sowinski, who was stupid. Kliszko [as mentioned earlier] was a broken man. Strangely enough, Gomulka believed very much in Moczar at first, which was another mistake. In a sense, you could say that [Golumka constituted] a faction, but the faction was composed of too many unproved and unreliable men. All the others were really not very helpful.

Dealing with subsequent developments, Rurarz reveals a number of previously unknown details concerning power struggles in the 1970s. It may be a surprise to many that, according to Rurarz, the Polish Prime Minister Jaroszewicz was able temporarily to dominate appointments at a high level and to keep the Polish party boss Gierek in the dark about his designs:

When the Natolin and Pulawska factions were competing for power. . . . both claimed not to exist at all. The Pulawska group was victorious at first but later [was] defeated, and subsequent factional rivalries are not as easy to discern. The Natolin group survived only as an orientation of sorts, while reformers were [also] unorganized. Later, people were not so stupid as to belong to an organized group, but took stances more or less on an individual basis. The most important thing for the Party boss to learn was who was holding the reins of power on behalf of these invisible factions. Gierek actually had much less power than many people believed; I think that Premier Jaroszewicz was far more powerful than Gierek, at least before the 1976 riots. When it came to economic problems, Jaroszewicz was almost always able to install his people, even ahead of Gierek's. For instance, Gierek learned from me that Kazimierz Olszewski, at that time the minister for foreign trade and maritime economy, and later Polish ambassador to Moscow, was about to be made Vice-Premier, without my telling him Gierek would never have known. Gierek was furious at the news, and told me, "No, Olszewski will never get that position." But two days later, he did.

Those who had lined up on the winning team's side made no secret of their new status. From Tadeusz Kucharski, we have a contemporary example of the reaction of lower echelons to Jaruzelski's takeover in Poland:

I was present [in the Polish embassy in Angola] when Jaruzelski took charge and martial law was imposed [in December of 1981]. The military staff was pleased that their man now had supreme power. As a result the military became the predominant force in the [Polish] embassy and became more arrogant. After martial law was declared the military staff acted as the supreme delegate of the army at the [Polish] embassy, which meant they no longer considered the ambassador as their superior. The ambassador at this time was no longer a general. . . . It became clear that the people who were sympathetic to Solidarity would be replaced. The period after martial law was declared was marked by a far greater arrogance on Warsaw's part. There was no place for dissent. Anyone who disagreed was an enemy.

Vignettes III. Nicaragua

The last example comes from Nicaragua. It also illustrates the concept that policy does not determine faction, but faction does determine policy. The classic archetype of this dynamic is the maneuvering in the Politburo between the death of Lenin and the consolidation of power by Stalin. In this process, Stalin, among others, considered domestic tactical advantages more important than ideological consistency.

Miguel Bolaños-Hunter gives a contemporary analogy from Central America. Speaking about the conflict between Borge and the Ortega brothers, Bolaños-Hunter states that, while all are Marxist-Leninists, they also disagree with each other. Their disagreements manifest themselves in a variety of fields. (His vignette is of interest also to students of disinformation and deception.)

> [Topics that constitute ammunition against rival factions include] foreign policy, domestic policy, in everything that is important, anything that is supposed to be coming from the national leader. That is what they are [really] fighting for, [namely, control of] the leadership. It is the ambition of one or the other to take control of policy decisions. . . . They are not "pragmatists," or "dogmatists." They are the same. There is no such things as a "soft-liner." It is just because of the [external] circumstances; it is a useful image to project. We in state security, myself and one other person, started the whole myth of dogmatists and pragmatists in the FSLN[68] because the CIA was interested in this. We made this a big issue ever since 1980. We created this and now the whole world believes it. . . . And we were the ones who created the whole thing.

International Linkages of Factions

As with appointments, there is a special international dynamic in factionalism. Factions in Moscow can spill over to other socialist centers— Warsaw, Prague, East Berlin, Budapest, and Sofia.

Two interviewees describe how these linkages contributed to Khrushchev's downfall. Gregory speaks of a channel which existed between GDR leader Ulbricht[69] and Suslov:

---

[68] FSLN, the Sandinista National Liberation Front.
[69] Walter Ulbricht, former party leader of East Germany; deceased.

The final straw in [Khrushchev's] dismissal was a result of a European trip. Adzhubey [Khrushchev's son-in-law] met with FRG officials and said that Khrushchev wanted good relations with them. Among other things, Adzhubey called Ulbricht an old idiot. The next day Ulbricht had a complete tape of the meeting and he called Suslov immediately. Ulbricht refused to have his scheduled meeting with Adzhubey and sent Suslov a copy of the tape. This was in late 1963 or early 1964. . . .

[I]t was well known that relations between Khrushchev and Suslov were not friendly. . . . I think Ulbricht talked to Suslov because he knew of this tension and he knew that Adzhubey was Khrushchev's son-in-law so he could not speak openly to Khrushchev about the problem. Suslov also supervised the two relevant departments [the International Department and the Department for Liaison with Parties of Socialist Countries, as it was subsequently named]. All these things gave Brezhnev his ammunition [against Khrushchev]. Of course the Politburo members had information about Adzhubey and they saw what Khrushchev had done [himself]. It was a very suitable time to dismiss him.

General Sejna asserts that Brezhnev had a sympathetic network within the Czechoslovak security police:

During the last years of the Khrushchev period, the Czechoslovak intelligence services collected information against Khrushchev during his travels abroad. Information was collected about what he said and whom he met, until there were pretty thick files on him back in Prague.

Rurarz describes solid links between the Soviet and Polish military leaders. According to him, General Jaruzelski felt himself more allied with Marshals Ustinov, Kulikov,[70] Ogarkov, and Yepishev[71] than with the very top of the Soviet Communist Party:

Apparently Jaruzelski's behavior in the presence of Brezhnev suggested that he had absolutely no respect for him. Ustinov, Kulikov, Ogarkov and Yepishev were present, and Jaruzelski would talk to them with his back to Brezhnev! And Brezhnev would tap him on the back, "Wojtek! Wojtek!" but Jaruzelski wouldn't pay any attention to him. I was astonished to hear this told, though not completely. What this meant was that Jaruzelski was dealing exclusively with the Soviet military, that [this] was what really counted for him, and that the party apparatus could be ignored.

I think that this was a reflection of a wider scheme: the Soviet army, as far as I know, has had for some time a somewhat different design in Poland than has had the Soviet party or even the KGB. This dates from the

---

[70] Viktor G. Kulikov, USSR first deputy minister of defense; former commander-in-chief, Warsaw Joint Pact Forces; member of the CC CPSU; marshal of the Soviet Union.

[71] A.A. Yepishev, former chief of the Main Political Administration of the Red Army; deceased.

wartime and was the idea of General Shcherbakov [then in charge of political supervision over the Soviet armed forces]. The Soviet military wants Poland stabilized, so that, in the case of war, the Polish army could fight the West German *Bundeswehr*, which has been its strategic assignment. The Soviet military is less interested in ideological affairs than the party or even the KGB, [which] presses for more political conformity. Jaruzelski, with the support of the Soviet army, could do certain things that would not please the Soviet party or the KGB. The Soviet military and secret police are more powerful than the composition of the Central Committee or the Politburo would suggest, since many party apparatus officers or state apparatus officers can in fact be GRU[72] officers or KGB officers under cover. When I was Gierek's adviser, it was because I was sent by the Polish military intelligence service to be his adviser. I was in fact accountable to them, not to Gierek. I was not afraid of Gierek at all.

Benemelis paints a picture of Cuban politics which indicates that, while Castro at one time looked to the West for help, he turned to the USSR at a time when certain factions were gaining power. At that point, national needs were secondary to the establishment of good relations with the rising factions in the USSR:

> Castro was closer to a group in the USSR which was gaining power. Grechko's [elevated status], Brezhnev's new [more militant approach], growing Soviet military power, and [the Soviet Union's] militant stand in the Middle East, all made Castro reflect. He also knew his chances for successful relations were few in the West. The U.S. was too involved in Vietnam to give Cuba what the Soviet Union was giving. . . .
>
> [While Andropov's relations with some Cubans were good], I do not know how Castro saw him. The relationship between the [Cuban] army and the Soviet Union was very strong. The relationship with the Soviet International Department was also very strong. . . .
>
> [The relationship between Pineiro, former head of Cuban intelligence and of the Central Committee's Americas Department, and Allende[73]] was not strong. Allende had stronger ties to other people in Cuba. . . . [Allende was close to] the old guard establishment of the party, and with Fidel and Raul Castro.[74] For functional purposes, Pineiro had to provide him with certain things. Allende was more connected to the Cuban political establishment than the operational machinery.

For Cuba, international relations beyond the Caribbean also became more important after 1968, when the Cubans became surrogates for the Soviet Union in Africa and Southwest Asia, as Benemelis points out:

---

[72] GRU, *Glavnoye Raznedatelnoye Upravlenie:* Soviet military intelligence.

[73] Salvador Allende, former president of Chile. He was overthrown by General Augusto Pinochet; deceased.

[74] Fidel and Raul Castro, Cuba's supreme leader and minister of defense, respectively.

There was a bitter fight between the Cuban ambassador and the military chief [in South Yemen]. The military chief had closer connections with the Soviet advisers. The ambassador was more aloof, because he was closer to the president [of South Yemen]. The Soviet advisers and the Cuban army were close to the first secretary, Abdul Fatah Ismail. That split reflected the differences of opinion inside Cuba and inside the USSR about South Yemen. . . . There was a crisis recently. Usually, unless there is a "high commissioner" to coordinate everything, it is done in Moscow. In Angola, Jorge Risquet has everyone reporting to him, because he is a Politburo member in Cuba. He is the direct connection to Moscow. It is an extremely high-level arrangement which goes beyond institutions. At the second level, there is more coordination between Cuban and Soviet military personnel than between the civilians. The emphasis there have more coordination than we had in the 1960s or in the other places.

Bolaños-Hunter describes the links between competing Sandinista factions, the KGB and the (Cuban intelligence service) DGI:

The DGI and KGB links to [the various Sandinista factions] were all the same: The Terceristas were linked to Cuba since 1960; and [the rival faction GPP leader] was linked with Cuba also since 1960. The DGI used to take care of these people. The DGI had special operations, and also had a section which is mixed with the Cuban Communist Party itself to take care of contacts like this.

Today, [the GPP's] Cerna maintains direct liaison with the KGB and DGI. The link is so natural. It's like working with your teacher. You tell him everything about the school. You ask him everything. This guy knows everything about you and the specific subject that you are studying.

According to Wolde, Ethiopian links to the top of the Soviet power structure are crucial for policy formulation. Instead of receiving instructions from the Soviet party *apparat* or the state, the Ethiopian general secretary received his instructions directly from the general secretary of the CPSU himself:

I do not believe that the Ethiopian embassy in the Soviet Union is involved in any policy formulation, although the post is very important as far as Ethiopia is concerned, particularly at this point in time. The relationship has developed over the years as a result of the direct bilateral contact between the leadership of the two countries, between the two general secretaries. And whatever has been decided at that level has been instrumental in shaping Ethiopia's foreign and domestic policy.

Clients of the USSR frequently maintain linkages outside the state-to-state frameworks. Foreign communist parties—those not in power—and national liberation movements have their contacts within the Soviet Union, which, as Shevchenko relates, do not always follow official channels:

I think [national liberation movements] have to rely for information on the KGB or the Foreign Ministry. They have some instructions which are: first, that some material can be sent directly in the diplomatic pouch. A second possible source of information is the two-way street between the communist parties of, say, France, or the [Syrian] Ba'ath or the PLO, and Moscow. These people come to Moscow and talk with Soviets and vice versa. Locally, the functionaries of the International Department go [to the countries concerned], and they might go there on behalf of neither the KGB nor of the Foreign Ministry. This touches on some of the delicate matters . . . raised [earlier, namely] whether Ponomarev would like to act in such a way as to avoid the KGB and the Foreign Ministry. . . . If he wants to contact Ba'ath, he will send a man like Brutents there, and formally no one will know that he talked with the secretary general of the Ba'ath party one evening and the next morning returned to Moscow and reported to Ponomarev. On this basis, Ponomarev can report to the Politburo. It is not necessary for the Secretariat [as a whole] to be involved.

Nomenklatura

Nomenklatura can be defined as the power to appoint persons to specific positions. This term has been used differently by some, including several interviewees in this volume, mostly to describe a leading group within the party, military and security organs. However it is more appropriate to use the term as defined above. The power to appoint, of course, is the power to control. Sejna describes this process:[75]

> *Nomenklatura* is not just the few top people, but the whole system whereby the party and the society are governed. So every level of the party has its own *nomenklatura,* its own power to appoint selected people to selected positions. Ministers fall under the *nomenklatura* of the Central Committee, whereas the promotion of generals is the *nomenklatura* of the Politburo. When I was first secretary of the party at the Czechoslovak Ministry of Defense, I had my own *nomenklatura.* The Minister could not promote anyone even to major without my consent, nor could he name a department head within the Ministry without my consent. . . . Regarding the actual appointment of personnel, the operative principle is that of cadre reserves. For every position currently filled, there must be two other people reserved potentially to fill that slot. The whole system of training and preparation works to serve this system.

Voslensky provides useful details on the *nomenklatura* of the various party strata, from the Politburo down to the *oblast* level:

---

[75] For a more detailed analysis of this view, see Jan Sejna and Joseph D. Douglass, Jr., *Decision Making in Communist Countries: An Inside View* (McLean, VA: Pergamon-Brassey's, 1986), pp. 61–63.

There is the *nomeklatura* of the Politburo, and there is the *nomenklatura* of the Secretariat. If an appointment needs to be made for chief of a department of the Central Committee, then it is sent to the Politburo. But of course they are clever, so they would informally tell the Secretariat. . . . And the secretary responsible for this department would sign the draft; the Politburo would not accept the draft without the signature of the secretary. . . He takes the responsibility for his appointment. He has proposed this appointment.

Q: What would be the highest level of appointment which belongs to the *nomenklatura* of the Secretariat and not of the Politburo?

Voslensky: A deputy minister of the Soviet Union, and the deputy—but not the first deputy—chief of a department of the party Central Committee.

Q: And what about the republics and the districts, the *oblast* level?

Voslensky: The first secretaries are appointed by the Politburo, and also the second secretaries—because the second secretary is Russian—and also . . . ministers and first deputy [ministers and their equivalents], department chiefs of Central Committee and first deputy [department chiefs], first secretary of the Central Committee of the Union Republics, and the second secretary . . . these belong to the Politburo. . . . [Almost] every first secretary [of an RSFSR *oblast* or *krai*] will be appointed [by the Politburo]. . . . I don't know whether all the first secretaries . . . . In any case, it is not a surprise for the Politburo. The Politburo would, at least, be informed.

Q: And that would be true not only of *obkom* [*Oblastnoi Komitet Partii:* Regional Party Committee] but also of *gorkom* [*Gorodskoi Komitet:* City/Town Committee] in Moscow?

Voslensky: Moscow, Leningrad, that is clear because the first secretaries of Moscow and Leningrad are almost immediately made members of the Politburo.

Q: Would you say that the *nomenklatura* of the Secretariat is kept essentially in [the hands of] the party Organization Department?

Voslensky: [That is not its only task.] The party Organization Department prepares different decisions of the Secretariat and of the Politburo concerning the organization, work, and structures in the party. So it is not just the *nomenklatura.*

Q: So in fact if one were to look for a file of the names, that's where it would be kept, essentially.

Voslensky: In the party apparatus. But, for instance, the ambassadors of the Soviet Union—this is another department, this [is] Chervonenko's department—the department of *zagranichnikh kadrov* [cadres abroad].

From Jiri Pelikan, former Director General of Czechoslovak television, a similarly detailed description was obtained of the *nomenklatura* in Czechoslovakia. There, little is left to chance—the rights to nominate are enumerated in detail with the force of law, albeit against the letter of the law:

Pelikan: [The clauses concerning the power to appoint were] very complicated, [appearing] in a party document in which . . . one by one different functions [were enumerated] which should be approved by the Politburo, the Secretariat, by the [relevant] department [of the party Central Committee]. Notice the three. That means, for example, [the] director general for . . . television must [be] approved [by] the Politburo, but, for example, the head of the news sections or of the economic section, or head of the studio, because we had five studios, . . . that was approved by the Secretariat. But [it was] on my proposal . . . that means I was . . . obliged . . . to nominate [such persons]. . . . I had to elaborate [each candidate's] biography. . . . And I gave it to the referent of the section and then [he] had to make his own investigation about the person . . . [He] would always ask the StB, the state security. . . .

If I said I want to nominate [a particular candidate, I would present a written] proposal or [state] this orally to the referent, who spoke with [others], who [then discussed it] among themselves and then told me, "We would not [advise] you to make this proposal because it would not be accepted by the Secretariat. We have to choose another [candidate]". . . . [S]ometimes, they themselves [presented] a proposal. Saying, for example, because we know this comrade [in Czechoslovak television] will [be pensioned] and we have a candidate for this position from Brno . . . I [would say] okay, it was a good candidate. If [this was] not [the case, I would reject the proposal]. . . . [I]n [that] case, they [had] no power to impose . . . this nomination.

Nomenklatura is taken undoubtedly from . . . Soviet practice but . . . it was applied in Czechoslovakia and it was applied in all countries, it is a system of appointing. . . . The *nomenklatura* was elaborated [in] great detail. . . . It is printed, but it is not published of course. It is actually a secret document. . . . It is top secret because it is actually against the law. . . . For example, I got the nomination as general director of television from the prime minister, who sent me [an announcement] which I have somewhere still: . . . "I nominate you general director of Czechoslovak television." But [de facto] I was already nominated one month before by the Politburo, I was already in my function when I got this [announcement]. . . . The Politburo decided, "we nominate Pelikan as the general director," but . . . the resolution of the Politburo would be written to comrade Viliam Siroky, the prime minister, [who was] instructed to make the [formal] nomination. . . .

The *nomenklatura* is [supposed to be] the system [by which persons] are appointed by the party. In this sense I said that it is against the law because actually even the appointments of non-party people are approved by the party.

[The *nomenklatura* lists of major appointments are available only to the] general secretary, secretaries of the Central Committee, members of the Politburo, . . . then heads of the [Central Committee] departments, . . . and then [the] first secretary of the committee [from which a recommendation originated, then the] first secretary of the [district] committee, and then the secretary or chairman of the local organization, but each of them [has] only a certain part of the document, according to their [jurisdiction]. . . . There are decisions by the Secretariat [according to] which certain bodies can be appointed without the approval of the Secretariat. . . . [F]rom 1948–68 there were some positions [that were left primarily in the jurisdiction] of ministers. . . . This *nomenklatura* is being changed every year.

Jiri Pelikan further explains that appointments for Central Committee secretaries, ministers and deputy ministers are presented to the Politburo by the general secretary rather than by individual Politburo members.

The *nomenklatura* at a given level is affected by certain administrative bodies which, if they cannot prevent a promotion or demotion, must at least be active in the process. Voslensky gives details of some of the duties of two of these bodies, the party Control Commission and the Department of Party Organizational Work:

> The party Control Commission is disciplinary [rather than being involved in] the decision-making process. . . . Theoretically, there is no [upper] limit [in the party Control Commission's intervention on personnel matters]. Practically, I would say that if they speak without the decision of the Polit-buro or at least the Secretariat, they would not say anything serious about a member of the party Central Committee.

Voslensky explains also that party members could not be put on trial and sentenced as party members. First they would have to be expelled from the party.

Voslensky goes on to stress that the Department of Party Organizational Work, as distinct from the General Department, or the Chancery of the Central Committee or the Personal Secretariat of the General Secretary, controls the regional party organizations:

> It . . . includes appointments, because . . . there is no longer a Main Admin-istration of Cadres in the party Central Committee . . . [While] the draft decisions on appointments are prepared by the respective departments, . . . [the Department of Party Organizational Work is] responsible for the *nomenklatura* of the party Central Committee, as far as the party apparatus is concerned.

Two Polish interviewees refer to the powers of the Organizational Department, which oversees the promotion of candidates to posts as high as the ministerial level. As Rurarz notes, the Organizational Department holds control over virtually all appointments:

> Any decision taken by the Personnel Department always had to be more or less [coordinated] with the Organizational Department, since in the *nomen-klatura* (in Polish, the *kartoteka partyjna*), once you entered that select

group of the elite—some four thousand of them—you were at [the disposal of the Organizational Department]. Thus whenever the Personnel Department wanted to propose somebody for a post, they needed to have Organizational Department's consent. Everything was sort of a double-track decision. I would rank the bodies that deal purely with party affairs in the following order: The Organizational Department is the most important, then the Personnel Department [once a bureau], and then the Chancery of the Secretariat (but again, among the people at the Chancery there are only three to four . . . who have real influence).

Michael Checinski, a former Polish military counterintelligence officer, confirms the importance of the Central Committee's Organizational Department, and explains its *nomenklatura*:

> You can't be a minister without approval by the Organizational Department. . . . All the deputy ministers must be approved [by it]. But the candidates [for these posts] must be proposed by the prime minister.

The CPSU leadership, the KGB, and the armed forces of the USSR, not surprisingly, play a major role in the affairs of other socialist states. Checinski believes that the *nomenklatura* of the Soviet Union encompasses most of the East European leadership positions. While there are exceptions, Checinski indicates that this has been the practice. He describes a complex system, in which various agencies and personalities, domestic and Soviet, vie for the advancement of their respective candidates:

> In the [Polish] Central Committee there is a Cadres Department which appoints lower-level personnel. The difference between the Soviet Union and [East] European countries is [that] the Soviet Union is independent, the [East] European countries are not. Not being independent [affects] the structure of the whole apparatus. That means that usually some of the positions are controlled by the Soviet Union—by the KGB, by the [International] Department, or [the] Department [for Liaison with Parties of Socialist Countries]. . . . And they try to put different positions into effect. This is a very hard battle between leaders of the [socialist] countries and the Soviet Union. This could be a battle even for leaders very loyal to the Soviet Union; they want autonomy for their governments as well. [They] are constantly under surveillance. [They] are not free. There is a gentleman's agreement regarding various positions and who will appoint personnel. . . . Specifically, head of the [state security] service, chief of [military] intelligence, chief of staff, some sections of the military, foreign affairs, the Central Committee's Administration and Organization Departments. [Both the USSR and the East European leaders] will try to put their own people into these positions in the Eastern European countries.

Ambassador Rurarz concurs with this assessment, and shows how Soviet control over top posts in Eastern European countries also affects appointments at lower levels:

> Before any decision is taken concerning whom to appoint to an important slot, the issue is discussed with the minister of internal affairs and in many (but not all) cases with the minister of defense as well. But even at this stage, the stage of preliminary discussion, the Soviets step in and interfere with the process, since both the Interior and Defense Ministries cooperate directly with the Soviets.

In Cuba, however, a different appointments process prevails. Juan Benemelis, in describing a process of replacement made by Castro, implies that the Soviet role in Cuban appointments is advisory only. Castro maintains a certain level of independence:

> *Q:* Was is possible that Soviet officials spotted Mendez when he was in the USSR and suggested to Castro that he replace Pineiro [head of the Americas Department of the Central Committee of the Cuban Communist Party]?
>
> *Benemelis:* No, they do not do that. They had a conservation with Fidel and Raul, and they left the decision to Fidel. Castro was the one who promoted him. No one else can make that decision. The type of person Castro proposes symbolizes whether or not he accepted the suggestion. By proposing someone like Mendez, he was saying he accepted it.

It may be argued that, irrespective of the political system in which they flourish, successful political careers have certain attributes in common, including personal determination and political agility. However, the editors, in section I of this work, focused on aspects of political life that are characteristic of closed societies. The interviewees corroborated one another in showing that such features as continuous factional struggles are attributes of the political system that their various countries have in common. They confirmed that, in the absence of a non-arbitrary, fully, fairly, and impartially implemented legal system, decisions on appointments, promotions, and dismissals inevitably are functions of extra-legal factors, including factional bonds (despite the fact that the CPSU has outlawed factions), and "connections."

2
Foci of Power

Since the Soviet Union and its allies are neither open societies nor constitutional states (*Rechtsstaaten*), politico-economic power is divided and decision-making authority is distributed not as a result of constitutional processes, but as a result of factional struggles among the elite. Consequently, as most students of Soviet-style political systems would agree, there exists a discrepancy between the official and the actual decision-making structures and hierarchies. Interviews with former party, government, military and state security officials represent an important tool available to Sovietologists who try to look beyond the official facade at the de facto foci of power.

The Triangular Power Structure

Virtually every model of decision-making in communist systems starts with a description of the triangular power structure, involving an uneasy and ever-shifting tripartite alliance between three dominant institutions: the *apparat* of the Central Committee of the Communist party;[1] the security organs; and the military sector.[2] Their relationship is one of mutual support, but also of

---

[1] It is important to remember that the communist parties in the Soviet Union and Eastern Europe are mass organizations, often involving around ten percent of the population. Naturally, only a very small segment of all party members has any input into the decision-making processes and one must therefore stress that virtually all power exercised on behalf of the party is vested in the central and regional party organs.

[2] After the 19th CPSU Conference, this model seems inadequate. The reform plan presented at the conference indicates that Mikhail Gorbachev intends to shift the responsibility for the day-to-day running of the country away from the Central Committee *apparat* to the state machinery of which he recently became executive chief as a result of a session which lasted some forty-five minutes. Naturally, the principle of the CPSU's leading role in the society will be upheld. This would indicate that one could no longer treat the CPSU and the Soviet government as one analytical unit, a view expressed in many standard works on the Soviet decision-making structures, e.g., in Roland J. Hill and Peter Frank, *The Soviet Communist Party* (Boston: Allen & Unwin, Inc., 1986). If Gorbachev's proposals are implemented, many otherwise reliable works of power relations in communist countries will have to be rewritten, e.g., Stephen White, John Gardner and George Schopflin, *Communist Political Systems: An Introduction* (New York: St. Martin's Press, 1987). Naturally, the material presented by the interviewees, and therefore this portion of the work, reflects the situation as it existed prior to Gorbachev's assumption of power.

mistrust.[3] None could survive without the other two, yet when one grows in power and influence to the point of threatening to overshadow the combined strength of the other two, the latter are likely to ally themselves against the former so as to restore the balance.

Of course, reality is more complex than this simplified model. It must not be overlooked that there is a great deal of overlapping between the party, the security and military institutions, personnel, and responsibilities. A good illustration of this phenomenon is the Main Political Administration (MPA), which is a military organ within the structure of the Central Committee of the party. Some of its workers conceivably work for the East European and/or Soviet security organs "on the side." Despite such overlap, the interviewees support the triangular model as useful in explaining the dynamics of Soviet and Soviet-style politics. The three elements of this power structure are in a permanent tug-of-war for authority. In the words of the former Czechoslovak Gen. Jan Sejna:

> Because the party bureaucracy is one of the three pillars of Soviet power—along with the armed forces and the KGB—it is continually posturing for greater authority.

Anatoly Fedoseyev, a former Soviet scientist, stresses that the three components of the triangular structure are not equal players. Except for brief periods in Soviet history, the Communist Party, to a significant extent, has penetrated and controlled the other two institutions. Fedoseyev presents his view of the mechanism whereby the party controls the other two elements of the triangle, using as a metaphor the concept of a hydraulic system. The various organisms that compose the Soviet body politic are dependent for nourishment upon supplies that flow from large pipes into feeder lines controlled by an elaborate series of valves. The organisms are kept alive by those who are in charge of the main valves. Since such personalities possess potentially dangerous power, Stalin kept rotating controllers of the main valves.

Compartmentalization can help to ensure effective control, and it is the party which assigns tasks to the various institutions. For example, it would upset the balance of power to allow the KGB, which has the means to implement operations, at the same time to formulate policy. Therefore, policy formation is kept in other hands, a phenomenon described by Orionova:

---

[3] Party/government/military relations are examined, for instance, by Dale R. Herspring and Ivan Volgyes (eds.), *Civil-Military Relations in Communist Systems* (Boulder: Westview Press, 1978), with relevant chapters by Roman Kolkowicz, William E. Odom, and Timothy J. Colton; interesting, although unverifiable assertions can be found in Victor Suvorov, *Inside the Soviet Army* (New York: Macmillan, 1982). Not enough has been done in the area of party/security organs relations since reliable information is scarce.

[Despite centralization], there are different bodies, pillars of power which compete with each other. The KGB doesn't deal in terms of defining Soviet policy toward a particular area, but in how to steal something and to point out areas where opportunities exist for Soviet policy. The realm of the KGB is more in operations and tactics.

In Eastern Europe, the same basic model holds, but with a number of important regional variations. For instance, in Poland during the Solidarity period, the party became almost immobilized and the armed forces took over significant sectors of the decision-making structure. Direct participants[4] have provided testimony to this effect. On the other hand, in Czechoslovakia, the military historically played a limited role during the period of the First Republic (1918–1938). Perhaps as a consequence, the Czechoslovak army (CSLA) has been less prominent in the decision-making process, as illustrated by Pelikan:

[T]he minister of defense was always appointed by the Politburo and by those people who were fully under the control of the party. The only exception was Cepicka, who was at the same time a member of the Politburo and who married the daughter of Gottwald, then president and general secretary of the party (KSC). . . . [A]fter his elimination, [Cepicka] was taken as an example that the minister of defense should not be a member of the Politburo and should not have such influence. . . . I think the only period when the army . . . used its influence on the political development of Czechoslovakia was in 1969, that means after the Soviet invasion. . . .[E]ven the army intelligence service has not had a [major] influence on the policy making of the Communist Party.

The example of Cuba stands as a further warning against any attempt to force one model, no matter how satisfactory it may appear, on all the countries under Soviet-style rule. The Cuban army has been deployed in a number of Third World countries as a Soviet surrogate. At the same time, the army is also an important tool in the hands of Fidel Castro and those of his colleagues who share the concept of Fidelismo. Consequently, the Cuban army commanders apparently enjoy significant domestic political authority. As described by Juan Benemelis, there are some analogies between the Cuban and Polish (as opposed to Czechoslovak) models:

The army is the only highly organized, powerful, pro-Soviet institution in Cuba. Other institutions just do not compare. [The Cuban security organs, DGI] are not as powerful as the KGB in the USSR. The Cuban army surpasses everything. An army general is always more powerful than a DGI officer. This is the Latin American dimension of Cuba and Castro's legacy.

---

[4] See Ryszard Kuklinski, "The Crushing of Solidarity," *Orbis* 32/1 (Winter 1988): pp. 7–31.

Eden Pastora Gomez points out that the concept of troika, consisting of the party, security, and military organs, may be more relevant outside Soviet-style political systems. It is more applicable, as a model, to authoritarian dictatorships. The totalitarian variety is considerably more complex, not only in the area of decision making, but also when it comes to population control. Totalitarian systems employ many more mechanisms to control their subjects, and their impact on daily life is deeper:

> The rightist dictatorships—the [classical Latin American] dictatorships—use three organizations to subdue the people: the security police, the party, and the army. The leftist dictatorships, like Nicaragua, have thirty-five organizations. The party, state security, and the army control sixty percent of the population. And the rest [the state] controls, by organizing the children, the women, the workers, the neighborhoods, the small producers, and the businessmen. [This system] controls national life.

The Party and the State

Conspicuous in its absence from the troika model is mention of the state—that is, government—apparatus. The interviewees generally believe that the government, more precisely the Council of Ministers, has little power of its own. They imply that it acts only as an appendage of the party in implementing the latter's dictates.[5] The deliberative bodies of the state structure, such as the Supreme Soviet in the Soviet Union, in fact had little authority and served to ratify party directives. (This constraint, however, seems to have vanished, partly because the chairmanship of the Presidium of the Supreme Soviet is now in Gorbachev's hands.)

Yet it is not simply legitimacy in the eyes of its people and of foreign states that the party seeks; it also needs scapegoats for its own mistakes. The guiding principle seems to be that the party accepts responsibility for successes while the government has to assume responsibility for all failures. Pelikan provides an overview of party/state relations:

> [I]n the system of the Soviet type [of] socialism, it is the party which decides everything, so the government is just the executive body of the party. That means that first of all the government is appointed by the decision of the Communist Party. That means the prime minister and all the ministers are approved by the Politburo and by the Central Committee of the party. And then, in fact, in its daily life the government is applying the decisions of the

---

[5] As indicated above, this may no longer be the case in the Soviet Union, where recently Gorbachev has assumed real power in his new capacity as executive head of government. The East Europeans are likely to follow suit; Czechoslovakia, Poland, and Hungary already have.

party. Not all of the decisions of the Politburo are automatically valid for the government and for the respective ministers who are instructed by a decision of the Politburo to do this or that. Also the heads of the departments of the Central Committee are actually chiefs of the respective ministers of the government. They communicate daily by telephone, they meet personally and so on. And they dictate what the minister should do.

Q: Given that all of the important decisions are made by the party . . . why do they [in Eastern Europe] keep the governmental hierarchy, why do they have it all?

Pelikan: Because it is a Soviet-type system, and they have adopted the same system as . . . exists in the Soviet Union. That means you have the party and you have the government.

Q: But since all of the decisions are actually made by the party, why keep the governmental hierarchy if it is in fact just duplication? For every important ministry in the governmental part of the power strucure, there is a department within the Central Committee where most of the important decisions seem to be made.

Pelikan: This is the Soviet type of socialism.

Q: Let me ask you another question; why do they have this [system] in the Soviet Union?

Pelikan: [T]he government has certain functions which cannot be implemented directly by the party apparatus. . . .[T]he party is in fact very satisfied that it is not responsible for everything, for [every] shortcoming in daily life. The governmnent can be made responsible. And this is why sometimes Novotny,[6] when he was the first secretary of the party and the president of the Republic, used to say [to] the Central Committee, "So, why does not the government govern? Why is not the government [doing] its duty, when there are so many shortcomings, for instance in the economy?" And of course, the ministers were very bitter about that, and they said: "We cannot govern because we are prevented from governing by the party." But the party said "you should govern better." We have taken the correct decisions, but the decisions were not correctly implemented by the government bodies.

Goshu Wolde's description of the Ethiopian party/state structure suggests a similar dynamic. It is interesting that Chairman Mengistu took the path toward accumulation of functions which General Secretary Gorbachev would later follow within his own power-stucture:

The party came into being only [recently], in September 1984. Before that there was COPWE (Commission of the Progressive Workers of Ethiopia), the

---

[6] Antonin Novotny was the first secretary of the Czechoslovak Communist Party, the KSC, and president of the Czechoslovak Republic. His fall in January 1968, is generally considered to constitute the first event of the so-called Prague Spring, which was terminated by the Warsaw Pact invasion in August 1968.

commission for organizing the party. Before the advent of the Workers' Party of Ethiopia, there was total governmental control by the Council of Ministers, or more specifically by the PMAC, the Provisional Military Administrative Council. It was the legislative and the executive arm of the government. Now that the party has come into being, it has begun to share power. Perhaps "share" is not the proper term. Under all systems of the Soviet model, power resides with the party. The party is the leading organ in both state and society. As such, the state organs are left to implement the decisions of the party. The party sets policy directives, [makes] the decisions and asks the state to implement them through its various organs. We now have, or will soon have, the Peoples' Republic of Ethiopia, where there will be an elected national assembly, the Shengo, a Council of Ministers, the Council of State and the president's office. It so happens that all of these are headed by Chairman Mengistu himself while he is general secretary of the party, so they are indistinguishable. Even if he were not the president of the Republic, or not the president of the Council of State or of the National Assembly, he would wield the same power and influence simply by being the general secretary of the party, because that is the real source of power.

The definition of the relationship between party and state often is (perhaps deliberately) blurred. There are large areas of overlapping responsibility; many leading personalities, sometimes the most powerful among them, serve simultaneously in the government and the party:

> [The Ethiopian Constitution] does not define in very clear, precise, detailed terms the working relationship between the party and the state. But it states what should be stated and it states the obvious. It says clearly and unambiguously that the WPE [ruling party] is the leading organ of both the state and society. And that is crucial because it means that it is that party which gives the directions. To go beyond that would perhaps help in bringing about working harmony in the operations of the system as a whole—in the party, the public and mass organizations and the government. But it does state the single most vital link and that is that the state and the society will look to the party for political direction. When I say party, it involves the Politburo and the Central Committee. [The term] party, it is taken for granted, refers to the Politburo and the Central Committee. Mozambique, Somalia, and others have gone to great lengths to avoid some of the tensions which exist in the system now. How does a party decision come to be? . . . Does it go to the Council of Ministers? What is the relationship between the party and the state and the mass organizations? These things should have been spelled out, but they were left deliberately vague. . . . [O]nce the element of party supremacy was included, that is what really counts. The state would then look to the party for ideological and political direction.

In any case, the interviewees leave little doubt that the government, that is to say the Council of Ministers, should be viewed as the junior partner in the arrangement. Indeed, according to Sejna's perception of the role of the government, it seems to be little more than a dumping ground for the incompetent:

> A party secretary or department head . . . [is] . . . appointed [but a] minister is [there] to be fired. It is as simple as that. The secretaries direct the ministers, and not the other way around. The ministers may have a good salary, but they have no power. . . . They make a good living, but they are there to take the heat that should be directed at the party. Once one has outlived his usefulness to the party, he is dismissed.

However, as the Soviet and East European political systems have developed, the party has found that it must rely on the government more and more for the expertise to implement policy. Because of this dependency, the state bureaucracy has gained a certain amount of influence. The following excerpt indicates that the system is not static. Hus, who is a former member of the governmental bureaucracy, believes that the trend is in the direction of more responsibility for the state apparatus. A former Czech national with experience in the foreign-affairs domain, he also mentions trends within the Soviet system:

> *Q:* Do elements of the state apparatus, for example the ministries, now have more weight in relation to party bodies, than they had twenty years ago?
>
> *Hus:* [T]wenty years ago, the ministers were little more than an external function of a [department] within the Central Committee. At that time the party leaders believed that they had all the answers. Life became more difficult. The leaders wanted to be in charge, but not take the responsibility if something went wrong. The ministers could fill this role. This change developed after Khrushchev, the last party leader who accepted such responsibility. . . . Ministries gained power as the Politburo became satisfied with establishing the main line of policy and leaving specifics to others. If a ministry suggested something [the Politburo members] did not like, they could overrule it. However, this [became] increasingly rare. In this way the ministries have become more important and everybody profits.

The party remains in complete control when it comes to appointments. This responsibility is not shared with anyone. The system of appointments is clearly defined and all entities of the Soviet-style system know exactly where such decisions are made, by whom, and who has to shoulder public responsibility. Hus continues on this topic:

> There is not a big fight over appointments. For example, now there is this "Americanist" clique [in Moscow]. The party is happy with these people. They come from the same background as the party officials themselves.

If there is someone the party does not like, he will be removed, without a quarrel. If the Czechoslovak Politburo as a whole, and not just Bil'ak, did not like Chnoupek,[7] they would not quarrel with him. They would tell him he may disagree, but he must follow the Politburo's policy. Even so, the Ministry will often be allowed to shoulder the responsibility for a policy decision. If it is successful, then the secretary responsible for that ministry profits, and if it fails, then the minister is to blame. In this way the ministries do not threaten the party officials but help them solidify their positions.

But nothing is uniformly applicable throughout the Soviet system. What may be true of the Soviet Union, Czechoslovakia or Ethiopia does not have to be true elsewhere. For instance, in Poland of the early 1970s, the state leadership appeared to be capable of out-maneuvering the party, but this may have been a reflection of personalities, rather than institutional design:

Kucharski: [Prime Minister] Jaroszewicz was a man of Moscow. He had been prepared since the war as a party and government leader. Clearly he was an agent of Moscow. He carried out Moscow's policy and followed all instructions from the Soviet Union. It is possible that he had more power because of this direct Soviet support. Also, he had the government's bureaucracy behind him and all of economic life under his control as chief of state. He could operate directly, while Gierek would issue instructions, which [did not go to] the enterprises directly. They always went through the ministries controlled by Jaroszewicz.

Q: In the Soviet Union . . . real decision making takes place in the party's Central Committee and the corresponding ministries in the government only supervise the implementation of party directives. On the basis of what you have just told us, in Poland it would appear that the ministry is more important than the party. Is that correct?

Kucharski: For practical purposes the ministries and the enterprises can conduct policy more or less independently from the party. There was no visible difference between Jaroszewicz and Gierek, because both were conducting the irresponsible policy of borrowing money from everywhere. They borrowed billions of dollars. They followed the strategy of the so-called dynamic development. They were willing to take money from anyone who would lend money to Poland. In that respect they were equally responsible, but in the end Jaroszewicz was ousted, because it was easier to put the blame on the government than on the party. The government was directly involved with foreign trade and investment policy. The party is only responsible for successes. There is always someone else to be blamed for failure. It is easier to blame the prime minister than the first secretary. It was a way to defend Gierek, yet it was short-lived. A few months after Jaroszewicz was ousted, Gierek was ousted too, with the rise of Solidarity.

---

[7] Vasil Bil'ak, former secretary and Politburo member of the Czechoslovak Communist Party; Bohuslav Chnoupek, former Czechoslovak foreign minister.

Kostov, speaking of Bulgaria, describes the relationship between party and state as highly complex, with areas of overlapping responsibilities and an unclear chain of command. Ultimately, Kostov affirms, the party retains control; in his view, the various organs of the Central Committee constitute the high court which decides which ministries work well and which do not. He also adheres to the theory that the party assumes responsibility for success, the government takes blame for the rest:

> The Politburo [decides whether a minister] works well or not. If he has to report to the Politburo, along with his report goes a report from the responsible department of the party, charged with overseeing this particular ministry. It is very hard for a minister to present his work as good if the Central Committee department says it is not. In this case, if they say that the ministry is working badly then the minister is guilty. But never the party man. The problem for the minister is that he must know how to maneuver [around] the Central Committee. It seems to me that this is one of the biggest problems of the Soviet system. They have units which do not take any responsibility but which are the jury that decides [who is] guilty.

Party control over the ministries is implemented through the Central Committee departments which serve as parallel apparati to direct and oversee each state office from the minister's level down. Voslensky describes the relationship between individual ministries and the appropriate departments of the CPSU Central Committee:

> *Voslensky:* The ministry is dependent on the [Central Committee] department.
>
> *Q:* Does a department usually have supervision over a group of ministries? After all, the number of ministries varies from sixty to eighty. With twenty-two or twenty-three departments, that is three or four ministries per department.
>
> *Voslensky:* Yes. The International Department, however, does not supervise ministries; it supervises functions. The Department of Heavy Industry, on the other hand, supervises different ministries; more than four ministries.

Yet party control is not applied without resistance. Because ministers know they will take the blame for poor policy decisions by the party, they try to circumvent party dictates which they believe will lead to problems later on. Checinski describes a constant flow of instructions from the Polish party to the government as well as the mechanism which Polish government members can use to resist instructions they do not wish to implement:

> The prime minister is the party secretary for economic affairs. He has all the ministers for culture, for education, but his main responsibility is the econ-

omy. He manages and is responsible for the working of the whole national economy. Each minister is subordinated to the department in the Central Committee that is responsible for, let's say, light industry, heavy industry, communications, and so on. They [are responsible to] the Central Committee. What is the difference between the prime minister and the Central Committee? The prime minister in the Soviet Union has a [council consisting of representatives] from the most important ministries. . . . Through these ministries he manages all the most important requests, especially when they conflict with each other. For example, suppose the prime minister has an instruction to kick out twenty percent of the bureaucracy because of a reduction in manpower. He has to get rid of twenty percent, but he can say in this ministry three percent, in that ministry thirty percent. What you can do is you can go to the Central Committee and claim on behalf of your department that you can't get the job done and ask for support. Not before the elected body [that is, the Central Committee as a whole], because they have no power, but to the party bureaucracy. So he goes to the appropriate [Central Committee] department that controls his ministry and says he cannot fulfill the plan because the prime minister has cut the staff by thirty percent. The prime minister could not throw out any minister without the approval of the department. He can go there and complain about his chief, without any fear for his job, because it is secured by the *nomenklatura* of the Central Committee. This weakens the power of the prime minister. But on the other side it makes the system more flexible. In Polish they say, "The Central Committee apparatus is for drinking, the ministries are for beating." Or as they say in the United States, "the party is responsible for successes, the government is responsible for failures." If Gorbachev is not fulfilling the plan, he will not say, "I'm responsible," but rather "the ministry is responsible."

As before, Cuba seems to deviate from the system described by the Soviet and Eastern European interviewees. In Cuba special areas of the government exist which are not under the control of the party, but under personal control of Fidel Castro. It seems that when there is a lack of uniformity or even similarity between various entities of the Soviet-style system, this tends to result not from a different design but from unusual personalities. In the following excerpt, Juan Benemelis describes the Americas Department, which Fidel Castro founded in 1969:

> It was officially under the Central Committee, but was not subjected to it. It is placed there physically, but it does not work [under] the party [bureaucracy]. If it worked for the party, it would report to the Secretariat. Instead it works for Castro. That is a source of conflict with Carlos Rafael Rodriguez, Valdes, and the Soviet Union.

As will be demonstrated, even within the party there are dynamics at work which tend to blur the chain of command and fracture the lines of control.

The Party Structure

Current knowledge of the structure within the party central *apparat* is imprecise. While the names and some of the functions of the party's decision-making bodies are known, their exact areas of responsibility and relationships to each other are interpreted differently by different witnesses. For instance, one might ask, does the Politburo or the Secretariat control the Central Committee? Is the Politburo the top policy-making body or an almost rubber-stamping collective for decisions made elsewhere? Is the general secretary "first among equals"; does he wield absolute power; or does the scope of his power lie between those poles? And what of the somewhat shadowy Defense Council? This section seeks to shed light on such questions.

The Politburo

The Politburo has generally been considered the focus of power in the Soviet politics examined here. Yet, for such an important body, little is known about the manner in which it actually functions.[8] The interviewees, to the extent possible, have shed new light on the nature, purpose and functioning of Politburos of the various communist parties.

The Politburo of the CPSU meets formally once a week. In client states this pattern is duplicated to some extent, but it is not identical. For instance, according to Hus:

> [The Politburo of the Czechoslovak Communist Party] meets once a week for four hours, as in the Soviet Union, but on Fridays instead of Thursdays. It meets after the Soviet Politburo, so that its members know the line that the Soviet leadership has taken.

According to Wolde, the Ethiopian Politburo meets weekly on Tuesdays, the Central Committee meets twice every year—little of substance is discussed—and the party Congress meets once every five years. Wolde states that these meetings have no impact on the direction of Ethiopian foreign policy:

> The Central Committee Secretariat is where department heads are represented, and the decisions are made, technically speaking . . . but in Ethiopia's case, the decisions are made [actually] by Mengistu. There are times when issues will be presented to him through the Foreign Relations Department. . . . There are those in the party who say that foreign relations, just like domestic relations, should be decided by the party. This is not familiar working procedure in Ethiopia, where we have never had a party, and where the

---

[8] A useful overview of the structure and distribution of power in the Soviet Union can be found in Wolfgang Leonhard, *The Kremlin and the West* (New York: W.W. Norton, 1986).

foreign minister always decided or formulated policy in collaboration with the head of state. It is Mengistu now who decides. There have been cases when I took issues to him, and he decided them, particularly on non-party matters.

The manner in which, indeed the extent to which Politburo meetings are held varies significantly, depending to a remarkable degree on the party leader's personality. Rurarz illustrates this point with respect to Poland, albeit during an earlier period:

> Under Gierek they [that is, the Politburo meetings] were [held weekly], but under Gomulka the Politburo never met in full, and when it met at all it was only once every three months or so. Gierek held meetings of the full Politburo every week, but Gomulka held only infrequent, abbreviated Politburo meetings. Gomulka simply never trusted anybody and preferred to make decisions on his own, occasionally asking Kliszko, Jaszczuk, Logo-Sovinski, or somebody else to handle some specific problem. But under Gierek, the Politburo immediately began to meet once a week, on Tuesdays.

Since the Politburo meets no more than once a week (perhaps with rare exceptions) and must address a huge agenda (the party is in overall charge of every facet of life, including items considered trivial in the West, such as what novel may be published), the question arises whether the Politburo really does make decisions, discussing agenda items in depth as opposed to merely placing a stamp of approval on policies that have been designed elsewhere. Stanislav Levchenko intimates that the leadership seems to devote time to frivolous or purely ceremonial activities:

> What I really do not understand is where they find the time and strength to discuss all this kind of nonsense in the Politburo. In one sitting of the Politburo they must approve at least one, often more, of these official congratulatory protocols. And Brezhnev, or when he was sick, Suslov was personally signing all these messages. They really spent a lot of time on this basic nonsense.

The Politburo and the Secretariat of the Central Committee, like other institutions in the Soviet system, have practical working arrangements that do not necessarily appear in institutional charts. Kostov, speaking of Bulgaria, describes such a situation:

> There is [an arrangement] as to which questions have to be decided in the Secretariat and which in the Politburo. The meeting is only for putting decisions on paper. During the week, for example, one [Politburo member] makes a proposition in his field. If he acts on this proposal and the Politburo

does not accept it, it will be a big blow for him. So before the [meeting], he will discuss it with other members of the Politburo, lobbying for his proposal. When there is a consensus inside the Politburo, a decision has already been made. This is how they make so many decisions in a small period of time. It happens that a person's proposal is turned back to him if the general secretary decides to show him the stick—to punish him for something. Everything else is fully discussed. This is the way it works in the Bulgarian system.

It is generally known[9] that certain Politburo members attend the weekly meetings only rarely. This has to do either with geographic limitations (for example, in the case of Kunaev, who would have had to commute weekly from Alma-Ata), or with the fact that such members are on the Politburo merely as "token representatives" of an ethnic minority and have little decision-making authority (true generally of Central Asians, to the degree that they are on the Politburo at all), or with membership intended primarily to indicate a link with the "heroic past" (such was the case of Pel'she, who had worked with Lenin). Kostov reports, however, that the Bulgarian Politburo, perhaps because of the country's small size, seems to meet in full:

I have the impression that in general all the members are present . . . In any case, the practice is, if someone must be absent he gets all the material in advance and others know if he agrees or has some remarks.

Voslensky concurs that most of the real decisions take place outside the framework of the weekly Politburo meeting:

[E]verything has been pre-decided. [The Politburo members] have the veto power. There is no particularly extended discussion. Everything has been prepared by the party apparatus. Should there be something that is indeed disputable, they would not discuss it within the official framework of the Politburo meeting, but rather outside the strict confines of an official meeting. Politburo members certainly discuss problems outside the realm of official meetings. The Politburo meeting is an official occasion. There are not only the members of the Politburo and secretaries of the CC, but also the chiefs of the [Central Committee] departments, if not of all departments. . . . It is by no means a small group. The [Politburo] meeting itself serves only as the opportunity to make official, final decisions. If a decision has not yet been finalized, the members will discuss it with the apparatus, with their assistants, with the ministers and among themselves. But when everything is more or less pre-decided, they will meet just in order to rubber stamp the decision. Should there be something wrong . . . I think that they would send [the material] back to a [Central Committee] department or to the Secretariat, where additional material could be assembled. They understand that it

---

[9] See, e.g., Michael Sadykiewicz, "Soviet Military Politics," *Survey* 26, 1 (Winter 1982): pp. 180–210.

is difficult to recall a decision taken by the Politburo; that is why it must be finalized before the meeting.

Shevchenko's view is that not all members discussed everything: indeed, most matters which were considered routine were not discussed at all. Since the Politburo's agenda is so extensive, involving perhaps two or three thousand issues a year, who has the final word when it comes to setting the agenda?

> The [general secretary], if he can function. When Brezhnev was absolutely incapacitated, there was always someone in the Central Committee who was considered to hold a nonexistent position but who actually assumed de facto Brezhnev's functions in the absence of the [general secretary]. Kirilenko was functioning that way and Suslov sometimes presided over [discussions], as did Gorbachev when Andropov was sick. The final word rests with him, but the handling of the growing agenda belongs to the *Obshchij otdel* [General Department].

Certain issues—most likely those pertaining to defense, intelligence, and some aspects of foreign affairs—do not appear to be discussed by the Politburo. Instead, Shevchenko reports that proposals on such matters are presented to various secretaries of the Central Committee and Politburo members on an individual basis:

> More decisions of the Politburo are adopted this way than at the meetings themselves. The meetings are once a week which means that all decisions which cannot be delayed for a week or two–three days are decided that way. . . . I would say that eighty to ninety percent of the proposals are never discussed in the Politburo. If something is really important, then usually the [general secretary] has already moved on it, and the others have theoretically read all the materials that support the issue. By the time of the meeting of the Politburo it's a very routine procedure.
>
> The Politburo is not a place where they fight each other. Moreover, there always will be an established policy. Any [general secretary], every one, would pursue the issue to be decided in the Politburo with as little debate and discussion as possible. First, for the simple reason [that] there is no time to do that. And, if the Politburo wants to retain its total control, its members have to adopt this procedure. Even if they approve of a given proposal, and even if they feel that this really shouldn't even be submitted to the Politburo, it's still better that it be submitted and everyone just goes along with [such a policy]. . . . [S]ome of the decisions are adopted [by the Politburo] in blocks; for example, Brezhnev would say, "[Regarding] agenda items 13 to 25, are there any comments from the members of the Politburo?" If not, that's it. They are all adopted.
>
> But on the other hand, there are some things which generate a lot of debate. They put every detail into proposals, [especially] if it's a controversial

matter, such as the invasion of Czechoslovakia, or the Afghanistan issue. The invasion of Czechoslovakia was a matter over which the Politburo was actually split. There were endless sessions of the Politburo, and until the last moment they fought over what they wanted to do.

Shevchenko notes that if dissension exists within the Politburo, it will not be noted officially:

Q: Is there a mechanism for recording a reservation by a member or members of the Politburo who say "Look, we go along with you but we want to state our reservations?"

Shevchenko: I never saw any such reservations. There could be different opinions, and maybe not everyone will have the same view. But the main thing is that in the record all that should be included is the final decision. There is no other way. They will not give a separate opinion.

Q: There are no minutes?

Shevchenko: There are no minutes.[10] The only way is if someone really wants that—and I never saw it done—you have to have a decision of the Politburo to include a separate view. Someone has to insist they do that and I doubt that any member of the Politburo would become so bold. At least I never saw it. So, the only thing stated is their position, and it's not really even necessary. Every decision will be known in the circle of the Politburo and when the decision is implemented, that's it. I don't think that, even for the sake of maintaining the image of the Politburo, there has ever been included in the hundreds and hundreds of decisions that I saw an indication of whether there was dissension or not. . . . There is no elaboration.

The result is an almost classical case of contradictions—the Hegelian dialectic at work. Shevchenko continues:

[T]here is a contradictory policy from the very top. On the one hand, the Politburo—or, for that matter, the Secretariat of the party, or the general secretary himself—wants to retain control over the most important issues. On the other hand, they realize and they understand very well that there is an enormous volume of proposals, of materials of absolutely different urgency, with different consequences. Either it's an economic problem or a social problem; but it's absolutely impossible for one body like the Politburo

---

[10] This may be a question of semantics. Arkady Shevchenko here apparently means that differences of opinion, arguments, etc., remain unrecorded; obviously there is a written record of decisions reached. The Politburo of the Czechoslovak Communist Party, for instance, did keep detailed minutes, i.e., records of its meetings. The minutes were promptly printed, inserted into the record, and deposited in the archives of the Central Committee. Karel Kaplan, the Czech historian now living in Munich, brought copies of such minutes to the West. See, for instance, Karel Kaplan, *Nekrvava revoluce* (Bloodless Revolution) (Toronto: Sixty-Eight Publishers, 1985). Michael Voslensky seems to support Shevchenko's view that the CPSU Politburo does not keep written records of discussions during its meeting.

to deal with it all. This is a continuous mass of work. I don't know whether Gorbachev will resolve it or not.

Situations can arise in which there is a lack of unanimity on the Politburo. In such cases there could be a genuine vote or, if there is an outright split, referral back to the Secretariat:

> *Voslensky:* [I]n such cases the secretary general or second secretary says: "Point number 25, the item is, you all have the documents, the draft decisions. Are there questions?" No. "Does anyone wish to present his opinion?" No. "Who is against it?" Nobody. If somebody says "No, I have such opinion," or if somebody says "I am against it," and explains why, then it is possible that there is a discussion. Then there would be a vote.
>
> *Q:* Would it be likely in such a case that they would simply send the document back to the [Secretariat] to be redrafted?
>
> *Voslensky:* If it was clear that there was in fact a split in the Politburo—not just one dissenter, some provincial who has not understood it.

Politburo members try to forestall rifts before a formal meeting takes place. In Czechoslovakia, former insider Hus states, staffers of various Politburo members play an important role in reaching conclusions while preparing the agenda:

> When there is a subject of great importance, the staffs of different members get together. They then work out the issue and present their solution to the Politburo, which then states its approval.

This does not always work out, and when contentious issues reach the Politburo unresolved, Hus reports that the leaders are compelled to devote a great deal of time to such problems:

> On issues where there is sharp disagreement, two full Politburo meetings might be taken up.

Politburo Agenda Setting. Setting the agenda is no mere logistical endeavor, and those who control it wield a great deal of influence. Gregory explains that this task is performed by the personal staffs of key members of the Politburo and Secretariat. Who sets the Politburo's agenda and what role does the General Department of the Central Committee play?

> *Gregory:* The agenda is prepared by the assistants of the general secretary, the assistants of the Politburo members, and the assistants of the secretaries [of the Central Committee]. They prepare the final draft of the agenda. The agenda must be prepared by the *apparat* of the Central Committee, including

the International Department. They must [determine] that there is . . . [a] need to discuss certain questions. For example, four from the International Department, three from the Ministry of Foreign Affairs, five from the party organs [Central Committee Department], and so on.

Q: Where is the final decision made?

Gregory: It is the personal secretariat of the general secretary. This has many "referents," not assistants, about twenty-five or thirty. They work for the general secretary and are relatively unknown. They prepare the agenda. They decide that say, alcoholism is first [on the agenda], then a problem with heavy industry, and so on. I knew one of these referents—Samyoteikin. He is now ambassador to Australia. He was the head of this personal secretariat [of the general secretary].

Q: Is this group completely separate from the General Department?

Gregory: Yes, absolutely. I would often talk with Samyoteikin, but he would sometimes not be able to meet me because he was preparing the agenda. Before the personal secretariat [of the general secretary] prepares the agenda, they would have to consult with the secretaries. Proposals would come from many organizations, including the Union of Journalists. Our plan would have to be approved—how many delegations we should have, how much money we receive, how much foreign currency and so on. We would send our proposals to the Department of Agitation and Propaganda or the International Department. Our proposals would have to be approved because without the decision of the Politburo, one cannot do anything.

Sejna confirms that precluding or, at least, diminishing the possibility for conflict within the Politburo is one of the key duties of those who set the agenda and who, in the Soviet case, are members of the Technical Group in the Secretariat, whose tasks include coordination between the various Central Committee departments. He indicates the extent to which performance of this task confers control upon the Secretariat and the other elements of the Central Committee bureaucracy:

[In Czechoslovakia, as in all communist countries], the real power resides in the hands of the party bureaucrats. . . . For example, I was summoned by the Czechoslovak Administrative Department of the Central Committee, which in the Soviet Union is the Administrative Organs Department, and told that I was to be elected to the Central Committee of the Czechoslovak Party. Being a rather naive provincial, I asked how that could be possible, and I was informed curtly that things had already been decided and that I could consider myself elected. That is how everything is done.

Sejna continues:

The most important people in the system are the secretaries of the Central Committee. Every week, before the meeting of the Politburo, there is a meeting of the Secretariat. The Secretariat meets first in an open session, with certain other [persons] invited to present their views, and then in closed session, with only the secretaries. It is there that the decision is made as to what the Politburo ought to consider, and it is there that the agenda is drawn up which will shape the Politburo decision. The Politburo can never make very detailed decisions. With the exception of the five-year plans and occasionally other important issues, no report to the Politburo [in Czechoslovakia] may exceed forty pages. And because the Politburo will consider between fourteen and eighteen such reports at each meeting, the members will never be thoroughly familiar with the details involved. Politburo sessions [in Czechoslovakia] begin at noon and often last until midnight. There is that much to cover. Furthermore, because of the overriding need for party unity, there cannot be struggles in the Politburo except [during] crisis [periods]. It is the responsibility of the party bureaucracy to cleanse the reports of everything that might be found controversial well before the document ever reaches the Politburo itself. In the Politburo, or in the Defense Council, the members do not fight for anything unless there is a crisis. The idea that the Soviet Politburo would routinely vote 10 to 5 or something like that is nonsense. I would like to see anyone vote against Brezhnev and keep his position.

Pelikan illustrates how agenda topics are prepared within the party apparatus, and how they are sanitized as they progress through the bureaucracy before reaching the Politburo. For instance, when the Czechoslovak Politburo was to consider the situation in agriculture, who prepared the agenda for the Politburo meetings?

[This task was performed by] the first secretary with the help of his Secretariat . . . and his assistant. . . . Josef Svoboda [for instance] was the Chief of Novotny's personal Secretariat. He was a member of the Central Committee but he also participated in the meetings of the Politburo. . . . [M]embers of the Politburo or departments of the Central Committee of the party prepared the [agenda]. . . . The way this was prepared was as follows: the minister of agriculture was asked to prepare with his staff the report about the [agricultural] situation. He had to submit this report to the head of the Department of Agriculture of the Central Committee of the party. Then this head of the Department would discuss the report and find that it is not well written or that there are some weaknesses, that there is too much criticism, or that there is not enough criticism and so on. So, he would return the report back to the minister, usually several times. After the report was approved by the head of the Department of Agriculture of the Central Committee, it was passed to the first secretary of the CC who again discussed this report with the head of the Department of Agriculture. . . . Then the first secretary would tell Svoboda to put the report on the situation in agriculture on the agenda of the next Politburo meeting. . . . Of course, it must have been always prepared in advance because the members of the Politburo had to have a chance to read this report. In general, for one meeting of the Politburo the members had about several hundred pages in front of them.

According to Shevchenko, the Politburo usually prefers not to be presented with several options. Therefore, the Secretariat's preparatory work is very convenient for the Politburo:

> You might submit a proposal to the Politburo and mention two or three options and even express your opinion that the first option is the best one. But when they come to the attachment where you have given two or three options, they don't like it. You can't go to the Politburo with three options. . . . Gromyko himself never [submitted proposals with several] options in attachments.

It seems, therefore, that the Secretariat is a major player in setting the agenda for Politburo sessions and there are eminently practical reasons for that. However, this does not mean that Politburo members are paper dragons. One must remember that the Politburo's key members are part of the Secretariat; moreover the Politburo's views are percolated through the system during the preparatory stage through the intimate involvement in the process of the personal staffs of the Politburo members. Members of the sub-elite, including also the staffs of Central Committee Departments will not assume positions which they know to be unacceptable to the top decision-makers.

Politburo Subcommittees. One topic of discussion among observers of the Soviet system has been the existence of specific subcommittees of the Politburo, or joint commissions of the Politburo and the Secretariat. The consensus of the interviewees seems to be that while such bodies have appeared from time to time, no clearly defined sphere of decision-making responsibility has been established for them. Some of the interviewees have referred to the appearance, from time to time, of an ad-hoc commission for foreign affairs.[11] Shevchenko, Gregory, and Sejna address this issue:

> *Q.* As far as you know, is there such a [body] as a joint commission of the Secretariat and the Politburo to deal with certain specific issues?
>
> *Shevchenko:* There is no permanent commission, though you can be confused by talking to different people because in different times of Soviet history, they have established commissions and then abolished them. They have changed their function all the time, as well. Thus, there have been Commissions such as the Commission for Foreign Affairs, Commission for Ideological Matters, which have been established and then abolished . . . essentially it is ad hoc. There might be some ad-hoc commission that existed for a number of years, not just for a few months or a few weeks. Actually it depends very much on who the [general] secretary is and how he conducts affairs.

---

[11] This is not to be confused with the Commissions of the CPSU, which the Central Committee brought into existence in September 1988.

Q: Do you know anything about subcommittees of the Politburo, do they exist, what are their functions?

Gregory: Khrushchev once organized subcommittee[s], but they do not exist anymore. There is also no foreign policy commission. There are only the departments [of the Central Committee], the Secretariat, and the ministries, but no subcommittees.

Q. [In Eastern Europe], are there permanent subcommittees of the Politburo, which might meet between the Politburo's weekly sessions?

Sejna: There are special permanent committees for the economy, agriculture, youth, and ideology, but they carry the title of Committee of the Central Committee, with no reference to the Politburo. The Secretariat handles these committees. In Poland right now, for example, there might be a special committee to deal with the question of labor since that is their main problem.

Q: And are Politburo members on these subcommittees?

Sejna: No, never. A Politburo member might be chairman of the Subcommittee for Ideology, in the same way that Kolder was chairman of the Subcommittee for the Economy in Czechoslovakia.

The General Secretary's Role. From the mechanics of the Politburo—when it meets, how its meetings are arranged, how it makes decisions, and the way in which the agenda is set for the meetings—one has to move on to discuss its internal dynamics, namely the relationships between the individual Politburo members and the obvious impact on decision making. At the center is the general secretary, who is usually much more than *primus inter pares:*

Checinski: I don't know what it is like today but I am convinced that the present situation cannot be much different than in the past. The Politburo is not a collective body. The [decisive] party person in all the socialist nations is the single leader. Take, for instance, Khrushchev. He was the leader, the single leader.

Q: You are saying that the Politburo is not a collective body.

Checinski: No, members of the Politburo are not equal . . . [some are] yes, more equal than others. You can't compare the members of the Politburo. So if you are talking about the Politburo, from my own experience, the [general or first] party secretary is the leader.

Q: Would you say that the general secretary [or first secretary] is a dictator?

Checinski: Yes, sir. The dictator could have different periods, when he is more [of a] dictator or less [of a] dictator. But he is a dictator. He has the main power. And if he is an absolute dictator, he has a chance to be one for a long time. He has to be a good dictator. . . . He is responsible for both the Politburo and the Defense Council.

Of course, the interviewees from the USSR and Eastern Europe do *not* imply that the general secretary holds absolute power at all times. As history has shown, a general secretary can be removed, an occurrence that is addressed later in this volume. In Cuba and Ethiopia, there are variations upon this theme. In these two states, the general secretary's powers are closer to the absolute:

Benemelis: Castro learned a great deal from [his] early experience. He decided not to make the party again as strong as ORI[12] was then. Actually, he does not have any really powerful institutions in Cuba. When he does not want one, he just cuts off their support. He manages institutions in a guerrilla style. For example, the DGI is not the only important intelligence service working outside Cuba; there is also the Americas Department. Everything depends, in Cuba, upon when Castro moves. Sometimes he will have individuals in the Cuban upper elite with no connections to intelligence, like Montane, doing intelligence work. And it does not concern Pineiro or the DGI; only Castro.

Q: In Ethiopia, is Mengistu as important as Castro is in Cuba, or has the party itself become the main power base?

Wolde: I think that it is Mengistu himself, rather than the party, as in Cuba. He is the general secretary of the party, the head of state, the head of government, commander-in-chief of the armed forces. The party is there because he wishes it to be there. In fact there are many issues which he does not even bring to the attention of party leadership. I think that Mengistu is fully in charge. Power is consolidated in him, and for the first time in the history of Ethiopia we have all power concentrated in one person. Even in the Soviet Union, one could say that the party is in charge, but the general secretary has greater influence than the others. . . . Even the leadership cannot talk freely about our problems in the Council of Ministers or in the Central Committee. Only the dictates of a few people count.

For those below the rank of general secretary, power and position are defined by a complex system of intersecting lines between party offices:

Checinski: Five [secretaries of the Central Committee are on the Polish Politburo]. These five secretaries who are members of the Politburo are really very powerful. There are some members of the Politburo who will never be secretaries but they are more powerful than some secretaries. The minister of defense can never be a secretary.

Q: Is the minister of foreign affairs more powerful than a secretary of the Central Committee who is in charge of the Foreign Relations Department?

Checinski: If he is a member of Politburo he is more powerful. . . . general secretary, the name tells you everything. He leads all the secretaries. They have to work under his supervision.

---

[12] Integrated Revolutionary Organization.

While individual boundaries within the system may appear ill-defined at first sight, Shevchenko assures us that within the Politburo each member is certain of where he stands in relation to every other member of the party bureaucracy:

> As far as I know, each member of the Politburo knows his position. There are a few members of the Politburo whose places are more or less fixed. . . . They would be the secretary general himself, the chairman of the Council of Ministers, and the chairman of the Presidium of the Supreme Soviet. In the Central Committee, it is more or less clear who is number two, and it's accepted. It's also known who is number three, more or less, and I would say that this is true of all the positions at the very top. Number five or six is no problem because it's known.

The Secretariat:
the Central Committee General Department

Some view the Secretariat of the Party Central Committee as an implementational arm of the Politburo, but a majority regards the Secretariat as being equal to—and occasionally more influential than—the Politburo. Cross-membership between these two organs is the rule, and those who hold the title of secretary while simultaneously being Politburo members are key personalities. The general secretary, of course, derives his title from his position as the leader of the Secretariat. Voslensky provides insight on the manner in which the Secretariat functions:

> Q. Do [the members of the Secretariat] meet regularly as a group, and if so, how often?
>
> *Voslensky:* Yes, once a week.
>
> Q: Is that before the Politburo meeting? Is there a regularly scheduled time?
>
> *Voslensky:* Yes. If I'm not mistaken, they meet at the beginning of every week, on Tuesday. I'm not quite sure. The Politburo meets on Thursday; practically all the decisions of the Politburo are prepared, typed, and classified secret, top secret and so on, and are then received by the ministries, and so on, on [the following] Monday morning.
>
> Q: On their way down, do these Politburo decisions go back to the Secretariat before they are passed on?
>
> *Voslensky:* No. The Secretariat and the Politburo are two parallel organs. The Politburo decides, or the Secretariat decides.
>
> Q: . . . I mean, on its way to implementation, does [a decision] go directly, for instance, to state organs like individual ministries?
>
> *Voslensky:* Yes.

So much for the downward flow, from decision to implementation. As for the upward flow of material to be submitted for decision, Voslensky draws attention to the role of the Central Committee's General Department:

> The [Central Committee] Departments prepare papers; the General Department manages the passing of these papers to the Politburo or to the Secretariat. And then, after the matter has been decided, the General Department sends it to all concerned, to those who have to implement it.

Voslensky makes the division of labor between the Secretariat and the Politburo explicit:

> *Q.* By what criteria would the Secretariat decide that a particular matter need not go up to the Politburo?
>
> *Voslensky:* The criterion is: on purely organizational matters—to the Secretariat, on matters of high policy—to the Politburo.

The Secretariat (particularly those secretaries who have interlocking simultaneous membership in the Politburo) is the organ which, *inter alia,* monitors implementation of Politburo decisions, especially those concerned with party affairs. Some decisions of the Politburo, it appears, are almost entirely in the hands of the Secretariat (and occasionally, of the CC department chiefs) for implementation. This pertains particularly to matters concerning the internal affairs of the party and the relationship between the Central Committee CPSU and other communist parties. Voslensky continues:

> The Politburo can also assign other tasks to the Secretariat, which, as a practical matter, is a subdivision of the Politburo for these very important questions.

Another issue regarding internal structure concerns the existence of a so-called second secretary or chief ideologist of the party. (As of this writing that second secretary of the CPSU appears to be Vadim Medvedev.) Voslensky warns that such a function is not officially recognized. He does not believe that the CPSU has a chief ideologist.

> No, there is no such thing. It is nonsense. There was certainly the ideological [department chief] of the Party Central Committee. But he [Suslov] was much more.

At the same time, Zdenek Mlynar, a former high-ranking functionary of the Czechoslovak Communist Party's Central Committee, relates what he learned in the Kremlin shortly after the 1968 Warsaw-pact invasion of Czechoslovakia. In December of 1967, when Brezhnev was told that Antonin Novotny was about to lose his position as the first secretary of the Czecho- slovak Communist Party, he asked: "*I u nikh, kto vtoroi* (who is their number two)?" Mlynar points to this as a manifestation of Brezhnev's imperial attitude toward Eastern Europe. He did not bother discovering that the Czech system never did have a *vtoroi,* a number two. This would indicate that the Soviet system around 1968, at least, included the concept of the Party's second secre- tary (presumably Suslov, in the case of the USSR). Pelikan asserts that the idea of a chief ideologist arose from the fact that the general secretary usually does not concern himself with ideological matters, but, at least in Czechoslovakia, "runs only one [Central Committee] Department directly. . . . This is the Organizational Department and sometimes also the Cadres Department, which means he is responsible for nomination and appointment of all [top] officials."

As with many of the institutions and offices in the Soviet hierarchy, the position of second secretary may be a product of personality and opportunity; someone may hold this power de facto at certain times and not at others. Power structures in the Soviet Union and Eastern Europe are fluid. What holds for one period may be inapplicable for the next.

Voslensky comments on the difference between having the title secretary and being an untitled Central Committee Department chief:

Q. Regarding the Secretariat of the *apparat,* there are unsolved problems. First, how does somebody who has the personal title of secretary differ from somebody who is a head of a Central Committee Department [without] the title of secretary? Are we to understand that if you have the title of secretary, then you are the super boss over a number of departments?

Voslensky: It is so. You are a boss, but it is possible that you have just one department. But you are the boss, and this is the difference between a secre- tary and a mere department head. The department head does not belong to the leadership of the Soviet Union, the Kremlin leadership. The secretary belongs to this leadership. This is extremely important. The secretary is elected, the department head is appointed—he is an employee.

Q: Appointed by whom?

Voslensky: Certainly by the Politburo. The chief of the Department is an employee—he is appointed. He belongs to the *nomenklatura* of the Polit- buro. But there is this difference between a person representing the party leadership and such an employee (even if he is an important bureaucrat); this is a very important step in the career, and every department head of the Party Central Committee has the dream of eventually becoming secretary.

Through the General Department, the Secretariat also controls a wide range of important non-implementational activities, as Voslensky points out.

To reach the Politburo's agenda, a proposal must pass through the General Department of the Central Committee:

> *Voslensky:* The General Department prepares the agenda of the Politburo. It certainly is true that if the general secretary wants to put a point on the agenda, he or his assistant calls the chief of the General Department and says, "Mikhail Sergeevich Gorbachev says that we must put this point on the agenda for the next meeting of the Politburo as one of the first five points, so please look at whom [to] invite on this point."
>
> *Q:* So in fact other members of the Politburo have very little control over the agenda?
>
> *Voslensky:* Well, they have specific interests. To put something on the agenda, they would first ask the general secretary; they would try to persuade him. If this were not so, the general secretary would come to a Politburo meeting and find unexpected points on the agenda.
>
> *Q:* The agenda goes back through the General Department for the necessary preparations. Is there any way of getting around the General Department?
>
> *Voslensky:* No, no, that's impossible.

In the General Department, proposals either await the regular meeting of the Politburo, or, in matters of particular importance and urgency, they are sent directly to the parties concerned for immediate action. The process of decision making outside official Politburo channels, which Shevchenko has mentioned, is directed by the General Department:

> They make twelve copies of proposals for the General Department and they are sent to all Secretaries. It is the responsibility of the General Department to be sure they're sent, marked "urgent" or whatever. Each member of the Politburo either initials it or if he doesn't initial it, makes some notes. Then the General Department collects them. However, it is not necessary to wait if someone is not involved at all and they know this in advance. If the matter is urgent, as in [the case of] Daniloff's arrest,[13] they will not wait for someone's approval. It would be Gorbachev, Ligachev, Shevardnadze, Gromyko, etc. that would look at this. It would go without Shcherbitsky and Kunaev. They [hardly participate in] any decisions. . . .
>
> If it's something [the leaders] want absolutely, then all members of the Politburo would be behind them, of course. Some matters have more urgency. Otherwise, Shcherbitsky can receive it with a delay of a few days and the decision will have already been adopted, and even implemented. He will receive the material of course, eventually. He complained about it in a few conversations with me. His foreign minister complained even more. The

---

[13] American reporter Nicholas Daniloff was arrested in Moscow on 30 August 1986, and released without trial on 2 September.

Ukrainian foreign minister complained and tried to convince Shcherbitsky who, frankly speaking, didn't have a great deal of interest [in many matters in Moscow]. He didn't care about some of the things that went on.

Shevchenko continues:

But there is a way to hasten matters which is usually the responsibility of the appropriate bureau in the Soviet system. For example, on foreign affairs issues it's usually a senior assistant to Gromyko—and the senior assistant now [to] Shevardnadze—who must ensure that [the item] will be on the [Politburo] agenda. He is supposed to know all about that. And he has the authority to be in direct contact with the people in the *Obshchij otdel*.

There are several levels, of course, because there are people in the General Department who deal with vaguer matters. They have a division, more or less, between who deals with foreign affairs matters and who deals with economic matters. Some others know a little bit more, if not the substance, then at least [they] recognize who is who. Thus Makarov, in my time, would maintain contact with the man who was responsible for all material, or a proposal, or anything which had been sent from the Foreign Ministry. And if the person [from the Foreign Ministry] assures Makarov that [the item should be before] the Politburo meeting, if necessary, then Makarov will attend to it also. If some of the [items] are not important, he will leave [them] to go [at the normal pace]. . . .

That's why on many issues, the matters which don't have any urgency can sit somewhere like the Central Committee for months sometimes. For a very long period of time, they can just be sitting there. This is one of the major problems of the functioning of the whole Soviet state machinery. This enormous centralization of power is a great handicap [to] the Soviet Union. The Politburo would like to put its nose [into] all these minor things, which number in the thousands every month. The delay is very substantial . . . in deciding [matters at] the Politburo [level]. They may have a situation when a person in the General Department hears from the Foreign Ministry that they want to vote tomorrow in the Security Council and they need a decision from the Politburo in a matter of hours. However, the Politburo is occupied with other business; there is a problem. What can they do?

The General Department also handles other duties which seem to be purely operational, but which carry with them a great deal of latent power. Gregory and Shevchenko explain:

Gregory: This department works for the whole Central Committee, not just for the general secretary. It coordinates all work for the CC.

Q: Who deals with the personal correspondence of the general secretary?

Shevchenko: It's one of the functions of the General Department. They have to combine it. They coordinate it as a special unit. They can do it themselves, but in most cases they would refer the answer to the appropriate departments. They also don't write themselves. The answer is that the General Department is just a coordinating body, deciding who should deal with the issue. Some of these letters will go to the [general secretary's personal] assistant to be answered directly by the general secretary, or if something is within the competence of some other department, it will go to the appropriate person.

Interviewees from outside the Soviet Union did not place such emphasis on the importance of the General Department. Jiri Pelikan points out that many issues are addressed both in the Secretariat and the Politburo:

I would say [that] although the Secretariat officially is there for the [implementation] of the decisions of the Politburo, there is some kind of double overlapping . . . for example, . . . the situation in agriculture [may be] discussed [both by the Secretariat and the Politburo].

Ambassador Rurarz's concept of the Polish Central Committee's General Department follows the lines of an administrative body concerned with paper traffic and continuity:

The General Department of the Polish Central Committee dealt purely with Central Committee administrative and internal matters, and did not interfere with anything of substance. There was an Organizational Department, which dealt with all organizational matters of the party including personnel for the party apparatus; but not for non-party bodies. For that [there existed] a Personnel Bureau.

The General Secretary's Personal Chancery

The USSR. The General Department of the Secretariat is not the only organ that handles the personal affairs of the general secretary and other leaders, and it may not even be the most important. Increasingly, the leadership has surrounded itself with informal personal chanceries made up of trusted persons and experts whose work, at least on occasion, seems beyond the purview of the party *apparat.* These groups act as independent bases of support, information gathering, and influence projection. Michael Voslensky spells out why the general secretary and others in leadership positions may need private chanceries in addition to the General Department:

The General Department is a rather huge organization. Practically every paper in the framework of the Party Central Committee comes through the channels of the General Department. If you write a letter to the Party Central

Committee it will be sent first to the General Department and they will decide what to do with your letter. . . . Personal secretariats are small, first of all; second, they consist of highly qualified people whom [the chief] trusts absolutely, and who work for him personally. They write his speeches [and] manage his time schedule and agenda. These are personal assistants.

The roots of the personal chancery may be found during Stalin's reign. During Stalin's later years, his personal secretary, Aleksandr Poskrebyshev, was able to control access to his boss. This applied to all but the most influential personalities, as Gregory describes:

When someone wanted to see Stalin, only Beria and Malenkov could go straight in. Khrushchev, Bulganin and everyone else would have to go through Poskrebyshev. If Stalin was at a *dacha,* for example, Poskrebyshev would decide who could see him. If Poskrebyshev decide[d] something was not important or that he should rest instead, Stalin would agree with him. Stalin believed in him. But I do not know how clever he was. When I read Bajanov's[14] book I suspect that he exaggerated somewhat, because he said that Stalin would ask him to review or prepare speeches. This is not true because Stalin never asked anyone to prepare his speeches; he always did it himself. This is quite different from Khrushchev or Brezhnev.

Peter Deriabin had personal insight into the activities of Stalin's chancery. He confirms the importance of personal relationships with Aleksandr Poskrebyshev. Deriabin sheds light on Poskrebyshev's role as an intermediary between Stalin and other Soviet leaders:

Q: How large was Poskrebyshev's secretariat, Stalin's personal chancery?

Deriabin: I am not sure, but it was quite small. Most of the actual work was done by Poskrebyshev himself. It is highly unlikely that anyone else would have known the secrets. There were typists and stenographers but Stalin even had his own stenographer; however, only rarely would Stalin use his stenographer unless he had already written, organized and prepared his thoughts. [This chancery] later grew much larger after I left. Some of the key people, such as Aleksandrov-Agentov[15] and Blatov,[16] remained in the organization from the time of Brezhnev to Chernenko. Andropov did bring in a KGB colonel with him but kept Agentov and Blatov. Incidentially, Alexandrov-Agentov's real name is just Agentov. When he was ambassador to Sierra Leone, he took the name Alexandrov; I do not know if he was

---

[14] Boris Bajanov, Stalin's secretary, defected to the British in January, 1928. See, Gordon Brook-Shepherd, *The Storm Petrels: The Flight of the First Soviet Defectors* (New York: Harcourt, Brace, Jovanovich, 1977), pp. 3–71.

[15] Andrei Mikhailovich Aleksandrov-Agentov, born 1918, aide to CPSU CC general secretary L.I. Brezhnev.

[16] Anatolii Ivanovich Blatov, born 1914, aide to CPSU CC general secretary, L.I. Brezhnev.

working with the KGB. When he returned to Moscow and was elected to the Central Committee, he was forced to adopt the name Alexandrov-Agentov that he goes by now.

Q: With whom did Poskrebyshev work other than Stalin?

Deriabin: He worked with everybody in some way. If someone could work well with Poskrebyshev, then it was more likely that he could get to see Stalin. It was just not possible, as far as I ever knew, that a Molotov or a Voroshilov did not go through Poskrebyshev to see Stalin. One also had to approach Poskrebyshev according to the circumstances: If he had been drunk the night before then it was probable that he would not see anybody; if he was in good humor and his health was fine, then one had a good chance to get in to see Stalin. Even in Malenkov's case, if Stalin wanted to see him, Poskrebyshev would call Malenkov and tell him; then Malenkov would come and go in and see Stalin. Beria was a special case because he was so often in and out of favor. In 1946, when he lost control of the state security organs, Stalin told Abakumov and Poskrebyshev that they no longer had to keep Beria fully informed. So we no longer wrote reports to Beria even though he would normally have been informed because he was a Politburo member. When I was in the Guards Directorate and in the First Chief Directorate it was the same: sometimes Beria was involved and sometimes he was not. For instance, if I wrote a report on Vismut[17] while in the Austro-German Department it would go to Beria as well as certain other Politburo members, such as the minister of defense, but usually not candidate members or the foreign minister. If the report was on Vismut production rates it would be routed differently than if the report was on the use of uranium in atomic weapons.

As Soviet power grew and the political life of the leadership became more complex, the personal secretaries grew larger and more important. The size seemed to vary with the historical period and with the leader:

Q: How large is the personal secretariat?

Shevchenko: In Brezhnev's time there were no more than eight [members], substantively speaking. For the clerical personnel, there are one or two secretaries who type records and who are tied directly to the office. However, even the office of the secretary general of the party uses a Central Committee [typing] pool. Aleksandrov or Blatov, or a younger guy, each [had] a clear-cut division of work to deal with the KGB, or the military, etc. For example, Aleksandrov would look at everything which was related to foreign policy, submitted by the International Department, or the Foreign Ministry, or something like that. They are quite busy since there are not many of them and I don't think they have much support.

---

[17] Operation Vismut, run by Beria, was the code name for Soviet exploitation of Saxon uranium after World War II. See Gavriel D. Ra'anan, *International Policy Formation in the USSR: Factional Debates' during the Zhdanovshchina* (Hamden, Connecticut: Archon Books, 1983), p. 89.

Gregory indicates that the important functions of the general secretary's personal assistants, included briefings:

[The general secretary's assistants] are very important. They are assistants, but not just technical assistants. For example, Gorbachev's answers to a correspondent from *Le Monde* would be aided by them. They would consult the appropriate department about the SS-24 and SS-25 or whatever. They would show the draft to Gorbachev and discuss it with him. Their functions include speech writing, prepared statements and briefings. They also control scheduling and access.

In response to a request for additional information on the background of the personal assistants, Piatigorsky states:

Piatigorsky: I know one of [Brezhnev's] secretaries [who] was a crony of mine. Also a couple of others from the faculty of philosophy. They were taken very young, right after postgraduate studies, straight from the university.

Q: Was that because of their specialization?

Piatigorsky: No. It was other things, maybe connections of their parents or their backgrounds. They were all good Russians of good origin, not bad university careers, and not at all stupid.

Q: Would they get some special primary training before being employed?

Piatigorsky: Never. They [were trained] during their juniorship in the Cental Committee.

Q: Does every member of the Politburo have his own personal secretariat, or is it only some?

Piatigorsky: Every member, of course. Each has his own chancery. Not just a secretary; he has his own assistant, first of all, like Aleksandrov was to Brezhnev. He was not a secretary, he was his personal assistant. He also has a responsible secretary and a referent. At least five people in all.

Ability is one of the key traits for anyone aspiring to work in the personal chanceries of the leading personalities of the Central Committee. It is insufficient to be well known and trustworthy; one must also be efficient. Some workers in the personal chanceries were so talented that they have survived several general secretaries for whom they had worked. It has puzzled students of the Soviet Union that several of the personalities whom Brezhnev had appointed remained when Andropov came in and stayed even under Chernenko. Some of them may still be in place in various personal chanceries of Politburo members. Why, when this is such a personal matter, would new leaders keep the assistants of their predecessors? Was it not to be expected that each new leader would bring in his own personal chancery staff? Michael

Voslensky, who knew Aleksandrov-Agentov personally, responds to this question:

> *Voslensky:* Yes and no. Aleksandrov-Agentov is an extremely able man; I know him very well. He is a nice man. When he got on the personal secretariat he got very bureaucratized, but in principle he's a nice, clever man, a diplomat.
>
> *Q:* Where did he come from?
>
> *Voslensky:* The Foreign Ministry.
>
> *Q:* Blatov also?
>
> *Voslensky:* Blatov also. I know Anatolii Ivanovich Blatov. He's a very cautious bureaucrat, but Aleksandrov-Agentov is an intellectual. Blatov is not very cultivated, but clever.
>
> *Q:* Did either of them have any previous personal acquaintance with Brezhnev?
>
> *Voslensky:* No.
>
> *Q:* So who chose them? It's a key appointment, after all.
>
> *Voslensky:* Yes. Both worked with Gromyko. Blatov was a department chief in the Foreign Ministry. He was chief of the Third European Department, and then the chief of the so-called OB—the Administration of Foreign Policy Information. I know that Aleksandrov-Agentov was personal assistant to Gromyko and Brezhnev. He was efficient.

Yet, ability alone cannot be the sole criterion for keeping on chancery personnel. The general secretary who is new to his job may wish to retain some members of his predecessor's personal chancery staff in order to exploit their knowledge of the tasks at hand and to maintain a much needed institutional memory, as Sejna points out and Piatigorsky confirms:

> *Sejna:* They are probably retained because of what they know, their institutional memory. Gorbachev was made general secretary because his predecessor had died, but when Brezhnev came to power after Khrushchev had been ousted, he could not phone Khrushchev to ask his advice. The personal secretariat provides continuity and advice.
>
> *Piatigorsky:* [Some people were retained] because they had absolutely immeasurable bureaucratic experience.

One other factor contributed to the development of a broader sphere of responsibility by the general secretary's personal chancery: as the General Department grew, it became more bureaucratized and less responsive. Michael Voslensky believes that the duties of the two institutions are delineated clearly enough so that conflict is minimal.

Voslensky: The personal [chancery] is indeed [the general secretary's] personal secretariat. . . . It's what belongs to him personally. . . . The General Department is a chancery of the Politburo and to the Secretariat. So it is not the persons [it serves] but the bodies, the agencies.

The General Department would certainly prepare a draft agenda [for the Politburo] and show it to the assistants of the general secretary. If these assistants have some questions they would ask them, even of the general secretary. Probably even the general secretary himself would read this agenda, even if only for three or five minutes. If he says okay, then it's okay.

Q: So you feel that the division of functions is clear-cut enough for there not to be any overlap?

Voslensky: Yes, I think they are clear-cut enough.

Arkady Shevchenko is inclined to downgrade the substantive weight of the General Department compared with the general secretary's private chancery:

The *Obshchij otdel* [General Department] never will go into the substance of a given matter. They don't decide on substantive issues. Essentially, [they perform] a clerical function. They receive all the proposals—*vsye zapiski TsK* [all the papers of the Central Committee]. [These] come first to the *Obshchij otdel* to be typed up. It's up to [the department] to circulate them properly, to decide to whom [they] will go and how a decision will be made. Either [they] will be distributed to the Politburo itself, or [they] will be sent to the . . . Secretariat of the party which is where some of the decisions can be made. On some things like health issues, it's enough that two secretaries of the party decide without submitting [the issue] to the Politburo. So, here it's a question mostly of typing—which is enormous because everything needs to be supervised. However, in the General Department there are no experts on substantive matters who could deal with specific issues. It's paperwork, actually.

Arkady Shevchenko points out, however, that the General Department can influence the outcome of a policy proposal by delaying the submission of certain items to the Politburo:

If the head of the [General Department] talks with the general secretary . . . the general secretary can then check on [the submission of the item in question to the Politburo]. Otherwise the *Obshchij otdel* can delay. The importance of the position of the General Department [chief] is that first of all he knows everything which goes to the Central Committee. The possibility of [preventing an item from reaching] the Politburo, or changing something (as Chernenko, who was a personal friend of Brezhnev, could do when he was chief of the General Department) can only occur by talking with the general secretary. Otherwise it's impossible for the department itself to stop [or] to [change items].

But there is a lot of delay because [the department members] decide the priorities, which sometimes might not coincide with the views of the respective ministers. So the ministry is very much dependent on the men who work there, who might say to the minister, "your proposal cannot go through the Politburo for a month for there would be an argument." So on the one hand, this looks like paperwork and clerical work, but in essence it could become important or sensitive.

Shevchenko gives an example of the options that the chief of the general department could exploit but for the constraints posed by the general secretary's private chancery:

For example, when Brezhnev put Chernenko in this position, Chernenko decided what was submitted to the Politburo. Chernenko knew that everything, from appointments to [passing on] the decision of the Secretariat, or the Politburo itself, or the secretary general, all went to the General Department and to the man who looks through all these documents. Nothing can go around [him] indirectly. So it's an . . . important position for any general secretary, including Gorbachev, if he doesn't want to have a situation where someone could create a little sabotage. . . .

Under Brezhnev—and I think under Chernenko and most likely under Gorbachev—the [general secretary's] personal assistants deal more with . . . substance. . . . While they cannot themselves change a proposal of the foreign minister, defense minister, or KGB, their function and role for the secretary general . . . is to screen papers and relay their opinion. For example, Aleksandrov could come to Brezhnev and tell him, "You have a proposal from the foreign minister, but my opinion is that it should be changed." He can draw [such matters to] the attention of Brezhnev or whoever the secretary general is. Thus the General Department usually will not embark on any kind of [designation of] proposals or [on presenting] a recommendation for the Politburo or [on persuading] the general secretary to change [proposals]. If such a recommendation came, it would be on a purely personal basis from the [chief] of the [general department] and he would convey it orally to the general secretary.

There is also a conflict between the personal chancery and the Central Committee's departments as a result of contradictions between the basic inertia of the system and the requirements of the leadership. Piatigorsky explains:

There has always been . . . a tendency [for personal chanceries to become more important than Central Committee departments]. It is an agency which is not mentioned in either the party statutes or the state Constitution. Only the official Central Committee departments are mentioned. Each official department has its own supervisor, who [answers to] one of the secretaries of the Central Committee. Not all of those secretaries belong to the Politburo. Each secretary is responsible for at least one department or more. I would like to stress that the personal secretariats [chanceries] of Politburo members are extremely personal, irrespective of their involvement in any other business, in which case [Politburo members] would [need] another secretariat side by side with the personal one.

Other Socialist States. The situation in Poland, Czechoslovakia, and Bulgaria mirrors that of the Soviet Union. There are large and influential personal chanceries assuming roughly the same duties as do personal chanceries in the Kremlin. In Poland, the personal chancery has official existence as an organ of the Secretariat, but in fact is an institution answerable exclusively to the general secretary. Rurarz notes:

> The chancery of the Secretariat is, in fact, his [the general secretary's] private chancery, but officially serves the Politburo and the Secretariat of the party. It plans the meetings of both the Politburo and the Secretariat. For instance, I planned the Politburo meetings when it came to economic affairs, although in fact I was involved in more than just that. . . . Equally important, the Chancery had the responsibility of choosing [the persons] to be present at Politburo discussions of a certain [agenda] item, which meant eliminating some people in advance and promoting others. No one of those invited was ever allowed to stay throughout the whole Politburo meeting. He would stay for a particular agenda item only.

In Czechoslovakia, the personal chanceries of Politburo members were large institutions. According to Jan Sejna, their duties included everything from situation briefings to the setting of the dinner menu. Sejna elaborates:

> I was chief of staff to the minister of defense and this was a . . . body that was only personal [staff] and had nothing to do with the general staff. I had under me five or six departments, which were for the minister of defense only. For example, since [General] Lomsky [the Czechoslovak defense minister, who resigned in 1968] never had time to read all the papers required for his role in the Politburo, members of this personal staff would go over the material and brief him on it. The same was true for the general secretary, with the difference that he would have that much more to cover. Therefore, his personal staff would have to be larger in order to do all the work for him. In the Communist system no one trusts anyone else. These staffs are personally loyal to their boss[es] and represent personal security within the system for the Politburo member. . . . The private secretariats also look after what the man eats, what gifts he should give or receive, who shall meet him or be present at various receptions and other such activities.

In Bulgarian political life, trust is a rare commodity. The personal chancery, therefore, serves as a protective shield for the leader. Vladimir Kostov likens the personal chancery to an illegal organization, with a cell structure:

The present leaders are used to big bureaucracies. When I entered the Komsomol, I joined a committee where there [were] over twenty full-time workers. I was one of them. They understand that the more functionaries . . . you have the greater your importance. It is not a coincidence that the personal secretary of Zhivkov, who started his career as the head of the personal secretariat, has a lot of power and is a member of the Politburo. Now he is called chief of the chancery. . . . I was taught that you can build the structure in different ways but that the ultimate aim is that no one should be responsible for more than ten people. Zhivkov is following the same rule no matter how many workers he has, he only comes into contact with a few of them. It is like the structure of the underground party.

In Ethiopia, Goshu Wolde states, there was no personal chancery at the time of the interview. The relevant tasks are performed by the Department of General Services, roughly an equivalent of the General Department in the Central Committee of the Communist Party of the Soviet Union.

The Central Committee Apparatus

The East European interviewees provided information on the composition and structure of the apparatus of the party Central Committees in Soviet-style states. In Poland, Checinski reports:

The Central Committee controls everything, all areas of life. Everything is . . . supervised by a specific person or department—economics, politics, military, etc. . . . Now, [in the USSR] there are two departments . . . which are the most important: the Organization Department and the Administration Department. These two departments are like the nerve system of the whole body. He who controls these two departments controls the party and the country. . . . [The general secretary has to control these two departments.]

While the Central Committee plenum as a whole consists of many prestigious party members, its plenary sessions do not really set policy. That function, to the extent that it is not performed by the Politburo, is filled by the Central Committee Secretariat and the individual departments of the Central Committee. Speaking about his experience in Czechoslovakia until 1968, Jan Sejna stresses that the Central Committee departments exercise direct control over Central Committee members:

Before the Central Committee meets, each member is called by the appropriate department and told what to do. The party bureaucrats then follow up later to see how well [the Central Committee members] are prepared; they do not leave anything to chance. . . . Let me give one example of the strength of the [Central Committee apparatus]. I was at Novotny's house during the period when the Central Committee was meeting to consider ousting him.

Novotny was fighting desperately to retain his position, but one evening he said to me, "Well, out of fourteen departments, nine have come out against me. I am finished." He never stopped to tally up how the members of the Central Committee would vote, since the departments control the members of the Central Committee. If one is a member of the Central Committee and from the agricultural field, the Department of Agriculture will prepare him for the meeting and will tell him what to say and when to say it. In fact, the members of the Central Committee are divided up into groups, into fiefdoms, and get instructions from different people.

Hus points to the dominant control mechanisms of the Politburo and the Secretariat over the Central Committee and its various departments:

> Every Department of the Central Committee is supervised by some member of the Politburo. None of these people will allow any other person to fish in his lake. The Central Committee is the body above all the ministries. The Minister of Foreign Affairs is a member neither of the Politburo nor the Secretariat. Bil'ak[18] was a member of both. Therefore, the minister was subordinate to Bil'ak and could not get involved with the International Department. Also the Ministry is part of the state apparatus, while the Department is part of the predominant party apparatus.

Jiri Pelikan, former director general of Czechoslovak television, outlines the respective functions of the various parts of the *apparat* and their influence on the modus operandi of the Central Committee:

> [The] Central Committee [has] very formal meetings, because the members of Central Committee actually have nothing . . . or very little to say about the [substance of the] political line, tactics and strategy of the party. The meetings of the Central Committee to which I was invited in my position as the general director of [Czechoslovak] television were usually very formal things, until . . . October and December of '67. There were always reports of the first secretary of the party or somebody from the Politburo. . . . [T]he discussion was prepared [beforehand] mainly by the secretaries of the party, [and detailed] the success of their party organization [during] that period. Then the meeting was concluded by [a] general resolution [approving] the report of the first secretary or of a member of the Politburo. . . . The same . . . also [held true] for the [party] congresses. The congresses of the party were . . . [theoretically] the [highest] policy-making body. But [the composition of the congresses resembled] the Central Committee. . . . It was a big event. There was a general report by the general secretary, then there was [the usual prepared] discussion. . . . Only people selected by the Secretariat

---

[18] Vasil' Bil'ak, born 1917, a former tailor's apprentice, member of the Czechoslovak Politburo since September 1968 and secretary of the Central Committee since November 1968, suddenly resigned all his positions on the Central Committee, KSC, 15 November 1988. See *Rude Pravo,* 16 December 1988, p. 1.

of the party were allowed to speak. The congress was mostly concluded by approval of the report of the general secretary of the party and by electing the Central Committee and the Control Commission, which were also chosen by the Secretariat of the party. In fact, the real body was the Secretariat of the Communist Party composed of secretaries of the [Central Committee of the] Communist Party and [members of] the Politburo.

For some, membership in the Central Committee can be an important part of their power base. For others, however, it can mean very little. Some Central Committee members serve what Sejna describes as a purely decorative function:

> Look, in the Central Committee there are people there because of their power, and [then] there are others there purely for decoration, such as . . . distinguished milkmaids.

Even those Central Committee members who are marked for upward mobility, indeed, particularly such persons, must obediently follow instructions they receive from the Central Committee departments, the Secretariat, and the Politburo. Sejna graphically illustrates this point:

> At my first meeting of the Central Committee I asked . . . "Comrade General, what does it mean now that I'm in the Central Committee?" I thought I was equal to him. He said: "Nothing. Just look around and shut up."
>
> [At a later Central Committee meeting] I criticized Jankovcova, a member of the Politburo. . . . She was in charge of our food industry. And, of course, she said there [was a lot] of fruit. . . . I criticized the situation and when I mentioned her name, everything was very quiet. Finally, I finished the speech. There was no applause. [Someone] called me to the conference room, and he repeated what I had done. I said, "What I said is true." He said that I was not in a meeting in my village. "You are in a meeting of the Central Committee and you cannot criticize members of the Politburo. We have selected you to rise very high and if you want to stay, shut up."

Michael Voslensky asserts that, while it is better to be on the Central Committee than not to be, one does not have to be a member to have access to higher party posts:

> [It] is possible for someone to become a chief of a Central Committee department without being a member of the Central Committee. . . . Look at Chernenko—he was the long-time chief of a very important department, of the General Department, but was not even a candidate member of the Central Committee.[19] Then he became a candidate; it is a very important first step.

---

[19] This statement is not corroborated by other sources.

In Bulgaria, the Central Committee apparatus functions as an informal governing mechanism, ever changing in size and influence, based largely on personal connections with the top leaders. Vladimir Kostov indicates that the work of the Bulgarian Central Committee apparatus reflects the shifting influence of personnel and the impact of various, often Western, theories of management; moreover, there seems to be a great deal of improvisation:

> *Kostov:* It is not possible to know [the number of Central Committee departments] at any given moment because they are changing it all the time. For example, a couple of years ago there was one Military Department, one Security Department, and one for Bulgarians working abroad. Now, as I understand it, all of this is in some super department. . . .

> *Q:* Was there ever [an] attempt, as in the Soviet Union, to have an International Information Department within the International Department?

> *Kostov:* As far as I remember no. [Where] Bulgaria is concerned I sometimes had the impression that such changes are made because of somebody who has good connections to Zhivkov. He goes and presents his ideas and says that he needs a department to carry out this idea. The next day, when he is out of favor, he is gone together with this [newly] created department. They do a lot of improvisation. Somebody, after visiting the Soviet Union, and seeing that there is something new, says, "Let's do it this way." In the last ten years or so, they are monitoring to get as much scientific information as possible, including the management theories in the Western countries. As far as I can tell, they are trying to implement some aspects of this in their work.

The State Defense Council

Relatively little is known about the State Defense Council (SDC).[20] Yet, at least in some East European countries, it may be as powerful as the Politburo itself and it exists in one form or another in every Soviet-style state.

The USSR

The State Defense Council's composition and its role remain obscure in official Soviet publications. The only regular mention one finds of the State Defense Council usually follows shortly after the ascension of a new general secretary, when a minor note will appear in *Pravda* announcing that he has become the head of the State Defense Council. The general secretary, some interviewees argue, is always the head of the State Defense Council of the

---

[20] One of the few authors who deal with the State Defense Council is Ellen Jones; see her *Red Army and Society: A Sociology of the Soviet Military* (Boston: Allen & Unwin, 1985), pp. 6–10.

Soviet Union, though such an ex officio position is not mentioned in the Soviet Constitution or any other known official document.[21] Jan Sejna elaborates on the general secretary's position:

> [When] the chief editor of *Pravda* was in Yugoslavia, he was asked whether it was true that Gorbachev was chairman of the Defense Council. The editor replied that once Gorbachev had become general secretary of the party he automatically became chairman as well.

Michael Checinski, with extensive experience in Polish intelligence, believes that the Defense Council plays a crucial role in decision making, particularly in the area of political-military issues. However, he stresses that the Defense Council is a state, not a party, institution:

> [The general secretary] is part of the Politburo, and he is [naturally] part of the Defense Council. He leads both. There is no difference here between Poland and the USSR. . . . In [*Perestroika*] there is a short biography of [its author] Gorbachev. [It] mentions clearly that he is the head of the Defense Council. If this is not important, why . . . is it mentioned? It not only exists, it plays a crucial, [even] dominant role in the political-military issues of the Soviet Union. But we have to make clear the distinction between the Defense Council and the Politburo. First of all, the [primary] difference. The Politburo is a party organ. The Defense Council is a government organ. People who argue that the Defense Council is a subcommittee of the Politburo have no idea what they are talking about. The Soviet Constitution . . . clearly [states] what the Defense Council is.

The membership of the State Defense Council, how many members it has, and by what criteria membership is established (for example, *ex officio*, or through personal influence) are elusive questions. Take, for instance, the case of Mikhail Suslov who was apparently a member of the Soviet Defense Council. Did he belong to it because of who he was, or because of his position as the so-called second secretary? Comments from Michael Voslensky indicate that members of the State Defense Council are partly important personalities and partly key office-holders. Voslensky is one of several of the interviewees who think that the peacetime importance of the State Defense Council is quite limited.

> *Voslensky:* I would guess [that] Suslov [was a member of the State Defense Council because of] who he was.
>
> *Q:* Which other members of the Politburo would have been represented on the State Defense Council?

---

[21] Mikhail Gorbachev's innovations provide for the chairman of the Presidium of the Supreme Soviet (in fact the general secretary, that is, himself) to be also chairman of the SDC.

Voslensky: The general secretary is automatically a member of the Defense Council. Also the minister of defense, who is practically his deputy [in the State Defense Council]. I would say Romanov is probably a member, representing the military-industrial complex.

Q: Gromyko?

Voslensky: I would not exclude the foreign minister. . . . The KGB chief would be there, as well as the chief of the general staff, Ogarkov. . . .

Q: [Would the] commander-in-chief of the Warsaw Pact [be a member]?

Voslensky: Kulikov, yes. It's possible. . . .

Q: Would the chairman of the State Defense Council carry the title in peacetime of supreme commander-in-chief of the armed forces?

Voslensky: Yes.

Q: [Why is it that] this title, if it appears at all, appears only a long time after someone assumes the position of chairman of the State Defense Council, and sometimes isn't published at all?

Voslensky: It's just for optical reasons. It doesn't look so good if the general secretary, the number one party man, has such a peacetime title.

Q: It's very often not mentioned in obituaries that the deceased was chairman of the State Defense Council; for example, in Chernenko's case. Gorbachev mentioned his two titles but not the third.

Voslensky: As I understand it, [that may be] because it's not very important. . . . The Defense Council is a theoretical organization. The Politburo and the Secretariat are the two bodies that matter.

Voslensky's comments raise the most vexing question concerning the State Defense Council, namely, is it at all important in peacetime? Some think that an organization so secret must be important. Others believe that the lack of information on the SDC stems from a lack of substance. They argue that, in essence, there is little to know. Voslensky elaborates on his disbelief that the SDC is some sort of extraordinary policy-making body:

Voslensky: [Any hard evidence of the importance of the State Defense Council] is practically non-existent. [The State Defense Council] exists [only] in order to make it official that the general secretary is the chief of the military. . . .

Q: There is a claim that the Brezhnev Constitution automatically makes the general secretary the chairman of the Defense Council. I have found no such reference anywhere.

Voslensky: In the Constitution certainly not, but I also have the impression that it is automatic. . . . Because the meaning of [chief of the SDC] is just this, commander-in-chief. . . . It's informal. They do not need a paper for it. Everybody understands. . . . My opinion [of the SDC] is based on the fact that one hears very little about this organization and as a matter of fact, everything is decided by the Politburo. . . . [Strategic] military planning is done [in the general staff]. . . . [There] is no body, no agency, in any communist system or any ruling communist party which could afford and could be allowed to make decisions excluding the Politburo. . . .

Q: Who would do the staff work for the general secretary and for other civilian members of the State Defense Council? Where would that staff come from? Would it come from the General Department, if it doesn't come from the personal secretariat?

Voslensky: But there is no practical work there, because the military-industrial complex prepares everything, all drafts, every sort of thing. It would be considered by the general secretary's specialists, and also by his assistants and he himself would look it through. You know, Brezhnev was a clever man—he looked stupid, but he wasn't. And even Chernenko—who looked extremely stupid, but was not—I would say, although certainly not an intellectual—he had been a peasant and remained a peasant—but even such things he would just review.

Q: So you would say that people like [Leonid V.] Smirnov, and later [Marshal Dmitri] Ustinov, would have prepared [such material] . . . by virtue of heading the Military Industrial Committee [VPK].

Voslensky: Well, yes. It could be the VPK, but in principle the military-industrial complex. Everything will be prepared there, under the general staff, or the VPK, or in the [appropriate] department in the Central Committee. It is not a matter of real policy—it is just a military matter, [while] the important policies are political.

Q: Who makes the decisions as to which items go before the Politburo, and which go before the State Defense Council?

Voslensky: The General Department.

Arkady Shevchenko also takes a dim view of the State Defense Council. He sees it as an organization designed for crisis situations but unutilized in peacetime:

Shevchenko: I don't think the State Defense Council ever really functioned, because the most important things [go] through the Politburo. I think this Council was established for an emergency. It was set up more or less for a wartime situation or a major crisis situation. . . . Any decision on military affairs always goes to the Politburo, and there is no reason why they should have such an enormous body like the Defense Council, which cannot function properly. It's not a body which was designed to function smoothly. In a situation where every minor detail on military affairs and foreign policy affairs still goes to the Politburo, it makes no sense.

Q: Could it be that it's a decorative title? By giving the general secretary the title of chairman of the State Defense Council, does it [not automatically] make him supreme commander of the armed forces?

Shevchenko: . . . It could be just a device to give him [that title], but in fact the general secretary has always been functioning in that capacity. This is all a rather minor issue, because whoever the defense minister is, whether a member of the Politburo or not, he is not the supreme commander. The final word belongs to the general secretary in all important matters.

Gregory is even more skeptical about the actual importance of the State Defense Council. In describing the genesis of the Council, he gives insight into its role, which had, in his opinion, more to do with self-aggrandizement than strategically important defense-related matters:

[The State Defense Council] was organized by Brezhnev because he wanted to be the marshal of the USSR. When he visited armed forces detachments, he was only a major general. He decided to organize the Defense Council so he could be marshal. If [a] crisis occurred, decisions would be taken by the Politburo. The Politburo is the ruling organization; it includes the minister of defense, KGB chief, etc. This Defense Council could not make a decision to go to war by itself; it is an artificial organization. Previously, it was headed by Stalin during the war. We were amazed when Brezhnev reformed it; there was no war. I had many friends in the Ministry of Defense, including a military journalist with *Red Star*. I asked them about the Defense Council and they said it meant nothing, a big zero. There is nothing in the Soviet constitution about the Defense Council—no law, no provision, nothing. It is really an artificial organization. It allows the general secretary to be an additional rank higher than the minister of defense in official, formal terms. I never heard of any meetings of this body and I doubt if it did meet regularly.

Among the Soviet interviewees there seems to be little disagreement concerning the absence of pervasive indications that the State Defense Council plays a significant role in peacetime decision-making. However, in communist states outside the Soviet Union, one finds a State Defense Council of a distinctly different character.

Allies and Clients

State Defense Councils in the various East European countries appear to resemble one another in structure. In fact, General Sejna states that "Right now all of the states of the Warsaw Pact use the same Defense Council structure." However, most of the information provided by the interviewees on State Defense Councils in Eastern Europe is limited to the Polish and Czechoslovak cases. According to Ambassador Zdzislaw Rurarz, the Polish Defense Council (KOK), holds substantial power. In the following excerpt, he provides insight into the formation of the KOK and its membership:

[The Politburo has become less important than the State Defense Council.] I keep saying this all the time and nobody wants to believe me. I can assure you that the Politburo in Poland has never discussed military affairs at all. The Politburo would discuss security matters, but only internal security, never military. Military questions were discussed by KOK, *Komitet Obrony Kraju,* the membership of which is secret in Poland as it is in the USSR. You'll know roughly who is a member, but officially you can't know. . . . Officially, KOK was created in 1967; but even before 1967 it already existed, although not under this name. The most important figure was ostensibly the party boss, although when Gierek came to power in Poland the chairman of KOK was not Edward Gierek but Alfred Jaroszewicz, the prime minister. For some time [the formal] head of the KOK was [the] premier. Jaroszewicz was one hundred percent a Soviet man, whereas Gierek was somewhat less so. Only several years later did Gierek take over from Jaroszewicz, but then everybody knew that the main figure in the committee was General Jaruzelski. It was said that Jaruzelski had an antenna set for Moscow and that he followed orders only from Moscow. The minister of national defense was at the time the most important person, and I think that now Jaruzelski is still the most important. As far as I know, the first secretary of the party, the prime minister, the minister of defense, the chief of the general staff, the minister of internal affairs, and in all likelihood the chief of the political administration of the army are the permanent members of the country's Defense Committee.

Michael Checinski elaborates on the Polish State Defense Council's membership and its role. He refers to other Warsaw Pact countries and the variations in their respective State Defense Council structures:

The permanent members [of the State Defense Council] are the general secretary, prime minister, the head of the Security Service, the minister of foreign affairs, and the minister of defense. Five members. There are also nonpermanent members, such as the chief of staff and his deputy responsible for military economic planning. Other additional members could be the head of the Organization Department or Administration Department. . . . The general secretary has to administer two bodies. On one side he has the Politburo, on the other side he has the Defense Council. . . . [W]e are talking here about the highest levels. The Secretariat [of the Central Committee] is not a decision-making body. . . . The Secretariat [of the Central Committee] is an operative body; it prepares information, proposals, agenda, but the decisions are made by the Politburo, [or] by the Defense Council. . . . The permanent members of the Defense Council are usually members of the Politburo. But not always. In the Soviet Union the minister of defense is not [necessarily] a member of the Politburo. But in Poland he is. In Czechoslovakia he is. Now the general secretary has excellent instincts where he can put forward his proposals or to discuss a problem—in the Politburo or in the Defense Council. This is his decision. When he says, "We should discuss this in the Defense

Council," he is probably sure that he will succeed. In discussing this in the Defense Council he prepares the material. The Defense Council approves it. If it is a very important issue [it] must be approved by the Politburo. Now I am asking you, who in the Politburo would have the courage to say no when he came to a session of the Politburo where the four most important members of the Politburo say they are supporting the move? Who would have the courage to say no?

Michael Checinski, who strongly emphasizes the Polish State Defense Council's role in decision-making processes, also points to the general secretary's need to seek a majority for his policies both in the Politburo and the State Defense Council. Despite the latter's importance, however, the Politburo, Checinski argues, has the final word:

> The Defense Council plays an extremely important role in pushing forward the ideas of the general secretary. [There] could be an extremely difficult situation where he feels that he may have some opposition in the Defense Council, so he will try to manage to have the majority in the Politburo. He may discuss some proposals privately with members of the Politburo and then he will put it in a session of the Politburo. Because the Politburo is a higher body than the Defense Council.
>
> Now, this is an extremely important instrument in the nuclear age. [In the case of the Soviet State Defense Council] you have to know the history of the Soviet Union and the history of the war economy to understand the importance of the Defense Council. [The Defense Council was created] during the war in the Soviet Union. . . . It concentrated the entire power of the country in one body. That means that both the government institutions and the party institutions, including the Politburo, were subordinated to the GKO [Soviet State Defense Council].

Zdzislaw Rurarz intimates that the Polish State Defense Council is more important than the Politburo of the Polish party. This is not the only occasion when two interviewees, former senior officials in the same country, disagreed in their evaluations of power relations in the system from which they escaped:

> Apart from the first secretary of the party, the prime minister, the minister of defense, and the minister of internal affairs if he was a Politburo member, it was not clear whether the secretary of the Central Committee responsible for military and police affairs was a permanent member of the Council. As far as I know, they would meet as the so-called reduced staff of three to four persons, never in full plenary, because the matter was considered to be much too secret for all of them. Furthermore, they never met in Warsaw, but always somewhere outside the city, perhaps believing that Western [electronics] might otherwise pick up the talks. . . . At any rate, according to the Polish Constitution, as amended in November 1983, it is absolutely certain now that the country's Defense Committee is more important than all the

other institutions. . . .[22] [From] what I can gather the Polish Defense Committee would seem to meet officially three or four times a year. In reality, of course, the Committee meets very frequently, on a weekly basis, according to what I know. In fact, it is the Collegium of the Ministry of National Defense which supplements the KOK and does the daily job.

According to Michael Checinski, the Polish Defense Council's role in decision-making has increased significantly since General Jaruzelski's action against Solidarity and the imposition of martial law on 13 December 1981. It played the key role in the administration of the Polish state:

The Politburo plays a secondary role [for example, during the Polish emergency period after Solidarity was created]. What happened at the time? The Politburo didn't function. It was the Defense Council. This is not only a formal body. It is an extremely important decision-making body in time of peace for all defense issues, but in times of war for *everything*. They take over power from the Politburo.

However, Checinski continues, even in peacetime, the State Defense Council plays a major, if not decisive, role in the formal policy-making process. This is especially true in the area of defense issues:

The role of the Defense Council is prepared in such a way that it has to play a double role in time of war. But at the same time, all [security] issues—foreign policy, disarmament, armament, mobilization policy, structural administration of the country, etc.—[are] decided by the Defense Council. Even if it is decided [later] by the Politburo, it is first discussed in the Defense Council. It is impossible that an issue like disarmament would be approved without the discussion of the Defense Council. . . . [The] Defense Council is operational. It is formally independent from the party because [it] is a government institution created by the government's highest body. . . . Now, [many] members of the Defense Council are simultaneously members of the Politburo. Not every member of the Politburo is on the Defense Council. [It is] a body exclusively for the discussion of defense issues. This means that the Defense Council is not duplicating the work of the Politburo, because the Politburo is deciding about the entire life of the Soviet Union or Poland or Czechoslovakia. The entire social, political, cultural, everything. The Defense Council has a very specific area of decision making. Only defense. . . . In other words, the Defense Council is a very specific body which has to act according to its task—defense issues—and nothing more. This includes

---

[22] On 21 November 1983, the Polish Sejm amended the 1967 Law on Universal Military Service which gave significant powers to the KOK. The 1983 amendment increased the powers of the KOK in times of "emergency," which had been redefined in the July 1983 session of the Sejm to include internal, as well as external aggression. On 22 November 1983, General Wojciech Jaruzelski was elected chairman of the restructured KOK.

foreign issues, defense issues. This is why in the Defense Council there are permanent members and non-permanent members. The general secretary is the head.

Michael Checinski adds a comment on the dynamics of Soviet-Polish relations:

In Eastern Europe [the Defense Council] is formally headed by the prime minister. And in time of war, the general secretary takes over the leadership of the Defense Council. Now in Poland, Jaruzelski decided formally, [and had] written in the Constitution, that he [would be] the chairman of the [Defense Council] and simultaneously the supreme commander of the armed forces. People do not understand why he did it. In my opinion [it was] an additional hold for him against the Soviet Union. I want to stress that. [Soviet leaders] don't like it. In Eastern Europe they want to have a different situation. They want the centers of power [in the client states] to be divided so they can play one against the other. This is why you have a different situation in Eastern Europe than in the Soviet Union.

Our information on the Czechoslovak Defense Council emanates largely from General Sejna, who says he was present at its inception. Unlike the Soviet and Polish councils, Sejna places the Czechoslovak State Defense Council's formation in the mid-1950s. Sejna seems to treat the Czechoslovak Defense Council as a party, not a state organization.

In 1956, when I was chief of staff [to the Czechoslovak Minister of Defense, General Lomsky], under Khrushchev's order we established the Defense Council of the Communist Party in Czechoslovakia. . . . At that time I was [the] secretary. . . . This was the most important position because all top secret, military intelligence, and counterintelligence documents do not go to the Politburo, but to the Defense Council. At that time we had just seven people and the Politburo had fourteen; these documents for the other seven were secret. Politburo members, like [Zdenek] Fierlinger for example, never knew what went on in this area. It was of great importance since not just Czechoslovak leaders, but many times Soviet officials, were present. They pushed their rights to [control] operations . . . and opposed discussions.

Sejna also makes clear that in the 1950s, State Defense Councils did exist in other states. In this claim he is supported by Zdzislaw Rurarz. Below, Sejna explains why Khrushchev initiated the establishment of State Defense Councils in Eastern Europe:

[It] was Khrushchev's decision to develop better party control over the military and the security service. In each communist state the Defense Council was reorganized. We got instructions from the Soviet Union to prepare the Statute for the Defense Council of Czechoslovakia. At the time, I was the chief of staff to the minister of defense. The secretariat of the Defense Council was in the cabinet of the defense minister, and so it was my job to prepare everything. The Defense Council would make the decisions, and although the minister of defense was officially secretary, in fact I did everything.

The membership of the State Defense Council reflects its dual mission. In times of peace it handles military matters, in times of war it takes full control. Some of its members are not in the Politburo.

Sejna: The minister of defense was not a member of the Politburo, and later on, [Lubomir] Strougal, the minister of the interior, was not a member of the Politburo. The single most important criterion for membership in the Defense Council was the authority to pass [on] Defense Council decisions . . . to oversee their implementation. They were the people who covered the most important areas—defense and intelligence. And in wartime everything is considered, which is why the chief of the State Planning Commission is included. He controls money and material. If he were not present, someone else would have to explain to him what must be done. These are the most important people. . . . What must be kept in mind is that the Defense Council handles matters so sensitive . . . that they are routinely kept secret from many members of the Politburo. The Defense Council is [there] to handle the conduct of any future war, like the *Stavka*[23] before [in the Soviet Union]. In the meantime, it is responsible for all of the most important military issues. Therefore, the members of the council are those who have power in the areas which are necessary for the implementation of the Defense Council's decisions. That is why the chairman of the Czechoslovak State Planning Commission (in the Soviet Union, the *Gosplan*) is represented on the Defense Council, although he is not a member of the Politburo. . . .

The chief of the KGB [or, in Czechoslovakia, the StB] is also a member of the Defense Council, as is the prime minister, since he has the authority to tell the other ministers what to do. In Czechoslovakia it is the minister of the interior. The minister of defense is the other most important member. . . . In Czechoslovakia, Jiri Hendrych, the deputy [of] the first secretary [of the Communist Party], later was made a member of the Council. That way, should the first secretary be unavailable during the war, or just sick or absent at a routine session, there would be someone from the party familiar with what was going on.

Q: Hence the unofficial concept of a second secretary [is manifested] within that committee?

Sejna: That is right. There is nothing written about a second secretary, but he is always at these sessions. Today, Ligachev is probably taking the place

---

[23] The Soviet supreme military authority in World War II.

that Suslov once held, just as Vasil Bil'ak has assumed Hendrych's spot. It is partly for this reason that the party will list as those present at a certain meeting the principals, "and others." That's a typical party trick, who can know who these others are?

As its Polish counterpart did during the Solidarity period in Poland, the Czechoslovak State Defense Council assumed power during crisis situations. General Sejna notes that international crisis which demanded the attention of the Soviet State Defense Council automatically caused its Czechoslovak counterpart to spring into action:

[D]uring the Hungarian Revolution in 1956, for example, and during the Cuban missile crisis, [the Soviet Defense Council] sat twenty-four hours a day. The same was true of the Czechoslovak State Defense Council, which was in close contact with the Soviet Council. Of course, that was during a crisis. During the Cuban crisis, the Soviet leaders were worried that war might break out and therefore kept their Defense Council working around the clock. People ate there, slept there, and naturally [they] expected us to do the same.

However, not all observers agree that the State Defense Council is of primary importance. Typically, the skeptics have a non-military background. Jiri Pelikan, the former director general of Czechoslovak television, gives the State Defense Council extremely low marks with regard to its power over the Politburo of the Communist Party:

Pelikan: [The State Defense Council] existed, but it had no influence on decision making. It is a very formal body.

Q: Is it at all possible that the functioning of this organization would be so secret that one wouldn't even know about it?

Pelikan: Yes, [but] only if it is dealing with [matters] of defense. That means they discuss the budget of the armed forces and they discuss some plans for the duties [of] the Warsaw Pact [forces], but it has no impact on the internal life of the party or of the state. At least [this is true] in Czechoslovakia, and I don't think that [the State Defense Council] has any impact in the Soviet Union. . . . [I]n general I don't think that it is correct to assume that the Politburo is excluded from the top secret [defense] problems, because it [deals] with [such] problems. But what is called the Defense Council is a kind of meeting between the General Secretary [Antonin Novotny, who, also being the president of the republic, acted as commander in chief of the armed forces], and some generals—you know, minister of defense, minister of the interior, some generals of the army and of the secret service. . . . [During] my dealing with the party [I never heard] of any decision of the Defense Council which would have had any [significant] influence.

Hus, a former Ministry of Foreign Affairs official, is more positive concerning the State Defense Council in Czechoslovakia, but only in the sense that it has power based on its expertise. If the Politburo wants to disregard the State Defense Council, it may do so:

> The officials in the Politburo try to deal with everything, and so they are not experts in anything. As a result, it is difficult for them to go against the [State Defense] Council, which does have a real expertise. The Politburo goes along with the Council most of the time. However, if there is some issue over which the Politburo really disagrees with the council, then [its members] will overrule it. It is not always a logical decision. It is also important in that it is the council which selects the ideas to be presented to the Politburo. It is the same as in the Foreign Ministry, where the director of a department will present an idea to the minister. The idea will not have originated with the minister. In this respect the director is more important in that he determines more specific policy, while the minister is concerned with the more general policy or big issues. It is the same with the Politburo and the Defense Council. The Politburo maintains its predominance over the council in that it appoints who is on the council and [it] can change [the Defense Council's] membership at any time.

Goshu Wolde, the former Ethiopian foreign minister, gives us his views on the role of the Defense Commission in Ethiopia. He sees some similarities between the Defense Commission and the Soviet Defense Council:

> *Wolde:* In Ethiopia we have under the new constitution a Defense Commission, which [is] headed by the chairman [Mengistu] himself. The one thing I know is that the composition of the Defense Commission of Ethiopia and of the Soviet Union, at the leadership level at least, is [dominated by] the security [services] and the [representatives] of the KGB [in Ethiopia]. [Participants] who occasionally came in and out, as the occasion demanded, made that clear. . . .
>
> [The Defense Commission] is intended to be an arm of the government which discusses security and defense matters on an ad-hoc basis. . . . For example, [it] would discuss the rearmament of the Sudan or Somalia, or the military threat from some of the Arab countries in the area and what type of weapons they have. [It did] not go into technical evaluations of available weapons, but [made] general evaluations of the potential danger to the country from the region. . . .
>
> *Q:* Who were the other members of the Defense Commission?
>
> *Wolde:* Chairman Mengistu, the minister of defense, the minister of the interior, the vice-chairman of the Council of Ministers and people who were involved with security and defense. . . .
>
> *Q:* Did you get any sense that this body was created to mimic in any way the State Defense Council in the Soviet Union?

Wolde: It is similar, but it is perhaps not as well organized and disciplined in its operations as the Soviet model. The Soviet Defense Council has a lot of history behind it and the Ethiopian one is fairly new. Since the threat to Ethiopia is not seen in the same way as the Soviet Union sees the threat to itself, I think it is very much governed by the perception of the chairman of the committee. It is his perception which really guides all the activities and the impressions of the Defense Council.

From the evidence obtained, it may be concluded that the State Defense Council in each country was either created or influenced by the Soviet Union. One can see the State Defense Council as an instrument of control by Moscow over client states—a way of securing power over the military and intelligence forces of these states. It keeps order during crisis, it facilitates an all-Warsaw Pact effort, and it can forestall any attempt to turn this organization against Soviet power.

A second important concept is the operational nature of the State Defense Council and its relationship to Moscow. If East European Defense Councils are in fact Soviet tools for implementing plans and policies arrived at in Moscow, they would be stronger where political control is weakest (as in Poland), less important in more stable countries (such as Czechoslovakia), and virtually impotent in the center, Moscow, where it is the Politburo of the CPSU that makes the ultimate decisions with the possible exception of military crisis situations.

Party Oversight: The Party Control Commission, the Main Political Administration, the Department of Administrative Organs, and the Department for Cadres Abroad

The Party Control Commission (PCC) is the self-styled organ of oversight. It belongs to the Central Committee *apparat,* but in some sense it stands above it because it is intended to discipline errant party members to a certain extent. Although the PCC is apparently important to deal with the top elite (the elected Secretariat and the Politburo), its very existence is supposed to protect the party's reputation by having enforcement of certain standards kept "within the political family." Arkady N. Shevchenko describes the issue of the PCC's jurisdiction:

Shevchenko: [The Party Control Commission] was more important in Stalin's day, especially before the war. [It now deals mostly with disciplinary matters.]

Q: How high up?

Shevchenko: It might include some of the members of the Central Committee . . . [but higher up] is out of the question. I think that it would be out of the question even for a chief of a department of the Central Committee. I would say that it is hardly likely that the *Kontrol'naya kommissiya* [Control Commission] would start any kind of procedure against the top people, not only above the high party apparatus itself but even at ministerial level. This is still a decision of the Politburo, and the reason is obvious: if a matter goes to the *Kontrol'naya kommissiya,* too many people would know—and they don't like for too many people to know. If it is a high-level [person], usually they will first go to the general secretary of the party to clear it with him. They will decide what kind of a procedure will be adopted. With other people who don't fall into this category, the *Kontrol'naya kommissiya* has quite a lot of power.

Shevchenko indicates that the PCC's task is to subject party members to disciplinary action by the party itself, rather than (or at least prior to) measures by the state:

The *nomenklatura* cannot even be prosecuted. If [a member of the Soviet elite] were to kill someone in the street, the *militsiya* would not actually arrest [him]. . . . The first thing the *militsiya* would do is to see what [his] position is. Then they would go and call the minister to find out whether [he] belong[ed] to the *nomenklatura* before taking any kind of action. They have no right even to prosecute those who belong to the *nomenklatura.* They have to refer everything to the Central Committee. Then, it can go to the *Kontrol'naya kommissiya* and they can decide on either criminal prosecution or civil prosecution. Whatever the state bodies can do, they [the Control Commission] will give authorization [for it] or not.

Michael Voslensky stresses that the influence of the PCC currently is fairly limited. He believes that the PCC is mainly an advisory body with fluctuating influence:

[The Party Control Commission] is a job that could become important in a certain situation; it is a job with possible prospects, but now it is not very important.

Voslensky agrees with Shevchenko that the jurisdiction of the PCC stops at a certain level of the Soviet power pyramid:

Voslensky: Certainly [the PCC does not reach the level of] the members of the Politburo.

Q: How about heads of departments [of the CC]?

Voslensky: [If the PCC discovered anything at that level], [it] would tell the general secretary [about it].

Q: But this is powerful stuff; you can intimidate people with this.

Voslensky: Of course; that is why I say it can become important. I do not think it is very important now.

Gregory also notes that the PCC is "not very serious" and has no influence at all over the KGB and GRU.

In Eastern Europe as well as the USSR, the party has created instrumentalities for oversight over the military and security sectors, as well as the lower echelons of the party membership. Checinski refers to the organ that has oversight over the armed forces:

> One of [the Central Committee] secretaries runs the party military department. There is not a party military department per se; the party Military Department is in fact a complex organization. It is first of all the [Main] Political Administration of the military, which is in fact one of the departments of the Central Committee. Its chief has a dual status as a deputy of the minister of defense and the head of the [Main] Political Administration of the army.

In this respect a more influential watchdog entity is the CPSU CC Department of Administrative Organs [DAO], which oversees some personnel aspects of the security and military organs. Gregory describes the DAO's functions.

> *Gregory:* [Nikolay] Savinkin [the head of the DAO] is not under the control of [Viktor M.] Chebrikov, [Eduard A.] Shevardnadze or [Geydar A.] Aliyev. His work [comes] under the direction of the general secretary and the full Politburo. He was [in the] KGB before, but now he has other obligations. Chebrikov can discuss questions with him; Savinkin [does not] outrank Chebrikov. They work hand in hand. The DAO has authority over the KGB. Their authority does not include [assigning tasks] but [is limited to] staff and personnel problems. For example, if I am going abroad under journalistic cover I cannot go to TASS because they know I am not a TASS correspondent. DAO would give me the proper credentials. If a GRU agent was going abroad as a military attaché, the process would be similar. If there was a reorganization within the KGB, the DAO would take care of the new assignments and other related matters.
>
> *Q:* In a hypothetical case, if the KGB were bugging the rooms of Politburo, would Savinkin be in a position to find this out?
>
> *Gregory:* No, he would never know about it. Somebody could report it to him but that is all. . . . Savinkin deals with staff problems: discipline, alcoholism, reorganizations, etc. In operations, the KGB is a sovereign institution. . . . If the KGB planned an assassination, it would not be known to Savinkin unless he heard about it afterwards. If a KGB or GRU man is going abroad, that is his business, along with the ID [International Department] and the Department of Cadres Abroad (DCA).

Michael Voslensky goes considerably further than Gregory in evaluating the power of the DAO. Ultimately, he believes, the KGB itself is an object of DAO surveillance:

Voslensky: It is [Savinkin's] job to control and check KGB activities. And if he is not able to do it, then he will be [removed]. He must have his informers on different levels in the KGB. I can imagine that . . . they would be prepared. They are all afraid of this department, the Administrative Organs. . . .

Q: [P]resumably [Savinkin] has some influence on appointments within KGB?

Voslensky: But of course, very important influence, because in the KGB the appointments of the *nomenklatura* position must be signed by Savinkin.

Q: So the relationship he exercises is very similar to that exercised by the Main Political Administration vis-à-vis the army.

Voslensky: Yes, but it's even official. The Main Political Administration is the military department of the party Central Committee. It's [exactly] . . . the parallel case. It is also impossible for the chairman of the KGB or for his deputies to [seek out] the [DAO] agents [in his] department, because then he would immediately alert the leadership that he [is trying to evade supervision] by the party. This shows that he probably has some plans. That puts [the chairman of the KGB] in a very difficult situation. He would probably be very glad to get rid of these characters who are spying within the KGB, but how?

The authority of the Department of Administrative Organs over the KGB and GRU within the Soviet Union is firm. Administratively, however, it ends at the border. There, a third organization, the Department of Cadres Abroad (DCA), takes over. Stiller elaborates:

[The Department of Administrative Organs] deals entirely with internal matters; [it has] no competence over KGB in the field. The most powerful organization is the Department for Cadres Abroad (DCA). Nominations for sending individuals abroad, from the level of attaché on up, were cleared through this department. All the diplomatic cadres had to be approved by the DCA. During my time in the field, the director of the DCA, Panyushkin,[24] came to Egypt. He was on a field trip of sorts, traveling about, checking on the personnel, and so forth. The KGB *resident* reported to him. . . .

Gregory presents a similar view. He adds details regarding the duties of the Department for Cadres Abroad. They cover a broad spectrum from travel briefings to monitoring the social habits of Soviet representatives who are sent abroad:

---

[24] Aleksandr S. Panyushkin, major general and ambassador, chief, Department for Cadres Abroad, deceased.

The DCA is a very large department [which is] responsible for approval of all personnel traveling overseas. No one can go abroad without approval from the DCA. When I went abroad as a TASS representative, I had to get approval from the DCA. . . . The relationship between the DCA and other departments is very complex. The KGB and the GRU members going overseas must contact their own party organization. TASS does not have its own similar party organization and any correspondent going overseas must get approval from the DCA. In one's first assignment abroad, one must meet an instructor who gives [one] detailed information about the proper behavior of Soviet citizens abroad. He presents a paper that must be signed. He then describes the professional duties one must perform while abroad. If something goes wrong, . . . some type of misbehavior, the DCA decides whether one can stay or if one must be recalled. The DCA is the organization that receives the letters and reports about the behavior of all Soviet personnel serving abroad. They also are responsible for the work of the party organizations abroad. For example, in Geneva we had a large party organization of more than six hundred members. The head was a member of the [CPSU] Central Committee but once a year a representative of the DCA would visit to discuss party matters. The DCA [monitors] party loyalty, family relations, drinking problems, etc. They receive . . . reports from the embassies about every Soviet citizen working abroad. The DCA makes the decision about which citizens to recall for "consultations." . . .

If someone is [going] to work abroad, he would have to see [Nikolay I.] Savinkin [former head of the Department of Administrative Organs]. Savinkin would prepare the details. The order would have to be in a Central Committee resolution and afterwards Savinkin would go to DCA and say, for example, "Mr. Petrov is going to be the first secretary in the U.S. embassy." The embassy section would know that Mr. Petrov was KGB but the Central Committee resolution [would be] secret.

Stanislav Levchenko indicates that power is flexible, and that one cannot state categorically that the DCA has unchallenged influence over personnel overseas. The interest of various institutions may clash and resulting problems may be resolved according to the varying degrees of influence of the leading officials in question.

[Departments] usually do not have any serious clashes. They can clash when the International Department wants to send somebody abroad and the Cadres Abroad Department says [that] they have a bad report on him. The question here is whether or not they can overpower the International Department; sometimes they can. They go to [other officials], not to Ponomarev.[25] He may decide that the International Department has no serious interest involved there. [Then there will be no clash.]

---

[25] Boris Nikolaevich Ponomarev, born 1905; chief of the International Department, CC CPSU from 1955; secretary, CC CPSU from 1961; candidate member, Politburo, CC CPSU from 1972. Now retired.

The Security Apparatus

Like other closed societies, the Soviet system devotes a great deal of energy to scrutinizing the loyalty of its citizens. While those at the bottom of the power pyramid on occasion may be exposed to random surveillance, members of the elite take for granted that they are watched closely. The organs responsible for surveillance of the elite inevitably discover much important information. Naturally, access to information translates into political leverage. Therefore, the security *apparat* is a significant component of the power structures of the Soviet Union, its allies, and clients. The business of watching the powerful is a delicate task: those responsible for such activities in turn are watched most closely. Michael Checinski, who had worked for Polish Security, stresses that, throughout his professional life in Poland, he had never enjoyed any privacy whatever. A great deal of internal surveillance is carried out by the "sword and shield" of the party, the KGB. In fact, many KGB assets are committed not to overseas work or counterintelligence at home, but to watching the Soviet citizenry, the Soviet military, the Soviet party elite, and the allied states. Orionova observes:

> To be a real KGB officer—not a sort of a mixture of an academic and a KGB officer—but to be purely KGB is a horrible life, seeing how they take four half-liter bottles of vodka to spend a weekend at their country house in the KGB village where all the generals do not even talk or drink with one another.

To be in the KGB means to distrust and to be distrusted. It is a life which carries special benefits, but also many onerous tasks. Involvement with the KGB begins usually with recruitment, always initiated by the KGB, not by the candidate. Orionova asserts that it does not necessarily hurt one's career to reject a KGB recruitment attempt:

> It depends on the person involved. I know that there are people who [refused KGB recruitment] and it did not hurt their careers.

Institutes and universities offer many opportunities for recruitment. Stanislav Levchenko explains that students are obvious targets since they live in a restricted world for a prolonged period of time. This renders the task of the KGB recruiter all the easier.

> *Levchenko:* The KGB and the GRU screen students very carefully. . . . In my university department I knew that there was one person in the Personnel Department who was undercover. He was at least a lieutenant colonel of the KGB from the First Chief Directorate's Personnel Department. The students were screened for several years. Now it takes five years to graduate from my school, but in my time it was six full years, which were barely enough to

absorb all the necessary information. From the point of view of the security personnel, it was very convenient, because within six years they could gather a thick file on every student and see from this file what kind of person he is. Then at the time of graduation they could approach those students whom they had targeted.

Q: If you say "no," will there be repercussions?

Levchenko: There will be no repercussions, unless you hit the recruiter with a chair. If you say politely, "I have different plans," then the recruiter may say, "Please think about it thoroughly for a couple of days and come back." Then in a couple of days, the student comes and says, "It is still no." The recruiter answers, "That's okay." It does not mean that in his future career this student will never be sent abroad. Not at all. And it does not mean that the KGB has become soft-hearted. No. It has just become more practical. They do not want people who do not want to work for them. Under Stalin, they said, "We want you," and you had to go, but [it is] not [this way] now.

Piatigorsky, a former research fellow of the Institute of Oriental Studies, concurs with this view. It was not uncommon, he states, to reject an offer from the KGB.

Piatigorsky: When a friend of mine was asked to become a KGB member, he was summoned to [the office of the Foreign Section in our institute]. A man appeared and started telling him about the importance of struggling against foreign spies. But he was not an intelligence officer. He was a KGB officer trying to recruit him into the KGB surveillance service. It is absolutely commonplace. . . .

Q: Was it possible for someone without strong protective connections to say no?

Piatigorsky: Absolutely, everybody could say no, without any problems. It is different for domestic KGB work. There they know how to recruit. They use threats. But foreign intelligence is a well-paid job. They usually asked for more people than they needed. If someone says no, it is no problem. I said no, and a couple of my friends—one a very active party member—said no because he had different prospects for his career. He did not want to spoil his chances of becoming a prominent professor. . . . [S]urveillance of foreigners [is a KGB function]. . . . Each time I received a foreign colleague, I was summoned to [the KGB] and told that I must write a report. I was not recruited, but each Soviet scholar officially receiving foreigners [is asked to] write reports on that person [for the KGB].

While the three interviewees cited thought that refusing KGB offers could be done with relative impunity, it should be noted that Stiller presents a differing viewpoint. He states that those who refuse may not have heard the last of the security services:

If you refuse [recruitment], you are a marked man. They will let you refuse—in fact, they may be glad you refused, because they do not have to go to all the expense of training—but one is then marked. When one becomes an employee of the Ministry of Foreign Affairs, the KGB then has a great deal of [leverage]—they can use you for whatever operations they have in the country where one is posted. The KGB will come to you and say, "Look, don't you remember so and so? Now, can you do this for me? How about it? Come on, let's go to a restaurant together." This is exactly what happened to me eventually. . . . There is always a percentage of the students who will not work for [the security services], but, as a result of that initial discussion, the KGB always has something to use later on. They would say, "We briefed you, we were there, we talked to you, and so you are with us." Later, it dawns on you, after having worked in an embassy a couple of months, that the only way you are going to get your career going is by collaborating fully.

For most recruits training is rudimentary; they may not become KGB regulars. They may act as adjuncts, aiding the KGB in their respective official capacities in the organizations for which they work. However, for the actual agents, training is extensive. Peter Deriabin describes actions to be taken within the Soviet Union and against Soviet citizens, not foreign agents. He presents insights into the complexity and intensity of the KGB's domestic operations:[26]

The core of the operational coursework was devoted to [the study of] working with agents. Recruitment of sources was taught in detail. There are three levels of agents: the lowest was the informer; second was the agent; and third was the *agent-rezident*. Since a case officer would not always run all agents himself, he would select the best of his agents to be *agent-rezident*. This person would run a group of informers and/or agents under the supervision of the case officer. The lower-level informants, as a rule, were recruited from party members, Komsomol members, and activists who would be approached and generally would readily agree to assist the organs of state security to root out anti-Soviet or nationalist feelings. The security organs usually possess compromising material concerning those who are approached for recruitment. People like this make the best agents for two reasons. First, a person has no choice; he must work with the organs, or go to jail, lose his job, etc. He is valuable because he has no way out; he can be ordered to do anything and he will do his best because he knows what the consequences of failure would be. Second, a person who is compromised often has the best contacts with those who the organs are after: he would know who has expressed anti-Soviet sentiment, who discusses Trotsky or Bukharin, which army officers oppose party work, etc.

---

[26] For more information, see Peter Deriabin, *Watchdogs of Terror: Russian Bodyguards from the Tsars to the Commissars* (New Rochelle, NY: Arlington House, 1972).

The *agent-rezident* is usually developed from an agent but not from someone who has been recruited through the use of compromising material or blackmail. It could be a loyal party member devoted to Soviet power, a retired KGB or SMERSH officer, a party official who has risen through the ranks to become personnel chief of a certain organization, and so on. *Agent-rezidents* were often recruited from the management levels of various economic enterprises. What is needed is someone with access to files, and someone who regularly observes and meets with the workers so he can run a number of lower-level agents in his own enterprise.

The next subject taught was the registration of the "enemies of the people," usually referred to as anti-Soviet elements. There were many different files that would be kept on certain population groups. For instance, if the subject was a factory, the first thing I would do is collect information and open an observation file on Factory X. Petrov is anti-Soviet; Ivanov is patriotic; Smirnov has family problems, and so on. All the employees would be separated in different categories: anti-Soviet; family problems; work problems; party problems; etc. There were about twenty different categories.

Next, and most important, is the agent development file. This file would be opened on a group of people, usually numbering from five to ten. It could be on a group which reads Western literature or criticizes Soviet literature, or it could be on a group of people that occasionally complain about food shortages, or similar groups. From this file comes the next step, separation of the people who will actually receive recruitment attempts. This file is called *delo formulyar*.

At this point the case officer would already know that the subject was going to be arrested sooner or later because of his anti-Soviet activities so the object is to take the time to develop him as an agent. The case officers must develop agents, otherwise they will be out of work—the enemies of the people exist and it is the security officers' job to find them. I should emphasize that when I attended this school, in 1944, we did study more than just military counterintelligence. We learned about general counterintelligence, what the NKGB did, and how to monitor civilian populations. Because the authorities knew that many of the cadre trained would later work in non-military CI, our training was more inclusive even though it was wartime. We also paid special attention to population control in what we called the freed territories: western Ukraine and Byelorussia, and the Baltic republics.

Gregory notes that his training placed emphasis on certain forms of active measures. Significantly, the actions he studied were taken against those who defected, a powerful disincentive for attempts to escape and more evidence of the lack of trust which pervades the entire *apparat*:

We studied the Cheka and OGPU operations very attentively, especially "Trust-style operations.[27] At that time there was a standing order that any

---

[27] For more information on the Trust (Trest) operation, see John J. Dziak, *Chekisty: A History of the KGB* (Lexington, MA: Lexington Books, 1988), pp.47–50.

anti-Soviet groups or individuals had to be silenced, whether through kidnapping, murder, or whatever. This was the reason for our rigorous training in special operations. We knew how the OGPU succeeded with Operation Trust, how they captured the British agent Sidney Reilly. The official version was that he was shot trying to cross the Soviet-Finnish border but in reality he was captured and taken to prison in Moscow. He was not executed but he died in prison after five or six years. His interrogator was Artuzov, head of the special department for liquidation and kidnapping.

We also learned about the case of Krivitsky.[28] He was killed by a KGB agent. We studied the case of [Georgis] Agabekov as well. Agabekov was killed in 1938, according to Brook-Shepherd,[29] when crossing the Franco-Spanish border. I heard another version. During my time at the Higher KGB School, we saw many people we called fighters. They were experienced KGB agents [who] would lecture in our classes. One of them was decorated with the Order of Lenin when Agabekov was killed. He was the man who liquidated Agabekov; his name was Sanakoyev[?]. He was from South Osetia[30] in Georgia. He explained how long the operation to get Agabekov was planned. He had been a close friend of Agabekov. Agabekov had been in Romania and was working against the Soviet Union and the Politburo gave the order to kill him. Sanakoyev told us he found a way to see Agabekov even though he was heavily guarded by the Romanians. He convinced Agabekov to see him alone and then he strangled him and propped him up as if he was reading. He then left and told the guard he would come back in a half hour. This is the story we were told and it is very different [from] the account given by Brook-Shepherd. I do not know if this is absolutely true but this is what we were told. I do know that the behavior of Agabekov as told by Brook-Shepherd is very strange for a defector, especially at that time.

We also studied the case of Konovalenko, the Ukrainian nationalist liquidated in Amsterdam by [Gen. Pavel] Sudoplatov. Sudoplatov later became the head of Department 13 of the First Chief Directorate but he worked under the special authority of the head of the KGB because his activities were so sensitive. Sudoplatov lectured at the school as did many others; we called them old Chekists. They were all people who had carried out special operations abroad.

Anatoly Fedoseyev, a senior researcher at the Soviet Academy of Sciences, describes surveillance activities at his institute and refers to the effect this has on personnel:

Every institute has a cadres division. The chief of this division is a KGB officer of very high rank. Everything is on file there. The party organization and

---

[28] Walter Krivitsky, a senior Soviet intelligence official, defected to the West from his post in Holland in 1937; he wrote *I Was Stalin's Agent*. His death in Washington, D.C., was officially called a suicide. For more, see Gordon Brook-Shepherd, *The Storm Petrels*, pp. 139–172.

[29] Ibid., pp. 95–111.

[30] Yugo-Osetinsk, a region in the northern part of the Georgian Soviet Socialist Republic.

the trade union have direct contact with these cadres. They certainly give more privileges—like maybe a rest house—to people they consider ideologically reliable, but it is not only ideological; it is conducive to work with the party line. In our institute, and in all other institutes, only very unusual cases were under special consideration by the party organization. Usually it goes much more smoothly, because the director is always a member of the party organization. They must consult and be together, because if they would not be, both would be punished.

How does KGB surveillance of the upper echelons of the *apparat* influence personnel policy? In Stalin's time the surveillance apparatus was an important tool in the maintenance of his personal power. Peter Deriabin provides a detailed description of this infrastructure:

Deriabin: During the time of Stalin, nobody was immune from surveillance and investigation; Stalin bugged whomever he wanted to. Lieutenant Colonel Karasev, chief of the MVD's Second Technical Support Department, was the man responsible for the electronic surveillance. He was shot two weeks after Stalin's death with the approval of Beria; Beria approved [of it] because Karasev's information was going to Poskrebyshev and Stalin but none of it was shown to Beria. . . .

Part of [the surveillance of high-ranking officials] was done by the SPU (Secret Political Directorate) but the most important organization was the OPEROD: Operations Department of the Guards Directorate. The actual bodyguards for an official would not be involved in collecting information on that official; on occasion [they] could give tidbits to the OPEROD but bodyguards were not supposed to report on their bosses because their bosses could find out, and that would undermine the position of the Guards Directorate. This prohibition of spying on your own boss was a strict regulation from Vlasik and his deputy chief of operations, Lynko. There were always enough agents and informants surrounding a Politburo member, his wife, his friends, and his favorite clubs that were willing and able to give the OPEROD information. . . .

[The] OPEROD was set up inside the Guards Directorate [in February 1947]. The OPEROD consisted of eleven subsections, all of which had agent networks—one for the Kremlin, the Council of Ministers, the Central Committee, the Moscow City party offices—in any place where full or candidate Politburo members or CC secretaries would be working. In charge of each of these places would be the commandant for the Guards Directorate and under him would be the OPEROD section responsible for collection of information from a variety of sources. Another section was responsible for arrest and executions under Stalin's personal orders. . . .

The leaders of all departments in the Guards Directorate under Stalin had a special kind of protection. Stalin had private meetings with them when they began work, so that if any minister or Politburo member complained to them or about them they could respond and say that they were working under the express personal orders of comrade Stalin. The arrest and operational work of the OPEROD was conducted separately from the work of Karasev's Second Technical Support Department of the MGB. Karasev's unit was separate—directly under Abakumov. All the transcripts from their wiretaps went straight from Abakumov to Poskrebyshev or Stalin himself; even the chief of the OPEROD would not have access to this information.

Stalin would occasionally use the material when meeting with Politburo members by bringing up something that they only discussed at home. When Stalin died Karasev was arrested and shot, and his department disbanded. . . . Most of the Karasev employees were thrown out of Moscow to the Urals because they were the ones who did the actual transcribing and they also knew too much.

Q: Why do you think Poskrebyshev did not meet the same fate?

Deriabin: First of all, he was very useful; all members of the Politburo wanted to know what Stalin had on them. Second, Poskrebyshev was a good organizer, even though he drank too much, and they may have needed him for that. Third, Poskrebyshev could very well have claimed that nobody could fault him for obeying orders and that he was polite, and that even though he knew everything, he did not make trouble for other members of the leadership. It was true that all the members of the leadership had to treat Poskrebyshev well, shake his hand, etc., but that is the way with any organization: if you go to see your boss, you say hello to the secretary.

Stalin's successors eventually took action against Stalin's minions, but the basic need for surveillance of the whole society in order to maintain power has not vanished. Michael Checinski gives an up-to-date picture of the tools used for this task:

The KGB collects information for all parts of the system. I can tell you from personal experience that party functionaries know that their offices are bugged. If they want to talk about something privately, they go out in the street. Everybody knows this. This is the system; they built it and they are subordinated to [it]. The KGB [collects] information about [one's] private life, and they will use it against [one]. . . .

Further, Michael Checinski stresses that the surveillance system is not at all simple. Not only does the party seek to control the security organs, they in turn try to penetrate those party organs which are in charge of security-related operations:

The Administration [Administrative Cadres, in the case of the USSR] Department [of the Central Committee] has control over the army and over the KGB, but only to a point. They do not control the activities of the KGB. Some [KGB operatives have infiltrated] the Administration Department, [and] the Organization Department too.

It must be noted that there are oases within the power structure that, due to personal circumstances, may evade the watchful eye of the security organs. Stanislav Levchenko explains that the International Department of the Central Committee may be one such sanctuary:

> The International Department is a separate entity in [the] community, and it is not controlled by the KGB. It is probably not the only such entity, but still it is the only part of the Central Committee which is free from KGB surveillance. . . . The KGB cannot start surveilling someone who is a guest of the International Department, without special permission. . . . The International Department itself does not have superior status with regard to the KGB.

According to Hus, the same dynamic exists in Czechoslovakia where the International Department enjoys a certain degree of freedom from interference by the Czechoslovak security organs (the StB). That the department was until December 1988 run by Vasil Bil'ak,[31] one of the most powerful men in the country, also played a role:

> To my knowledge, no one who worked in intelligence at the Interior Ministry ever worked within the International Department of the Central Committee. If Bil'ak ever discovered that an intelligence officer was in the International Department, he would have the interior minister fired. Bil'ak is very jealous of his position.

Hus indicates that oases free from surveillance were to be found not only in the International Department, but also in any area in which a Politburo member had a personal interest:

> When one was in the Central Committee apparatus, in an area controlled by a Politburo member, one did not even have to worry about the minister of the interior. If Bil'ak ever learned of an intelligence officer interfering with an officer of the International Department, the Interior Minister would be reprimanded. It is not that Bil'ak is so touchy, but he does not want to create any precedent that could lead to the subverting of his position.

In Poland, according to Michael Checinski, the security organs can influence even the Politburo. This happens, in part, because the security organs control the flow of information, in and around the party central organs:

> I think that the secret police has many ways to influence the policy of the Politburo or the Secretariat, because they are [the ones] who give to the

---

[31] For Bil'ak's political philosophy, see his work *Pravda Zostala Pravdou* (The Truth Remained True) (Bratislava: Pravda, 1971).

members of the Politburo and the general secretary or first secretary [day by day] the background information about what is going on in the country and in the world. That means that each member of the Politburo receives a special bulletin made by them. [T]here are different kinds of bulletins [for different levels of the *apparat*]. . . . I received the [bulletin] for middle functionaries.

The Czechoslovak StB, through its role in protecting the members of the Politburo, Central Committee Secretariat, etc., is able to obtain accurate information on the personal lives of top officials. According to Pelikan, this information can be crucial in a power struggle:

[State Security could] destroy [a Politburo member]. It depends on what kinds of arguments they would have, but they usually have very good information about the private lives of the members of the Politburo. . . . [U]sually the driver was [an] employee of the StB, [and] the cook was [an] employee of the StB, because the food must be controlled. . . in order [for them] not to be poisoned. The secretary was usually employed by the StB, so [the security service] knew about the private life of these people. And if they knew about some . . . extra-conjugal relations or that the man is starting to drink too much, then it was sufficient to send such a report to [Antonin] Novotny and the man was finished.

Michael Checinski believes that a similar situation exists in the Soviet Union. He observes that for the security organs adequately to protect members of the party upper elite, they must gather information on it which, of course, could be used against the elite's members. The result seems to be a cycle of permanent spying, under another name:

Q: [D]oes the KGB dare to collect [damaging] information against the Politburo, the Defense Council, and the general secretary?

Checinski: Yes. But [the head of the KGB] will not make it official. He will not order his subordinates to collect information on the general secretary. That would be dangerous. But because he has to protect the general secretary he has to know who is calling him, who is writing him, who he is talking to. Protecting him means collecting information on him.

In Cuba, Juan Benemelis describes a system in which Fidel Castro has separated his personal security from the DGI altogether.[32] By setting up a personal guard, he attempts to protect himself from all threats, including potential danger posed by his own DGI watchdogs:

They [the special units] were not under the DGI; they are called the special troops of the Ministry of the Interior. Their chiefs are Raul and Fidel Castro.

---

[32] General Directorate of Intelligence, the Cuban state security apparatus.

They only follow their orders. They are not DOE.[33] Their job is working as Castro's bodyguard, training, and very special operations. They are smaller than a division, but [they consist of] more than one thousand men. They are Castro's personal military reserve unit if something happens to him in Havana. There are people from this unit who operate in the intelligence services doing special missions for Castro. Nobody else touches these missions, not even the DGI or Pineiro.[34] About twelve hundred of these troops were sent to Angola. Sometimes Castro lends them to foreign visitors inside and outside Cuba as bodyguards.

In Poland, Zdzislaw Rurarz argues, the military could ultimately prevail over the civilian security organs. In the party/security/military power struggle, the military arm has a clear advantage, states Rurarz:

[T]he commander of a Polish army garrison will order the arrest of anyone from the Ministry of Internal Affairs whom he suspects [of] secretly monitoring the reliability of his unit. Many such Internal Ministry officials have sat in jail for forty-eight hours with no official reason given. The military simply mistrusts them. That's what happens in Poland. Maybe the same isn't true in the USSR . . . but I would not underestimate the Soviet army.

Most of the interviewees believe that the supreme control over society resides with the party. Still, the balance of power in any political system is fluid, in the closed society more so than elsewhere. Given the opportunity, KGB officers can try to extend the influence of their services, as described by former Soviet researcher Piatigorsky:

They tell you that the party controls the KGB. This is true and it is not true. Yes, the same level of the KGB is impotent against an equal level of the party. In other words, a KGB head of a [union] republic is impotent against the general secretary of that [union] republic. But he is not powerless against the secretary's deputies and [against] the whole party apparatus subordinate to the party secretary. In other words, each level is controlling different things. The head of the KGB is selected and approved by the general secretary and the Politburo. But once he is in that position, he has . . . an incredible apparatus available to him, for surveillance, recording, checking everything. Everyone fears him but officially he is subordinated to the party general secretary. If the general secretary feels that there is something wrong with him, however, he can finish him. So, the head of the KGB is very careful not to be in conflict with the general secretary or other powerful members of the

---

[33] Department of Special Operations, the department of the Cuban Ministry of the Interior that carries out special operations, such as sabotage.

[34] Manuel Pineiro Losada, Head of the Americas Department of the Central Committee of the Cuban Communist Party; in charge of coordinating subversion in the Western Hemisphere.

Politburo. Yet he knows what everyone is doing, as compared to the Politburo, which does not.

According to Stanislav Levchenko, the struggle between the security and the party has continued under General Secretary Gorbachev. He refers to the various tools the party maintains in order to control the KGB. Levchenko seeks to show the fine line the party treads between preserving the KGB as an effective instrument of power, on the one hand, and placing itself in danger on the other.

Levchenko: The KGB has become increasingly involved in domestic investigations, such as bribery, because [Soviet leaders] cannot trust their own police. The police were rotten. The minister of interior, a four-star general, got himself involved on a large scale, [in] the Tsvigun affair. I think that the greater participation of the KGB in controlling the country is primarily [due to] domestic problems. [Soviet leaders] want to feel more secure. They do not realize that there is no way for them to cope with bribery, and so they try. At the same time, because the KGB is throwing people in jail, they need to create a better image. . . .

The [members] of the KGB [were] very unhappy about de-Stalinization and they were trying to change it. Andropov was chief for fifteen years. He knew more than anyone else [about] the KGB's longing for a more important role. As a result, he displayed the KGB more in the Soviet Union. Internationally, it will not make a difference, because the KGB is already well known. . . .

Q: What about the question of ultimate party control? And what about the other branch that has been negatively affected by the increase of the KGB's prestige, the armed forces?

Levchenko: I would be cautious about saying that the armed forces lost power to the KGB, but the party undoubtedly has. [Soviet leaders] are clever enough not to let the KGB become too powerful. That is one of the reasons they gave top officials from the KGB important party positions; to give them a stake in the party. Gorbachev needs time to clean out a few hundred places for his people. His new people will try to clean up what was left from [Konstantin] Chernenko's and [Leonid] Brezhnev's time. Over the years he will feel more secure as the Soviet leader. He will not give the KGB a chance to control the country. Anything is possible, but they will never get rid of corruption. If you want to know the main cause of the socialist system's death in the Soviet Union, look at corruption. It is not only material corruption, it is also moral and political corruption. Whomever Gorbachev brings to power will be the same type. . . . They will start with a little graft and then get into even greater corruption. The role of the KGB in this respect is prominent, because that is the segment of the Soviet government that, while still corrupt, is less corrupt than all the other segments, including the party. [Gorbachev] is also increasing the prominence of the KGB to [enhance his own power].

The power struggle between the security organs and the Red Army leadership manifests itself primarily as a conflict between the KGB[35] and military intelligence, the GRU. Gregory points out that it is in the interest of the KGB to keep the GRU under scrutiny:

> The GRU has been and will be under the careful surveillance of the KGB. It does not matter if [Ivan] Serov or anybody else is the head of the GRU; the KGB is the dominant intelligence service in the Soviet Union. The KGB has its own agents among the GRU and the armed forces. It is possible that Serov was appointed to increase KGB dominance over the GRU. The KGB is responsible for counterintelligence within the USSR and abroad. This mandate includes watching the GRU. If a GRU officer plans to defect and is discovered, the KGB takes action, not the GRU. The GRU has no counterintelligence service. The GRU is a very large and important service; its intelligence gathering, especially in high-technology areas, is vital. But only the KGB does counterintelligence work. I do not think the Politburo will ever [assign] another service with counterintelligence [duties].

Yet, Zdzislaw Rurarz notes, the GRU is not defenseless. While it may lack the broad scope of the KGB counterintelligence apparatus, it has other assets with which the KGB cannot compete:

> People in the West generally underestimate the efficiency of the military in the USSR, and point to the role of the Third Department of the KGB (which officially does not exist) in penetrating the army. But, of course, the GRU tries to penetrate the KGB in return. It is not irrelevant that when Beria was arrested in 1953, it was done exclusively by the military. Because the military controls Soviet strategic forces and airborne divisions, their officers are best trained (and armed), which gives them tremendous power; I think this is often underestimated. KGB officers sent to watch the Red Army inevitably grow terrified of the GRU and the Soviet army in general. Hence, they may be less loyal to the KGB than many believe.

Thus, in the surveillance struggle, each group—party, security and military—has its own unique advantages and disadvantages, strengths and weaknesses. Stability of the whole system (to the extent that it remains stable) derives not so much from a lack of conflict as from a relative balance of power between the competing forces. Yet, the ultimate dominance of the CPSU over the Soviet state remains unquestioned on the part of most insiders. In some East European countries, this seems far from clear. In Bulgaria, the party and the security service seem well integrated. Kostov says:

---

[35] The Third Chief Directorate of the KGB is charged with the task of oversight over the Soviet military establishment.

My opinion is that these two organizations are very closely connected and integrated. I would say that the question should be who are the watchdogs of Zhvikov in the party and in the DS?[36] Tomorrow if somebody replaces Zhvikov, the DS will become the watchdogs of this person. I do not have the impression that the party is over the DS or vice versa.

The Nicaraguan example is striking for its puritan tone. Bolaños-Hunter explains that the security organs were virtually unnecessary as far as watching the party was concerned. Instead, each party member was counted on to watch the person next to him, and the results were satisfactory, at least for the vigilant:

With their [the Cubans] encouragement we started increasing what we called revolutionary surveillance among us. We watched and listened to the colleague next door and reported anything wrong. If there was something wrong with somebody, even just a drinking problem, there was the possibility of it getting more serious. We would discuss the problem in the meetings of the party militants—the very dedicated cadre of party members—who would then decide on an investigation and who should carry it out. I was a militant. . . . There was no special group in state security for this revolutionary surveillance; the party militants took care of it. From the advice that the Cubans gave us, apparently they had similar cases, but they never said so directly. The Cubans are cautious about that. . . . Revolutionary surveillance involved matching people to a profile, for example, watching out for symptoms of bourgeois consciousness—expressing material desires, being late for work or with reports. These things get the party militants worried. . . .

The DPEP[37] has an internal function. They are the ones who monitor the people in Nicaragua: the psychology; the perceptions of how everything is going; where they have to put more emphasis or use more of one type of propaganda. It is also the main department that carries out the Marxist instruction and political education of the militants and the members of the FSLN,[38] and controls the implanting of communist or Marxist theory in the schools and public life.

Two final notes on domestic surveillance systems. The first has to do with the creeping bureaucratization of the security services. Given the amount of information the KGB must process, it has developed a massive, and highly bureaucratized infrastructure. The new KGB professional is not the old, hardened NKVD man who had served at the front in World War II (meaning

---

[36] *Durzhavna Sigurnost,* Bulgarian state security.

[37] Department of Propaganda and Political Education; in charge of Sandinista internal propaganda.

[38] The Sandinista National Liberation Front.

mostly the domestic front) and had been trained by tough and experienced Chekists. Instead, he was probably trained by career-minded bureaucrats and party members more concerned with promotion than with their tasks. There seems to be a shift in tone in everyday KGB operations. A. Piatigorsky shares his experience:

> I was investigated . . . twice by the KGB. I cannot compare the two investigations. I was [first] investigated at the end of the Stalin period. Those who investigated me were, in a way, SS men—sadists, very cruel people. When I was investigated in 1973, they were two absolutely plain bureaucrats, not at all cruel or active, thinking only of money and promotion. They did not give a damn about me. They would not beat me or touch me. They wanted to get it over with as soon as possible. Absolutely lower middle-class bureaucrats.

Michael Checinski gives a sense of the fatalism of these watchers, who know that they themselves are objects of the trade they practice:

> *Q:*   Did you think that when you spoke with your wife that you enjoyed privacy?
> *Checinski:*   Never in my life have I enjoyed privacy. I was directly involved in all these things and I have no doubt that I was watched. I have no illusions. My house, my telephone, my letters, everything. It's like you get used to living with insects. They are part of you, like in the jungle. . . . It's a part of life.

3
Exoteric and Esoteric Communications

Channels of Communication

The Structure of Communications

Information constitutes power in every political system. In closed societies, those who control, supervise and monitor information are careful to ensure that it flows only through approved channels. On a mass scale, this is implemented through control of the information media—newspapers, magazines, books, radio, and television. Historical as well as contemporary state and party documents also are closely controlled. Internal publications and broadcasts are censored, while those originating abroad are banned or jammed at least intermittently. Since about 1986, the attitude of the Soviet leadership toward mass media has been changing, allowing some latitude internally and more access to external sources. It remains to be seen whether these positive developments constitute an irreversible trend. However, the interviews cited here were concerned less with the flow of information to the masses, than with the circulation of information within the policy-making and -implementing hierarchy.

The material presented below focuses on the flow of information in the Soviet Union, Eastern Europe, and client states in the Third World. The channels of information are complex and depend on many variables. Even the sub-elite in the Soviet Union does not enjoy automatically guaranteed access; rather, each morsel of information is allowed to pass through the official channels on a case-by-case basis, as explained by Gregory.

Q: Would a distribution list be composed for each specific item, or would there be simply general categories, such as a very limited Distribution List A and a Distribution List B?

Gregory: There are [general] guidelines and there are categories which are set in advance. But in each particular sensitive case, [persons] in the [Ministry of Foreign Affairs] are trained so well that they are [very] discerning about distribution. For instance, a former senior diplomat [in the Ministry] understood that a Dobrynin-Kissinger conversation should be delayed and discussed before [a] decision [was] made. They have good . . . judgment and usually, whenever they have the slightest hesitation in the [Ministry of Foreign Affairs], they know that it is better to ask . . . and [to] bring it to someone's attention.

They have general guidelines. . . Thus, when secret negotiations are involved [their contents] might not go into general distribution. They know who is important. They knew [by experience] that SALT negotiations were in a separate category, that generally Kissinger was in a separate category. Sometimes Makarov[1] himself would get involved [in deciding on distribution].

The General [Department of the CPSU Central Committee] has a team that works with all the "cables" and makes a [digest] for the Politburo, three to four issues a day, out of about one hundred cables, . . . a five-page summary.

The Politburo members, then, have regular access to information. Other Central Committee members, however, do not enjoy this privilege, as Gregory explains:

Membership in the Central Committee gives . . . a certain status. [Members] can go to the central Committee without ordering a pass in advance. Or they can go to some special stores. But that has nothing to do with the distribution of information or knowledge. That is not decided on the basis of [membership in] the Central Committee. For example, the second and first [*obkom*] secretary in Irkutsk . . . might be a full member of the Central Committee, but he may never see . . . cables from any ambassador. There are [persons] in the Academy of Sciences or in the Writers' Union . . . who don't have access. It is decided separately in each individual case.

If . . . communications from the center [are to be distributed to] the Foreign Ministry and the Politburo [and] Soviet ambassadors, [this would constitute] a wide group, [not to mention] all the [Institutes of the Academy of Sciences]. . . .

There is fear that there will be a leak; the Arbatov institute cannot be considered [secure]. The more places you have on a distribution list, the greater the chance of a leak. [Moreover, another] consideration is that information is power. Beyond the need . . . for certain persons to have access, [it is considered undesirable] to give information to [individuals] who are not involved in the process.

Gregory further points out that restrictions at the Central Committee level are tougher where domestic rather than foreign information is concerned. This indicates the nature of the most significant knowledge, that is, information that can affect the closed society from within.

---

[1] The senior assistant in the Ministry at the time.

Q: Concerning the four separate edictions of TASS—with an escalating degree of secrecy classifications—is it correct that most of the more highly classified material, in fact, doesn't deal with Soviet affairs, but concerns the outside world? Would the top personnel at an institute like Arbatov's[2] have access to the most highly classified version of TASS, or would that be reserved entirely for members of the Central Committee?

Gregory: Arbatov himself might [have access], by virtue of the fact that he's [simultaneously] a member of the Central Committee. Some of the [individuals] in the institute will have it, but most will not.

Q: Did you, in your role, have access to such documents?

Gregory: Yes. I had no problem whatsoever. . . being a part of the inner circle of Gromyko, I could read everything which Gromyko read.

Q: Were you permitted to take material like that outside the office?

Gregory: No. In the Soviet Union, you are not supposed to take out any documents, not only top-secret ones, but resricted ones as well. Israelyan[3] has been violating this [restriction].

Q: Because of the photocopy machine, has this approach become even stricter?

Gregory: Yes.

Q: Did you ever find [anything about the Soviet Union itself] in the most highly classified versions, or was it entirely material [concerning] the outside world?

Gregory: TASS? Entirely about the outside world.

Q: There is no internal distribution of highly classified material about the Soviet Union?

Gregory: There is [this kind of] information, but only for the Central Committee. In the Central Committee, they don't have a [classification] system, top secret, etc., for information from outside the Soviet Union. But there is [such] a code system for information coming from within the Soviet Union. The first secretary of a region will [send classified material] to the Central Committee [concerning] the domestic situation [in his area].

In Cuba, according to Juan Benemelis, there are three basic security classifications for information in the official channels:

> There were three classifications: top secret, which went to the chief of state, secret, which went to the ministry, and confidential, which came to me.

---

[2]Georgii A. Arbatov, Central Committee CPSU Member, director of the USA and Canada Institute of the Soviet Academy of Sciences.

[3]Viktor L. Israelyan, former Soviet U.N. Representative and member of the Kollegium of the Soviet Ministry of Foreign Affairs (MFA).

I could give the confidential material to a section chief or an analyst if I wanted [to]. I could read secret material, but I had to go to the minister's office [to do so]. I had to sign for it and sit there [and] read it. If the vice-minister called me in, sometimes I could read top-secret material.

In most countries, one needs a security clearance before gaining access to classified documents. Michael Voslensky relates that, unlike in the U.S., where the individual under investigation is given a personal interview to clarify information received from various references, the person under investigation in the Soviet Union is given no opportunity for personal input:

> I was not interviewed for . . . special clearance. Security clearances there are not like they are here; there is no dialogue. You give them your curriculum vitae, answer questions, and wait six to eight weeks. Under Stalin it took three months.

Of course, even in the Soviet Union the security system is not fool-proof. Stanislav Levchenko mentions a Soviet official who was so lax with classified documents that he actually shared them with underlings as a matter of convenience:

> Kovalenko, who is basically a Soviet military person, leaves top secret documents all over his huge desk, which is against all regulations, but at least he felt comfortable. He is not supposed to show these things to people in his section, but he and others did, because they want their staff to know what is going on [so as to enhance] their work. I would say that the handling of paperwork in the International Department is fairly liberal, as compared to other Soviet organizations.

Access to foreign media, while less constrained, is not unrestricted, except at the top levels of the CPSU. It would be a mistake to assume that Soviet top leaders receive as little intelligence concerning the West, as Western leaders are able to obtain concerning the Soviet Union. The Soviet Union may remain an enigma to Western statesmen as long as it is a closed society, but, to the Soviet leaders, the West is an open book. Deriabin notes that this has been true since the Stalin era.

Q: What kind of publications did Stalin receive?

Deriabin: Both his office and his *dacha* had large libraries. Almost all types of publications were delivered to him, from books on shoemaking to Clausewitz. Some of them Stalin looked at right away and others were shipped out after a month or two. There was also a regulation established that outlined the distribution of books and other materials. I am sure that this was done with Stalin's approval. Politburo members and heads of Central Committee departments would receive many publications at home and free of charge. High officials in the KGB, trade ministry, CC CPSU staff, etc., would also have publications delivered, but would have to pay a reduced fee for them.

All kinds of publications were sent out this way: encyclopedias, political material, Nobel prize literature, etc.

At lower levels, Western periodicals are made available, albeit with a certain degree of censorship. Censorship is a centrally controlled process—literature passes through the censor's office before being passed down to institutes and libraries. In theory, according to Galina Orionova, the process is straightforward:

We have *Glavlit*.[4] The censorship department has definitely defined subjects which must be [deleted from dissemination]. In fact, all the literature in the department [of an academy institute to which] one required special access was marked with a [hexagon]. But literature which is particularly sensitive [had] two [such hexagons]. So the librarian at the institute who received [this material knew] how to sort it out. One [category went] into the safe and [the other went] onto the shelf.

Access to materials at IMEiMO, according to Voslensky, is not limited according to degree of security clearance. Rather, Western materials were provided on a need-to-know basis. Censorship does, however, have its place.

Voslensky: The Western publications are not classified officially as secret. They are classified "for service use only." That means it was not necessary to have a special security clearance to read them, just the permission of the director of the institute. So we all automatically had permission.

Q: Would that also have applied to publications that dealt with internal affairs of the Soviet Union?

Voslensky: No, not quite. About the Soviet Union, yes, it is possible to read what it says [in Western publications, but not what it prints about individual Soviet leaders and their factions]. *Glavlit* cuts out all [such] articles. Well, certainly . . . the Foreign Ministry [and the CPSU] Central Committee [were exempted from such censorship]. But at our institute, unfortunately, we were always very dissatisfied, not because we wished to read [such] articles, but we considered [offensive] that they [censored them]. They did the same in the Sovinformburo. I think . . . exemption [from] this [censorship] rule [applies] only [to] the Foreign Ministry and certainly [to] the Central Committee, and KGB.

---

[4] *Glavlit,* Main Administration for Safeguarding State Secrets in the Press, previously called Chief Administration of Literary and Publishing Affairs. It is in charge of censorship.

Anatoly Fedoseyev gives details of the relatively large flow of information that he, as a scientist, needed and was able to obtain:

Every institution like ours had its own special service. After some time a special information institute in Moscow was created. It began to copy magazines and to issue them to every institute. I even got those magazines to my plant by personal subscription. I received the proceedings of the American Society of Engineers and Electricians, for example. I do not remember all of them, but I got about ten different . . . magazines at my plant. When I was looking at the magazines, I noticed that some pages were missing. I complained, without any results. I discovered that there was censorship, which resulted in the removal of those pages. The same institute produced some translations. There also was an information service at several levels: One at the level of directors, which we were in, one at the ministerial level, . . . and I suppose there were some issues for the Politburo. I would say that we were much more up to date about American technology and science than the average American engineer or scientist.

Galina Orionova also enjoyed access to Western press and other materials. In her testimony, she reveals the complexity and stratification of the system which provided researchers in central institutes of the Soviet Academy of Sciences with information:

The IUSA, as well as all other institutes, including IMEiMO, had an absolutely insane system of information. We worked mainly with information from daily TASS bulletins in Russian, which were printed on cheap yellow paper. I am not sure whether it was classified TASS, and I do not know which TASS this came from. I've never seen another TASS because whenever I needed some other file, I would go to the IMEiMO library, which had much better files made up of TASS, *Newsweek* and *Time* clippings [which the IUSA did not have]. Here I would see the same sort of TASS. This contained information mostly on Soviet statements. . . . [O]ne needed a special permit to read it, so it may well have been [classified]. . . . At the same time, we had the TASS bulletin which was published twice a week, a little yellow book; we also had the blue edition, which we used to read every day. We had only printed matter, no broadcast information from the U.S. But everyone listened to [Voice of America] or BBC.

All in all, Galina Orionova describes a system which allowed her access to the greater part of the information she needed. But even Academy of Sciences researchers had to put up with censorship. On occasion, it turned out that the system was designed mechanistically and was, therefore, prone to embarrassing errors, as in the case involving the *Village Voice*.

Orionova: We even had the *Village Voice* because they took it as an agricultural newspaper! Once I joined the institute, I only went to an outside library once or twice, because we were self-sufficient. . . . [T]he shelves contained regular journals dating from 1968. Every journal was in the special collection of the institute. Each had a special stamp with a number inside and, if it was controversial, like something by Solzhenitsyn for example, it would be put into a special safe. If you wanted to read a particular newspaper, you would either be given a part of it or you would be shown the article you needed. Sometimes you would be able to read the censored material. I first saw Solzhenitsyn's memoirs this way because it was printed in the *New York Times* in large excerpts. If it is really hot . . . you still can get a magazine because sometimes [the censors] miss things. For example, I found a wonderful piece in the *Far Eastern Economic Review* where Kosygin, Brezhnev and someone else were swearing at something, using four-letter words. . . .

   I used *Orbis,* because it is very good at [dedicating entire issues to] a particular subject. . . .

Q: *Orbis* in the mid-1970s would have had some very critical [pieces] on the USSR. If you picked up *Orbis,* would there be articles missing?

Orionova: Yes. The institute was very lax in regard to some of this, though. I used my bosses to [take] this literature home, because I was not allowed [to but they were].

Orionova found that the institute's library resources were adequate. However, when it came to copying, the institute maintained close control over the technology.

Q: How is copying done at the institute?

Orionova: By Xerox. But as far as I remember, we never used the Xerox for typed material . . . only for printed material. You could cheat by using a carbon, because you [could not obtain access to] the Xerox at the institute. No one [was] allowed, except for the man who [worked] on it. There was a special room which was always locked. To get [access to] a Xerox, you needed a special permit signed by one of the deputy directors and by the First Department.

Stiller reminds us, however, that a watchful eye ensures that only those who have a legitimate need to know actually obtain classified information, and that sometimes having a need to know did not guarantee one would see the required documents:

I know that at the end of [our] course there were requirements for those students who could not get an internship overseas—those who had to stay in the Soviet Union. There were requirements for them to read various [editions] of TASS, and from what I understand, they had trouble getting them there. It was not that easy. There are different grades of TASS denoted by color. The problem was that some graduates needed information, and they had a hard time getting it; we knew where it was, it was in a room by the cadres department, right by the KGB.

The Media—Censorship in Bulgaria

Censorship worked differently in Bulgaria, according to Vladimir Kostov. It was not under the control of a central organ, such as the Soviet *Glavlit;* instead, individual editors were required to ensure that only the official party line would be expressed in the print and in the electronic media. The trend is toward self-censorship, that is, each writer understands he has to adapt to the official position. Otherwise, his career is at stake.

Kostov: The Bulgarian leadership adopted a more economical way. It liquidated the *Glavlit.* The editor-in-chief played the censor. He got his instructions from the Central Committee of the party. If he did not do the job according to these instructions he would be fired. You often read that the leadership boasts that there is no censorship. It is true. The editor-in-chief is the censor.

For example, in 1969 after the Prague Spring, I was responsible for information on Bulgarian radio. Up until then, everything that went on the air had to have three persons give their approval. I said, "I want to make my commentaries on [certain subjects] without the approval of anyone." The boss said, "Excellent! Very good! You know what the game is. If you make a mistake, it will be the last. You are out." So the editors and their assistants are excellent censors because they do not have regulations. They simply know if what they are doing will be disliked at the top it [will be all] over.

Q: Would the editors and chiefs have a meeting of the kind that exists in the Soviet Union—with someone in the *apparat* of the Central Committee?

Kostov: First of all, they have meetings on a regular basis. Second, they also have [special] meetings when it is necessary. Third, each of these persons is allowed to approach every member of the Politburo if it is reasonable and proper. When I was responsible for information on the radio, if some event occurred which was a surprise, my task was to call [my immediate superior]. But if he was out of reach, I could try to contact the secretary of the Central Committee, a member of the Politburo who was overseeing the media. At any given moment, when it is necessary, the editor-in-chief can consult the top.

At the regular meetings, there is a list that is presented of people who must be invited. There is also a list [of persons who may] deputize [for] the editor-in-chief if he cannot come. All of these persons are known by sight by the security services [and] [v]ery often they do not [have to] ask for credentials. I am saying this to stress that there is very strict control over [participation in] these meetings. If the editor-in-chief wants to send a person who does not regularly attend, he needs special permission.

Access to various newspapers of different sensitivity, like access to classified documents, is not so much a function of ex officio power as of personal position and influence. The short list of persons with access to foreign press in Bulgaria is subject to change.

> *Kostov:* The classification [of Bulgarian Press Agency editions] is the same . . . as in the Soviet Union. The most highly classified document is what the foreign press is writing about Bulgaria. The bad news is that what the foreign press is writing about the Soviet Union cannot be found . . . in Bulgaria.
>
> *Q:* To get the most highly classified edition do you have to be a full member of the Central Committee?
>
> *Kostov:* No. The highly classified documents are not limited according to certain position . . . [they are limited according to certain individuals]. By the person, not by the position: [in general, mostly] members of the Politburo, heads of the departments of the Central Committee, the bosses of the secret services, the bosses of the army, the Soviet embassy. Between 100 and 150 persons. It is not a constant number [because not all individuals concerned enjoy such prerogatives of rank].

Telephones

In *Nomenklatura,* Voslensky describes in detail the role of telephones in the Soviet Power structure.[5] Telephones are symbols of power and of influence. For instance, when a Western television crew was admitted to the office of the former Moscow party chief, Boris Yeltsin, its members found that he had six telephones on his desk—indicating that at the time he occupied a powerful position.

Each phone has a distinct purpose. Some handle only incoming calls, usually from superiors. Others are connected only to certain departments. Two of the Eastern European interviewees commented on the internal phone network. Jiri Pelikan, as director general of Czechoslovak televison, had access to the so-called Cernin telephone system; the Cernin telephone directory is classified as secret.

---

[5] Voslensky, *Nomenklatura,* pp. 207–213.

Pelikan: [I had the] regular telephone, yes, and I had [the] Cernin, the special line.

Q: Special line for what?

Pelikan: For communication with the [top] *nomenklatura.*

Pelikan also explains the configuration of the phone system at the apex of the power pyramid.

> *Q:* I hear from others that the general secretary has four different phones whereas a Politburo member has only three, and I wondered if you know anything about the special telephones they have.
>
> *Pelikan:* I think that the general secretary and maybe some other secretary, the second one, and [the secretary] who is responsible for [the] international section, have special telephones for connection with Moscow. But in general this line [functions well], this so-called Cernin, so it is just enough to have two telephones, one in your office and one in your home. I don't know about other telephones. If there are some special telephones [for] the secret service, I don't know.

In Poland Michael Checinski dealt with three phone lines, each with a special purpose. The most secure of these, Checinski states, was controlled by Soviet specialists:

> When I was in . . . counterintelligence, there were three lines. One was a normal telephone. Second was a military telephone direct to military leaders. I could dial direct, with a code number, or I could go through an operator. The third was a red telephone. It was secure and from it I could call for secret information. The service of that line was in the hands of the Soviets. It was by cable but it was secure, it could not be bugged. I could call any place that also had one . . . all the party leaders, etc. They had a special list of all the persons who had a secure phone. This book had all the numbers. Later there was another line, for the government. It connected only to Polish government leaders. It did include the security [personnel], though. The more important the personality, the more telephones. In my time we could not speak openly, even on the secure phones.

Jan Sejna explains how East European party leaders communicate with the CPSU general secretary:

> Regarding the broader question of party affairs, there were direct phone links between the Soviet general secretary and the first secretary of the Eastern European parties. For the implementation of important decisions, this hot line would establish immediate contact with the necessary leaders.

I was in Novotny's office many times during direct conversations between Novotny and Khrushchev or Brezhnev. Of course, the use of this line was generally one-way only. Most satellite first secretaries would not dare to interrupt the Soviet general secretary, except to convey birthday wishes. Day-to-day affairs, Jan Sejna says, are handled separately.

Sejna: Phone links with the Soviet general secretary are the exception. Generally, for day-to-day affairs, instructions are conveyed either through the Soviet ambassador or between the Soviet party departments and their counterpart departments in the Czechoslovak party. For example, the Czechoslovak Administration Department [of the party Central Committee], which controls the military and the intelligence service, maintains direct contact with the Administrative Organs Department in Moscow.

Q: Is this done generally by phone and are the lines considered secure?

Sejna: There are special phones, which only those with the highest clearance can use, and Moscow is convinced that this system cannot be bugged. The Soviet troops laid the cables for these special lines, which run from every Eastern European capital to the Soviet Union. On more important matters, the Eastern Europeans will be called to Moscow, and on average issues the Soviet ambassador will deal with the party first secretary. One can see in the local party paper that the Soviet ambassador calls on the first secretary an average about once a week. Such meetings are usually reported in the open press.

In the case of some countries, however, concessions must be made to geographical location and technical limitations. Goshu Wolde states that there was no red line between Moscow and Addis Ababa. Instead, the Soviet embassy served as a communication link between the Soviet and Ethiopian decision-making elites.

Coderooms

The most closely guarded information is that which flows from the Soviet Union to its embassies. The reason is clear: given the importance of intelligence centers, the sensitivity of the information coming in and going out, and the proximity of foreign intelligence operatives, coderooms in embassies must be given special attention. Levchenko describes the arrangements for obtaining access:

It is a very limited number of persons who have access [to the coderoom]. Anybody who is not himself involved in the actual coding or decoding would not be allowed in the room except the ambassador. The *rezident* can go into his code clerk's rooms.

Even the highest officials in Soviet embassies must have a need to know in order to gain access to cable traffic. Levchenko elaborates on this requirement:

> [The traffic one is allowed to see] is assigned by the ambassador. It is carried physically from the code room to the office and back again. It is not supposed to be left in your possession alone. . . . The system is quite simple. The code clerk has an attaché case in which he keeps all the incoming and outgoing traffic. He goes to whomever needs the information, for example, the ambassador or the *rezident*. He tells them he needs them to read something and to take action. He is supposed to stay in the room while it is read, but I do not think he really stays there. If it is a large room, with fifteen persons in it, he cannot stay, but he is around. As soon as the person is finished working on the cable he calls [the code clerk], gives it back to him, and signs for it. Even the *rezident* and, probably, the ambassador, have no right to stockpile cables in their own personal safes. The code room is not just locked, it is also guarded twenty-four hours a day by an armed guard.

Levchenko explains how the Soviet embassy in Japan handled security of the coderoom:

> For purely MFA persons, there is a room adjacent to the code room with a little window through which a specific cable is handed. They read it, sign for it, and hand it back. This system depends on the country. For example, in Japan there were two KGB code clerks in a fifty-person residency. They worked twelve hours each day, because there is a lot of traffic. The embassy's personnel is far larger. Usually it is thirty-five to forty percent KGB, which is a large figure, but there are still about one hundred "clean" [i.e., non-KGB] persons. It would be impossible for an MFA code clerk to chase around after everybody. There is probably about ninety percent of the cable traffic which a certain level of MFA persons never see at all. The code clerks have their assignments and know whom to call. Instead of running around the embassy they will call the recipient of the cable. The person will come and read the cable. The KGB does not use this system; things are much more personal there.

Stiller states that both the KGB and the GRU have their own separate coderooms and that the codes are different:

> The Ministry of Foreign Affairs has its own [code], KGB has its own, GRU has its own. The Central Committee's International Department might have its own. I am not sure about how the communications worked, or on what level of classification the whole system was organized. [The person] in charge of the coderooms would be a Ministry of Foreign Affairs person. Under his umbrella would come the facilities for the KGB, GRU, economic

counsellor, and so on. . . . All the arrangements such as placement and allo-cation of space were his responsibility.

He further details the procedure for reading various cables from all the coderooms:

First of all is the sign-in book. In that book every cable you read is regis-tered; whenever you read something, you sign the book. They know exactly which cables you have seen—in case you leave, or for counterintelligence. There are various levels of classification. Some of the cables can be checked out for several hours and read in an adjoining room. Some . . . could only be opened, read, handed back, and the book signed. Some were totally con-trolled in this manner.

Stiller describes communication between the Soviet consul general in Alexandria and the KGB *rezident* in the Soviet embassy in Cairo:

Let's say the consul general and the KGB *rezident* in the embassy needed to communicate; this could not be done simply by telephoning the embassy or through the airwaves. The only way to communicate was to drive to the *rezidentura* in Cairo and communicate there. There were not many emer-gency trips of this sort by the KGB *rezident*, or by KGB persons from Alex-andria to Cairo. This would suggest that the KGB in Alexandria had partic-ular guidelines as to the general direction they were to [follow]. Any time an emergency arose, the KGB persons in the consulate would just travel to Cairo, leaving very suddenly. This was not more than three or four times a month. There were frequent trips by the KGB *rezident* out to Soviet ships, however; I do not know what sort of communication took place there.

Soviet security requirements are tough even by East European standards. Kucharski, who served at the Polish embassy in Luanda, Angola, enjoyed more latitude of movement than his Soviet counterparts:

The Soviet embassy's staff is located in one building. They are not allowed to have apartments throughout the city. It is easier to keep track of them if they are all together. It is this way in all Soviet embassies. Also all staff members must take direct Aeroflot flights to or from Moscow. There is not even a possibility for a Soviet citizen working in Angola to stop in Warsaw, Budapest or other socialist capitals on the way home. While I was in Angola, I returned to Poland for vacations. On the way I would stop in Rome or Paris. I never went directly. I could not have flown directly if I had wanted to. The closest thing to a direct flight went through East Berlin.

Published sources reveal that the Soviet penchant for the physical isola-tion of personnel as a means of information control finds it most extreme expression in the fate of GRU coderoom clerks, who are prohibited from leaving embassy compounds and are never allowed to attend embassy functions when foreigners are present "even if they are Bulgarians or Mongolians."[6]

The Message

General

Propaganda is an important tool for the transmission of the party line to lower-level party workers, as well as to the allied countries and sympathizers abroad. The use of the word propaganda here follows the older definition of a method for spreading or propagating a particular set of ideas, principles, or information, rather than the more colloquial meaning of false information. Jiri Pelikan points out that what is known in the West as propaganda is regarded different in Eastern Europe.

> *Q:* What is the difference between agitation and propaganda?
>
> *Pelikan:* [Agitation] means publishing posters, leaflets, influencing public opinion . . . producing propaganda material. . . . Whereas propaganda is the education of the [party] members . . . in Marxism-Leninism.

In the Soviet Union, propaganda is controlled by several specialized institutions. Internal propaganda, which includes placing reactions to events outside the Soviet Union in a context suitable to the party line, was handled until recently by the Propaganda Department (formerly *Agitprop*) and by what was, also until recently, the International Information Department. (These activities are handled now, respectively, by the Ideology and International Departments.) Stanislav Levchenko explains the genesis and activity of the former International Information Department, information that remains topical since it sheds light upon the manner in which Soviet policy goals affect bureaucratic organization:

> I did not witness the creation of the International Information Department in 1978, but undoubtedly it must have been a bureaucratic nightmare. Like the International Department, it is based on geographic divisions, but it also includes functional ones. Ponomarev and Zamyatin are the key figures, and . . . many officials of these departments try to convince them to follow their ideas. . . .
>
> The International Information Department was brought into existence not to react to what the West does, nor to initiate, but primarily to provide

---

[6] See Viktor Suvorov, *Inside Soviet Military Intelligence,* (New York: Berkley Books, 1984), pp. 101–102.

better coverage of foreign events for Soviet domestic propaganda. This was a bad idea from the very beginning, because it is virtually impossible. In 1978 or 1979, . . . instead of something being published a week late, it was published two or three days late. Soviet officials understood quickly that reaction should be as fast as in the case of the BBC, Voice of America, or Radio Liberty. They started to think about what else they could do that would be useful for the Politburo. Then they started to influence the foreign media and its representatives in Moscow with their information and responses. . . . At the same time, I have no facts, but there is no doubt that around 1979 or 1980, they started to get involved in active measures as well. Mr Falin[7] [now head of the International Department], an ambassador who allegedly speaks beautiful German, almost moved to West Germany as elections approached. The story was that he left Germany and became a journalist. Falin's example [indicates] that the International Information Department was involved in active measures, [and thus] overlaps with the function of the International Department.

Gregory sees the former Internal Information Department as a quick-reaction mechanism, an institution capable of rapid response to external events. His description of the complex mechanism whereby personal and organizational relationships interact remains relevant for the contemporary scene:

The International Department [ID] has major responsibility for communist parties abroad and cannot concentrate all its energy on the media and propaganda. [In this area] control was given to the International Information Department [IID]. The IID provides coordination but it is not an institution [that] merely [coordinates] between the media and the ID; the ID and IID work together very closely. [Leonid M.] Zamyatin[8] clearly has less importance than [Boris N.] Ponomarev but has more responsibility for the media. The ID sets the overall strategic themes and the IID coordinates the various media channels.

The IID can give articles directly to the media outlets. It is not that Zamyatin needs permission from Ponomarev to publish an article. The IID has direction and, because [its members] are experienced journalists, they can implement the general themes without needing constant approval. Zamyatin will confer with Ponomarev but would not got to [Vadim V.] Zagladin because Zamyatin has an important position in and of himself. His deputies are also experienced . . . they know their subjects well. Zamyatin has discretion. The ideas come from the Secretariat; they prepare their own articles.

---

[7] Valentin M. Falin, former chief of the bureau of *Novosti* news agency, former ambassador to the FRG, now member of the CPSU Central Committee and chief of its International Department.

[8] Leonid M. Zamyatin, former chief of the International Information Department of the CPSU Central Committee.

The IID fulfills the need for a rapid, counterpropaganda response. Many of the persons that work there, such as Falin, are journalists. For example, if Reagan makes a statement, IID writes the article responding, not *Pravda* or TASS. They are responsible for reacting immediately.

The transmission of propaganda to the West was originally the task of the *Sovinformburo,* organized during World War II to inform the world of the struggle against fascism on the Eastern Front. Deriabin sketches its origins and first chief:

> At the outbreak of the war [Shcherbakov] was the secretary of the Moscow party committee; then he was made chief of the political administration of the Soviet armed forces. Later he was in charge of the Soviet Information Bureau (*Sovinformburo*), which informed the world of the Soviet view of the course of the war. He had sole approval of what went on the radio and what went into the newspapers. If there was a defeat at Smolensk, for example, it would be called a tactical retreat; language would be manipulated in order to announce events differently. He was a very hard-working man but also in poor health; he was very fat and drank a lot. . . .
>
> For a variety of reasons unknown to me, Stalin liked Shcherbakov[9] quite a bit. He was in Moscow during the war and he did a very good job in misleading the Western world about the conduct of the war. Shcherbakov also organized propaganda within the USSR: placards, slogans, pictures, leaflets, and entertainment for the soldiers. Stalin must have liked his hard work, but eventually Shcherbakov just drank too much and killed himself.

A successor to the *Sovinformburo,* which operated through the 1950s, is the *Novosti* press agency. Michael Voslensky points out that when the KGB becomes involved in shaping Soviet propaganda, as it probably does through the *Novosti* agencies, propaganda stops being merely a tool for exerting Soviet orthodoxy. It becomes a channel of disinformation:

> [The *Sovinformburo*] was not dissolved, rather a new agency—*Novosti*— was created under Khrushchev in the early 1960s, approximately 1962. [Staff] from the *Sovinformburo* came over to *Novosti* automatically, and they brought on more personnel. It was just a continuation of the *Sovinformburo* under a new label and was much more closely supervised by the KGB. The *Sovinformburo* was [in fact] an agency of the party Central Committee, of the International Department. In the beginning [it was] even located in the same building [as] the CPSU Central Committee. Then [it] moved to the former German embassy.
>
> I believe that the KGB was engaged in the creation of the new agency

---

[9] During the bogus "doctors' plot," concocted by Stalin, Kremlin doctors, mostly Jewish, were accused of having killed leading party personalities, including A.S. Shcherbakov.

Novosti. This was unexpected. The atmosphere of *Novosti* was [very] different [from] that of *Sovinformburo*. It is huge, impersonal, less responsible than *Sovinformburo*. *Sovinformburo* was a responsible agency, acting [formally] for the Council of Ministers of the USSR. It was, therefore, an official representative of the Soviet government. . . . *Sovinformburo* was not officially tied to the Ministry of Foreign Affairs, except as much as there was a "personal union" with Lozovsky.[10] Lozovsky was the deputy foreign minister and at the same time, chief of the *Sovinformburo*. . . . *Novosti,* on the contrary, does not belong officially to the state and it is able to write absolutely irresponsible [material]. This was a result of the participation of the propaganda and disinformation organs of the KGB.

There also developed a connection between *Novosti* and the Journalists' Union. In any case, practically all the representatives of *Novosti,* like TASS representatives, are secret service personnel.

According to Gregory, different interest groups among the Soviet elite set differing objectives for professional propagandists:

[There is a] problem with the persons who are, in the Soviet Union, called propagandists. It is a term which is often used in a . . . derogatory sense. Gromyko, for example, had a much deeper and more substantive view of what . . . can affect Soviet-American relations. . . . Together with the [more] reasonable [circles among the] military and with Brezhnev at the top of the Politburo, [these groups] saw in SALT a vehicle which would be strategically important for the Soviet Union. It would permit the Soviet Union to continue some of its programs while directly affecting American military thinking and future American military programs. [The Americans, as a result, might even cut some programs, as was the case with ABM treaty under SALT I.] They saw the advantages [of arms control] for the Soviet Union and the ways it would affect the military and strategic posture of the [USSR].

But the propagandist has an ideological view. He has to appeal to the masses, which is an important element of the whole strategy of the communist movement. The more serious persons look at this [more primitive approach] and say, "All right, you can continue this propaganda, but what is more important if we take a long-term view: to continue this propaganda campaign, which might be a failure,"—and there are often diplomatic failures—"or, to get results?"

In the view of the serious persons, propaganda [has] an important . . . pragmatic [dimension] because it [can be] used to help in negotiating. [Therefore, they] don't see propaganda as a goal in itself. . . . [For the propagandists, on the other hand,] propaganda is more important than . . . substance . . . such as arms control. In the International Department, for

---

[10] Solomon Lozovsky was executed in August of 1952, in Stalin's purge of the members of the Jewish Anti-Fascist Committee, set up during World War II.

example, they [had] a very superficial view [under Ponomarev]. They [did not] even have experts on arms control, but [stuck] their nose in anyway. . . .

Let's take the present situation . . . as an example. At this stage, propaganda and deception are extremely important, and for Gorbachev, at this moment, [that] may even be more important than substance on arms control or strategic weapons. But the whole [situation] could change; . . . after the propaganda barrage, [with] . . . the possibility of influencing liberal elements or neutral elements in the United States and the West, exhausting all the means of splitting the U.S. from the European allies, and trying to work on the Congress through . . . influential persons in the United States, it could come to the point where the Soviets really would wish to have an agreement on SALT. At that point, they can . . . diminish the role of propaganda.

Czechoslovakia has a Department for a Special Propaganda that spearheads disinformation campaigns. Such departments exist throughout the Eastern bloc, and they have tasks both in peacetime and in wartime. Jan Sejna describes these tasks:

In Czechslovakia new steps were taken [in the late 1950s]. . . . In the military forces, Departments for Special Propaganda were set up, patterned on the Soviet model. In the Soviet Union the head of this department was General Shevchenko, and in Czechoslovakia it was Colonel Bucek. Operating by a decision of the Defense Council, these new departments answered to two supervisors—the chief of the Main Political Administration and the chief of the GRU, depending on whether the civilian or military intelligence was involved.

The main reason for the establishment of these new departments was the desire to prepare deception for both peacetime and wartime. The military enjoyed a lot of influence within industry and among the masses, and sought to draw upon these resources to help prepare deception.

The Soviet [counterpart department], the Main Administration for Special Propaganda, is divided into sections that cover every zone in the world. Of course, in Czechoslovakia we were mostly oriented toward NATO, including the United States and Canada. Officers in these departments would collect information on political parties, the military, the police, the justice system, individuals, etc., and would pass this information on to the highest party and military leaders each month.

This information would then be used in the preparation of disinformation regarding these organizations or individuals, for use in peacetime or saved for wartime. This involved secret printing systems, mobile printing systems, radio and television, and pamphlets to be dropped. There were even lists of persons in the NATO countries, primarily West Germany, to be executed by Field Courts in the event of war. . . . The party must have propaganda ready to explain . . . why it was necessary to execute (such persons]. . . . Czechoslovakia . . . had twelve [officers] studying the United States and Canada. They were in Moscow, officially [attached] to the Military Political Academy. They analyzed this information and some they used in peacetime against leadership parties or opposition parties. They prepared for wartime or revolutionary situations to be ready in case the war starts. . . .

Sejna stresses the importance of semantics in Soviet operations:

Within the [Warsaw Pact] long-term strategic plan, there was a subheading called Political Organizational Work. No communist agency can ever bear the title Department of Disinformation, because in the communist lexicon disinformation and deception are crimes which only the capitalists practice. What Political Organizational Work meant was that there were instruments available that could help bring about the goals of the strategic plan, such as foreign communist Parties, propaganda, and disinformation.

Sending the Message Abroad

The mission of the party press is not so much to inform as to instruct. In other words, its objective is to ensure that communist cadres conform with the current party line. In that context, *Pravda* was not intended to be a newspaper in the Western sense, although it appears it has functioned, according to Hus, as a collection of marching orders in journalistic dress:

Czechoslovakia after 1968 would not deviate at all from Soviet policy. Czechoslovak leaders followed what they read in *Pravda* and heard from Soviet leaders. . . .

Naturally, the Soviet Union has not confined coordination and communication with its East European allies to *Pravda's* editorials. Hus describes some of the channels of communication between Moscow and the various East European decision-making institutions:

The officials involved in foreign policy formulation read *Pravda* very carefully. They also occasionally go to Moscow for instructions. There is, of course, coordination between the various intelligence services and, to a lesser extent, the International Departments. However, the Czechoslovak and Soviet foreign ministers would only meet once a year. When there is an international conference, then there is coordination between the deputy foreign ministers before each new phase of the conference. At such meetings the Soviet Union makes certain that everyone agrees ahead of time. Even on the issues of the United States and China the experts only meet once or twice a year. That is all the coordination there really is. . . . Gromyko informed Chnoupek of the Soviet position on important issues. He would set priorities. It was not a meeting to coordinate foreign policy on specific issues, as local situations changed. The Soviet Union expects that the Eastern Europeans will read *Pravda*. . . . Further coordination occurs at the level of Czechoslovak embassy officials in Moscow. Diplomats there meet regularly with the equivalent officials in the Soviet Foreign Ministry.

Semantic Plots

Naturally, Soviet operational directives are given in esoteric terms—at least to the unindoctrinated observer. Tone and special terminology are key ingredients in conveying effective instructions, which means that one can understand the direction of Soviet policy only by monitoring such communications over an extended period. Tadeusz Kucharski, speaking about the Czechoslovak crisis of 1968, notes:

> The Polish leadership actively paid attention to Moscow's line. Gomulka and Ulbricht played an active role in pursuing [Soviet] policy. They were clearly cooperating with Moscow. [Polish and East German] propaganda was clearly anti-Czechoslovak . . . as early as May [1968]. From that alone we suspected there would be an invasion.

Levchenko reports that at certain times a specific signal acts as a flag, informing those in the field that a new campaign is about to begin:

> Around the time when a major operation is planned against the Chinese, a cable will be sent quoting not only Marx and Lenin, but even Gorbachev. It will [indicate] what the Soviets want at that time [to be the] result of the operation. [Their precise operational goal may not be stated] during the training period before [a Soviet emissary] goes abroad, but [will be enunciated subsequently] in the context of a specific operation.

Soviet leaders comprehend the importance of terminology in political struggles. In part, they seek to influence Western perceptions through the repeated use of words and phrases calculated to tinge objective events with overtones sympathetic to the Soviet view of the world. This is a subtle, long-term process, but it can be effective. Tadeusz Kucharski illustrates the key technique:

> The propagandists are well trained. They know how to use words. . . . The Western press has bought some of these terms. Then half of the work is done. If the West accepts Soviet terminology, then Soviet objectives are already partially achieved. Persons talk about the white minority government in South Africa, but what about the minority government in Poland? It is such a small minority that it does not even constitute one percent of the population and yet it has been in power for almost forty years. Jaruzelski

will be in power as long as he lives. Also there is the Angolan [resistance] movement, but this is [ignored]. Many . . . in the press say that the U.S. should not undermine the legitimate government in Angola, but this government could not exist if it were not for Cuban troops. How can that be legitimate? Respect by the Western press for the government in power can aid the Soviet Union a great deal.

I received instructions to call specific movements the only legitimate movement. Those movements selected were Marxist-Leninist and had been selected by Moscow. All other movements were puppets and agents of the CIA. In Angola the only legitimate movement was the MPLA, a minority movement. In Zimbabwe it was ZAPU, also a minority movement. The MPLA prevailed, because of the Cubans. ZAPU failed because ZANU had a larger base, since its support came from the Shona tribe, while ZAPU's support came from the Ndebele.

General Sejna explains other terminology biases:

Already by the early 1960s, the Soviet Union decided to put terrorist groups into two categories. First, there are terrorists for progressive action, whom they do not call terrorists at all. They call them fighters for freedom, etc. They only call the right wing, the fascists in Italy, for example, terrorists.

Kucharski adds:

[Terminology was] designed by Moscow to give the impression that [whichever] progressive movement . . . had been chosen, [it] was a national movement that could incorporate different ethnic and religious groups, economic classes, women, etc. [In fact, that] movement was prepared to take and keep power according to the Soviet example.

Sejna recalls a briefing by Mikhail Suslov before the Consultative Committee of the Warsaw Pact, another channel of communication between the Soviet Union and its allies:

[In the early 1960s,] peaceful coexistence was just a deception. [It served to convince the rest of the world] that now communists wanted to get along with the West; that they no longer wanted to liquidate persons, that they wanted to be friendly, etc. When Suslov met with us two years later at a meeting of the Consultative Committee, he analyzed the situation for us and said that criticism of Stalin had been the best possible step, that it had worked better than they had expected. Of course, all of these men had been associates of Stalin's all their lives. It was no personal pleasure for them to denounce him, but it was part of the policy of deception. . . .

Special terminology may be used also to coordinate disparate facets of foreign policy. A state may be waging a proxy war against another state, but may wish to gloss over this fact, especially if it might be bad for business, as Kucharski points out:

> In order to maintain good relations with her, Portugal would not be specifically mentioned [in the context of anticolonialism in Angola or Mozambique]. Poland sold ships to Portugal, even though there were no relations between the two countries. At this time, they would not talk about "Portuguese imperialists" or "Portuguese colonialists;" they used the phrase "forces of imperialism and colonialism."

The USSR strives for terminological coordination. A single term or phrase is to be employed for a particular development everywhere at the same time. This can cause problems when an operational agency is not sufficiently informed of the nuances of the current line. Levchenko describes such an incident:

> I understood that the KGB *rezident* gets a cable [concerning a shift in policy affecting his area of operations] for his eyes only. He must decode this message himself and then destroy it. The main document that the rank and file sees is the annual plan for active measures. . . . This document shows, without any rhetoric, what [is planned. The officers on the spot] write this document for themselves, although it is approved by headquarters, where some changes are made. Usually, headquarters agrees with the basic sense of the plan, because the persons in the field know what the Soviet Union wants and because of the experience they have developed through their years of service.
>
> Probably the *rezident* gets a more general plan, but if it concerns a dramatic operation, then headquarters explains what they want. They know that it will be very difficult for the officer to implement a plan if he has no [comprehension] what it is for. One funny example I remember was during the campaign against the neutron bomb. Headquarters chose a nickname for the weapon that would appear humorous to the Japanese. They wanted to belittle the weapon. They did not explain this to the *rezidency,* which thought it was a joke. Therefore, nobody moved a finger to introduce this nickname. It was a mistake by headquarters. We also had absolutely no idea about how the neutron bomb was presented by the Soviet Union in Europe. This prevented us from applying the European case to [the line contained in] our instructions [for Japan].

Media

Stanislav Levchenko states that in some cases a certain amount of variation in the tone of Soviet media is allowed:

> In certain ways [the Soviet media] are operating separately from each other. However, they are subordinated to the same part of the Central Committee

[of the CPSU]. The language they use is different, and the authors are quite different. . . . They want them to sound a little bit different. That is why *New Times,* regardless of all kinds of idiocy, is a very unusual Soviet magazine. There is nothing that resembles it. *Novosti* does not have anything like it, while I know that *Novosti* does all kinds of things on radio and elsewhere that *New Times* would never do. [*New Times*] is a combination of the International and the International Information Departments' activities. It is well organized. There are persons who are responsible for each magazine or organization in both departments. They have everyday contact with them, as well as with the Secretariat of the Central Committee. They know what the hot issues are. . . .

There were . . . a few cases when they had to destroy almost two hundred thousand copies [of *New Times*), because that very day someone in [the] Central Committee would disapprove of an article. Actually, *New Times* is a very nervous publication, because of . . . its coordination with the International and International Information Departments. The role of the censors is minimal there: to be sure that [the periodical] never mentions Soviet military affairs or new types of weapons. But politically, the censor plays no role . . . because it is censorship by [the editors of *New Times*] and by the Central Committee. *New Times* is a large organization, with many high-ranking persons there.

If a senior officer, the deputy of Ponomarev for instance, says that an article was all right for yesterday but not today, then they destroy the whole issue. It is all Soviet propaganda, but the magazine is different from others. There are fewer polemics. It is the only Soviet magazine which publishes letters from foreign readers, ninety-nine percent of which I am sure they invent in the office. I would personally recommend to any student of Soviet [affairs] to read *New Times* regularly, because in many cases they think that they have rebuffed questions in a smart, convincing way, but it is really a childish affair. Yet it is important to understand the logic of Soviet propaganda. For instance, they have a couple of Jewish persons write vicious articles about Israel. One is Volski. He does not have an exit visa, because he is a Jew, but they keep him because he writes very fiery articles [denouncing Israel].

The journal *Problems of Peace and Socialism* communicates the CPSU Central Committee line to foreign communist parties. Most of these parties have little or no influence in their home countries, and are entirely dependent on the Soviet Union. Hus notes that there is little question as to whether they will go along with Kremlin policies:

Because [these parties] were only a minor part of the electorate in [their] countries, my task was quite simple. At one point or another, someone from each of these parties traveled to Prague, and I would meet with them. Almost all of these parties have a representative at *Problems of Peace and*

Socialism [*World Marxist Review*] in Prague. They would just inform me of the situation.

The American communists are probably [promoting peace issues and organizations] on their own. Persons like Gus Hall can travel to Moscow or anywhere in Eastern Europe whenever they want. They have a very good life, but to maintain it they mŭst be perceived to be important to Moscow. To achieve this they must follow Moscow's line. Therefore there is no real need for direct supervision by Moscow. Its views are being put forth anyway, without such direction. The International Department in Moscow expects and works with certain parties and movements to achieve foreign policy objectives. When these persons travel to Moscow they are received at a high level. . . . In this way they are given a general framework within which to act. I never heard anyone in Prague specifically tell the Americans what to do and I was never ordered to do so.

Stanislav Levchenko adds the following observations:

[*Problems of Peace and Socialism*] is the only available official guideline for foreign communist parties. . . . I read it regularly too. More or less everything is in conformity with Soviet policy, but sometimes I [would] run into a part of an article that is interesting. [It would typically have a] different form. It rarely [would be written by] only one person. [Such articles] are often written by teams from unrelated communist parties.[11] They are involved in obvious self-censorship, because if one tries to write something that contradicts Moscow's line, the other two or three comrades will prevent him. I think that these collective articles are reflections of certain problems they have there, among persons who are prominent representatives of their parties.

One must be able to distinguish between policy directives and information which is intended for deception. *Pravda* may be useful for discerning Soviet policy, but the Soviet leaders understand that all Soviet publications come under scrutiny in the West. This fact was a source of some amusement for Kucharski:

Some responsible scholars in the U.S. . . . analyzed the program of the congress of the Communist Party. They analyzed everything very seriously. This was ridiculous. The program is elaborated upon only to be published. What is published is not secret. . . . Actual activities to pursue Soviet objectives are very important and are not published. . . . The published program is propaganda that will feed off the wishful thinking of others. No one in the East would believe it, but serious Western scholars will see it as sincere expression of Soviet, Polish, or any other Eastern-bloc country's intentions.

---

[11] During the 1960s, there were instances in which an individual communist party (e.g., the Syrian CP) would publish a sharp dissent from CPSU policies in *Problems of Peace and Socialism*. However, this privilege was not extended to pro-Chinese parties.

Implementation

Once the general line has been promulgated, those responsible for implementing it go to work. For many, Jiri Pelikan explains, this means adapting general party instructions to their specific circumstances, then passing them further down the chain of command:

> As I was nominated by the Politburo [to be director general of Czechoslovak television], I was responsible to the Politburo, and I was, I would say, the communist who was in charge to develop or to apply the line of the party in the field of television. . .
>
> For example, when I was at the congress of the [Czechoslovak] Communist Party, [there] was no real discussion of real decision, but the report of the general secretary was approved. So, I had to read this report very carefully and to take notes and to establish from this what were the probable consequences for the general work of television. For example, [the general secretary] said we have now the problem to convince the peasants about the advantages of the cooperatives. So . . . now we have to . . . show [on the news] examples of those cooperatives which are functioning well. . . .
>
> [From time to time, I convened] my collaborators, sometimes all collaborators, which [meant] several thousand [persons]; twice a year we had plenary sessions. . . . [I met in] weekly sessions [with] the heads of the respective departments, [such as] the heads of news, of drama, of the music program, of the youth and so on, I explained . . . the consequences [of directives] from the Central Committee or from the congress of the party. [I told them to emphasize one aspect or delete another. They might make suggestions concerning implementation and then they would sit with their production teams to discuss how to translate my direction into a final product. Sometimes they would elaborate upon the general directives. We had annual, monthly and weekly plans. Much depended] on my own application of the [party's] instructions. . . .
>
> There are some weekly [deliberations] in the Central Committee . . . [such as when] the Politburo changed the [education] system so that the secondary schools [would] be opened to everybody. . . . So I discussed, for example, the consequences with the head of the school department—how this should [be made] known, or [how to] prepare the public . . . for these changes. . . . [Money was outside my competence;] we had a budget, and sometimes the budget was very low, especially foreign currency. If . . . for example, [I was told that there would be an] important meeting with the prime minister of India and the Politburo was interested, . . . [I would respond], "Okay, we can send two or three persons to India [for] . . . reportage about India, but for this we need a special allowance in foreign currency." [This would be discussed then] in the Central Committee, and if told there was agreement, [I would write] a letter to the minister of finance, saying that we have approval and he [would give] us the necessary money.

For some propagandists the task is to present the line authorized for foreign visitors, especially journalists and academicians. The point is to give them the impression that they are getting an inside story. Upon returning home, Galina Orionova points out, such visitors relate the line they heard in the Soviet Union with greater authority, thereby becoming unwitting extensions of the propaganda network.

Q: Is it an aim of the people at the institute [for the USA and Canada] to play on the vanity of foreign academics?

Orionova: Oh yes. Absolutely. But it is not only vanity. On returning to the U.S. [such visitors] can claim that though [they] may not have brought back anything concrete, [they have] the feeling that the Soviets have confided in them. . . . [I]t will always work, and you will never stop it. That is why it was so successful, except for 1980, when there were only four or five visits to the institute as a result of Afghanistan. It is the Soviet view that many persons on the right are more important than others on the extreme left, who may not be very significant anyway.

Orionova gives an example:

[When dealing with] an entire Japanese delegation or a group of, say, American senators . . . and you know that there will be some difficult questions on the agenda, all those [from the institute who will be meeting them are coached] to give a unified answer as to why the USSR [follows] a particular [policy]. During the Carter administration [the emphasis] was [on] the neutron bomb. [Then] it was Afghanistan, and now . . . I believe it is that the Soviet Union cannot cope with the Vietnamese, which is partially the truth. . . . I don't want this to apply to all members of the institute, because you must always keep in mind that there is a group of persons on the level of Trofimenko and several others, [sent to] attend conferences [abroad], and it is that part of the delegation [which has primary] responsibility for answering questions. This group will go to a particular section of the [CPSU Central Committee International Department] and get instructions on how they should deal with a certain sort of question. The entire delegation, however, as a rule, goes for a one to one-and-a-half hour briefing at the Foreign Ministry, to get a more general instruction on how to deal with difficult questions.

The USSR has tried to leave little to chance in contacts with Western delegations and individual visitors. Gregory's experience with the Union of Journalists indicates that there were a conscious effort to supplement the usual channels of propaganda through individual contacts. In 1957, Gregory officially left the KGB to become the deputy general secretary of the newly created Union of Journalists. He was asked why was the organization created:

Gregory: It was the decision of the Central Committee of the CPSU to devote more attention to our relations with foreign journalists. There was an International Organization of Journalists [IOJ], but in 1955 or 1956 it was divided; it had headquarters in Prague and we needed a UJ in order to have relatons with the IOJ. That was an institutional reason but the main reason was to use the UJ to spread our propaganda and counterpropaganda. This meant that we would have to invite foreign delegations. *Pravda,* the party newspaper, or *Izvestia,* the government newspaper, could not do this—the UJ could.

Although less important, another reason was the desire to organize some courses for Soviet journalists. This was an internal problem; we wanted to educate them so they could better communicate the decisions [of the Central Committee] to the Soviet people. The most important reason was to organize an international department within the UJ that could be used effectively by the KGB, both the First and the Second Chief Directorates.

Q: What was the institutional relationship between the UJ and Ponomarev's International Department [of the CPSU Central Committee]?

Gregory: We worked under the supervision of two departments of the Central Committee. First, the Department of Agitation and Propaganda [Agitprop] and the ID. The former supervised the internal operations and the latter supervised foreign operations. The UJ was divided into external and internal sections; I worked in the former. I had daily contact with the ID. We would discuss what kind of delegates we would like to see in Moscow, prepare the plan for receiving delegations, and so on. All my work was closely coordinated with the ID.

[Depending] on the situation, I would consult with the appropriate geographical section. Proposals would be made for the next year to the ID.

Communications with the Allies

Daily Directives and Supervision

The day-to-day business of communication with the Soviet Union's allies is carried out in a more direct manner. Specific and urgent directives cannot be sent through regular channels. This would be too slow and, moreover, given the scope of Soviet intervention in allied operations, it would be impractical. Instead, each Soviet party organization or state agency has links to the corresponding institution in every allied country. Michael Checinski describes the mechanisms whereby Moscow communicates various guidelines to its allies:

There is a very complicated system of channels. First, there are connections between the Soviet party and the East [European parties]. Each [Soviet] department has its counterpart in Poland. So they are always in touch about issues of concern, say, [to] the International Department of the Soviet Central Committee and the International Department of the Polish Central Committee. This is why they build the party structures almost identically.

And this makes communication easier. On very important issues, communication can also be carried out indirectly; it could also run through the general secretary. The Soviets can also use their agents within each of the departments, so if there is some issue that is particularly important to them, they can use these hidden channels to get what they want. So one channel is direct, the other is secret.

The KGB has its own unofficial channel. The Soviet embassy has its hand in everything that is going on in the country. Reporting to the embassy is like reporting to the minister of foreign affairs. The second [channel] is the [International] Department in the Central Committee, the third is the secret channel of the KGB. So they are writing three different reports and sometimes one doesn't know about the other.

You also have a very important [direct official] channel between the KGB and the security organs of the particular country. In Poland, it is the Ministry for Internal Affairs.

Michael Checinski further notes another level of communication:

Of course, [Poland and the USSR] have ministry-to-ministry [communications]. They are not able to make decisions, but they have links. Both are impotent; if they want to make a decision they go to the Central Committee.

Eden Pastora Gomez reflects on the mode of communication between the Soviet Union and the Sandinista regime in Nicaragua:

The [channels of communication] are very formally organized. The military talk with the military, the politicians with the politicians, the economists with the economists. All the political matters were . . . discussed between the [Sandinista] national [directors] and whoever their Soviet counterparts were.

Of course, the channels are not always so well defined. Zdzislaw Rurarz states that members of the Soviet decision-making hierarchy would on occasion communicate with their opposite members in Poland, without the knowledge of General Secretary Edward Gierek:

Coordination with the Soviet party takes place at the level of at least a deputy head of the [Central Committee] department, sometimes even without the knowledge of his superiors. Gierek, head of the party, for instance, was unaware of how frequently his subordinates and his chiefs of department were visiting Moscow or hosting their Soviet counterparts. There was a constant shuttle between the two capitals, not to mention the active role of the Soviet embassy.

The flow of instructions is always one-way, according to Michael Voslensky.

Q: Why was it necessary to subdivide [the original International Department]? Was it a question of overwork, [having to handle] relations with parties in power and relations with parties not in power?

Voslensky: These problems are actually quite different. The parties in power are semi-colonies of the Soviet Union; they are more or less marionettes, with the exception of China. China was nevertheless handled by the Ponomarev [International] department, not this young department [for liaison with Communist and Workers' Parties of Socialist Countries]. . . .

In 1957, when this other department was created, the China desk moved there, but there also existed a Chinese or Far Eastern desk under Ponomarev. At that time I think Ponomarev was more important [with respect to China] than Rusakov [who was the head of the new department. That new department was not really dealing with international affairs]: To talk to the Czechs, this is not foreign policy; it's administration.

Before Khrushchev rose to power, the Soviet ambassadors to client-states were, as General Sejna says, watchdogs for their superiors in the Soviet Ministry of Foreign Affairs and other institutions in Moscow:

The Soviet ambassadors were required to receive a copy of every piece of paper that was to come before the . . . Politburo [of the country to which they were accredited]. It was as though the Soviet ambassador was a part of the Czechoslovak Politburo. He received everything to be dealt with on the Politburo's agenda. When Khrushchev assumed control, he stopped this practice, but the Soviet ambassadors continue to be fully informed on what is taking place at the Politburo level [in Prague]. [The Soviet leaders] always have their own agents and their own means of finding things out.

On matters of security, Soviet control mechanisms are even stricter. Without the approval of the Kremlin, Jan Sejna states, the Czechoslovak Defense Council would not even consider an agenda item:

Every document presented to the Defense Council must have two important paragraphs. First of all is the issue of whether the Soviet Union was consulted on the matter in question. If not, the [Czechoslovak] Defense Council would not proceed on that item. The second key paragraph must say that "The Defense Council recommends to Comrade Novotny (or Husak) that information be conveyed to the Politburo" on whatever the decision was. If this paragraph is not present, then the matter is [kept] secret from the Politburo.

When the party is in danger of being compromised, Jan Sejna tells us, the party leadership must authorize actions of the intelligence services:

[T]he party must give its approval for any members of the party newspapers (*Pravda, Rude Pravo*) [to work] as agents abroad. KGB or GRU authorization alone is insufficient since the party could be compromised. Also, when the possibility of a scandal exists, top party approval is required. When Czechoslovak agents recruited [a leading Indian statesman], for example, Defense Council approval had to be given.

Jan Sejna also indicates the route the [annual] Intelligence Plan of Czechoslovakia had to follow when he was in a position to know, as secretary of the Czechoslovak Defense Council:

> [T]he Intelligence Plan must go to the Soviet Union before it can go to the [Czechoslovak] Defense Council. Before we could even prepare the plan, we had to go to the Soviet Union, where they told us what it was that they wanted from each Eastern European intelligence service. Furthermore, GRU and KGB advisors were on the spot every day and they would observe exactly how Soviet instructions were implemented in Czechoslovakia, Poland, and the other satellites. There was very little that we could do without Soviet knowledge or approval.
>
> . . . [I]dentification of objectives [in the intelligence report] must indicate the concurring guidance of the Soviet Union. Soviet approval must be there.

With regard to security, the Soviet Union is elusive not only vis-à-vis adversary governments, but also vis-à-vis its allies. When a crisis arises, the strength of the Soviet system is put to the test. Such a crisis occurred in 1968, when the Warsaw Pact forces invaded Czechoslovakia. Hus contends that the crisis came to a head partly because of a communications failure:

> The Soviet leadership tried for a long time to communicate to the Czechoslovaks that they should go no further. . . . That the whole Soviet Politburo went to Cierna showed not only that they were not yet decided over whether to invade, but that they were going to great [lengths] to [avoid] such an invasion. They were trying to show the Czechoslovak leadership how serious they were, but instead the Czechoslovak leaders felt that this was the final proof that there would not be an invasion. The price of the invasion was heavy for the Soviet Union. International communism is dead. . . .
>
> Brezhnev and Dubcek had both agreed to curtail attacks on [each] other's country in the press. When Dubcek tried, Czechoslovak press sources, such as *Literarni Listy,* complained of censorship and immediately launched another attack against the Soviet Union. To the Soviet leadership it looked as if Dubcek was either not in control or not carrying out his promise. If the Politburo had not invaded and the situation [had become] worse, several people [in Moscow] would have lost power.

When the Warsaw Pact invasion of Czechoslovakia was set into motion in August of 1968, some of the participants did not even know they were engaged in hostilities. Zdzislaw Rurarz explains:

I checked with military intelligence, and found that even they had not been informed in advance. What had happened was that the order came from Marshal Yakubovsky to the operational divisions from the Silesian military district as though it were only an exercise. When the Polish parachutists landed in Czechoslovakia and took one military compound, they thought it was just a war game. Only later did they realize it was an intervention.

Stanislav Levchenko says that the invasion showed the skill of the Soviet military in rapid mobilization and swift, unobtrusive troop movement. However, the low level of awareness among the troops regarding the objective for which they were being deployed indicates that Soviet military planners had doubts concerning the reliability of their soldiers:

I was in the International Department with one of the fronts at that time. They kept the plan very secret. The presence of a few thousand Soviet tanks in the Ukraine cannot be kept secret, but Czechoslovakia never knew. The Soviet Union was smart. Troops were not on the border of Czechoslovakia; they were somewhere around Kiev. Mobilization was [undertaken] as a part of constant maneuvers. From Kiev they made a forced march under the cover of night. It was quite devious. I strongly doubt that too many persons knew of it. . . If army units had been told that they were going to Czechoslovakia to take over, some probably would have been sympathetic to the Czechoslovak cause. Many probably would have hesitated to shoot, if they had known a few days in advance and had some time to digest it. It was not really our of secrecy that the troops were not told, rather it was that the USSR wanted to avoid conflict within the Soviet [units].

In Czechoslovakia, secrecy aided the Soviets. In Angola, however, it did not. A Soviet-sponsored coup attempt against the socialist leader of Angola, Agostinho Neto, by another Angolan party member, Nito Alves, failed because the Soviet leaders did not inform their principal surrogates in Angola, the Cubans. Tadeusz Kucharski was on the spot:

[The Soviet-sponsored coup against Neto] was not coordinated with the Cubans and they put a stop to the coup, because they did not know of the Soviet sponsorship. For a few hours, Alves was in control of the radio station in Luanda, until the Cuban troops intervened on the side of Neto. This was a case of a lack of coordination between the KGB, the Soviet ambassador, and the Cubans. Because the coup could prove to be a major embarrassment for the Soviet leadership, they neglected to inform the Cubans. Their love for secrecy was so great that only Nito Alves and his group knew of it. After a few hours, Castro gave orders for the Cuban troops to help Neto and a half hour later the coup attempt was over, because there was no counterbalance to the Cuban troops in Angola.[12]

---

[12] For further details, see the section on Shaping the Agenda for Decisions in International Affairs in chapter 4.

Kucharski further notes the causes and consequences of the Soviet failure in Luanda:

> The Soviet failure resulted from two things: secrecy and over-centralization. Coordination is always conducted at the level of the center, and not at the local level. Decisions are always made in Moscow or Havana. There was no coordination in place. There is also a great deal of suspicion within the socialist camp. This was present in Angola, for example, between the Soviet and Cuban communities.
>
> . . . [The Polish embassy was] caught by surprise. We did not know anything about the coup ahead of time. General Paszkowski was in close contact with the Cubans. He coordinated more closely with the Cuban ambassador and military officers than with the Soviet ambassador. Perhaps this was because the commander of the Cuban force in Angola, Tomasiewicz, was of Polish origin.

Despite such occasional failures, communications at the level of implementation, for the most part, are handled well between the Soviet Union and its allies. Thousands of routine decisions and directives are transmitted daily, and, while the working relationship may not be close, it *is* effective. However, the system of communication between the Soviet Union and its allies does not handle crises well. In such situations, control passes directly to the Kremlin, and the matter is resolved at the top of the power structure. The fact that Moscow can take control keeps the Soviet satellites in orbit, and prevents them from failing to follow the stream of directives from the center.

Esoteric Communications

Introduction

The founders of the Soviet Union understood the value of words better than most of their contemporaries. Particularly Lenin and Stalin realized that language was "an instrument of struggle."[13] It can be used directly for *exoteric* communications, such as in the *Communist Manifesto,* whose authors postulated complete frankness: "Communists disdain to conceal their views and aims. They openly declare their ends can be attained only by forcible overthrow of all existing social conditions."[14] But as soon as the Bolsheviks

---

[13] See the collection of articles on language by J.V. Stalin, as they appeared in *Pravda* between 20 June and 2 August 1950, and were published in the USSR as a pamphlet in 1954; currently available as Marxism and Problems of Linguistics (Peking: Foreign Language Press, 1972), p. 23.

[14] Karl Marx and Friedrich Engels, *Manifesto of the Communist Party* (Peking: Foreign Language Press, 1975), p. 77.

established themselves in power, openness gave way gradually to indirection or secrecy. This chapter focuses on the indirect, *esoteric* use of language and extra-linguistic means of communication by the Soviet and East European elites.

Why, it may be asked, does the top leadership in the Soviet Union not communicate openly with its subordinates throughout the country? As William Griffith has demonstrated,[15] esoteric communications have been characteristic of all closed societies. Historically, what often presented itself as a scholastic debate (religious or secular) in reality involved concrete power interests, with political and economic results. But ideologically oriented societies, whether religious or secular, must hide the existence of conflict among their leaders since conflict seems incompatible with the myth that the state is run either on the basis of an non-improvable divine revelation or in such a scientific manner that no rational person could manage it any other way.

Yet, closed societies, as Franz Neumann demonstrated in his analysis of the Third Reich in *Behemoth,* are plagued by factional struggles, which are fought out in secrecy. This phenomenon is not at all confined to the Soviet orbit. However, the absence of a normally functioning, open society, with regularly scheduled elections, a legal opposition, a free press, and legally operating interest groups, makes factionalism a permanent attribute of the political system in Moscow and Eastern Europe. Members of various factions within the top elite must communicate with their clients among the sub-elite; at the same time, they must maintain the required degree of secrecy. (For an analysis of the phenomenon of factionalism, see the section of Factions in chapter 1.) Hence, esoteric communication.

Pictorial Communication

This form of communication may but does not have to involve the use of language. For instance, the order in which Soviet, Eastern European or Cuban leaders appear in ritual appearances is a time-honored and easily ascertainable esoteric signal. The same applies to the seating order during party congresses, or Supreme Soviet meetings. Photographs of the Kremlin leaders standing in ceremonial order on top of Lenin's mausoleum are published after every May Day and October Revolution parade, a fact which by itself indicates that this contains an important message for the guidance of the sub-elites around the country and in the Warsaw Pact countries. Virtually nothing is left to chance; the diplomatic protocol is strictly adhered to and so are all party

---

[15] William E. Griffith, *Communist Esoteric Communications: Explication de Texte* (Cambridge, MA: M.I.T. Press, 1967).

and state-related rituals. Stanislav Levchenko confirms the significance of studying esoteric signals:

> I never cease to be surprised by the number of rituals in the Soviet Politburo. It is very important to see who walks first and second.

Of course, some of these signals may be so esoteric that an outsider may not be able to interpret their true meaning. However, as indicated above, the need for communication from the apex of power to the sub-elite is real. Therefore, the signals must not be totally arcane since they could miss their intended targets. According to Levchenko, a pictorial analysis of leading Soviet periodicals, that is, watching who appears where, next to whom, and who does not appear at all, is part of the ordinary chores of officials pursuing their careers:

> If one is in the position of an important cadre and wants to ensure his own future, he will pay careful attention to who is going up and who is coming down. By the mere [sequence] of where people are, one can see who is friendly or not so friendly to number one. . . . If someone sees Tikhonov take one step back, then they might assume that he is in ill health and will die soon. There will be immediate speculation.

Since the order in which the leaders appear is so important, it would make sense to assume that whoever determines that order is powerful. But the Soviet system is not simple and facile assumptions of one kind or another usually do not pay. It seems that the order in which individual leaders line up on the mausoleum is determined by the general secretary who, however, has to consult with other powerful personalities:

> It is not as if the [general secretary] says, "Tomorrow, Mr. Tikhonov, you will be the fourth." That may be the way he finally [puts it to] him, but first he must make phone calls to some of his buddies on the Politburo and explain why he wants to do this.

But exactly how is it done? Does the general secretary consult with eight or nine individuals in order to change the standing of two or three members of the elite? Could anyone be asked to accept his own demotion? Stanislav Levchenko admits that this remains unclear:

> The question here is, who is the person in charge of rituals? I do not know.

General Sejna, relying upon his experience within the Czechoslovak system as well as on his frequent trips to the Soviet Union, agrees with Levchenko that such decisions are not taken unilaterally but reached at the highest level. Can a Politburo member be told: "Well, you've been number two, but from now on you'll be number four"?

Only the general secretary and the secretaries of the Central Committee can do that. That is, Gorbachev could do it, but he must first have the agreement of the party secretaries.

Surely such a demotion would be an emotionally wrenching experience, and a setback one would have an impulse to resist. Yet Michael Voslensky notes that a person being demoted has an interest in complying with reality. When one's ranking changes from fourth to sixth on the mausoleum during a parade, just how is that done? And why does the demoted individual accept his new ranking?

Do not underestimate the elasticity of these people. . . . [The person being demoted] understands. Maybe his good friend will say to him, "You [stood in the place] where the chairman of the Council of Ministers normally stands" or "You [stood in the place] where the second secretary stands." He understands [that these are messages to tell him that it would be no longer appropriate for him to occupy such exalted spots]. If he insists [on continuing to appear in the previous order of rank] then he'll have difficulties. . . . He tried. He has more to gain by going back to the sixth place than by disappearing from the mausoleum.

Reading the mausoleum signals, then, can provide a great deal of insight into changes in the power structure of the Soviet Politburo. Client states have adopted this practice. Tadeusz Kucharski confirms that strict adherence to the protocol and signals-watching spread also to Angola:

Yes, Angola followed the example of the whole Soviet bloc. One's importance was determined by where one stood [on the dais]. If someone's position changed, then [his] power had changed.

Most witnesses agree that the order in which top leaders appear is significant. Yet Arkady N. Shevchenko points out that there are definite limits to using qualitative content analysis techniques to judge relative power.

Shevchenko: [I]t is my view that in some other cases, particularly if you are talking about candidate members [of the Politburo] and the order in which they stand on the mausoleum, it could be a mixture which is not of great significance.

Q: I have seen some changes back and forth [as far as lesser leaders are concerned] within the same month.

Shevchenko: In my personal opionion, [the candidate members] don't decide and don't attach very great importance to the order, at least after the people who are at the very top. Their position is more or less defined. It's clear to everybody that the order should be for the first four or five; but as to the order after that, I would caution people who study such things not to jump to the conclusion that something happened because maybe Aliyev was standing [in one position] in November, and then next May or some other time he moved a little bit. You know, it might even be the case that they simply would like to talk with each other. I know that on some occasions Gromyko told me that he wanted to talk with someone. So he can choose with whom he would like to stand. Therefore, changes in the order can sometimes take place just for practical reasons.

It would appear, therefore, that while significant changes in the power structure among the very top leaders would generally be reflected in the order in which they stand on the mausoleum, at lower levels this does not have to be the case. In some instances, such as when meeting with a delegation from another country, the host agency may inform the guests of the seating (or standing) order. Of course, this does not mean that the agency concerned necessarily determined that order.

When Sejna arrived in the Kremlin with a Czechoslovak delegation, it was his impression that the seating order had been arranged by the KGB, since he was aware of a previous instance, in which a Czechoslovak delegation coming to visit Khrushchev had been shown to their places by KGB officers. Of course, it seems unlikely that the KGB had prepared the seating order for the delegation without consulting the appropriate, and so far unidentified, entities of the CPSU Central Committee. But, says Sejna, "the specific order of appearance [was] handled by the KGB."

Based on his first-hand experience, in case of a visit to the Kremlin by a fraternal party, it is the Soviet side that determines the order in which the guests will be received:

> The Soviets . . . will say to the minister precisely where to stand and they will do the same with the deputy secretaries of the party. When we were to be received by Khrushchev, I was told to stand next to last.

The number of times one appears in photographs—whether actually present when the picture was taken or not—also provides an important signal. Goshu Wolde, formerly the Ethiopian foreign minister, notes that Gorbachev, a rising star, was not given ample opportunities for visibility during the periods before and after his patron, Andropov, was in power:

> The most interesting point is that when either Brezhnev or Chernenko was in power, Mr. Gorbachev's presence was not very visible.

Occasionally, there are public relations drawbacks to appearing in every photograph, as Levchenko points out:

I want to caution you that when you see Soviet newspapers with all of the leadership gathered to see someone off, some of the faces have been inserted afterwards. They face a strange situation with their own people in the Soviet Union. Quite a few people started to write to Soviet newspapers asking "when do [our] leaders work, if they are all going back and forth to the airport all the time?" Nothing was explained and it continues [in this way]. Actually they aggravated the issue by adding faces [after the fact].

A photograph appearing in a publication communicates more than its contents alone. The size and location of photos in the newspaper also are important signals. Jan Sejna notes contrasting treatments of transfer of power in recent Soviet history:

When Andropov was made head of the Soviet party, for example, the first page of *Pravda* bore his picture, along with an account of the decision of the party, the recommendations for his accession, and his speech. It was the same thing for Chernenko when he came to power, but when Gorbachev was made general secretary, his picture was only in the lower corner [of the front page]. The party decision was the major headline and his speech was on the third page. Whoever does not understand the system will not notice anything odd. For those who understand the system, however, it is apparents that the party bureaucrats are running the show. Gorbachev is not in complete control, and he cannot be until the party congress.[16] Only at the party congress will he have the chance to bring the party under his sway. Today [1985] he stands a long way from full power.[17]

The Written Word

The order of appearance in official ceremonies and other occasions, such as cultural events, is an important tool of communication between the elite and its clients. But for day-to-day guidance regarding the correlation of forces among the top political elite, members of the sub-elite in Soviet-style countries must look to the printed text. The unexpressed, or the hidden message, can be vitally relevant. Vladimir Kostov, referring to Bulgaria states:

It is important to read between the lines for somebody who wants to understand. For a person who wants to move up in his career, it is important.

Kostov also stresses the importance of the order in which names appear in the official press, and gives us some insight into the process whereby this

---

[16] The interview with Gen. Jan Sejna preceded the 27th CPSU Congress of 1986.

[17] For a similar analysis, see Zhores A. Medvedev, *Gorbachev* (New York: W.W. Norton & Co., 1986), pp. 3–21.

was communicated in Bulgaria. For instance, if an individual used to appear in the third place, but now is supposed to be listed as number five, who conveys this to the official media, and how?

> There is a very strict order on the subject. The secretary of the Central Committee, who is responsible for the information, tells the general director of the Bulgarian press agency, who is usually a member of the Central Committee itself, what the order is. . . . And everybody understands. Sometimes it happens that the radio or a particular newspaper makes a mistake. It is seldom, but it sometimes happens. If this mistake is not repeated, it means that it was a mistake and the person who is guilty will be punished. If, however, there is some change in the order, it means that the secretary of the Central Committee for Information has directed it. This secretary is the unofficial spokesman for the party leadership. It is absolutely impossible for him to do the changes on his own.

Vladimir Kostov further confirms that such changes are done impersonally. One is not told that an individual is no longer in second place; one simply receives a new list. Tadeusz Kucharski also corroborates that every effort is made by the media to avoid errors regarding the order in which names of leaders appear. Journalists in the Soviet bloc know that they must take their instructions seriously:

> In order to know who is more important, it is necessary to look at the newspapers. They will never make an error, [since] the order of names in the paper is done very carefully. The order in which the leadership appears in articles or photographs directly corresponds to their power.

While lists are important, they cannot be relied upon to tell the sub-elite *why* a certain change has taken place. In order to elicit such aspects one must take into account word choice, phrasing, tone and many other intangibles, the meaning of which can only be discerned as a result of long familiarity with the topics, personalities and style of the publication in question. Peter Deriabin shows how such communication was handled in the struggle between Beria and Abakumov during the late 1940s:

> Abakumov became minister of state security no later than April 1946. In October or November of 1946 (the signed letter was dated February 1, 1947), he issued an order in the form of a long letter describing what he found out about the old NKGB. The letter started with the words "While taking over the NKGB, the former People's Commissariat of State Security, it was discovered that the old leadership, Merkulov, the former people's commissar of state security, and their operational personnel forgot about the anti-Soviet elements: the old Trotskyites, Bukharinites, and other counterrevolutionary elements." The letter cited the example of Bukharin's sister

who lived near Moscow but was not discovered until the present leadership of the MGB took over. The letter ended with a statement, "according to the decision of *instantsiva* [higher authority, usually meaning Stalin] the following measures should be taken: review of all the files of the Trotskyites, Bukharinites, nationalist groups, and all other counterrevolutionary elements to evaluate the possibility of discovering active agent networks through surveillance and other means."

The most interesting aspect to the letter was the implied criticism of Beria. The tone of the letter suggested that it was done with Stalin's approval and the criticism seemed to go beyond Merkulov himself. We were surprised at the time how the letter seemed to be directed against Beria even though he was not mentioned by name. . . . As I mentioned before, Beria also was gradually cut out of the information flow. Abakumov of the head of the directorate would say a report was to go to all addresses except "Number Two." Everyone knew that this meant excluding Beria but his name was not repeated because it could be spread around and Beria was still a Politburo member; it does not matter who your boss is, you still have to respect a man on the Politburo.

Jan Sejna supplies another example:

To discern true splits in the leadership it is necessary to read between the lines. Jiri Hendrych,[18] for example, was Novotny's protégé and was originally elected to the Czechoslovak party Central Committee over the objections of some that the had in the past worked with Slansky. Only Novotny's insistence got Hendrych into the Central Committee and further. Later on Hendrych began to realize that Novotny was in trouble and that it would be only a matter of time before he would be finished off. Therefore, as early as two years before the Prague Spring, he began to work against Novotny. Of course he did not just stand up and say, "Novotny must go." He was far more clever than that. Instead, he repeatedly referred to Novotny in his speeches only when referring to a problem. When he had to go before a group of workers to tell them "You must work harder and produce more," he would not fail to add "as Comrade Novotny has always stressed." Or, "a Comrade Novotny insists, we must accept the increase in the price of food." Novotny was incapable of seeing that Hendrych was making a fool of him.

Sejna offers a more contemporary illustration:

To understand what is really going on one must pay attention to details. For example, recently the Soviet commentator, Bovin, referred on Soviet televi-

---

[18] Jiri Hendrych was a life-long functionary of the Czechoslovak Communist Party. As secretary of the Central Committee, Hendrych was considered by many as the second most powerful man in Prague during the 1960s. His career was brought to an end in the Prague Spring in 1968.

sion to the upcoming Geneva summit with the United States as well as to the meeting with the French in Paris, but he did not say one word about Gorbachev. This should show the trained observer that there is still substantial opposition to Gorbachev within the Soviet *apparat,* and that it is not yet clear how long he will be able to remain in power. Intrigue is a big part of the game, and those who know what is happening quickest will have the avantage over those in the system who do not.

Subtle signals are often the most effective. To attack someone openly not only jeopardizes the position of the attacker by unmasking his intentions, but also contributes to the possibility of creating turmoil among the sub-elites. For example, it would be unwise to announce openly that a purge was about to commence; however, the same message could be communicated cryptically and without the attendant troubles. Sejna further illustrates how this can be done:

> [J]ust recently I saw that the Czechoslovak Politburo sent a letter to the regional party leaders calling for renewed efforts to combat alcoholism and to restore discipline. Well that means that a new purge is going on, although its extent is hard to gauge. Now if the party wants to dismiss someone, they just accuse him of being an alcoholic or of having bad discipline.

In some cases even the presence of a single word can be a strong signal. A. Piatigorsky says that "[i]n party language, there is nothing more terrible than the term 'superfluous.' It is worse than 'wrong.' " For the work or even office of a party member to be termed "superfluous" is tantamount to two-weeks notice.

In attempting to understand relationships between the Soviet Union and its client states, analysts for many years could count on two dates, May and November, when the Soviet leaders issue official slogans which may indicate changes in the relationships between the USSR and other countries. These slogans until the late 1960s signalled the direction of Soviet foreign policy to leaders in the countries mentioned (or omitted), as well as to leaders of other states, communist parties and other political groups, and to Soviet diplomats, advisers and operatives inside the countries concerned. At the same time, analysts could judge which elements of the Soviet leadership were rising and which were becoming less influential. Stiller notes:

> [T]he slogans were carried in the Soviet newspapers on a daily basis, and every Soviet embassy had "information sessions" once or twice monthly— essentially briefing the personnel, based on Soviet newspapers. This ensures that everyone will read the Soviet newspapers, as well as [ensuring] that all the diplomats understand what the current line is and begin thinking in those terms.

Sloganeering then is part of the regular transmission of the party line, a part of the propaganda function as mentioned in the previous chapter. Changes in slogans can be reliable indicators of future policy shifts. For example, those who followed the Soviet war in Afghanistan saw important changes in the offing when "fraternal greetings" to Afghanistan disappeared from the slogan list in May 1987. Policy changes towards Afghanistan and the Afghan war became explicit shortly thereafter. This was no coincidence.

Who prepares the list of slogans? The answer from the interviewees is ambiguous, but it appears that the CPSU Central Committee's International Deparment may be the institution responsible for the list of slogans. Stiller speculates:

> The Ministry of Foreign Affairs would not have been doing this. I can only speculate that the slogans were most likely conceived by the International Department.

The slogans issued since 1967 have been far fewer in number, and less specific. Arkady Shevchenko explains why:

> It has always been debated from two points of view. One is that some of the countries friendly to the Soviet Union change their policy suddenly and often even their leadership, e.g., in a military coup. There were a lot of [discussions] between the Foreign Ministry and the International Department, asking, "Should we be so detailed?" It looked very awkward when in May [a particular state is treated as] a very friendly country, given brotherly salutes, and then in November, [it] disappears from the list. This reason had very little to do, really, with policy. It just was a consideration that if you go too much into details, all these shifts in emphasis and changes in relations with these countries make it very noticeable when [Soviet leaders] don't want to use such warm words to describe these countries.
>
> Also, the people in the Foreign Ministry were saying that these slogans were becoming known in the [countries concerned]. This has some consequences. You can make an ambiguous statement and everybody will forget about it. But when they carry one sentence, which is easy to understand in May but [do not include it] in November [it can cause friction with the country or movement with which the slogan deals, and] this is one of the essential reasons why they don't want [slogans to be] too specific.

In essence, this sort of communication was no longer "esoteric," and, paradoxically, had lost its communicative value as a consequence. Monitoring the shifts in foreign relations became more complex as the slogans increased in number during the early 1960s. Michael Voslensky notes that the CPSU Central Committee's International Department devoted a great deal of attention to slogans:

They work on this steadily throughout the year. It's their day-to-day job.

Unlike watching photographs and reading slogans, which appear regularly but infrequently, day-to-day signalling takes other forms. The reader may be more familiar with the concept of esoteric communication in this guise, often referred to as "diplomatic language." Whatever one calls it, the process is the same, namely, to communicate an attitude to a friend or foe without stating it in so many words. Consider Shevchenko's comment on the implications of an official Soviet greeting to Libyan leader Muamar Qaddafi:

> I think that some of the things going on with Libya and Qaddafi gave credence to those who think the Soviet Union should have a more balanced policy in the Middle East. I don't know if you've had a chance to see the information on the occasion of the seventh anniversary of Qaddafi's seizure of power. It is the coldest message I've seen! There is not a single word of praise for Qadaffi. He is not mentioned. It is addressed to him but he is not mentioned. That is unbelievable.

The study of esoteric communication is both an art and a science. For the modern Sovietologist, to separate the central from the marginal, the relevant from the trivial, constitutes the essence of his work. From the material the interviewees have revealed, it is apparent that esoteric communications are adapted to the changing needs of the Soviet system.

4
International Relations
Decision Making

Decisions in closed societies tend to be made behind the scene by a changing cast of characters, rather than by a single formal institution or several formally established and coordinated bodies. This applies to international policy no less than to other issues. The formal roles, of course, are assigned to the Politburo, the Secretariat, and the appropriate departments of the Central Committee. The testimony presented below indicates major fluctuations in the roles of various actors, varying with the passage of time, the specific country examined, and, above all, the individual personalities involved and their respective places on the pecking order in any particular phase of the decision-making process. The editors, of course, are fully aware of the structural, as well as substantive differences between international policy formation in the USSR and in Eastern Europe. In most cases, however, the similarities outweigh the differences.

Locus of Decision Making

The Formal Institutional Structure:
Politburo and Secretariat

Arkady Shevchenko explains that, in the 1970s, foreign policy matters were held over for the weekly plenary sessions of the Politburo. On occasion, this meant delaying urgently needed decisions:

> I did have a feel for how the Politburo functioned in the seventies. . . . [F]oreign policy matters were considered in the . . . plenary meetings every week. It caused a lot of trouble, because of delays in some of the urgent matters. Sometimes Gromyko himself had to intervene, as a last resort, [on behalf of] the Foreign Ministry. But this excludes any [sub]committees [of the Politburo].

Stanislav Levchenko, with background in the Soviet intelligence apparatus, views the situation from a different perspective. In his experience the

Politburo orders drafts of opinions on international affairs from the International Department of the Central Committee and other appropriate bodies.

> *Levchenko:* I do not think that every member of the Politburo reads comprehensive reports, but the foreign minister and the chief of KGB read them, because it is their offices that will implement these directives. The other members of the Politburo will probably listen only to a five- or ten-minute presentation. For instance, if it [involves] an "active measures" campaign conducted by Chebrikov, then they will trust his views. He knows the key points of his plan, and will draw attention to them because he does not want to get in trouble. They will approve it in principle. . . .

> *Q:* Is . . . that the reason why the Politburo in a single few-hours session a week can cover so many areas [because the members usually rubber stamp proposals rather than deliberate]?

> *Levchenko:* Yes. [However] . . . [i]f there is anything really serious [the Politburo] will spend the whole day there. If there is something, such as a new development in Afghanistan, they will spend as much time as they need. . . . The cannot be lazy. At the same time five or six members of the Politburo have daily access to secret information on international events. Other people do not. I do not think someone will say "I need more information". . . . It follows the traditional Soviet compartmentalization principle. Five or six members of the Politburo or their people are involved in international affairs in one way or another. But when they are specialists in Soviet agriculture or heavy industry, it is not their problem. They just will not get this information. By information I do not mean just the three-page-long daily intelligence digest, but information coming from important confidential sources. I do not have too much knowledge about [the] Foreign Relations [Sub]Committee [of the Politburo], but logic [suggests] that these [five or six Politburo members] meet more frequently than other parts of the Politburo and that is how they are able to push some issues and [resolve] some clashes of opinion.

Concerning a tradition that the CPSU second secretary, subordinate only to the general secretary, is in overall charge of the Party's foreign relations, Michael Voslensky makes the following comments:

> *Q.* Would it be correct to say that the proper description of Suslov was that he was "super chief" of both the Ponomarev and Russakov departments [of the Central Committee]?

> *Voslensky:* Yes.

> *Q:* He [Suslov] was the party's foreign minister.

> *Voslensky:* At the same time he was responsible for the world communist movement. He was considered the "second 2nd secretary" of the party Central Committee.

> *Q:* Although, formally, such a title has not existed.

Voslensky: Formally, no, but practically he was considered as such. In the apparatus people said there were two second secretaries—Kirilenko and Suslov.

Q: Kirilenko dealing essentially with internal administration?

Voslensky: Yes, organization and so forth. Right now Ligachev is automatically second secretary. The ideological and political secretary since 1947 was Suslov.

The Foreign Relations Commission

In addition to the formally established entities of the party Central Committee that deal with international affairs, the party leadership from time to time refers particular issues to an *ad hoc* Commission on Foreign Affairs. That body apparently reports to the Politburo and is to be distinguished from the Joint Foreign Policy Commission of the two houses of the USSR Supreme Soviet, an entity lacking meaningful substance, at least until recently. Neither of these two commissions should be confused with the International Policy Commission of the CPSU Central Committee, established in 1988.

According to Michael Voslensky, a Commission on Foreign Policy was established in 1948 to prepare foreign policy materials prior to decisions of the party leadership. As to its membership, he says:

The chairman was Suslov and his deputy [Boris] Ponomarev. . . . I presume the foreign minister is a member of such a commission. The chairman is probably Ligachev as the second secretary. Probably the minister of foreign trade, the KGB chief, probably the minister of defense. . . .

Zdzislaw Rurarz also alludes to such a committee:

In Poland there was such a commission, so there might also be one in the Soviet Union. The commission in Poland was headed, after December 1971, in my time by Franciszek Szlachcic, who had previously been head of the Ministry of Internal Affairs, and later a Politburo member and one of the Central Committee secretaries. The commission included the minister of foreign affairs (who was a member of the Politburo but not of the Secretariat), as well as the secretary of administration, who was at that time [Stanislav] Kania. As far as I know, the chairman of the Council of State, Henryk Jablonski, attended on an ad-hoc basis, but that was only for representative purposes.

Arkady Shevchenko speaks of such a commission in the past tense, however, and suggests different dates.

Shevchenko: There was actually a joint commission when Suslov was alive. It was a Commission on Foreign Affairs which considered some things, particularly national liberation movements. This commission even looked at appointments of the senior diplomats. That's why Suslov asked me for [a meeting] before the meetings of the Politburo. . . .

It was quite an important commission. It is my impression that it no longer exists, or if it exists it is a dormant commission. I think that after Suslov's death, no one replaced him. On this point, it has depended on how the general secretary would like to conduct these affairs. Either he wants to keep more authority among his personal assistants or to delegate some power to the Central Committee. In the case of this foreign affairs commission, it was a peculiar situation, because even Brezhnev had to respect Suslov's position. It is my understanding that this commission's authority went down considerably.

Q: When was it established?

Shevchenko: I would say that it existed at least since 1966 or '67. It was already functioning when I became [Andrey] Gromyko's adviser in 1970. When it was previously established I cannot tell because I was in such a junior position then and not in a position to know. . . . [W]hen Gromyko became a member of the Politburo, he was on it. Ponomarev was there from the Secretariat, and the heads of [appropriate] departments, and the head of the Cadres Abroad Department [of the Central Committee]. . . . The membership [was] rather flexible. It depended very much on Suslov.

As the Commission's functions, Shevchenko says:

. . . policy dealing . . . with the countries of the Soviet bloc, . . . dealing with the other parties (not the communist movement itself, but with social democrats), and the whole spectrum of political affiliations like women's movements, peace movements, and so on. . . . The importance of the commission was that some of the appointments of some ambassadors didn't even go to the Politburo. . . . Only the most important ones went before the Politburo.

Gregory, with his background in intelligence and journalism, acknowledges only the existence of an unimportant Foreign Affairs Commission of the Supreme Soviet.

Q: What is discussed by the Commission on Foreign Affairs in the USSR Supreme Soviet?

Gregory: . . . The Commission on Foreign Affairs [of the Supreme Soviet] would gather, hear a speech from Suslov and nod their heads.

Sejna states that he knows nothing of a permanent subcommission on foreign affairs.

Sejna: Suslov and Ponomarev never felt as though they needed such a body and if the issue was terrorism, then the Defense Council would deal with it.

Q: Would you say that, in Czechoslovakia today, Bil'ak and Fojtik preside over some kind of fiefdom in the Central Committee that deals with foreign affairs?

Sejna: They have responsibility for foreign affairs but that does not mean that there is a special committee. The responsibility goes through Bil'ak's being a member of the Politburo. It is from there that he derives his authority. It is the same thing with Shevardnadze today. . . .

In Czechoslovakia, the policy formation process resembles roughly its Soviet counterpart. According to Hus, there is no such Committee on Foreign Policy, certainly not in an official capacity.

Q: In Poland there is a Foreign Relations Committee at the Secretariat level, which included the ministers of interior and foreign affairs and the head of the International Department. Was there any such body in Czechoslovakia?

Hus: Not in Czechoslovakia. Debate on foreign policy takes place between Bil'ak and Chnoupek on important issues, and in the ministry on lesser issues. If the director of certain departments disagrees with members of the ministry within the ministry, he must yield to them as they are senior to him. However, if they are uncertain about their own views, then they will be more likely to heed his opinion.

The Secretariat and the Departments of the Central Committee, especially the International Department

The Secretariat of the CPSU Central Committee plays a significant role in the process of formulating international policy, as outlined by Levchenko.

Levchenko: The Secretariat reads the [text of a submission to the Politburo] when it is a draft. It actually functions as a censor and makes certain that nothing slips through. Let me repeat that at least five members of the Politburo, who are directly or indirectly involved with foreign affairs, will read the whole report and usually these members are a little younger than the others.

Q: Voslensky mentioned a Foreign Affairs Commission of the Politburo and the Secretariat [working] as a joint body. Is this what you mean?

Levchenko: That I do not know, but it sounds reasonable. He was in a position to know. We know from Khrushchev that there were subcommittees of the Politburo in Stalin's day, but they were peculiar. There was a Politburo Subcommittee on Foreign Affairs and the Economy, which [embraces] practically everything. I presume the subcommittees meet more frequently now.

Two witnesses give us an indication of the role of the Central Committee's International Department in foreign policy matters. Zdzislaw Rurarz comments on the basis of his experience in the Polish party central apparatus as well as his membership in two Warsaw Pact think tanks:

> The Soviets have two Central Committee Departments for international affairs, [the International Department, then under Ponomarev, and the Department for Liaison with Communist and Workers' Parties of Socialist Countries, then under Konstantin Rusakov], and since we were discussing not only the problems of the ruling communist parties but of the outside world as well, I think that Ponomarev ultimately was in charge. . . . I gathered that it was strictly Ponomarev's affair in the end, though somehow filtered through by Rusakov beforehand.

Kucharski adds to this perspective:

> One member of [the Foreign Department of the Polish Central Committee] directed the secretary general of the [Peace and] Solidarity Committee. He related to me the organization of this department. . . . One of the secretaries . . . is assigned all foreign policy. In the Soviet Union it [was then] Ponomarev. In Poland there is also such a secretary. The person in this position would change from time to time. When I was in the Solidarity Committee, the responsible secretary was Franciszek Szlachcic. The Foreign Department in the Central Committee was under him. The head of this department was the man who, on a daily basis, supervised the Peace and Solidarity Committees. He also gave guidance and information to the Foreign Ministry. For some time this [man] was Wlodzimierz Natorf. . . .
>
> The staff [of the department] was divided according to geographic regions. There were four or five sections. One dealt with ideology and cooperation between communist parties. For example, it dealt with the East German and Czechoslovak Central Committees. Geographically speaking, this was really the division of Central Europe and the Soviet Union. The other sections dealt with different geographic regions. . . . At this time the size of the Foreign Department's staff was more than twenty people.

All the interviewees agree on the role of the International Department (ID) of the Central Committee, including policy decisions, agendas, communications, and implementation. According to Stiller and Gregory, the ID is a direct successor to the Comintern.

> *Stiller:* I think that the ID is most likely just a new label on the old Comintern, and that later on it was reorganized into the International Department, with two subdepartments to deal with socialist countries and communist parties of non-socialist countries.
>
> *Gregory:* The ID was formally set up in 1955. The Comintern was set up to be the common organization of the foreign communist parties. The ID was established as the successor to the section of the party that dealt with

foreign communist parties. Now the ID plays a very important role in Soviet foreign policy. It does far more than maintain contact with foreign communist parties. It is an integral element of the CPSU Central Committee structure.

Michael Voslensky expresses the opinion that the Central Committee's International Department focuses on non-conventional diplomacy:

[T]he Foreign Ministry is sovereign only in the area of diplomacy. Soviet foreign policy uses both conventional and non-conventional forms of diplomacy. Non-conventional diplomacy does not come under the Foreign Ministry, but rather under the International Department. The ID is the Foreign Ministry for non-conventional foreign policy.

Voslensky further explains that Soviet foreign ministers are important only by virtue of membership in the Politburo:

Gromyko [was] a full member of the Politburo, but as an individual [rather than by virtue of being foreign minister]. [Vyacheslav] Molotov was also a member of the Politburo. (Andrey) Vishinsky was not; neither [Georgy] Chicherin nor [Maxim] Litvinov was a member of the Politburo. . . . [I]n any case, the International Department is an extremely important organization.

However, Voslensky adds some caveats, drawing upon his knowledge of Soviet international policy formulation by the CPSU *apparat.*

Voslensky: Soviet diplomacy also [comes under the heading of] political warfare. . . . The Soviet Foreign Ministry has the right, and makes use of the right, to go to the Politburo and the Secretariat with [its] problems, without passing through the normal way, through the [International] Department.

Then the Foreign Trade Ministry [comes] also to a certain extent [under the heading of] political warfare. But I had the impression that the International Department [was] . . . disinterested in foreign trade. The activities of the GRU [Soviet military intelligence] also . . . are not connected with the International Department because [its work] is purely military and technological. . . . The International Department is certainly very instrumental and important in . . . political warfare. If we look for one organization that could be considered the main organization [on the] political warfare front, it is the International Department. . . . But it does not mean that all of this front is fully concentrated in its hands. Ponomarev would like to do it, but he cannot.

Q: You mentioned that the departments prepare papers and the General Department manages the [flow] of these papers to the Politburo or the Secretariat. Could you give a concrete example of this process using the International Department?

Voslensky: This is the routine. [International] issues must come to the [International] department. The department prepares the draft decision. As long as the department has not prepared the draft decision, the item will not be put on the agenda [of the Politburo].

Q: Does the International Department draw up an annual plan of the goals it wishes to achieve during any year, what its activities will be in different parts of the world?

Voslensky: There will be a plan of work for the International Department, which will be approved by the Secretariat. The Secretariat also includes the general secretary, the second secretary, all of the senior secretaries. Practically, it is the Politburo, or at least the most important part of the Politburo. If there are some questions connected to KGB activities, it would include the KGB chief, [Viktor] Chebrikov; [Vitaliy] Vorotnikov is not important because he [represents] the RSFSR [Council of Ministers], which gives him little to do with the [International Department]. [There] is a practical, bureaucratic routine. It is impossible just to send something to the Politburo. . . . If by mistake [the Politburo] should receive something [via] the General Department, the assistants there will immediately, automatically send it back to the department from which it [originated]. There must be certain . . . documentation [comprising] the draft decision, signed by the responsible secretary of the Central Committee, by the chief of the department or the deputy chief, if the secretary is also department chief; and also by the chief of the [department subdivision]; and the necessary material, the explanation . . . [of] not more than five typewritten pages. If necessary it might also include the opinion of the ministries [concerned] or some other expert opinion.

Q: What sort of [items] would the ID be sending the Politburo, apart from the annual plan?

Voslensky: There are questions which arise in connection with the activities of the ID with [individual communist] parties, or . . . the convocation of an international conference of . . . communist parties. This requires Politburo approval. The decision to hold an international conference on a specific issue using a front organization, for example on Palestine, would be approved at the Politburo level. In the case of the World Peace Council, it is possible that the Politburo would approve a list of the conferences planned for the upcoming year, as opposed to approving each conference individually. The Politburo understands that the International Department knows better about the specifics of these decisions. The ID, however, needs the formal sanction of the Politburo . . . in order to prevent trouble should there be something wrong and they could be accused of having [acted] without the approval of the Politburo. The Politburo members understand that the activities of the World Peace Council will be organized at such and such a session—for example a conference of the World Peace Forces. It will all be decided within the framework of the budget.

Hus addresses the size of the Czechoslovak equivalent of the ID and discusses the framework of the organization:

There are about fifty staff members there. They are organized along geographic lines. [They comprise] the core of the department. There are geographic departments for the Soviet Union and Eastern Europe, the Third World, and the West. Then there are functional departments. These include the Department of International Organizations and the Department of Consultants. These consultants work on global questions, such as the Socialist International or problems of the Third World, including liberation movements. There are only three of them. One of them is responsible for all communist countries, one for the West, and one for the developing countries. Another functional department is the Cadres Department. Their concern [covers] only those [individuals] who go abroad or work on foreign policy issues. They are in charge of processing [cadres].

Stanislav Levchenko provides an estimate of the size of the Soviet ID:

The staff of the International Department is not that large . . . only two hundred people. Many of them have very prominent positions. To achieve [a goal] through their trusted contacts and their personal networks in different countries, they must discuss many issues [that] will never be [addressed] by any other Soviet official.

Speaking of fronts manipulated by the ID, Levchenko says:

[I]n the 1960s, [the Afro-Asian Peoples Solidarity Organization—AAPSO] was very important because of a division of labor between the World Peace Council, where they were disarming people, and AAPSO, which was a militant organization. What is interesting is that they never really made a secret of it. Yet there were some very serious gaps in American knowledge of the fronts. AAPSO openly declared its support for any national liberation movements. It openly said that it would provide them not only with food, but arms, uniforms, and everything else which is needed for guerrilla warfare. They were very vocal in their support of the national liberation movements in international organizations. Soviet fronts would pick up their political issues and try to bring them to the U.N. The PLO would not have been . . . successful in the late 1960s without direct Soviet support and contacts with people like Arafat. AAPSO was a very important organization [because] at that time quite a few members of AAPSO were also members of different countries' governments. It was just overlooked here [in the West], but it was important.

Concerning relations between the International Department and the KGB, Levchenko states:

[I]t would be a very rare case when International Department people go to work for the KGB. The KGB, Soviet research organizations, and the Ministry of Foreign Affairs are all likely places for the International Department to recruit new cadres. If somebody works for the KGB and gets a job in the International Department, he will then quit the KGB. It is a must.

While the ID seeks to avoid having operatives of the secret police in its midst, it has a good working relationship with the secret police, particularly with regard to active measures, including disinformation.

Gregory: [Disinformation under Major General Ivan Agayants and the ID] worked very closely together but this does not mean that Agayants was under the control of the ID. The KGB will never be under the control of the ID because the KGB chief is a Politburo member and has much power of his own. Agayants could contact Ponomarev or one of his staffers for special questions but Ponomarev could not tell Agayants what type of disinformation to work on. The type of disinformation to be spread is so important that it is a question for the Secretariat and the Politburo. In general, the KGB did its own work on disinformation.

Q: Was there any kind of breakdown between strategy (ID) and tactics (KGB)?

Gregory: These questions can often be decided collectively. The MFA [Ministry of Foreign Affairs], the KGB, the ID and other high-level officials can discuss these very important issues. The KGB is very careful to protect its sources and assets so this can serve to limit the [discussion], especially on sensitive matters.

Arkady Shevchenko stresses the division of authority between the ID and the MFA. He emphasizes that the ID does not have authority over the Ministry, and that certain operations, such as active measures, were handled by Anatolyi F. Dobrynin, by virtue of his personal influence, rather than because of his formal position, at the time, as chief of the International Department. He adds:

Dobrynin has never been a man who fit [the position of chief of the ID], never has had the mentality, and never has been involved in this work with the communist parties. . . . He was only marginally involved as an ambassador. He has wider interests. . . .

Gorbachev understands very well that Dobrynin is not a man who will run the International Department [in accordance with what] the Department's function has been. He put Dobrynin there to cool the heads of the orthodox ideologues . . . to shut them up for the time being. At this moment, there's a tactical change in the whole of Soviet foreign policy. . . . I don't think Gorbachev wants within the leadership a strong leader in the International Department like Vadim Zagladin. . . . He [Zagladin might] become a secretary of the party and eventually an alternate member of the Politburo who would [have] a very strong voice . . . on foreign affairs. . . .

[To give an analogy], when Brezhnev wanted to make some compromise at the expense of, say, the Communist Party of France, when he wanted to disregard the interests of French communists and have relations with DeGaulle . . . [Boris] Ponomarev was [like a small dog who barks]. I think Dobrynin [was made] head of the International Department deliberately to avoid having at this time a hard-line ideologue who would intervene in [international policy].

Michael Voslensky believes that the issue is "whether the ID will now become a semi-official agency of Soviet diplomacy, or whether it will continue [the traditional] Comintern line."

The Ministry of Foreign Affairs and Other Central Organs (in the USSR, Poland, and Czechoslovakia)

The Soviet Ministry of Foreign Affairs should be viewed in comparison to the ID, so that the division of functions becomes apparent. Stiller explains:

In the Ministry of Foreign Affairs, the most powerful organization is the *Kolegium*. It is selected from all the directors of departments of the Ministry of Foreign Affairs, though there are exceptions to this [such as one of the deputy directors who was appointed to the *Kolegium* because, for some reason, he had more power than well known directors].

Hus, with a background in Czechoslovak diplomacy, describes the division of labor between the ID and the Ministry of Foreign Affairs:

The International Department ran relations between Moscow and Eastern Europe. The Foreign Ministry does not make policy in this area. It only goes through the diplomatic motions. In the case of relations with the West, the situation was the exact opposite. This was primarily the sphere of the Foreign Ministry. There would be an officer in the embassy to handle relations with the communist party of that country, but his role was a minor one. [Anatolyi F.] Dobrynin was not concerned with meeting Gus Hall. The Foreign Ministry was concerned with state-to-state relations, and the International Department with party [-to-party] relations. It was the same in Prague. Because relations with the West were considered more difficult and more important than interbloc relations, the least capable people were usually assigned to handle bloc affairs.

Gregory also comments on the respective roles of the ID and the Ministry of Foreign Affairs:

The MFA has an important role in formulating foreign policy but U.N. organizations, Soviet embassies and consulates are all under the control of the CPSU Central Committee. Not the entire CC but the International Depart-

ment (ID) and the Secretariat. . . . Both ID and DCA[1] have their representatives in embassies—including Washington, D.C., London, Paris and the
U.N. Mission in New York. They [give support] but at the same time they
are controllers. I do not remember that any ambassador ever [came into con-
flict] with a representative of the CC. . . . In some cases, an ambassador
would recommend something but it would be modified by the CC representative. The ambassador would never do anything without consulting the CC
representatives. If, for example, the MFA decided to send a note of protest
to a government, it would have to be approved by the CC. But before the
CC would make a decision, the ID would read the note. This is how the
process works. Of course, [Andrey] Gromyko [was] a great figure but he was
under control of the CC of the CPSU. When he became a Politburo member,
it did not mean he became completely independent because international
questions are still international questions. One man, even a Gromyko, cannot decide policy in this area.

Voslensky indicates that the relative power of the ID and the Ministry of
Foreign Affairs fluctuates, depending upon the personality of the chief.
Voslensky asserts that the ID has no direct control over the MFA.

Voslensky: The Foreign Ministry is the exception to the general rule. When
Molotov, as the number two in the Soviet Union, was minister of foreign
affairs under Stalin, it was ridiculous to send a paper from the MFA with
Molotov's signature for the approval of Grigoryan, who was the chief of the
ID at that time. Then Gromyko also did everything necessary in order to
maintain this system, so that the MFA had the right to address the Politburo
and the Secretariat directly. This is an exception to the rule. The MFA is not
more important than the ID, but the ID does not have any supervisory
function over the MFA. There are tensions between these two offices, but at
the same they are both very cautious not to bring differences to open conflict
because the bureaucrats in the MFA understand that the ID is very close to
the leadership and that they are not so close. At the same time the ID is
always very cautious in the party apparatus. They consider the MFA to be
a useful organization, particularly as consultants.

Q: Would you say that, now with [Dobrynin as] the new head of the ID,
the MFA has gained the upper hand, having, in effect, one of their people
now in charge of the ID?

Voslensky: We must see if it was a very clear choice. Frankly speaking, I
think [the situation] will be difficult for Dobrynin, who was in America for
twenty-four years, and practically knows America better than he knows the
USSR [and] who had absolutely no formal contacts with the communist
parties; because he must work now as chief and supervisor of all the communist parties. I think Dobrynin's appointment was a very unusual choice.

---

[1] Department of Cadres Abroad.

Tadeusz Kucharski describes the international affairs chain of command in Poland along lines that resemble Voslensky's presentation of affairs in the USSR:

> The foreign minister could be guided by the first secretary of the party or his deputy, the secretary [in charge of] foreign affairs, but he cannot be guided by the head of the [party's] Foreign Department. The head of the Foreign Department is usually a Central Committee member, but not a Politburo member. The minister is usually a Politburo member. The Foreign Department can give guidance and instructions to department heads in the ministry. A great deal depends on the rank of the minister, because sometimes he is not a member of the Politburo. Then his standing is much lower [and] instructions can go from the Foreign Department to the ministry, but instructions or guidance would never go from the ministry to the Central Committee. It is impossible. The Minister cannot give instructions to the Central Committee staff. They answer only to the secretaries. . . . [With regard to functions rather than who outranks whom,] I would say the Foreign Department's function is much larger in scope than the ministry's. This is because it incorporates all unofficial liberation movements and all . . . movements which are not officially recognized by Poland through the Foreign Ministry. For example, [prior to Angolan independence] Poland could not both officially recognize the MPLA[2] and have diplomatic relations with Portugal. Therefore, it is the Central Committee of the party which incorporates everything.

Hus addresses the relationship between the party's International (or Foreign) Department and the Ministry of Foreign Affairs from the Czechoslovak perspective:

> The roles of these two bodies [the MFA and the ID] are not well defined. [Who is more important] depends on time and personalities. At one point when [Bohuslav] Chnoupek had surrounded himself with better people than [Vasil] Bil'ak had, he was more involved in foreign policy issues, even though he was officially less important than Bil'ak. Bil'ak's people could not challenge Chnoupek's. When Bil'ak had evened this out, then the International Department became more important and Chnoupek was forced to reduce his [staff] within the ministry. He was ordered to reduce it from about ten people to five. In this way Bil'ak's position was strengthened.
>
> On important issues, the Foreign Ministry formulates its view, which is then sent to the least important official at the International Department involved with this issue. He is usually at the rank of senior associate. He then takes it to the deputy or chief of International Department who then takes it to Bil'ak, the secretary in charge of international relations and number two man in the Czechoslovak party. The senior associate will often change parts of the report before it is presented to Bil'ak. Bil'ak will rarely disagree with

---

[2] The ruling Popular Movement for the Liberation of Angola.

[the material] presented . . . if the matter is routine. Everybody who works for Bil'ak knows his line and will not challenge it or let a report challenging it pass. The associate [is more likely to] point out that the Foreign Ministry [staff members have] not been principled enough as communists. The senior associate will inform the deputy foreign minister or department head that the comrade does not like the report and it must be revised. Everybody knows who the comrade is.

Therefore the International Department is more important, but only rarely are foreign policy reports initiated there. They are first formulated in the Foreign Ministry. Everything originates there, because the International Department does not have the staff. I was responsible for the United States, Canada, Great Britain, and Scandinavia at one point. Toward the end of my tour with the International Department, I was responsible only for Great Britain, Ireland, the United States, and Canada.

Levchenko supports the view that the International Department holds the upper hand:

There is not a doubt as to how important the International Department is in the scheme of Soviet foreign policy. It is apparent that the International Department is where the action is and not the Foreign Ministry.

The relative power and extent of authority exercised by other central organs in the USSR and Poland were also commented upon by the interviewers. Rurarz addresses the role of the Polish Council of Ministers in implementing international policy decisions:

When the [Polish] Council of Ministers knew that a certain item would also be discussed by the [Polish] Politburo, they would take only preliminary action. Only after directives had been [given] by the Politburo would the Council of Ministers move ahead with implementation. On those occasions when the Politburo [dealt with] an issue which had not been discussed at the Council of Ministers, the Politburo often simply sent its instructions directly to the various ministries involved, which were then committed to carry out the directive. But I can assure you that nobody ever bothered to control whether the directives were implemented or not. Officially, the departments of the Central Committee were obliged to monitor whether the implementation in fact took place, but (at least in my time) they never did. On two occasions, though, the Politburo specified (on my suggestion) that the implementation be monitored and that a report be made to the Politburo. But that was the exception.

Gregory notes that the roles of the Soviet Council of Ministers and of the Supreme Soviet in foreign affairs are largely cosmetic:

The Supreme Soviet does not mean anything, but [its members] have to do something just because they exist. Deputy chairmen of the Supreme Soviet are the chairmen of the Supreme Soviets in the [Union] Republics. They would rotate on a monthly basis through Moscow simply for show. It is really a farce. When we organized the Journalist Union, we had a Secretariat with the secretaries of the Journalist Unions from the [Union] Republics. We called it "duty-time." They would come to Moscow for one month to "work." It was a good holiday. . . . How could they know anything if they come from the Kirghiz Republic? They got an office, telephone and took themselves seriously. It is the same with the Supreme Soviet. They have no real power; they are a mere facade. . . . The Soviet leaders obviously do not like widely representative bodies. They want decisions highly centralized in the Politburo. The Council of Ministers can meet, discuss, whatever, but they cannot spend one kopeck without the approval of the Politburo.

Decision Making in Other Socialist Countries

Generally, the decision-making processes concerning foreign policy in Soviet client states mimic those in the USSR. Ethiopia is no exception, although there are some differences, as outlined by Wolde.

[In Ethiopia] [w]e don't call it the International Department. It's the Department in charge of Foreign Relations of the Party. This department is just another arm of the party, like the Ideological Department, the Nationalities Department, the party Control Commission, and others. . . . These are departments of the party, and of course the one that closely worked with me [was] the Foreign Relations Department. In Ethiopia, we found this party/state structure very difficult, because one begins to worry about the other and cooperation between the two [suffers]. Theoretically, it's the party [that] formulates foreign policy. While the Ministry [of Foreign Affairs] may be responsible [for articulating] it, it is the party which sets it. When I speak of the party, I mean not just a specific department, but the party structure as a whole, through its permanent committees, the Politburo, the Central Committee.

Juan Benemelis explains the policy-making infrastructure in Cuba, which is sui generis:

In Cuba, one will find foreign policy institutions with their own infrastructure, because they each have their own policy. When the army became more powerful in the early 1970s, it [followed this example]. . . .
There are power groups which create Cuban foreign policy. They compete among different personalities for influence. [A leading personality might be] given a whole continent. Now the areas are divided differently among new people. In that respect, Cuban foreign policy is less institutionalized than

the Soviet foreign policy. It is more ad hoc and more dynamic. They set up the *Tricontinental* magazine and published a lot of books through [Gian-giacomo] Feltrinelli, the person in charge of publishing all *Tricontinental* materials in Europe.

Categories of Decisions

According to Stanislav Levchenko, there are basically two categories of decisions:

> In one category are issues of great importance to the Politburo, and in the other is everything which is the reflection or interpretation of those decisions. In the second category, changes are very difficult and slow. There are very few examples when decision making becomes quick. It is one of the features which characterizes the nature of the Soviet system: that is, to be very slow in the changing of the long-standing positions.

Jan Sejna, drawing upon his Czechoslovak experience, sees three categories based on degrees of confidentiality:

> There are three different kinds of decisions which the Politburo can take. First, is a decision which is published openly for the whole country to note. Second, is a decision which is for the information of the party only. They are made known to party members by the so-called party letters or by blue bulletins. Those are periodically sent to the regional party Secretariats along with instructions on how to proceed and how extensively to disseminate the information. Third is a decision which carries the label "Secret" or "Top Secret." Each such decision is recorded in a special document which specifies at the end whether the decision of the Politburo had been approved by the Defense Council, the Secretariat, or the individual Secretaries of the Central Committee. Previously, officials in various Departments of the [KSC] Central Committee could disclaim knowledge of a certain directive. There was no way to tell whether they had in fact been informed or not. Now the fact of Secretariat approval is recorded.

Shaping the Agenda for Decisions on International Affairs

Stanislav Levchenko explains the way the agenda for foreign policy decisions is shaped.

> *Q:* If the [CPSU] International Department [wishes to bring] a major issue . . . [to] the Politburo, does it have to go through the General Department or . . . [does it go] through the private secretariat of the general secretary?

Levchenko: Probably it goes either way. If it is really something significant, [Boris] Ponomarev will get it in his hands. He will bypass [the private secretariat of the general secretary] and bring it to the Politburo personally; he will give them copies. He will do everything to show that he does not discriminate among them. . . . Routine matters will go through the whole process. . . . Sometimes there are conflicts with [Ministry of Foreign Affairs]. . . . On a daily basis . . . there are contradictions in putting together some proposals, or in approving and disapproving some actions. There is nothing dramatic in these differences, because they are natural differences between [diplomacy] and . . . an organization [like] the [CPSU] International Department. The MFA is always trying to soften [language] and actions. It is not because they are ["soft"], but because in some countries they have spent years seducing people to establish diplomatic relations or to sign an agreement with them, and they do not want some "guerrillas" from the International Department [to undo what diplomacy has achieved]. [The MFA has its] own diplomatic interest. . . . However, in most of the cases the International Department has the power. In principle, the International Department is the mind and consciousness of the party, while the MFA are the people who execute orders. Each time I witnessed differences, it was nothing overly dramatic. Usually it was only at the level of chief of section. He would call the chief of the Geographical Department of MFA and in a polite way say we discussed it here, so if you do not mind, we will still [go ahead]. The attempt is made to prevent two options from being presented to the Politburo. It will be a single proposal, rather than two. . . .

Q: Are there never cases where two options come up?

Levchenko: I do not know, but it is unlikely. There has to be a very deep difference of opinion for this to happen. [The leading members of the Soviet *apparat*] usually spend weeks putting together papers. They go to each others' offices, phone each other, send messengers, and things like that. They have time to settle differences. With a major disagreement, they may present two different points of view, but this does not happen too many times a year.

Hus comments upon decision making in the Czechoslovak Ministry of Foreign Affairs:

The decision-making process begins at a lower level. The officer responsible will draft a report or position paper. As this report progresses up the hierarchy, the officers checking it will change the style. Some of the low-level officials have achieved their positions through nepotism and are not well trained. Their work must be doubly checked. The process rarely starts from the top and works down. . . . In important cases, however, such as the visits of other foreign ministers, then the impetus for work comes from the top. . . .

On more important issues, reports from below are only used as rough drafts. Only ten or twenty percent of the [original] report, [mainly] factual [information], is used in the final report. When I was with [Bohuslav]

Chnoupek's[3] Ministry within the Ministry, all we used were the facts from the reports we received, because some of the reports that came up were extremely unprofessional and primitive. Using the facts we would reach our own conclusions. The foreign minister, a former journalist, did little beyond reprimanding his subordinates if they did not live up to his expectations. He never changed radically the substance of any of the work of the Foreign Ministry within the Foreign Ministry. There were some exceptions, such as relations with the United States, Austria, or Germany. It is in these areas that Bil'ak and Chnoupek became involved. What they decided was then communicated to the "Ministry within the Foreign Ministry" and to the pertinent department. These bodies then carry out the decisions.

Foreign Policy "Constituencies," particularly the Military

Stiller elaborates on group interests and how they affect the Soviet foreign policy formation process.

Stiller: [There is a] Middle Eastern lobby within the Ministry of Foreign Affairs and the Institute of [World Economics and International Relations] [that] has a great degree of influence in determining the outcome of Soviet policy vis-à-vis the Middle East. . . .

Q: [Concerning the desire of] the Soviet military to "go overseas", and the justification this offered for expansion [did this thrust emanate particularly] from Gorshkov, who was building up the navy?

Stiller: Yes, definitely. Gorshkov was in Alexandria, Egypt, for a visit, in fact. I was there and took the delegation for bathing and nightclubs. One perceived a great need to [insert] more and more Soviet [personnel] overseas. Gorshkov was, of course, building the fleet at that time, and I suppose there were a lot of Soviet submarine officers and political officers in the fleet who just cherished their overseas duties. Their conditions weren't so bad; compared to American duty they were, but compared to [the Soviet] internal service, it was just fine.

A sensible foreign policy attempts to operationalize strategic priorities. However, the policy must be flexible enough to adapt to local conditions. Sometimes this is not the case, as revealed below in an extended discussion with Shevchenko.

Shevchenko: Actually, [adapting policy to local conditions] almost doesn't work. And it almost doesn't work because the criteria for what is already

---

[3] Chnoupek was Czechoslovak minister of foreign affairs following the Soviet-Warsaw Pact invasion of August 1968.

established policy in the Soviet Union are very ambiguous. To decide anything, even in foreign policy, is difficult. For example, let's assume that there is some new development in South Africa. Now, Soviet foreign policy on South Africa was established long ago from A to Z, but [there] could be a situation [which] you really can't fit . . . into the usual mold. Often, for some tactical reason or because some new element appears in the relationship that needs to be evaluated, it is left for the foreign minister or deputy foreign minister to decide. Then he will go to the chief of the department.

Most of these people don't like to take the responsibility for deciding what is and what is not in the established policy. The result is that everyone tries to obtain a consensus before initiating anything, and no decisions are made except at the highest level. After a reminder from the Politburo, people become a little more careful, but soon they are back to passing everything on to the Politburo. . . . During my period of [Soviet] service . . . there was quite a substantial revolution in the relationship between the military experts (and the military as an institution) and those on the political side: Foreign Ministry, Politburo, civilians, etc. Actually, it is triangular: Purely military, the military-industrial complex, and the civilian political leadership.

When I joined the Foreign Ministry and at the beginning of my career . . . civilians particularly in the Foreign Ministry had almost no say in anything at all [with regard to arms control or arms transfer negotiations]— neither technical matters or political. They were absolute prisoners of the military. The military dictated whatever they wanted and, in fact, it was accepted by the political leadership. It was a reflection of the enormous influence of the military over all the tactics and substance of negotiations for the Soviet Union.

Slowly, the changes occurred. [Nikita] Khrushchev overruled [them on] a number of things that the military didn't like, such as the idea of general and complete disarmament. But he did it, irrespective of them. There was a little bit more of a role for the Foreign Ministry after many of these Khrushchev initiatives. On the killing of the negotiations on [arms control] there was a lot more influence by civilians who asked whether it was time to discuss control. The military always opposed that until the very end. They even opposed the [1972] Moscow treaty. But still it was done.

So, slowly the process went on. I would say the turning point was the beginning of SALT I. The civilian side acquired a little bit more independence and an ability to talk, if not entirely as an equal, at least as a partner who did not have to accept inevitably whatever the military wanted. That was the first agreement in which they were no longer able to withhold [military] information from a restricted group of civilians. (I am not talking about all military planning.)

Prior to that, the civilians who participated in the negotiations were not really informed at all about the Soviet military systems. I'm not talking about what was in the planning or experimental stage. We were not ever informed of what was already in operation. They avoided talks with the civilians even about some of the things that Western intelligence knew. . . . Western intelligence knew about the characteristics and deployment of some of the weapons. But still the Soviet military preferred not to talk to their civilian counterparts. You can imagine to what extent the civilians were out of the negotiation process.

Gradually, by the 1970s—when SALT I and ABM were negotiated—I would say that [the civilians] had a very strong voice. The military still [was able to keep back quite a lot of things but the civilian part of the negotiators had become a real partner. They could even overrule [the military] and could be separate and independent. It would have been unheard of in the 1950s for the foreign minister to submit something [on arms control] to the Politburo without the signature and full support of the general staff and the military. At the beginning of the 1970s, it could occur or at least [Andrey] Gromyko or [Deputy Foreign Minister] Semyonov or someone else could speak in the Politburo or participate in some other [meetings] and disagree. They could bring the disagreement into the Politburo. There had been a long period when the civilians did not dare to disagree or have strong feelings. But that had changed by the beginning of the 1970s.

It has progressed further and further and I think this will continue. I think the military lost control, if not completely then to a substantial degree. [I am referring throughout to] Soviet arms control negotiation policy, not other programs, of course.

There has been a qualitative change in military policy. What they have achieved now is almost real parity which was nonexistent in the midseventies. Thus, in the early seventies, there was no argument that the Soviet leadership was behind the many new weapons. They were far behind the U.S. They had to have all these new programs. By now, to a considerable degree, this is all but eliminated. Now there is an economic priority. What is more important for the Soviet Union? Just to think in terms of military superiority which, by the way, might be wishful thinking since it might not be achieved, is problematic.

I think that both the civilian and military have influence now. The military can still very much influence and delay decisions, but they no longer control them.

Q: Why do you think that a number of the military ended up supporting SALT if they were [originally] reluctant and they were powerful?

Shevchenko: The number of [people in] the military who ended up supporting SALT did so because of more sophisticated people like Ogarkov and others who had a much better grasp and understanding than you could expect from Grechko. They saw that SALT I really didn't prevent them from achieving what they wanted to achieve.

However, there were some military people who didn't have a good understanding of what was going on. They wanted to have an absolutely free hand. These military officers had a completely different understanding. . . .

Q: You said that these arguments were ironed out in debates. . . . Where and at what level did the debates take place?

Shevchenko: Most of this kind of debates took place in the Foreign Ministry at a senior level office or in Gromyko's office, less in Gromyko's office because he didn't like having the military in his office. . . . If Brezhnev were there or Ustinov, Gromyko could find a common language much more easily than with Grechko. . . . He didn't like to engage in discussions with Ogarkov or other senior men who were members of the Soviet delegation and their representatives who were equal in level. That was [at levels such as deputy chief of the general staff].

These discussions were usually in Vladimir Semyonov's[4] office. During the time when they had intervals between the sessions, it was Semyonov who was responsible for preparing the instructions for the new round. About ninety-nine percent of the preliminary discussions were held in his office with the participation of all the [officials cleared for that purpose]. Usually there were about five to eight military representatives and an equal number of civilians, the members who participated on the Soviet delegation (not junior members, not first secretary level). Ogarkov participated, as well as the chief of the International Department. Occasionally . . . Georgy Korniyenko[5] or Viktor Komplektov[6] [participated. There was] always someone from the American Department. Occasionally I participated and very seldom some people from Policy Planning. All in all, the largest group was no more than seventeen to eighteen people.

There were arguments. Semyonov and the civilian members of the delegation wanted to know to what extent the military were willing to go and to get [the military] to do something. It was next to Mission Impossible. . . .

Q: How does one threaten the Soviet military?

Shevchenko: You could because they didn't like [stalemate] either. The arguments would go to such lengths that there would be a complete deadlock. Semyonov would say okay, we can't do anything. Let's end this discussion. That would be the point when they would go back and discuss, discuss, discuss, and come back with one step more . . . the only tactic [was] to threaten the military with "Okay, good-bye. We can't do anything. But I have to report to Gromyko." Believe it or not, at this point in the early 1970s, it was a minor threat to them. They understood that they would have to explain it to their own people but the biggest threat Semyonov could use, which he did occasionally, was that he would talk to Brezhnev. Or he would refer to Gromyko's talk with Brezhnev, saying "I understand that on this matter, we have to . . ." Their reaction was to either [comply] right away on certain things or to defer, saying they had to consult with their people.

Communicating Decisions

Foreign Policy decisions are communicated much in the same way as others. (See chapter 3 for a discussion of exoteric and esoteric communications.)

---

[4] Vladimir Semyonov was deputy foreign minister in charge of German affairs.

[5] Georgy Korniyenko was deputy foreign minister specializing in American affairs.

[6] Viktor Komplektov was deputy foreign minister and, previously, chief of the Ministry's American Department.

However, the following comments made by the interviewees are worthy of note.

Michael Voslensky shows that the long-term goals of Soviet policy are not spelled out when instructions are given for the implementation of a particular policy directive.

> *Q:* [With regard] to the issue of overall Soviet political strategies, strategies on international relations: In the institutes, did you ever receive a long-term guidance paper, which said "the party views the development of affairs in the next decade as following this or that outline. Your work has to be understood as falling within these parameters." Have you ever seen what you [would] regard as an overall strategic document, that deals with world affairs as a whole?
>
> *Voslensky:* No, certainly not. It would be impossible. First of all, I am not sure they have such a strategy. And second, it is enough to have the orientation of the official documents published by the party. This is enough. If it's necessary to ask for some details, the party apparatus in the Central Committee would explain it to you to a certain extent. But it is enough for any practical purposes, since all these institutes, as a matter of fact, make propaganda. And propaganda changes with the party line.

Tadeusz Kucharski addresses the issue of conveying the party line both for propaganda and operational purposes:

> There was the Propaganda Department [of the Polish Party Central Committee]. . . . It prepared the statements of the Solidarity Committee against imperialism, colonialism, and in support of the just struggle of the African liberation movements, or anything else which was needed. These same statements, which were issued in accordance with the party line, also appeared in Prague, Budapest, Moscow and other socialist capitals. Statements of the Solidarity Committee were always published in the central press; in *Tribuna Ludu, Zycie Warszawy, Sztandard Mlodych,* and *Zolnierz Wolnosci.* Those statements were elaborated according to the party line. If the head of the Propaganda Department had doubts, then he would contact the head of the Central Committee's Propaganda Department in order to choose the right words.
>
> Another department was the Administration or Operations Department. It was responsible for daily operation and for funding the visits of the liberation movements. Both of these departments got their instructions from the general secretary as well. All three departments were on an equal footing.

Piatigorsky relates his experiences, in which instructions were passed on through briefings and reports:

> For instance, it started with *spravka,* the briefings. For two weeks, everyone was involved in reading English newspapers, Bengali newspapers, Madras

newspapers, and Delhi newspapers. Then two or three people would write reports. . . . Sometimes they were asked to work not in our common rooms, but in secret rooms, if the information was regarded as secret. In point of fact, it was not secret at all, but it was regarded as secret. Not because the sources were secret—they were foreign journals—but sometimes there were reports from the Foreign Ministry. Then it was officially classified by the special section as Secret. One would be given permission to read it only . . . under their supervision. These were Foreign or Defense Ministry reports, or any other secret information. In normal cases, magazine, journal, and newspaper articles were commonly available. Two weeks pass and they give all their reports to the chief of *spravka,* the person responsible for that particular task.

Instructions directed to East European military leaders were not handled as state-to-state directives. Rather they followed Warsaw Pact channels, as Gen. Jan Sejna states:

In the military realm, the conveyance of directives has nothing to do with the military attaché of the Soviet embassy. Rather, it centers around the representative of the supreme commander of the Warsaw Pact. All communications would pass through the Prague office of this representative. By contrast, at least until 1969, the states of the Warsaw Pact had only a "mailman" in Moscow, a colonel who would deliver mail from the country. There was no staff in Moscow at all.

Kucharski describes how the AAPSO received its instructions:

The Solidarity Committee [AAPSO] was directed by one man in the Foreign Department of the Central Committee, who gave instructions to the Solidarity Committee's secretary general. The secretary general then implemented those instructions, as well as those he received from [Boris] Ponomarev when he visited Moscow. There was also a section with the Foreign Department for relations with bloc parties, but I do not know its name.

Kucharski, who had served as a member of the international observer team in Vietnam on two occasions, recounts how Hanoi received information and instructions at the height of the war:

Q: Was there a direct connection to Hanoi or would all information go back to Warsaw, then to Moscow, and Moscow would choose what to send to Hanoi?

Kucharski: All intelligence activity was done under Warsaw's instruction. Information was then sent to Warsaw. Warsaw was not really interested in what was going on in Vietnam, and sent the information on to Moscow. There was cooperation between the intelligence branches of the Soviet and Polish general staffs. Contacts were between the centers, not on the spot.

There were no Soviet agents in Saigon, only in Hanoi. Our officers did not even have contacts with the military attaché of the Soviet embassy in Hanoi. All coordination was done from the center, even if the information was urgent and time sensitive. If it was really urgent they had a way to get the information coded and to Warsaw on the same day. The next day it would be in Moscow. . . . We were only supposed to send reports blaming the South Vietnamese army. There were clear instructions about this from Moscow. Any attempt of objectivity within the Commission was blocked at the site by us.

Oversight

In the USSR, the transmission of the leadership's foreign policy directives through the appropriate channels is monitored by specific entities. Below, Shevchenko describes the oversight apparatus.

Q: Is there somebody who monitors implementation and reports back to the Politburo?

Shevchenko: This is a function of the General Department. The procedure is the following: Each ministry has a unit which might be called the general secretariat, although it might have a different name to handle [such functions]. This unit in each ministry, or in each state committee, or whatever, is in charge of receiving the orders from the Politburo or Council of Ministers, etc., and distributing them within the ministry according to a special list which is appended to the list produced by the Politburo and sent by the General Department. For example, in the Foreign Ministry, if several departments are involved in implementing a proposal, then all their names are listed. It is up to the general secretariat of the Foreign Ministry to check all the dates of implementation. They regularly come to the department with all the lists and all the decisions are in books.

They might come to the American Department each month or every couple of months. [An official] from the general secretariat comes to the assistant to the chief of the department and they look through the list of deadlines. If one is delayed or something, they have to explain it. The same procedure applies to the General Department of the Central Committee. The General Department also, on a regular basis, checks with all the various ministers.

Once instructions have been received, they must be interpreted. General Sejna illustrates how this is done:

The body which is responsible for overseeing the implementation will be the relevant Department of the Central Committee. If the directive were to deal with the Ministry of Defense for example, then the Administrative Organs Department would control the implementation.

What is perhaps even more important is that the relevant Department also has the responsibility of explaining "what the Politburo meant." The Politburo decision may be only one or two sentences: "The Politburo resolves that the State Defense Council shall give the Ministry of Defense instructions to support the guerrillas in Guatemala." But what exactly will happen? The Administrative Organs Department would summon the minister of defense, who may not be a member of the Politburo, or the chief of the General Staff and explain in precise terms what the Politburo directive really meant. This is operational interpretation: send one thousand rifles, fifty radios, and so on.

The reporting process is not always efficient at the local operational end, as Stiller elaborates.

Q: How does the monitoring process work? How does Moscow keep watch over progress in the field?

Stiller: It begins at the local level. Any time I had a meeting or a conversation with a foreigner, I had to write a note and send it along to the censorship office. I didn't like to do this, really, but once in a while I had to, just to show I was following the rules. I knew some conversations were always censored, in my case, by the consul general; he would initial his approval before any further meetings or conversations could take place. Any reports I wrote went to the consul general for his approval.

At the level of the embassy, the ambassador did not have to approve everything. Instead, there was one man who approved most of the political reporting; he looked at everything written and was in charge of all political traffic. In the embassy, one had more latitude in what one wrote, simply because of the volume of material being written and sent. There was far too much paperwork for one man to check; the ambassador thus delegated the authority, and those at the lower levels to whom the responsibility fell were not particularly interested in checking everything that was reported.

In the other direction—from Moscow back to the field—there was a yearly evaluation in which there would always be a paragraph on each employee, assessing his performance. You had no idea who had evaluated you; if you were with the Ministry of Foreign Affairs, then you knew it had come from someone in the Ministry. But that was all. I think this worked to keep the system going; when you didn't know exactly who was going to be writing your report, you had to stay on your toes.

5
Direct and Indirect Implementation
The Role of Allies, Surrogates, Clients, and Fronts

The importance of a decision depends on the quality of its implementation. In this context, it should be noted that the USSR has a penchant for implementation by indirection, that is, using allies, surrogates, clients, and fronts to carry out tasks, particularly with regard to the whole array of active measures, low-intensity conflict (including surrogate warfare), influence and other covert operations. However, this requires a Soviet *apparat* to ensure appropriate monitoring and supervision of allies and clients. The Soviet machinery for this purpose is surprisingly convoluted.

In certain cases, Soviet personnel is directly involved in implementation, including indoctrination, training, and arming of clients, ensuring political and organizational coordination with (and between) clients, and establishment of fronts.

Implementation of Policy Decisions by Soviet Personnel

Teaching and Non-Military Training

What does the Soviet Union seek in groups that show some potential for being useful to its international operations? Kucharski explains:

> [Soviet decision makers] are cynical enough to support anyone, even a rightist group, if [it] can be infiltrated, its orientation changed, and it has the best chance to win. . . . They [do not] abandon a movement. Once they start to support it, they stay with it. They will not [switch] their support to another movement. This has been the case with the MPLA, ZAPU, SWAPO, and the ANC.[1] This is also the reason why the ANC is reluctant to seek Western support, other than financial support from Scandinavian countries and the U.N. [It] knows the West has no consistent, long-term policy. [It] could be abandoned by the West at any time, while the Soviet Union does maintain long-term support.

---

[1] MPLA: Popular Movement for the Liberation of Angola, ruling Marxist party in Angola; ZAPU: Zimbabwe African Peoples Union; SWAPO: South-West African Peoples Organization; ANC: African National Congress.

Which Third World groups seek Soviet help and why? Kucharchi offers some interesting answers:

> The Soviet model is the only political model which secures power for the handful of people on top as long as they desire. The leaders of liberation movements are not always so enthusiastic about Marxism-Leninism. They are enthusiastic about holding power. . . . This is perhaps the main reason why so many liberation movements embrace [the Soviet cause] so eagerly; this [includes] SWAPO and the ANC . . . not because they want to lead the population along the glorious path of socialism, but because they know [that once they take over] they will keep power and Soviet support for the indefinite future.
>
> The kind of aid the Soviet Union provides is not limited to [material] and advisers. Far from being just an arms dealer, the Soviet Union gives its clients fringe benefits [they] may or may not seriously want. Military training is something nary a country in the throes of conflict would turn down, but political training in communist theory may not be the most desirable benefit.

The Soviet leaders realize that some of their clients' best students—the most likely to be sent to the Soviet Union for training—have severe reservations about attending Soviet institutions. Michael Voslensky explains how the USSR deals with such inhibitions:

> Lumumba Univesity[2] follows a . . . cautious line. Lumumba is the only university, the only higher school, in the Soviet Union where the curriculum does not include any Marxism-Leninism. There is no Marxism-Leninism, no history of the [CPSU]. The Soviet Constitution is included in the curriculum, though, and the most important parts of it are put into the heads of the students. The impression [the USSR wants] to give is that the university has nothing to do with political schooling and preparing political cadres. Certainly the KGB meets people there from bourgeois origins who are not ready to go to a communist school. But the university is not so straighforward; [its administrators] are cautious. The [prospective] leaders [among the students] . . . are prepared at the higher levels—the party schools—after their . . . selection. I must emphasize that it is a long-term investment.
>
> [T]here was a party committee [at Lumumba], but the rules forbade the faculty from discussing the existence of a party organization with the students. We played it down. The slogan was "a university as any other"— no different from other Soviet universities like Moscow State University, but also no different from foreign universities like Dakar. The students were

---

[2] The Soviet institution of higher learning established in Moscow specifically for Third World students, resulting in de facto segregation and mockingly called "Apartheid University" by some of these students.

not supposed to get the impression that they were at Patrice Lumumba to be Sovietized or made into communists. That is why there were no courses in Marxism-Leninism.

Attending Lumumba University had definite advantages for those students of client states who desire leadership positions.

Voslensky: You can be sure that Soviet embassies are always informed about Lumumba graduates. I am sure that there is feedback from the embassy to the center [in Moscow] about which jobs [those graduates] have and what they are doing. . . . [S]ome will become members of communist or pro-communist parties, and they could be sent by their respective parties back to the Soviet Union for training. Then they will be considered as future leaders of these parties and potential leaders of the country, in the case of the overthrow of the non-communist government.

Q: So after [some] years, these graduates might return to the Soviet Union for advanced training. Can you identify the kinds of schools to which they might return?

Voslensky: First . . . I believe, would be the Insitute of Social Sciences of the party Central Committee. This is the party school for foreign communists, delegated by the communist parties of various countries. It is only for communists of non-ruling parties. There are no Soviet officials who attend this school; nor are there officials of peoples democracies. There are only people from the so-called capitalist countries. They may also be from feudal countries, but in any case, not from socialist countries. Its mission is to be the continuation of the Comintern school for foreign communists.

Q: How important is Lumumba to the Soviet Union? Was the growth of certain institutions like Lumumba an important development in a broader Soviet policy?

Levchenko: Yes. Lumumba was put together within record time. In the United States . . . you would not have a Lumumba, but rather foreign students would go to different universities. [In the USSR], money, resources, teachers were all allocated to Lumumba, and within a few years the whole thing started to work.

There are times, Levchenko points out, when it would be preferable for a student to attend school in Prague, or in Bulgaria, rather than in the USSR:

Yes, it is possible that a kid who is a member of the South African Communist Party or an ANC leader will go not to Moscow, but to Czechoslovakia or Bulgaria. This is to avoid any direct connections with Moscow. In the Grenada documents [captured in 1983], there are the letters from the Grenadian ambassador in Moscow to Grenada, in which he discusses the successes, or [failures], of young Grenadian students at the Lenin School, where all of them had assumed names. The naive ambassador put their real names on the same paper. . . . In Grenada, in those years, they did not have any serious reason to hide the fact that they went to study in the Soviet Union. [However], it is a Comintern tradition to act as if [such training] is a military operation and make it secret.

In the following, Stiller describes the selection of Egyptian and Palestinian candidates for higher education in the USSR.

Stiller: There was no process of submitting recommendations, or of checking out political reliability. The [Soviet] embassy [in Cairo] had the authority to make that sort of judgment, but there were so many going through that as a practical matter it wasn't done. I think . . . the assessment was done after they got to the Soviet Union. There were a number of programs taking students to the Soviet Union, bringing them into the Academy of Social Sciences. They were evaluated there, and then sent out to other educational facilities. Many of them didn't speak any Russian when they got there, of course, so first they had to have language training. This gave the Soviets a year to assess them, and decide where they should be sent. For example, when we were at [IMEiMO], we would be sent to Moscow University to practice our languages—in my case, English and Arabic—in the foreign students' dormitories. We established contacts with various Arab and English-speaking black Africans, and made profiles of them. I am sure those profiles were used to spot students who would be good candidates for further training. This was way back in 1963–1964. The lowest level was Patrice Lumumba University—it was a cattle ranch.

Q: When these [students] were brought into the Soviet Union, was there an attempt made to push them away from their religion?

Stiller: No. In fact, there was an effort to [avoid] insulting their religious feelings at all. At the institute we often came into contact with these students, as part of our own training. We were always told, "Please, one thing you never do is to insult any religious feelings. All you are to do is expose them to the virtues of Marxism-Leninism, and its advantages over capitalism."

Goshu Wolde, former Ethiopian foreign minister, describes the selection process for Ethiopian students.

Q: How were Ethiopian students selected to be trained in the Soviet Union and the East bloc?

Wolde: It used to be that the Ministry of Education selected them. I was chairman of the Higher Education Council at that time and it used to be done through this council, when I was minister of education. But the moment [the ruling Ethiopian] party was created, the party took over.

There is now a requirement whereby any youth who goes to the Soviet Union or to other socialist countries not only for ideological training, but also for vocational or other academic training, [must] be a youth member of the party.

Arming, Advising, and Military Training

Stiller describes herein the selection of Middle Eastern cadres for military training inthe USSR.

Stiller: Those who went to the Soviet Union [from Egypt] for training were generally mid-to-upper-rank officers. I travelled back with some of them. They were good pilots, with ranks up to lieutenant colonel. The Egyptians complained that the Soviets made them study Marxism-Leninism too much.

Q: Did . . . GRU personnel determine which of the Egyptians or Palestinians should be sent for training?

Stiller: The GRU were military attachés. They would evaluate the lists given to them by the Egyptian commanders. For example, in Alexandria the Egyptians had their headquarters in the old winter palace of King Farouk. They would sit down there with the Soviet personnel and give them lists of the people they thought were good prospects that ought to go to the Soviet Union. In many cases, bribes were assumed [to have been offered by] the Egyptians who wanted to go. Also, the military attachés, in both the consulate and the embassy, would perform a sort of on-the-spot assessment of what sort of training was required, and would write their report accordingly. For the most part, however, they just rubber-stamped the list suggested by the Egyptians.

For the Palestinians, the submission of a high school transcript, of all things, was required. These came to me. Of course, I did not have any idea what they meant, aside from saying that this guy had gone to school somewhere. . . . But that was the criterion; one had to have some sort of papers and passport.

Stiller addresses the weapons transfer process, particularly in Egypt, the area in which he was working.

Q: In the area of arms transfers, was there a distinct escalation in the quality of weapons sent to Egypt after the 1967 war, a move from weapons that were on the verge of obsolescence to advanced hardware?

Stiller: Yes, this was just before the 1970 *Okean* maneuvers; that was the turning point, I believe. I do not know the reasons for this, whether the Egyptians had finally become dissatisfied with the material they were being given, or if it was felt by the [USSR] that [the Egyptians] were ready. By that time they had two or three years of training since the 1967 war, and perhaps it was felt that they were ready for the second stage. . . .

At the port of Alexandria, there was a . . . strictly . . . military pier. Ships from the GKS (State Committee for Economic Relations) could dock there and be unloaded at night—without having to go through customs, of course. The material from these ships would be loaded [onto] . . . whatever [vehicles were] available at the time, and hauled away into the desert somewhere, where it would be put under the supervision of Soviet advisers.

As far as my role was concerned, I saw the bills of lading for all the ships. They were all from the GKS. Several types of Soviet ships were used for this purpose: Liberty ships, merchant marine ships, generally of a larger tonnage than regular merchant vessels. . . . I would have to go on board. We dealt directly with the GKS representative, not the captain. The KGB was always on board as well—first or second mate, usually. The KGB was aware of all shipments going to Egypt. I would not say they exercised control over the shipments through this presence, but they were certainly aware of what was coming in. Some material came in by air as well; not as much, but I was only directly concerned with the marine shipments. Besides . . . the director of the Cairo airport was our man, and so there was never any trouble getting things through the airport.

[Responsibility was divided] between GRU and GKS. It was a strange situation. We had a GKS representative in Alexandria who had a diplomatic passport. He reported to the GRU and the consul general at the same time; he was in charge of military cargoes coming into Alexandria. At the same time he was interested in the procurement of students to be sent to the Soviet Union. So I think there was perhaps a package deal going on: on the one hand, [the USSR] would be sending arms, and on the other [it was] training people back in the Soviet Union to use those arms.

. . . Specific [protocols of implementation of overall arms transfer] agreements were not necessarily negotiated at the highest levels.

I remember that [the Egyptians] were receiving surface-to-air missiles— SAM 2, SAM 3. At the same time, these were pretty advanced. The Egyptians also wanted a . . . guided surface-to-surface weapon. It would fly six or ten feet over the water and dive just before the target, guided all the way. It was still quite secret . . . within the Soviet Union. I do not know if they got it or not.

Zdzislaw Rurarz, former Polish military intelligence officer, describes weapons transfers through Lebanon:

Lebanon was a major conduit; I was in Beirut four times, and I knew that a lot of Polish arms were going through Beirut in small shipments. Arms were shipped to South Yemen as well, though I don't know who the ultimate recipients were. When I was in Aden I saw many Soviet MiG-23s, North Korean personnel and so on, but that was only several years after the arms sales to South Yemen had begun.

Rurarz also speaks of supplies to the ANC and SWAPO:

The actual provision of arms was probably done through the military establishment with direct orders from the Central Committee of the party. The [Afro-Asian Peoples] Solidarity Committee in Moscow was only a body that coordinated such support. Actual aid was given through the usual channels. This was usually through the military attaché at the embassy who would supervise the receipt of arms at the port destination.

Levchenko explains the complexities of military and other aid to national liberation movements, including terrorist organizations:

> My impression is that the Soviet Union prefers not to train classic terrorists on [its] own territory. [The USSR] still train[s] the PLO although [that project] is not a major factor anymore. [The USSR] also train[s] people from Angola, the MPLA, SWAPO, and Mozambique. There is a facility close to Moscow, and the KGB and GRU have another facility in the south [of the USSR], for the same purpose: guerrilla warfare. Of course, the difference between terrorism and guerrilla warfare is very loose because both activities include sabotage, instruction in blowing up bridges, and so on. . . . I do not think that they bring professional terrorists into Soviet territory for the purpose of training them. They are doing it through surrogates like the Bulgarians, who represent a small country, but are quite vicious. The Bulgarian secret service [DS] has diversified its approach. It now also deals in drugs, which brings [it] into contact with dangerous characters who are terrorists by nature.

Stiller provides further insights:

> The KGB was in charge of monitoring, assessing, setting up [these training camps]. There were camps in Turkey, for example. I could never figure out how the Soviets could set up a camp in Turkey, which in our eyes was American soil. I think the KGB was also in charge of "equal opportunity" in the procurement of students. But the GRU began taking over some of these functions. Both KGB and GRU had to fill quotas. . . . of Palestinians to be sent for training. The Palestinians were all given Jordanian passports to get to the Soviet Union. I think the technical training on arms was the responsibility of GRU.
>
> GRU would also have had an oversight function with military advisers as well. These advisers were, of course, military officers. The GKS was in charge of procurement. The KGB was more interested in the development of linkages, of communications, and with keeping the GRU in line, which is one of their major responsibilities, at home and abroad.

Levchenko speculates about Soviet motivations concerning such activities:

From the [general] point of view of Marxism-Leninism, the more unrest one can generate in the West, the more beneficial it is. . . . The West German terrorists, such as the Baader-Meinhof group, were able to terrorize the whole country and even to spread their activities across the border of West Germany . . . it caused many problems for one of the major adversaries [of the communist states] and diverted it from the East-West issues. . . . I do not believe that [the Soviet leaders] provide direct assistance to the Irish Republican Army. The logic says that is should be so, but I do not believe it. It could be discovered by others too easily. The vital interests of the Soviet Union are more important than support for terrorists. If [a] tie between terrorists and the Soviet Union is exposed, then it would be very damaging for the Soviet Union. Therefore, [the USSR] uses surrogates.. [Soviet leaders] do not have one point of view or one policy on this question. They will determine whether to indirectly support the terrorists, to train them, or to stay away from them, on a case-by-case basis.

Arkady Shevchenko asserts that Soviet decision makers have little sympathy for terror methods currently in use (particularly hijacking), at least when they could threaten the USSR itself. The Soviet Union, he says, may be involved in some activities that assist terrorists, but prefers to use surrogates for such purposes:

Even if there is no question of direct Soviet involvement in training in terrorist techniques either within or outside the Soviet Union, why are the Soviets [involved at all]? They aren't doing it for the hijacking of planes and explosions at the airports. They are doing it for what they call liberation movements. And they realize they're losing control over it. They train all these people and [the latter] go back to the Middle East and join . . . terrorist organizations [involved in hijacking and attacking airports]. Instead of doing that, the Soviets expected that [these trainees] would . . . be engaged in the Arab struggle with "Zionism" against Israel, or with SWAPO against South Africa. . . . But there are not supposed to be all these kidnappings, bombings, and hijackings, because the Soviets may suffer themselves. . . .

Terrorism is justified [from the standpoint of the Soviet leadership] if it is used to overthrow a government where the Soviet Union would like to promote its interests and establish its dominance. . . . But how it's been used by some extremist, radical Arab elements is considered wrong.

So there are two [factors]. One: [Soviet leaders] consider that type of terrorism wrong. Two: there is a lot of evidence that the Soviet hand is there and they would like to protect themselves [by being able to claim]: "No, we are not involved."

So, the Soviets do train and sponsor terrorist organizations, but because those groups have begun to . . . [stray] from "acceptable" methods, the Soviet support is not as [strong as] in the past.

Levchenko, summing up, discusses specifics:

Basically an organization like the Japanese Red Army is dangerous to the Soviet Union as well. In Japan the KGB was trying to watch the activity of this group, just to be sure that they did not aim any actions at Aeroflot or the Soviet embassy. Also, the [Japanese] Red Army is not a political organization, it is really a bunch of mad dogs. There is no political place for them. I [would] never [have] believe[d] that young Japanese men and women would die for a Middle Eastern cause. They [had] never been there before. The KGB does not work against such groups, but they watch them.

On terrorism, from the point of view of Marxism-Leninism, naturally unrest in the West is very desirable. This unrest shows that capitalism does deteriorate and that bourgeois freedoms actually do have a price. Lenin developed this theory long ago.

There are probably some terrorist organizations that receive Soviet support in a limited way. The Soviet Union does not want to provide special training to the terrorists on the territory of the Soviet Union. They provide guerrilla training, which is not too different. For example, it includes sabotage. They still consider it paramilitary or military training of the self-proclaimed officers and soldiers of the PLO, MPLA, or people from Mozambique. There are thousands of people involved. The PLO consists of twenty-two loosely connected organizations. Even if they train a few hundred or a few thousand of them to fight in the Middle East, there is no guarantee that some of them will not become individual terrorists or become attached to an existing terrorist organization. Therefore, by providing paramilitary training and assistance, it is indirectly supporting terrorism.

I do not know if they do direct training of terrorists, but if they do it is probably somewhere else, like Bulgaria, where the service is small and very vicious. Maybe the Czechs are involved. The North Koreans, a controversial case, may recommend some people to be trained. . . . The North Koreans have their own very specific ways of thinking. I would not be surprised if Czechoslovakia, East Germany, and Bulgaria provide training for European and Middle Eastern terrorists. Also Cuba, which has its Department 13 for terrorist training, is probably the closest the Soviet Union gets to the direct operation of terrorists. The DGI is entirely paid for from the Soviet budget. And if they own the thing, they know what it is doing. In surrogate countries, such as Czechoslovakia and Bulgaria, they exist close to the KGB and under its control, but are still formally paid for through their own government's budget.

Jan Sejna refers in fact to Czechoslovak assistance for the IRA (Irish Republican Army):

Czechoslovakia had the most contact with [the IRA], especially the anarchists and the communists who participated. What was going on there was not too much of a secret. There was some supply of explosive materials, radio stations, and equipment, as well some supply of money. . . . In 1963, the relationship was already very well established.

(For testimony concerning the training by Cuban special operations—
DOE—of M19, Tupamaros, Monteneros, ETA, and Red Brigades, see the
section on implementation by surrogates in chapter 5.)

Stiller addressed the effect of the Sino-Soviet conflict and of Soviet
interagency stresses upon involvement with "national liberation" entities,
especially when both guerrilla and terrorist aspects are concerned:

> The original [training] camps [for Middle Eastern national liberation enti-
> ties], from what I understood, were in Kuwait. There were some established
> in South Yemen by the Chinese immediately after the British withdrawal.
> Our concern there was how to get reliable people away from the Chinese.
> They were training various groups, including some of the PLO factions; they
> were also training the government of Aden. Hatred of the Chinese over-
> whelmed Soviet policy in this regard. It didn't matter what the Chinese did
> or said, before or after the Cultural Revolution. . . . Based on meeting two
> people . . . who kept shuttling back to Beirut, and based on a statement by
> [a] GRU [official] that "the only way to get rid of the Chinese is to give more
> and more arms to the factions, to train them on the Soviet side," I would
> make the conclusion that there would have been some training facilities in
> Iraq. Second, there is the possibility that Lebanon was at that time being
> considered as a potentially strong base for training activity; . . . Syria was
> the recipient of the largest arms shipments in 1969–1970. The channel of
> supplies was through Syria.
>
> . . . In about the spring of 1968, a relationship was established between
> the Soviets and the PLO. This was a very strong commitment; for example,
> the establishment of quotas of Palestinians to be sent back to the Soviet
> Union for training. . . . There were rallies organized [so-called] cultural
> centers—"solidarity with the people of Palestine." . . . A very grandiose
> political support structure was being established through the cultural
> centers. The ID [International Department of the CPSU Central Committee]
> also had a hand in this, though I never had a feeling that the ID was working
> directly with the PLO; that was the domain of the KGB and GRU. In Cairo
> I remember that there was a KGB operative who handled PLO problems.
> There were two operatives shuttling back and forth from Cairo to Beirut;
> they were in charge of liaison, setting up PLO organizations in Beirut, and
> so forth. They were very tough guys, young guys, from the KGB, but from
> a different department. . . . They looked military . . . but they were KGB,
> I'm sure. . . .
>
> Originally, the commitment was to the PLO as a political force that
> would be able to take over the occupied lands. There was a campaign to
> build up the PLO and the Palestinians as a great political force; this began
> in the spring of 1968. They saw the PLO as a very good vehicle to establish
> Soviet popularity among the Arabs. . . . Military support was conducted on
> a much more clandestine level than the political connection, even among
> ourselves . . . never once did we acknowledge that the Simferopool
> Agricultural School (in the Soviet Crimea) was not really an agricultural

school, even among ourselves. And of course, at this time larger and larger numbers of PLO members were going there for training. . . . To begin with Egypt was a fairly hostile territory to the PLO. . . . So the main route of supplies to the PLO became Syria. . . . The Soviets began developing a very strong organization in Beirut; they started courting George Habash.[3] There was . . . a continuous increase in the number of PLO members going to the Soviet Union for education, not only to Simferopol, but to Land Grant University, to medical school, to Patrice Lumumba [University in Moscow].

Prior to September of 1970, PLO cadres went directly from Amman to the Soviet Union; afterwards, they went through Kuwait or Beirut. They were diffused from Amman. The Soviets made a deal with the Kuwait government through Sheik Sabah in which the Kuwaitis would be paid to allow the use of a route through Kuwait to Basra and Baghdad and then to the Soviet Union. When I got to Kuwait, I was responsible for some of this movement, but a lot of it was also done directly through Iraq.

. . . The PLO became a central theme of [front] rallies. It became the center of the joint Soviet-Arab fight to liberate Palestine, to push Israel back. By Soviet standards, that meant back to the pre-1967 lines; by Arab standards, that meant into the sea. Whatever the case, the PLO cause became a central theme for the fronts.

Direction and Coordination

Many of the Soviet activities that fall within the category of surrogate operations have to do with front organizations. This is an imprecise term covering entities run and organized by—or on behalf of—the USSR and its allies, and also organizations whose members, for the most part, are not consciously pro-Soviet at all, but who sincerely support causes with goals that converge, at one time or another, with the tactical requirements of Soviet political operations. These activities, however, are not devoid of problems for the Soviet bureaucracy.

Levchenko delineates the division of power between two very different Soviet front organizations, AAPSO[4] and the World Peace Council (WPC):

In the 1960s, [the AAPSO] was very important because of a division of labor between the World Peace Council, where they were disarming people, and AAPSO, which was a militant organization. . . . AAPSO openly declared its support for any "national liberation" movements. It openly said that it would provide them not only with food, but arms, uniforms, and everything else which is needed for guerrilla warfare. They were very vocal in their support of the national liberation movements in international organizations. Soviet fronts would pick up their political issues and try to bring them to

---

[3] George Habash, leader of the Popular Front for the Liberation of Palestine.
[4] Afro-Asian Peoples Solidarity Organization.

the U.N. The PLO would not have been any [more] successful in the late 1960s without direct Soviet support. . . . AAPSO was a very important organization. At that time quite a few members of AAPSO were also members of different countries' governments. It was just overlooked [in the West], but it was important.

[The inability to keep the functions of different fronts cleanly separated, however,] is a bureaucratic phenomenon of the [CC CPSU] International Department, and of the Soviet leadership, which they cannot overcome. For instance, if one is supposed to say a few special words for the North Koreans, this policy will automatically run through all the fronts, even those fronts which [have no] logical . . . interest [in] Korea. It is almost a rule. The World Peace Council's role is still to convince Westerners that unilateral disarmament is the only solution, but . . . after the 1973 Arab-Israeli War, the World Peace Council conducted conferences for the PLO. . . . It was part of the major coordinated effort by all the Soviet fronts. . . . Also, one front will hold a conference, and all other fronts will send delegations. That is routine. They were pretending that AAPSO was a soft organization from the very beginning. By the latter half of the 1970s when AAPSO declined, it was the WPC that had to pick up the slack, but [subsequently] AAPSO bounced back.

Goshu Wolde describes Ethiopia's attitude toward such groups.

Wolde: [Member groups of AAPSO] were all guests of the Ethiopian Solidarity Committee. But once they came, they wanted to meet with many people, including me and my department heads; they also wanted to meet with the chairman. The ANC president, Mr. Tambo, for example, regularly meets with the chairman. They meet with the party functionaries, they meet with the head of the Ethiopian Solidarity Committee, it all depends on what type of delegation it is. Normally Ethiopia supports them politically; political support is there, moral support is there, and there was a time when Ethiopia supported them by training Zimbabwe's freedom fighters, and that's all. It did not commit troops.

Q: Was Ethiopia's policy towards these groups . . . coordinated with the Soviet Union?

Wolde: No. At the time when the Soviet Union and East European countries were supporting Nkomo, the Ethiopian government at that time was supporting both [Zimbabwean factions], but was more inclined towards Mugabe in the Zimbabwe conflict. The Soviet bloc as a whole . . . was committed to Nkomo. . . .

Stanislav Levchenko addresses the issue of geniune grass roots organizations:

[Soviet influence operations target] American public opinion or public organizations [particularly when it concerns] a grassroots organization. The

Soviet Union [does] not sponsor [such organizations]. [Soviet operations chiefs] are smarter than that. They usually try to find a grassroots organization that has already established itself. . . .

In response to further questions concerning this particular type of manipulation of Western public opinion, Stanislav Levchenko responded:

I would put it in the category of classic grey "active measures" and grey "propaganda." [The Soviet agencies may wish] to place an agent there, but if they cannot, they will still try to manipulate the organization in a subtle way. The members of the organization really want to understand what the Soviet Union is presenting to them.

Now let us be cautious with the term "under Soviet control." I mean under Soviet direction or influence. It is as simple as that. You can question why people get fooled that easily. It is a story of psychological warfare. After World War II, the World Peace Council started to operate in 1949 or 1950, playing upon the great exhaustion which the whole of Europe experienced as a result of the war. Everyone wanted peace. Everybody wanted to relax and live out their lives peacefully. That was why the World Peace Council was so successful in its first years. It tried to manipulate situations in such a way that the U.S. appeared as a warmonger. The objectives [of such operations] are much different [from] . . . the fronts in the Third World, the objective [of which] is the seizure of power. . . . If you look at the United States and Western society, . . . you are not going to topple the system or seize control, but you are going to slow down the response to Soviet military policy.

Michael Voslensky sheds light upon the problems involved in Soviet influence operations:

[There] is [a] weakness [in] Soviet management of . . . movements [like the Pugwash and *Pacem in Terris* movements]. And here is the point [at which] they fail. Because [the Soviet side] is a bureaucracy. There are these people, liberals from different countries, idealists and so on, in Pugwash. Now what can the Soviets demand from them? Only to accept practically every Soviet proposal and every Soviet formula. . . .

The question is whether this is reasonable or not. I was for instance always against it and I was not alone. Nevertheless, since [the responsible Soviet officials are part of a] bureaucracy, they could not do it in another way. Because they must present their results to the party Central Committee. . . . The only means the [CPSU] CC had do [decide] whether or not we had been successful at a given conference was to judge the final documents approved there. These had to repeat official Soviet positions.

So they need written resolutions and the Soviet formulas [to] appear, adopted by Pugwash. And they do it in Pugwash. . . . But the result is the decline of the importance of the Pugwash movement.

Voslensky mentions the religious factor in such Soviet operations:

They began to make use of the Russian Orthodox Church—but not all other churches in the Soviet Union or in the satellites—in their peace movements rather early. It began under Stalin. It was only logical to create their own organization for all these . . . church groups.

Implementation by Allies

Jan Sejna depicts the transmission belt through which agencies in Warsaw Pact states receive decisions from the USSR for implementation:

[Once instruction is received from the appropriate Soviet entity, e.g., the Administrative Organs Department of the CPSU Central Committee, the implementation] plan is presented to the Czechoslovak Defense Council, whether it is long-term, a one-year term, or just an operation-specific plan. In Czech the name for the Defense Council in the late 1960s was *Vojenska komise obrany ustredniho vyboru strany* [the Military Defense Commission of the Party Central Committee]. . . .

[The plan] contains guidelines for the [pact allies] and how [they are to] participate. Then the chief of general staff and the minister of the interior from the . . . country [in question] are called to Moscow. At the same time [the Defense Council of the client state] calls the Administrative Organs Department in the Soviet Union and [the latter] calls the chiefs of the Administrative Organs Department of [the client state], like [Miroslav] Mamula [in Czechoslovakia], the Moscow. [The Soviet Administrative Organs Department conveys the CPSU view, since] the party does not trust . . . the Soviet GRU or KGB [to give directions appropriately]. . . . While the [Czechoslovak] chief of general staff and intelligence chief are receiving their instructions, the [Soviet] party, through the Administrative Organs Department, is giving its own [directives]. [Sometimes, members of the Soviet Administrative Organs Department] visit Prague, Warsaw, or Budapest, and give briefings.

If [the Soviet officials] make changes [in existing plans] I would take notes, come home, write a report, and bring it to Mamula if . . . he was not present at the discussion. I would give him [also any] decision of the [Czechoslovak] Defense Council because it controls how [implementation is to] proceed. Then I would take the [various] documents and burn them immediately. [Such] meetings take place in the [Czechoslovak] Central Committee. In [a particular case], the [Czechoslovak] Defense Council might decide to steal computers or buy them illegally and transport them across the border to Czechoslovakia. In an important operation [involving personalities of standing], Leonid Brezhnev would be involved. If [anyone claims that] Brezhnev did not know [of such operations], it is baloney. . . . If there is such an operation, the Defense Council decides. The plan must be reported to the Defense Council, maybe twice: once about how it will [be implemented] and then how it finally was done. If it is just an average operation, the minister of defense and the minister of the interior in Czechoslovakia must present a report every six months to the Defense Council on how the plan has been implemented [or] how they are proceeding [with] the plan. . . . The [Czechoslovak] first secretary has a report every morning from both intelligence services on what happened the previous day. The embassies or trade missions use many agents for these operations.

Sejna proceeds to address the international division of labor amongst Warsaw Pact countries:

Each satellite got responsibility for a particular project or country. The Soviet Union always divides responsibility among the satellite states, giving a particular assignment to whichever country has the best chance for success. It does not mean that these countries do not operate in other places, but, for example, Czechoslovakia mainly worked in Latin America, Austria and West Germany. . . . India, like the United States, was pretty clearly the responsibility of the Soviet Union. Yet by 1958 or 1959, Czechoslovakia had been successful in recruiting [a senior official] in India, and so they gave us the responsibility because of the earlier success. Later on, Soviet intelligence took him over because of a larger strategy. In the beginning when someone had completed an operation, they gave him more responsibility. Who else could be a better agent than such a person?

. . . Czechoslovakia had most of the more important countries in Latin America: Mexico, the Dominican Republic, Guatemala, Argentina, Brazil, and in Africa: Ghana and Guinea. Ethiopia, Egypt, and Afghanistan as well. Czechoslovakia had the first 100 officers in Egypt, during the Suez crisis.

Tadeusz Kucharski presents his insight into the division of labor among Warsaw Pact countries:

[In Angola] military training was a monopoly of the Soviet Union and Cuba. They also had a monopoly over the delivery of arms and munitions. The East Germans had a monopoly in dealing with the Angolan security forces, and Bulgaria and North Korea were responsible for agriculture. Also the establishment of a voluntary youth organization was an East German specialty. Groups came from Germany to help with the economy, and members of the Angolan youth organization went to Germany. Another Cuban specialty was to provide medical assistance. For this there were Cuban doctors and nurses. The Soviet Union and Poland also sent [a few] doctors.

Wolde notes that the East Germans have a special task:

The East Germans are in the police force. There is coordination between the KGB and the East Germans. The East Germans are perhaps the more efficient of the two. They have single-minded determination to organize the point of perfection. It amazes me. Every time [Erich] Honecker comes to Ethiopia, if he says he will arrive at 9:00, he does. Not one minute earlier or later. And this is true of East German workers' efficiency. I think Honecker is also very deeply committed to socialism in Ethiopia. Once he makes a decision, there are no questions.

Jan Sejna describes the Soviet-Czechoslovak machinery for arms transfers to recipients primarily in the Third World:

The whole thing is orchestrated by the Soviet Union. It is handled [in Czechoslovakia] by the Department of Foreign Technical Assistance, *oddeleni zahranicne technicke pomoci* [of the Czechoslovak Defense Ministry—MNO]. . . . It [has] the responsibility for training foreign students in the new technologies and military equipment. It also procures the equipment from the factories and military warehouses. The Foreign Trade Ministry is also involved, which is administered by the military and run by General Macek. They handle the business and legal end of the matter, drawing up the contracts, etc.

The Department for Foreign Technical Assistance [of the MNO] is not involved if it is illegal to pass weapons to the group involved, such as . . . in the Dominican Republic, or to the PLO. In those cases [another entity] takes charge. . . .

That is why equipment has been placed in Third World countries: to help in . . . battles [that] will not be fought only in Europe. If one expects to fight in India or the Middle East, [the] equipment [is] there already. The Soviet military knows that the client state can never hope to use these weapons effectively. . . . One cannot seriously believe that the thousands of tanks and other equipment shipped to these Middle Eastern countries will actually be used by the Arabs. They are far more likely to be used by Soviet airborne brigades from the Caucauses or elsewhere.

Hus provides more information on Soviet coordination of Czechoslovak arms transfers. Unlike Sejna, Hus believes that the Ministry of the Interior, rather than the Ministry of Defense, is in charge of such activities.

Hus: Providing support, such as the export of arms, to a liberation movement is again the responsibility of a department within the Interior Ministry. Czechoslovakia will sell arms to anybody, at times even to groups which are fighting each other.

Q: To what extent were these arms sales coordinated with the Soviet Union?

Hus: When the Soviet Union wanted Czechoslovakia to sell arms it would contact the Czechoslovak Interior Ministry, possibly through the Warsaw

Pact offices in Moscow. The Interior Ministry had much closer contacts with Moscow than either the Foreign Ministry or the International Department [of the party—KSC]. This is because they are operatives, under close Soviet supervision. The Soviet Union would let it be known to whom arms should be sold. However, the Czechoslovaks expect to be paid for the arms. The arms sales are an important source of hard currency for Czechoslovakia.

Voslensky refers to an arrangement coordinated by the Soviet Union in which instruction is given in educational institutions of other Warsaw Pact countries as suitable substitutes for Lumumba University.

Q: Who pays for the education of the students who come from a country that does have a special relationship with the Soviet Union?

Voslensky: The Soviet Union pays one hundred percent of all costs. The local government will never pay any of the costs. I speculate that [sending students to Bulgaria] is to demonstrate to those in Moscow that Lumumba is better than Sofia. Bulgaria is just a country where the Soviets implement their dirty affairs.

Hus comments on the monitoring of foreign trainees in Czechoslovakia:

Q: Who would be responsible for [foreign students] who . . . come to Czechoslovakia for training?

Hus: It would be the responsibility of the Interior Ministry. The International Department [of the party] . . . would not be responsible for this. [It is] only responsible for the political aspects of the relationship. Everything that is political is run through the International Department. For such things as training it is done by the Ministry of the Interior. The International Department member is likely to find out more about such training from the [trainees] involved than from the Interior Ministry. It is not his business to know.

Implementation by Surrogates

Miguel Bolaños-Hunter, former Nicaraguan counterintelligence officer, describes the division of labor among non-Warsaw Pact communist and non-communist forces in surrogate operations, including military, guerrilla, and terrorist elements:

[In Nicaragua there were] Libyan[s], . . . North Vietnamese, North Koreans. The Vietnamese were in the military—in the army. The Koreans were mainly with the infirmaries, the hospitals and clinics of the Ministry of the Interior; [they] were mainly medical personnel. The Libyans were also with the army, but were also in the special operations team within the Fifth Directorage responsible for operations such as kidnapping and killing.

. . . The PLO was involved mainly in training the Salvadoran guerrillas. Wherever Cuban special operations—the DOE—was involved it was in terrorist training. This includes the training of Salvadoran guerrillas, Colombian M-19, Tupamaros, Montoneros, and so on. From Europe we had the Italian Red Brigades and the Spanish Basques—the ETA. I don't remember any Japanese. All these groups have offices with representatives there . . . , and they were available if needed. I know that the ETA was involved in the Costa Rica penetration operation, very involved.

The presence of terrorists in Nicaragua is confirmed by Eden Pastora Gomez:

Even the Italians, the Red Brigades group, [were] there.

Benemelis emphasizes the Cuban role in international terrorism:

If one looks at movements connected to the Soviet bloc in the 1960s [that] used terrorism, one will find the roots of that in Cuba. Cuba had more experience in terrorist tactics than any other country in the Soviet bloc. [Castro's] experience went beyond guerrilla warfare to urban warfare. Those tactics were later taught to the Monteneros and the Tupamaros. Groups in Castro's forces which fought against Batista were later used for terrorist training. They specialized in hijacking, bribery, and kidnapping. This was all highly developed in the fight against Batista. Raul Castro used it to kidnap the people from Guantanamo Naval Base. Fidel learned these methods . . . through his connections to criminal gangs in Cuba. Cuba was able to use this experience to teach terrorist organizations.

Eden Pastora Gomez confirms Miguel Bolaños-Hunter's account of the surrogate division of labor, and notes also the presence of Warsaw Pact elements.

Q: Aside from East Germany, do any other East European states have a significant presence within Nicaragua?

Pastora: Yes. Bulgaria was in charge of the economy. . . . The division was such that Cuba had the army, Bulgaria had the economy, and the PLO the air force. Khaddafi and the Ayatollah [were] also starting to get very involved.

[The PLO provided] pilots. . . . [After the Sandinista seizure of power], they went in the air force and they are still there. I could almost say that the PLO controls the air force. . . .

When I was there, the Nicaraguan pilots were being trained in Bulgaria.

They should be trained by now, and they should be keeping up their practice in Cuba. . . .

The PLO was trained by Syria, Libya, and by the Russians. The pilots were working for Arafat before. Now they're at the disposition of the Nicaraguans. But their most basic relationship is with . . . Habash.

Benemelis reinforces the testimonies of Bolaños-Hunter and Pastora on the division of labor among the surrogates:

Soviet bloc personnel [is] deliberately divided. East Germans [in some cases handle] security. . . . The Koreans [in some cases] were a fourth element, in addition to the usual three—Cuba, GDR, and the USSR. There were more Koreans than Germans in countries where Cuba was present, with the exception of Angola and Mozambique. Wherever you find Cubans, there will be North Koreans. They tend to focus on the air force, though in South Yemen there were also Cuban and Soviet advisers there.

Stanislav Levchenko focuses on the intelligence role played by surrogates of the USSR:

In Nicaragua, the KGB has made its presence known through surrogates. [According to Miguel Bolaños-] Hunter's . . . figures it [seems that] for every six officers in the Nicaraguan security force, there is one officer from the Soviet Union or a surrogate to provide guidance. The number of Soviet advisers there is not as large as the number of Cubans. In Nicaragua now, for example, the Cubans are running the service entirely.

I do not know if [the Cubans] have some intelligence officials in Angola, but I would not be surprised if they do. In Ethiopia they definitely have them. In Afghanistan they own the whole service. With the exception of [the] East German intelligence service, there is no surrogate country's intelligence that is as close to the KGB as the Cuban DGI is. Since the enhancement of intelligence, the Soviet Union started to train local intelligence services in the KGB's traditions. The DGI and the East Germans have very well diversified intelligence services scattered all over the world. They assist the Soviet Union in training Third World intelligence services.

Benemelis provides details of surrogates in actual combat:

The Cubans sent a tank brigade [to the Golan Heights]. It was an international unit. There were some North Korean drivers in Cuban tanks. This was [at the end of the October 1973 war]. I also heard that a small Korean air force unit provided cover for the tanks. It was a coordinated operation. So, long before Angola in 1975, there was Cuban-Soviet-Korean coordination in the field, in the Middle East, South Yemen, and Somalia. The Angolan pattern was created long before. The use of surrogates started in 1972. Angola was just a larger operation, not different.

Pastora discusses Cuba's role in Latin America:

[The Cubans] don't participate in the guerrilla activity in El Salvador. They are basically in charge of the propaganda and information . . . [but] when I was in Nicaragua, they were training Salvadorans and . . . [a Cuban was] in charge of logistic supply to Salvador. . . .

The Soviet bloc and Soviet Union . . . authorized [using Nicaragua as a funnel for weapons to the Salvadoran guerrillas]. As far as Cuba is concerned, they're totally, totally committed to helping the Salvadorans. In fact, it was their idea. As far as what Managua gives to the Salvadorans, what I can tell you is that I wish the United States had given me half of what Managua is giving to the Salvadorans.

. . . The FAL guns which Fidel gave went to Salvador. Also the M-1s, the Garands, went to Salvador. So did the G-3s which we had bought. The M-16s which came from Vietnam stayed behind. The machine guns, M-60s, and . . . rockets, fundamentally that. While the air is the most common route to get the weapons there, they'll also cross the Gulf of Fonseca in small boats.

Pastora elaborates on Nicaragua as an arena of surrogate activities.

Pastora: [Soon after Somoza's overthrow] when I went to the [Sandinista] command bunker, there was a large group of Cubans whom I had never seen before. On the same day, an airlift from Havana to Managua was installed.

. . . [Then I found] the East Germans . . . in charge of giving advice to the security police. They teach how to interrogate, how to use psychology, and how to use fear. The Cuban . . . in charge of the security police was trained in East Germany. All of the Cubans in the security police have been trained in East Germany.

. . . When they first came, the [Cuban] advisers started to select people to be sent to Cuba for training and then later to other countries in the Soviet bloc.

Q: What were the criteria for this?

Pastora: They chose people for tanks, artillery and aviation. Aviation to Bulgaria, and artillery and tanks to Cuba.

Q: How did they decide who should go?

Pastora: Two factors: ideological commitment and physical condition. . . .

Africa has been an arena for Soviet surrogates over many years, as Kucharski explains.

Kucharski: ZANU, Mugabe's movement, has always had strong links to Korea and China. Tanzania has also had strong links to these countries.

Q: Personnel from communist non-Warsaw Pact countries, such as North Korea, Cuba, and in some cases, Vietnam, [was] used for training and establishing a presence. Was this done so that it appeared as an independent non-Warsaw Pact action?

Kucharski: Yes, that is one reason. Another is that since they are not white they are more acceptable in black Africa. However, I saw no Vietnamese in Angola. . . .

The Cubans were used as a result of Soviet interest and the Cuban need for success, to demonstrate that Castro was a statesman. Also, it was better for Neto and the MPLA to have troops from a smaller country involved. It would be much more acceptable for the Angolan population than to have a superpower's troops involved.

Benemelis comments further on Cuban involvement in Africa.

Benemelis: The pilots used in Uganda and Chad must have been Soviet. The Libyans [had] only a few bad pilots. The Cubans built the road from central Libya to the southern border with Chad which the Libyans later used for the invasion. It ran south from Kufra.

Q: What do you know about the decision to commit large Cuban units in Ethiopia?

Benemelis: The Cubans acted openly as Soviet surrogates. There were some good Cuban generals there, but an even larger group of Soviet generals [was] in command of the operation. They only used Cuban infantry troops in very difficult situations like crossing the Marda pass. It was a Cuban paratrooper operation. They used about ten thousand Cuban infantry. It was . . . the turning point of the war. General Petrov was in the field commanding it directly. I talked to several Cubans who fought in Ethiopia who said their commanders were Soviet officers. It was all planned and directed by Moscow. The advantage they had was that a lot of Soviet and Cuban personnel stayed in Somalia until the last minute. They brought a lot of information on the Somali army back with them. It was very useful for the offensive.

Miguel Bolaños-Hunter adds:

In the first place, the Cubans numbered about fifteen thousand at the height of their involvement in the Ogaden war, but gradually they came to a lower number, now only a brigade. And there isn't so much Cuban presence as to be a bother. Those that are there have a Latin temperament and they like to sing, drink, play and dance. They are very jovial in many respects. By and large they are liked, unlike the Soviets, who keep very much to themselves. The unpopularity of the government is reflected on the Soviets.

Benemelis gives details of early Cuban training of Africans.

Benemelis: The training of Africans in Cuba started very early, even before I went to Africa [early in 1962]. It began in 1961, or the end of 1960. The trainees were from Zanzibar, Senegal, Tunis, the Congo, Namibia, Zimbabwe, and Cameroon. . . .

The Cubans and the Algerians established a training camp somewhere in Algeria; a huge one for Africa. This was at the end of 1962. Abdul Aziz Bouteflika was later the ambassador to Tanzania. He knew about the coup [in Zanzibar in 1964]. He was still chief of intelligence then, later he had some problems at the end of the Boumedienne era.

Q: Were the Cubans at the training camp?

Benemelis: Yes. They set up their most powerful intelligence center outside the western hemisphere. They would bring guerrillas from black Africa to this camp.

Benemelis continues:

Benemelis: The Cuban army handled . . . [the] training [of] Palestinians [in South Yemen] . . . [belonging to the] Habash [group]. The first secretary of the party and the real power in South Yemen, Abdul Fatah Ismail, was like a brother to Habash. Both belonged to a commando unit of the Marxist international movement in the 1950s and 1960s. One of Habash's headquarters was in South Yemen, even though he did not use it as a base. He had facilities there, with Cubans doing the training. There were also North Koreans there training people. East Germans were involved with communications and security. There were Soviet advisers in the training camps, but they were less heavily involved than the Cubans or the Koreans. The Soviet advisers were more involved with the Yemeni army. The DGI [Cuban intelligence] people were there for intelligence gathering. South Yemen and Somalia were run under one command by one general who moved back and forth between the two places. The DGI chief ran the centers in both countries also.

Q: Who received training?

Benemelis: North Yemenis, Dhofaris, Palestinians, Eritreans, Somalis from the Ogaden, and some Chileans. I did not have access to other facilities. I knew there were Europeans there, but I did not see them. There were Iranians there who had strong connections to the Cubans. I think they were leftists from areas of Iran near the Persian Gulf. They had been in Great Britain before. I knew some of them. The Palestinians came from

Habash's group, and Fatah. At that point, the training had not grown to include other factions.

Miguel Bolaños-Hunter also refers to the involvement of Middle Eastern elements:

The PLO opened an office in Managua within a month of the revolution, but PLO members had already been involved with the Sandinistas. In the last offensive, for example, there were three or four PLO members fighting as combatants with the international brigade in northern Nicaragua. I don't remember any internationalists fighting from the United States. After the Sandinistas took power, the PLO's role was to assist in training for special operations such as kidnapping, killings, and so on. . . .

[T]here were quite a few Sandinistas with PLO training. These relations date back to the 1960s. The PLO was not directly involved with the training of the FSLN itself, such as its intelligence officers. The PLO did assist the FSLN in the training of Salvadoran guerrillas.

6

The Soviet Union, Its Allies, and Other Partners: Coordination, Control, and Dissonance

Already during the closing years of World War II, Stalin was at work planning the construction of a Soviet-controlled zone in Eastern Europe. He had achieved his objective by 1948. Despite the Yalta agreement, which had called for the establishment of Eastern European governments "broadly representative of all democratic elements" and selected "through free elections," the region from the Baltic to the Adriatic Seas had fallen under Soviet domination. From the 1950s onward, the Soviet Union continued expanding its influence further until it established a sphere of at least partial control along such a broad geographic spectrum as to cover Vietnam, Cuba, and Ethiopia. The current situation is very fluid. It should be borne in mind at all times that the interviewees speak with authority only about the periods in which they were members of the party, military, or intelligence elites in their respective countries.

Eastern Europe

The Soviet empire, perhaps the only contemporary empire, is very diverse and in a permanent state of flux. Moscow's control over its allies is far from absolute and has changed over the decades from rigid day-to-day rule by Soviet *diktat* in the early fifties, to a more indirect system of suggestions and instructions to indigenous, powerful, well-entrenched bureaucracies, and the establishment of transmission belts, such as various "mass movements." These developments notwithstanding, few would doubt that the Soviet empire is not grounded on the consent and self-interest of its subjects. Therefore, Soviet decision makers have to rely on an elaborate, multilayered system of channels through which they seek to control their allies. The very existence of this network is resented by most of these allies and clients. This resentment has serious consequences, because the Soviet empire is probably the first empire in which the central power, the Soviet Union, is viewed by many inhabitants of the subject countries as culturally and economically less developed. Among our interviewees, Zdzislaw Rurarz, the former Polish ambassador to Japan and officer in Polish military intelligence (Z-2), describes this image of the Soviet Union in the early 1950s:

> When I was in Moscow in 1953, I saw barefoot people in Red Square, prompting some of our colleagues to say that they really liked this freedom, that you could walk barefoot in Red Square!

By the time Rurarz saw the bleak reality of Soviet society, Moscow's grip on Eastern Europe seemed firm. This appeared to be due to Stalin's ability to plan farther ahead than most of his contemporaries. Peter Deriabin, a former officer of the Kremlin Guards Directorate, describes some of the first steps taken by Stalin to develop a network of East European collaborators under Soviet control.

> *Deriabin:* SMERSH began to collect information on present and potential leaders in 1943. By the end of the war, the files were quite extensive. For example, a man like Ulbricht was well known: his abilities, political attitudes, and so on. Many Germans had been used in the Free Germany Committee in Ufa; they were recruited and cultivated. Later, these informants continued to supply information from Germany about government leaders. . . .
>
> *Q:* Were any people or groups of people, particularly in the leadership, exempt from surveillance by the security organs?
>
> *Deriabin:* First of all, externally the goal was to surround any satellite country's leadership with informants, agents, and, where possible, electronic surveillance. During Stalin's time, all leaders of allied governments were supplied with a bodyguard adviser who worked in the respective countries and only took a small staff of two or three people with him; the countries included Eastern Europe, China under Mao Tse-tung, North Korea under Kim Il Sung, and Tito's Yugoslavia in the beginning. The bodyguards were not instructed to gather information on their subjects, simply because many in the profession are ignorant of everything except protection.

Our interviews did not focus on the exact anatomy of Soviet take-overs. Nevertheless, the basic contours emerged clearly: once the first elements of Soviet presence in a country existed, in most cases through the insertion of the Red Army, Moscow tended to focus its main resources and assets to develop control over the local police, security, and intelligence organizations. In Gen. Jan Sejna's words:

> The Soviets are smart . . . they built up the military forces and the secret police right away. Those are the institutions of control. In Czechoslovakia the Soviet advisers went first to the Ministry of the Interior, since under the

communist system the security service controls even the military forces and military counterintelligence. They do not have anything to do with the Ministry of Defense. Therefore, step number one is to consolidate the police and the secret police.

Once the Soviet leaders established strong influence in a target country, they moved gradually from direct control to rule through trusted local elites. Rurarz, himself a former officer of Polish Military Intelligence, the Z-2, mentions this shift:

When Polish military intelligence was reestablished after the war, it went through various phases. At first it was totally controlled by the Soviets, and later controlled by the Poles. During Stalinist times, nineteen senior officers were executed and seventy others were sentenced to death. They had been interrogated by Soviet officers. They were mostly intelligence officers.

Michael Checinski, a former officer in Polish Military Counterintelligence, assumes that the USSR continues to be directly involved in controlling that service, the WSW. Other branches of the intelligence sector appear to be in Polish hands:

Military intelligence, or Z-2, is attached to the general staff. [While in the Soviet Union] counterintelligence . . . is part of the KGB, in Poland it is a totally separate organization. It is not . . . formally subordinated to the minister of defense. In fact, [it is] not subordinate to anyone in Poland, but only to Moscow. It is not like the civilian security service in Poland, which is made up of Polish communists and a number of Soviet advisers. The security service has to work with the civilian population. They must know the conditions in Poland. They must know Polish. They must know a lot of things that are connected with the fabric of society. . . .

Currently there seems to be an uneasy balance between the local intelligence personnel and its Soviet advisers. As tends to be the case whenever European countries are involved, historical memory plays an important role in shaping present-day perceptions. Rurarz, whose background was in military intelligence, not counterintelligence, does not believe that there is a direct Soviet presence in Polish military counterintelligence, the WSW:

KGB advisers are officially stationed at the Ministry of Internal Affairs. I never heard of any KGB advisers in military counterintelligence, on a permanent basis. There are contacts, of course, exchanges of information and so on. The Polish officer corps remembers the period of severe persecution, and they would be very uneasy to learn that such [persons] are returning once again.

Such a complicated web of channels, jurisdictions, and conflicting institutional as well as national priorities is more than likely to produce a Kafkaesque result. According to Michael Checinski, Polish military counterintelligence, the WSW, contained a subsection the purpose of which was to guard those who guarded the Polish military. This must be one of the best examples of the ultimate police state in which all but a very few are simultaneously jailers and inmates of the same system:

> Inside military counterintelligence was a special section which was a counterintelligence section against the counterintelligence service—a so-called Soviet section. The head of this section was responsible for knowing everything that the Soviet officers in our section were doing. All Soviet officers feared them horribly. The head was a Soviet officer named Colonel Sheligin. He was in direct contact with Moscow.

For prompt, accurate, and perhaps detailed information on top Polish officials, Rurarz argues, the Soviet Union can rely, probably in addition to other channels, on the *Biuro Ochrony Rzadu* (Office for the Protection of the Government). The BOR is within the chain of command of the Polish Ministry of Internal Affairs, but its chief commander is the general secretary of the party. It is responsible for the physical protection of important personalities. These bodyguards appear to have been given unusual responsibilities. All in all, Rurarz paints a depressing picture of a Hobbesian system based on permanent spying of all against all:

> The *Biuro Ochrony Rzadu* protects the top party officials: every Politburo member, alternate Politburo member, and secretary of the Central Committee is given full day and night protection. Many others are protected on an ad hoc basis. The party buildings themselves are guarded by BOR, as are private apartments and dachas of top people. . . .
> What was astonishing to me was that the bodyguards, the *Biuro Ochrony Rzadu*, BOR, [remained] almost always the same. The security officers, many of whom I knew, and were guarding [Boleslav] Bierut from 1954 to 1956, were the same people who later guarded [Edward] Ochab, [Wladyslaw] Gomulka, and then [Edward] Gierek.[1] When I returned to the party apparatus almost twenty years after 1956, these same officers were still there. I was amazed. . . . [T]he BOR . . . was, in fact, therefore, subordinated to the Soviet KGB. In fact, right after the war, head of the BOR was [a] Soviet colonel . . . though of Polish extraction. Thus, whenever Gierek would leave his office for a moment, the security officers would look through his things; I never dared to speak with him frankly, because these BOR people would know exactly what I had said. Gierek didn't understand these [matters] at all,

---

[1] Bierut, Ochab, Gomulka, and Gierek were leaders of the Polish Communist Party from the 1940s to the 1970s.

and he sometimes wanted to discuss very delicate [matters] with me, which I would have to evade. I was not afraid of what Polish intelligence or counterintelligence would find out about me, but about what the Soviets would. And of course the KGB was in fact suspicious, because later they pressed me to relinquish my position with Gierek.

The Soviet Union seems successful when it comes to keeping an eye on members of the top elite in Poland. But the lower levels of society appear to be more and more difficult to control. In the following analysis, Zdzislaw Rurarz describes the prospects for a reestablishment of comprehensive Soviet control over Poland after the imposition of General Jaruzelski's martial law in December 1981.

> *Rurarz:* The Soviets are now trying to reestablish control over Poland; whether they will be successful is an open question. I think they've run out of agents, and recruiting new ones is not easy. Those that they recruited in the war are retired or dying. The new effort to recruit does not include beatings and torture, which the NKVD used routinely to recruit Poles during the war. But the new recruits are not necessarily reliable.
>
> *Q:* But wouldn't they also use the enticements of stature and material gain in the recruiting effort?
>
> *Rurarz:* Yes, but if you recruit cynics, people who aren't motivated, or are fearing you, how useful will they be? That is a dead end for Moscow, especially when it comes to the Poles. The Soviets are strenuously trying to recruit more, but to my knowledge they are not very successful. There was the German bogey right after the war. No one really believes anymore that Germany is a threat to Poland, while everybody sees that the Soviet Union is having economic and political problems. So I don't think that the Soviets can be as successful now as they were during and right after the war.

Despite such difficulties, the degree to which the Soviet Union is informed about developments among its allies is impressive. Moscow can rely on a variety of channels of information on official as well as personal and private lives of top decision makers in Eastern European capitals. At the same time, one of our interviewees pointed out that on the political management level, the Kremlin is as inefficient as it is efficient on the level of intelligence gathering. Hus, with his background in the Czechoslovak Foreign Ministry, argues that several of the Eastern European crises resulted from a lack of management on the Soviet side, rather than overmanagement, as is commonly assumed:

> The Soviet Union was overconfident concerning Eastern Europe. There was no management of it. No one [in the Soviet Union] was dictating to Eastern Europe after Stalin [died]. This led to 1956, to 1968, and to Solidarity.

Under Stalin there was [stringent] control. In 1956, and shortly before that, the Soviet Union was [actively] involved everywhere in the world, except Eastern Europe. Khrushchev was involved in domestic conflicts and was negotiating the Austrian [State] Treaty [of 1955]. He had no time to be adequately concerned with Eastern Europe. In 1968 the Soviet Union was concerned about China and about negotiations with the United States, and was surprised [by events in] Czechoslovakia. In 1980 there was Afghanistan, the boycott of the Olympics, and the [US-imposed] trade embargo. The problem was not overmanagement; the problem was negligence and Soviet incompetence. That is why Gorbachev is now meeting with Eastern European leaders much more often. For the first time since Stalin, Soviet control over Eastern Europe is becoming technically better organized. Even now, however, the Soviet Union assumes [too] much about Eastern Europe. . . . It may be unpleasantly surprised later.

Hus points out that some members of East European elites on occasion reject Moscow's instructions as a betrayal of "true faith." They do not tend to survive in their positions for long. For instance, Vasil Bil'ak, described in the following statement by Hus as being sometimes more orthodox than Moscow, was eventually forced to resign in December 1988 from all official positions in Czechoslovakia:

Then there is the question of interpretation of Soviet policy. This is done by [Vasil] Bil'ak and [Bohuslav] Chnoupek. Sometimes even Bil'ak, who is the most loyal to the Soviet Union, will not agree with Soviet policy. He, at times, felt that Moscow was betraying the true faith. There is no real attempt on the part of the Soviet Union to try to outline how Czechoslovakia should take part in every detail of Soviet foreign policy. Under Stalin everything was by command. Afterwards, Soviet leaders, until Gorbachev, rarely met with Eastern European leaders. Gorbachev is binding Eastern European leaders much closer to his policy again. There is now coordination through summits.

Despite periodic outbreaks of unrest, the Soviet Union so far has maintained its grip on Eastern Europe. Rurarz states that Moscow continues to treat its East European allies in an imperial manner:

There is not the slightest doubt that, as with the non-Russian Soviet Republics, the East European states are treated as a kind of colonies.

One of the reasons why the Soviet bloc remains under Moscow's control appears to be a lack of unity among East Europeans. Divided by long and complicated historical developments, aware of territorial and ethnic conflicts which set them apart in the past, Warsaw, East Berlin, Prague, Budapest, and Bucharest continue to suffer from disunity vis-à-vis the Kremlin. Speaking about the 1968 Warsaw Pact invasion of Czechoslovakia, Zdzislaw Rurarz describes elements of a different current:

> I heard later that when the Polish troops realized what was going on, they slowed down the march toward Prague; Prague, as far as I was told, was supposed to be taken by Polish troops, to antagonize the two countries. So when the Polish troops learned what their true mission was, they slowed down enough so that the Soviets had to take Prague themselves. One of the colonels who participated in the invasion told me that the mood of the troops was such that if there had been any resistance in Czechoslovakia, the Poles would have joined the Czechs.

To guard against any untoward developments involving the Polish military, the Soviet presence is deployed in such patterns as to make anti-Soviet maneuvers by the Polish army impossible. According to Rurarz:

> Soviet troops are deployed close to Polish communication centers, officer schools, and equipment depots. In case there were any signs of revolt in the Polish forces, the Soviets would probably blow up such places. Furthermore, the entire Polish air defenses are directly subordinated to Soviet Marshal Koldunov, commander of the PVO, making their independent use impossible. Because of the near rebellion of the Polish army in 1956, the Soviets are determined not to repeat that mistake again. Even the minister of defense could not singlehandedly order a revolt against the Soviets, because his authority over the armed forces is so fragmented that he would have to have the cooperation of at least seventeen other people. It is out of the question that Soviet counterintelligence would not learn about it. The minister's authority stops short in many places, even in his capacity as commander-in-chief. I do not know whether the same is true in the USSR, but it probably is. The Soviets are quite clever about these things.

Periodically, however, Moscow is forced to deal with broadly based East European movements which threaten the stability of the whole Soviet empire. East Germany in 1953, Hungary in 1956, Czechoslovakia in 1968—each ended with the Soviet leaders opting for a military solution to the crisis at hand. Perhaps the greatest challenge to date developed in Poland during the Solidarity period. Rurarz provides information on Soviet crisis-management preparations:

> As far as I know, the Soviet had three headquarters prepared for the intervention in Poland: the main one was in L'vov, the second one was in Legnica, and the third one was in Warsaw itself. When I was in Moscow in June 1981, on my way to Poland following the plenary session of the PUWP [Polish party] Central Committee, I was told that [General] Rusakov went to L'vov, to oversee the Soviet intervention, but that as of that moment the USSR did not have enough troops ready to intervene in Poland quickly. My Soviet col-

leagues told me that to do away with eventual Polish resistance would require one million Soviet troops, and they didn't have that many in position. As early as autumn 1980, the Soviets began a partial mobilization to intimidate Poland, but there were many deserters—seven thousand or more.

Meanwhile, the Soviets must have been urging [Gen. Wojciech] Jaruzelski[2] to declare martial law. On 27 March 1981, for example, I received in Tokyo a cable from Warsaw, informing the embassy that in the event of a general strike in Poland, following the Bydgoszcz provocation, a state of war would be declared. Accordingly, I was instructed to proceed with certain precautionary measures. Later, the general strike fizzled out, but the precautionary instructions were never rescinded. When I was back in Warsaw I wanted to learn whether martial law would be declared, but none of the top people could give me a straight answer; things were very confused. When the Western media talked all the time about possible Soviet intervention, they were diverting attention from the internal intervention which was building up at the time, and which was the real threat.

The point is, I don't think the Soviets would really have intervened militarily in Poland at that time, even if Jaruzelski had refused to declare martial law. The Soviet army could of course have beaten the Polish army; there is not the slightest doubt about it. But the Polish army has 4,000 tanks, and to defeat 4,000 tanks you have to lose almost 4,000 tanks, especially if the tanks are in a defensive position. That would not be so easy for the Soviets.

Michael Checinski demonstrates the complexity of relations between the Soviet Union and its East European allies when he points out that Gen. Wojciech Jaruzelski has to resort to complicated legal maneuvers to guard himself against being totally enveloped by the Soviet web of controls. This might surprise those who prefer to think of him as merely a Soviet general in a Polish uniform:

> Jaruzelski changed the [Polish] Constitution to make himself simultaneously general secretary of the party and the head of the Defense Council.[3] . . . And in my opinion he did it so as not to give the Soviets this instrument to play against him.

Regrettably, there was no East Germans among the interviewees. Thus information on that country in this book is derived only from secondary sources. The former Czechoslovak General Sejna stressed repeatedly that, until the mid-1960s, East German intelligence had not been allowed by the Soviet Union to operate on its own, but had to work as part of a larger Soviet framework. Zdzislaw Rurarz also believes that the Soviet Union is very cautious when it comes to East Germany:

---

[2] General Jaruzelski has been in charge of the Polish party and state during the last decade.
[3] See section on the State Defense Council in chapter 2.

The East German army is directly commanded by the Soviets and treated more or less like Soviet divisions. Poland has some operational independence, but not East Germany. If that is the basic characteristic of the East German army, then the same must be true about military intelligence. They must be under tighter Soviet control than any other East European service.

The Oral History Project did not obtain access to first-hand sources on the situation in Romania. As in the case of East Germany, only secondary sources were available. Gregory, a former Soviet KGB officer and TASS correspondent, points out that security service contacts between Moscow and Bucharest exist, but remain strained:

> Like the one between Romania and the USSR, the relationship between their service and ours was troubled. There were many problems but we did have some contact. The links were not nearly as close as those with other services. As today, officially relations were good but there was much tension behind the scenes. Ceausescu was once told by Brezhnev that he knew what would happen if he tried to leave the socialist camp. I heard this from an aide to Brezhnev.

Cuba

Political developments between Moscow and Havana represent some of the most complicated and controversial aspects of international relations. On occasion, Havana has been allowed a great deal of latitude by Moscow. At the same time, Cubans have acted in several Third World countries as loyal proxies of Soviet imperial policy. The interviewees tended to stress the uniqueness of Fidel Castro's personality. The powers of party chief, guardian of pure ideology, head of government, chief of intelligence, commander of the armed forces, and perhaps a few others, merge in the person of Fidel. According to Juan Benemelis, a former official in the Ministry for Foreign Affairs in Havana, the Soviet leaders are willing to put up with Castro's idiosyncrasies in return for being able to work with him toward achieving the objectives Castro and the USSR share:

> The Soviet leadership understands Cuba and Castro very well. They are extremely patient with Castro and always accommodate him. They do not try to counteract his moves. To reach their final goals, they do things Castro's way and make concessions to him.
>
> Cuba has no one like [Boris] Ponomarev or [Yuri] Andropov. There is only Castro, who is all of them in one. Castro is the real chief of intelligence. You cannot say that about [Leonid] Brezhnev or [Mikhail] Gorbachev. The plans are laid down by Castro. He knows the operations and directs the foreign policy, also. Castro's personality is an important factor in . . . intel-

ligence and . . . foreign policy; that is Castro's style. It was important for Castro to be the only alternative for the Soviet Union in Cuba.

Juan Benemelis stated on several occasions that Castro is to a great extent his own man, not a mere puppet playing a predetermined role in Soviet designs. In fact, he knows how to use esoteric signals to indicate to the Cuban people and the Soviet leadership alike that nobody can take him for granted:

> One day there was a big front page report in *Gramma* on the Soviet oil indus-
> try, including how it had been growing, developments in the industry, and
> the tonnage of the ships. Further down there was another report in which
> they said that, because of negotiations between Cuba and the USSR, the
> Soviet Union decided to reduce its oil shipments. The Soviet excuse was that
> they were repairing one of their refineries. It was felt in Cuba.

Friction between the two countries is not limited to the apex of the power pyramid around Fidel Castro. In the following excerpt, Benemelis describes clashes between the Cuban intelligence service, the DGI, and Soviet advisers in Angola. According to his account, some of the Cubans were not prepared to be exploited by their Soviet colleagues:

> [The Cuban advisers from the DGI] used to tell us to be careful with the
> Soviets, not to give them certain [kinds] of information. The Soviets would
> then come around trying to get it, not to advise us, but to get information.
> The Cubans used to tell stories about the Soviet attempts to control them and
> how it almost reached a fighting basis. The friction was that high sometimes.
> One of the DGI men wanted to fight one of the Soviet advisers. He told us,
> the Soviets are good people and that they try to help each other, but they are
> too smart. They want to take advantage of everything. Also, when we
> received advice from the Soviets on two or three specific cases, the Cubans
> would say the next day that we would not take the advice.
>   That is how I found out that the Soviets were just taking our work and
> using it for their own purposes. They were already recruiting a CIA person
> while we were just trying to meet this person, or to get some information
> about him. They already recruited him so we were wasting our time. Not
> only that, but it was our target and our case, and they took it over. It was
> complete interference and then the Soviets would come in and say, "Why
> didn't you do this?" They got uncomfortable if we didn't do what they
> wanted. In that specific case, Soviets went to the office of our chief and tried
> to get him to follow their plan. He called the Cuban adviser into the office
> also and the Soviets lost because my chief backed the Cubans, but the friction
> was there.

In the 1960s, China emerged as a serious and independent international player. It became an alternative focus of influence among the Soviet allies and, more importantly, clients. Juan Benemelis shows how complex was the system of competing loyalties:

> After 1965, Fidel had a big quarrel with Mao. He tried to diminish the Maoist influence in Cuba, especially in the intelligentsia, despite Ché Guevara's favorable view of China. Ché was less influential inside Cuba than outside. Despite Ché and the Maoists' influence in the army, the Cuban intelligentsia never embraced Maoism fully. They thought they already had something important in Cuba with Fidel. Why then go to China? . . . I was a Maoist; but only up to a point. During the Sino-Indian war, I was on China's side, because the Soviet Union was backing India. I was not attracted by all that Mao said. I thought he had developed a personality cult around him; and, because of that, I had little respect for Mao or Kim Il Sung. Fidel did not respect them either, nor even Nasser. And so, I also did not respect Nasser. Such was Fidel's personal influence. He made the Soviet Union a target for criticism without using the Chinese or Yugoslavs.
>
> The Soviet Union was not very upset about that as long as Cuba did not deal much with the Chinese. They were afraid of a Mao-Castro combination in the Third World. It would have been a serious blow for them and for their prestige then. But they did not mind as long as Castro did not play games with their biggest rival, China. They did not like Ché Guevara. Not because of his guerrilla focus, but because he was voicing a pro-Chinese, anti-Soviet position. They also debated the effectiveness of guerrilla warfare.

The insertion of the Chinese factor into the global power equation complicated matters significantly. On occasion China became the main rival of the Soviet Union and Cuba in the Third World, specifically in Africa, almost replacing Moscow's publicly declared primary opponent, the United States. Benemelis comments again:

> I do not know if the Soviet moves were a reaction to the Chinese, but they were very worried about it. I did not discuss foreign policy with the Soviet officials because they were obsessed with China. Angola was viewed very differently in Cuba and the USSR, than in the West. Angola was not a Cuban victory over the U.S.; it was a victory against China. The first Soviet and Cuban moves in 1974 were not a response to Western moves. They were aimed against China. The Soviet Union and Cuba saw the heavy hand of China behind the FNLA.[4] They knew about Chinese influence in the MPLA and that Savimbi was pro-Chinese. That was the common perception. They knew about the U.S. role, but it was considered even more dangerous for Angola to fall into Chinese hands. The same thing happened in Somalia and South Yemen. The Chinese were very active in Africa then. It was more a material [support] policy than a propaganda policy. The Soviet Union wanted the Cubans in South Yemen to counter the Chinese.

---

[4] The Angola National Liberation Front, FNLA, fought the Marxist MPLA (Popular Movement for the Liberation of Angola) for many years, particularly in northern Angola.

Gradually, North Korea emerged as yet another power which became part of the already complicated knot of Cuban loyalties vis-à-vis the Soviet Union and China, respectively. Juan Benemelis describes a shadowy North Korean presence in various aspects of Cuban life:

There was not too much respect at first for Kim Il Sung and the way he projected himself. He was strongly criticized by the Cuban elite for his cult of personality. This is still true. On the other hand, I found there was more than what the public press was projecting. It was stunning for me, because one usually has a clue on the political side. . . .

The real relationship started in 1962–63, when Castro wanted to establish a "third position" inside the Soviet bloc. He got mixed up with the Koreans then. A strong Korean presence in Cuba started, especially in heavy industry, the production of nickel and iron. In the army, there has always been a strong Soviet presence, but from time to time one sees Korean specialists hidden away there. They were in aviation. They are very difficult to spot. One would not expect that, because there was not a big show of close Cuban-Korean relations.

In foreign relations, I never had instructions to tell the embassies to associate with Koreans. But somehow the Koreans always seemed to be around the Cubans in everything. In spite of their position in Asia, I thought they were very close to the Soviet Union. Korea has always been an enigma for me. I did not know about the intelligence connection, but I knew about the training connection, training in Korea and in Cuba. People said later that they worked for the Americas Department. The connection was with Pineiro. That was the subversion aspect outside the army.

Experts seem to agree that among Moscow's clients, North Korea enjoys perhaps the greatest degree of independence. Stanislav Levchenko indicates that the Soviet and North Korean agendas are hardly ever identical. From the perspective of control, North Korea is an unpredictable part-time partner, rather than an ally or client:

It is a nightmare for the Soviet Union because they cannot control Kim Il Sung. Not at all! There is nobody in the Soviet Union who can really push him into doing something which they want done. When North Korea goes more or less in a direction which is beneficial for the Soviet Union, they join it right away and try to enhance those operations. When it goes entirely in its own direction, there is not much the Soviet Union can do.

Africa

On the African continent, Soviet presence has been most strongly felt in Angola and Ethiopia. Tadeusz Kucharski, a former Polish diplomat who sought asylum in the West after Jaruzelski's declaration of martial law, proved to be very knowledgeable about the Soviet modus operandi in Angola. Speaking about the situation as he saw it before his departure shortly after General Jaruzelski's coup d'état, Kucharski presented his insight into the conflict in Angola, a country with a large Cuban military presence as well as Western business influence:

> Angola does not have an independent capability to extract oil. It is dependent on Western technology, equipment, and expertise. Since before independence Angola has been dependent on Gulf Oil in Cabinda and later became dependent on Texaco and Elf Aquitane. These are the three main oil companies, which extract the oil that Angola sells. The Angolan government could not survive without this money. Oil constitutes ninety to ninety-five percent of all Angolan revenues. Without the oil from Cabinda, Angola could not exist as it does now. The money from oil kept the country going and enabled the government to import several billion dollars worth of arms to maintain power.
>
> Most food is also imported as a result of the war and inefficient agricultural policies, which have led to severe shortages, while under the Portuguese there were many surpluses. For example, coffee production in 1984 was twenty times lower than in 1974. This was blamed on the departure of the coffee specialists. However, there is no doubt that government policy discouraged coffee production. The price set for coffee is so low that in real terms it is worth only a few cents a pound. The Angolan currency is practically worthless. Therefore, there is no incentive for anyone to increase the output of coffee. This is the case with many other agricultural products, leading to the need to import most food.

The ability of Western oil companies to coexist peacefully, or even to cooperate on occasion with Cuban expeditionary forces, stands in contrast with the apparent lack of coordination between the Soviet Union on the one hand and its allies and clients in Angola on the other. Kucharski presented an interesting example of a lack of coordination between Soviet security and the Cubans. Moscow's addiction to secrecy and its failure to consult with the Cubans resulted in a major embarrassment in Luanda. Kucharski talks about Nito Alves' attempt in 1977 to overthrow the Neto government:

> The coup was organized because the Soviet Union felt that Alves would be more obedient and less nationalistic than [Agostinho] Neto. Neto had disagreed with some Soviet policies and it was felt that Alves had a good chance to succeed. Alves was always the commander on the spot and popular in Luanda. Neto was the symbol of the movement, but had always worked from abroad. . . . [Alves] worked for the security apparatus. . . . Nobody knew about the coup in advance, including Fidel Castro. It was not coordinated with the Cubans, and they put a stop to the coup, because they did not know

of the Soviet sponsorship. For a few hours, Alves was in control of the radio station in Luanda, until the Cuban troops intervened on the side of Neto.

This was a case of a lack of coordination between the KGB, the Soviet ambassador, and the Cubans. Because the coup could prove to be a major embarrassment for the Soviet leadership, they neglected to inform the Cubans. Their love of secrecy was so great that only Nito Alves and his group knew of it. After a few hours, Castro gave orders for the Cuban troops to help Neto, and a half hour later the coup was over, because there was no counterbalance to the Cuban troops in Angola. We heard Cuban voices on the radio and then an announcement that the counterrevolutionary bandits had been defeated. Immediately afterwards, the Soviet ambassador was recalled by Moscow, and it was a long time before a new ambassador was sent. . . . The previous one had been too involved in the attempt. The Soviet failure resulted from two things: secrecy and overcentralization. Coordination is always conducted at the level of the center, and not at the local level. Decisions are always made in Moscow or Havana. There was no coordination in place [in Luanda]. There is also a great deal of suspicion within the socialist camp.

Kucharski further indicates how a common ground was found on the oil fields of Angola for the self-interests of the Angolan political elite, the Cubans, the Soviet Union, and Western oil companies:

The Soviet Union knew that Angola could not continue to extract oil or receive revenues on its own. They did not want a country with no money. Angola gets one to two billion dollars in cash a year [from oil revenues]. Then the Soviet Union can sell arms [to the MPLA] for hard currency. The terms of credit differed. Early on, when things were easier for Angola, the credits were for three years. Later they were extended to five, then seven, and more years because Angola became increasingly short of cash. . . . Everybody is interested in protecting the oil fields in Cabinda. This is the main reason for the stationing of Cuban troops there. Without this production Angola could not exist. Also Angola pays for all the expenses of the Cuban troops in Angola. Cuba needs this money, and so it is also interested in the uninterrupted flow of oil. The other sources of revenue—diamonds, coffee, sea salt, cotton, fruit, and fish—diminished considerably and are no longer counted as serious sources of revenue. This factor made oil revenues that much more important.

Goshu Wolde, the former Ethiopian foreign minister who was educated both in Great Britain and the Soviet Union, is exceptionally qualified to describe the structure of Soviet control over Ethiopia. In the following excerpt, Wolde analyzes the uniqueness of the Ethiopian case and sets it in the context of other Soviet involvements on the African continent:

The Soviet Union has invested a great deal in Ethiopia. Quite apart from the fact that it will want its money back, it will want its money's worth of influence in Ethiopia. It also has the objective of seeing to it that a country in which the Soviets are spending quite a lot of money will behave in a manner which will serve its political and ideological objectives. Ethiopia is now [deeply] in debt . . . on the military side, and also [accepts] a significant amount of military assistance. We have . . . Soviet personnel working in Ethiopia and also a formal military presence at service facilities on the coast of the Red Sea. And more importantly, thousands of cadres have had training and indoctrination in the Soviet Union. They may perhaps have also been recruited to serve the Soviet interest. I would be very surprised if the Soviets would simply be quiet if something were to happen in Ethiopia. True, they had invested more heavily in Egypt, the Sudan, Somalia, and they did leave [those countries]. But the situation in these countries is markedly different [from that] in Ethiopia.

In Ethiopia, it has not gone to the extent of South Yemen, but Ethiopia now has a fully established political party machinery, which embraces all parts of the society, and is digging in its heels and spreading its influence throughout the society. And in the armed forces particularly, there is not only [an overt] Soviet presence, but [additional] Soviet influence through [the use of Ethiopian] agents. [Soviet officials] could fight back through domestic contacts, through domestic agents. I doubt that they would leave without a fight, because the [opposition] is not well organized. We have only one ruling party, the Workers' Party of Ethiopia, and if the people are disarmed for all practical purposes, when something happens they will try to find an Ethiopian leadership which is to the liking of the Soviets. Whether they would succeed is, of course, anybody's guess. Nobody knows what the political factors would be; nobody knows how the [Soviet leaders] would play their cards; nobody knows what the internal situation would be.

Wolde further indicates that the Soviet Union and Cubans are perceived quite differently by the Ethiopian population:

[T]his has something to do with national temperament [and] national character. . . . The Cubans are friendly, sociable, and so on. They drink, they play, they like music. Because of this character of theirs, they are seen on favorable terms, whereas the Soviets are slightly—no not slightly—very aloof, perhaps deliberately so. Soviet military personnel are perhaps instructed to stay aloof, but . . . the [Soviet] diplomats, I think that they are not that bad. It may be fear, but generally speaking, they keep to themselves. And as a result of the perception by the Ethiopian people that with socialism there is misery and famine, this perception has hurt the Soviet image in Ethiopia— not amongst the leadership, but on the part of the general population, particularly in the cities.

Finally, Goshu Wolde describes how the non-aligned movement has become a tool in the struggle for influence on the international arena. He views the movement as diverse, but the Cuban foreign policy apparatus seems more vigorous and willing to take charge and control than truly non-aligned countries:

> Contact with Cuba is regular, not only for the non-aligned movement, but for general policies. The Cubans are very, very active in the non-aligned movement and in international relations on the whole. Their foreign ministry is very vigorous, very active, as are their embassies in many of the Third World countries, Their communications are very fast. There is . . . coordination at all levels. Particularly in the non-aligned movement, theirs is a dominant role, along with Yugoslavia and India. When Tito was in power, Cuba tried to take the non-aligned movement in a direction leading toward closer ties with the Eastern bloc.
>
> The composition of the non-aligned movement is very diverse. They are more or less like what you find on Noah's ark. There is a large collection of people who are very sympathetic to the United States and the Western position—Pakistan, Indonesia and many others in Latin America, for example. There are those who are also extremely close to the Soviet Union—Cuba and North Korea and so on. The trouble is that some of the countries on the right are not active, whereas Castro and the Cubans and others are so active. They see to it that they attend all committee meetings at all levels. The others send their third- and fourth-level people and it is very difficult to push through a resolution. The left is a tightly organized group. It is very disciplined and has a set of political objectives. They are in the movement for a particular purpose, and they are out there to secure their purpose. The others are divided and not organized.

At the inception of the new Soviet empire after World War II, Moscow attempted to rule its clients rigidly, with little, if any, latitude. Gradually, it became apparent that this approach was neither practical nor productive. Soviet objectives could be achieved even if the various players were permitted to develop separate agendas, so long, of course, as these conformed broadly with overall Soviet international goals. The material presented in this chapter demonstrates the degree of common ground found by the USSR, its East European allies, Cuba, and North Korea in their operations in various Third World arenas. At the same time, the interviewees indicated that these relationships often were less than harmonious, because of differing economic, political, and even ideological objectives.

7

Soviet Analysis and Perceptions of International Developments: Apparatus and Concepts of Policy

How does the Soviet Union perceive and analyze international developments? Do Soviet decision makers apply the dialectic and try to determine the identity of the "primary adversary," or do they view several competitors as posing challenges of similar magnitude? Within the parameters of this book, of course, it is possible only to sketch a mere outline of the answer. Do different entities within the Soviet Union perceive international developments in a similar fashion? What are the institutions that play a major role in preparing analyses which can aid decision makers?

Perceptions and Actions

At the end of World War II, Stalin gradually elevated the United States to the level of the Soviet Union's primary adversary. Gregory refers to the confusion that prevailed among Soviet officials during the period of ideological transition, 1945–1947:

> [Pre-1947, c]apitalism and capitalist countries were classified as the enemies; the U.S. or Britain were not identified by name. We were told that we would have to fight and destroy capitalism. At this time we were not told that the U.S. was enemy number one. . . . We were told that the U.S. and the allies aided us considerably. We saw American cars and American canned meat. We loved the American products that we saw. So it was difficult to destroy the fresh memories that we had. It took time. [Then] we were told that the U.S. had started the [cold war]. In September 1947, the Soviet Union started a joint political and military information service, the Committee of Information [KI]. I worked there for a time. The head of this committee was [Vyacheslav] Molotov;[1] his deputies were [Andrey] Vyshinski,[2]

---

[1] Vyacheslav M. Molotov, former member of the Politburo, CC CPSU; former Soviet foreign minister; deceased.

[2] Andrey Vyshinski, former candidate member of the Politburo, CC CPSU; former Soviet foreign minister; former Soviet prosecutor in the show trials of the 1930s; deceased.

[Yakov] Malik,[3] [General Aleksey] Yepishey;[4] . . . Panyushkin was also involved. . . . By 1947, we were being mobilized for the new cold war but we had been increasing our intelligence capability already for two years.

Sejna discusses the role ascribed to the principal adversary by Soviet military and political leaders in the post–World War II era:

A Soviet military leader does not concentrate on lesser enemies, but rather on the principal adversary. [Soviet leaders] do not want to destroy Europe, [but rather] to seize the West European economies intact. . . . If they destroy the United States' [military power], who will fight for Europe? Nobody. [Therefore,] that is what they seek to achieve.

Sejna explains shifting approaches toward the adversary under Khrushchev and Brezhnev:

I think Khrushchev in the beginning tried to present . . . peaceful coexistence policy [as] a major strategic deception [to convince the West] that he is different and communism is different. . . . Later on, in the Brezhnev years, [it was felt that this approach] was not realistic because [while] . . . [a] change [of] image was [useful in deceiving] middle-class journalists, [it did not affect the] aggressiveness [of] imperialism [as such]. This is why [Brezhnev] decided to put through the so-called strategic initiative, [which involved] sabotage and other [activities], while Khrushchev, for example in 1959 and 1960, [preferred] espionage [and] stealing as much technology as possible.

Shevchenko addresses more recent Soviet approaches:

The Soviet leadership understands the seriousness of [a] commitment [made by the U.S. and that Washington] will respect it in almost every case, and [this Soviet belief is not due simply to] trust in the American leadership. The Soviets understand that if an American administration makes a strong commitment [and it] becomes [widely] known in the United States, it is very difficult [for a U.S. administration not to abide by it] because of the American system and because of public opinion. They were absolutely right, particularly in the Cuban crisis.

Not only do Soviet leaders view the West as composed of states that can be played off against one another, but they regard individual countries as containing strata with incompatible policy preferences that can be exploited. In Sejna's opinion:

---

[3] Yakov A. Malik, former Soviet deputy foreign minister and Soviet representative to the U.N.; deceased.

[4] Aleksey A. Yepishev, army general; former chief of the Main Political Directorate of the Soviet army and navy.

The [Soviet leaders'] major goal was to influence the middle class: journalists, scientists, and [other] influential people. They seemed to think that the working class was more or less content and had no impact on policy. Khrushchev and the others thought that the middle class in the West had more influence even than the politicians. I remember how they discussed the strength of the media in the United States, for example.

According to Arkady Shevchenko, Soviet support for anti-nuclear movements is meant to weaken the West economically as well as militarily:

If we talk about the peaceful uses of nuclear energy, . . . oil will not last forever and [anti-nuclear campaigning] will undermine the West economically in the long range.

Stanislaw Levchenko speaks of serious research and analytical work carried out in connection with Soviet efforts to manipulate American public opinion:

The KGB *rezidencies* in Washington and New York . . . probably [make] their own surveys of American public opinion and analyze them. Without this they could not start a campaign [to manipulate opinion]. They obviously took some time to get into the grassroots movements to determine how serious they were, and how responsibly [in KGB terms] and their leaders were acting. They would then write a comprehensive paper on what the weak points are in the United States and the importance of public opinion. They do a lot of research. The neutron bomb campaign was a huge, multi-level operation in which many people took part at all times from the preparation to the implementation.

According to Shevchenko, the Soviet view of Western public opinion holds that self-deception in open societies forms an indispensable base for such Soviet campaigns:

Time and again, I heard in conversations with people in the central Committee or the Foreign Ministry, that even if the Soviet Union were to stop all its propaganda and all its deception campaigns, still [views prevailing in some sectors] in the West would do the job. Moreover, there is an even more cynical view held by [those Soviet officials] who laugh sometimes at the Soviet propagandists who try to deceive . . . the West. They mock [such propagandists], saying, "You guys will never be able to do a deception like the Americans do to themselves." Without any Soviet involvement—this is one point.

A second part is coordinated efforts between . . . [Soviet officials and those in the West who] accept what the Soviets are always telling them. Some of [those Westerners] are sincere, and some of them are just ignorant and don't know who is who.

Misjudgments

Soviet understanding of the West, however, is not flawless, as Sejna explains:

> When the Vietnamese came, the Soviet Union pushed them finally to stop the war or at least to open the second or political front. They had to talk to Americans to exploit [the war] for propaganda and deception. The Vietnamese did not want to hear that. They just wanted to fight and . . . [they believed that the] Vietnam war would destroy the United States economically and politically. The Soviet leaders laughed at how the stupid Vietnamese wanted to destroy the U.S. But they were right. You know what damage the Vietnam war did in the United States? From a current . . . and political point of view, we still have trouble getting out of [its psychological aftermath].

There are also instances of Moscow's failure to predict accurately American reaction to Soviet moves. Kucharski points to the invasion of Afghanistan as an example:

> Nobody [in the USSR] expected a strong American reaction. The Soviet Union has acted with impunity on its borders [in the past] and had not been seriously challenged for such actions.

Kucharski refers to conspiratorial interpretations in East European circles, following the election of a Polish Pope:

> Officially, especially among the security personnel, the reaction [to Cardinal Wojtyla's election to the Papal throne] was one of dissatisfaction. There was a general feeling of uneasiness among the Eastern bloc embassies as a result of the Pope's election. The Soviet officials did not hide their opinion that it was a CIA-sponsored action to disrupt the Soviet bloc.

Jimmy Carter's insistence on linking human rights with arms control took the Soviet leaders aback, but, as Shevchenko states, they recovered quickly enough:

> I think the transition from the Nixon to the Ford administration was more or less smooth, with some initial turmoil. But it was more or less smooth because of Kissinger. I cannot say that during this period of time there was any major trouble. The major trouble was with Carter. That was entirely new. . . . The first really astonishing thing was when [Soviet officials] found that Carter was not only just talking about human rights, but had ideas that the whole process of arms control could be linked to it. They had thought these were just words or propaganda. But they found that it meant something. The didn't know what to do, until they found the weaknesses. They found that with all the human rights policy, Carter was a "minute man" who

was so idealistic that he really believed that the real [threat] had passed and that conventional relations could be [established]. [This attitude] could be exploited.

First, there was an initial period when [Soviet officials] were very concerned. Then they discovered such an enormous weakness. From intelligence sources they became aware as I did, that Carter had been talking about having relations with the Soviet Union like those with the British. This was not just a marginal statement. Then, when he turned [his criticism] back on the U.S. [as well] and said, "We are also bad guys. We all have to improve ourselves. [The Russians] too, are human beings. They are normal even if there are certain ideological differences," I think that at a certain stage [the Soviet leaders] knew [they had found Carter's weakness].

Hus states that Czechoslovak and Soviet leaders severely underestimated President Ronald Reagan's determination to change the course of U.S. policy when he was elected in 1980:

I predicted that relations would be tougher. [Vasil] Bil'ak did not think this would be the case. Of course, relations turned out to be more difficult, as was reflected in some negotiations between Czechoslovakia and the United States. The [Czechoslovak] leadership was unprepared for that, after [having assumed] that the United States was in decline. They did not believe that the United States could become more assertive again. It was a miscalculation. . . . Also, at the time, it would have been almost impossible for anyone to expect such a major change in the United States. After all, at the time of the Carter administration, it looked as if the United States was in the process of decline as predicted by Marxist-Leninist [theory]. A very early prediction by [Anatolyi] Dobrynin to the contrary would not have been supported by theory nor by the events of the 1970s.

I asked some Soviet officials why they were so inflexible in 1983, and I predicted that the United States would deploy Pershing IIs and cruise missiles in Western Europe without paying too great a price for it. They replied that they were trying to punish the United States for its anti-Soviet policy. They did not care that it would only make the situation worse for them. They did not want to appear to be soft towards the United States and they did not believe [America] would [recover]. Now that Dobrynin is [back in Moscow] he can make more realistic comments on foreign policy. . . .

In a communist system, one does not start a struggle with others for foreign policy reasons.

Hus further explains shifts in Soviet approaches to arms control in terms of the Soviet perception of [U.S.] high-technology advances:

Now arms control seems to be . . . no longer the tactical Soviet move of earlier years, such as détente. . . . Although arms control would appear to serve the tactical aim of increasing congressional [constraints] on [the] president's military buildup, the motivation seems to be Soviet [concern] about the advances in United States' military technology. The Soviet Union does not have the scientific capability to compete. [It has] become increasingly paranoid that the United States' scientific community can do whatever it wants. Arms control becomes a means of slowing down this process.

Soviet Perceptions: Europe

Great Britain plays a lesser role in Soviet plans than some other Western countries, perhaps because, since World War II, it has followed America's lead on most foreign policy issues. Prior to 1947, however, the Soviet perception was different, as Peter Deriabin notes:

In the [pre–1947] period, Britain was clearly the main antagonist . . . for a couple of reasons. First, the emphasis was on Churchill. . . . This was true especially after his Fulton speech. Second, the U.S. did not have any colonies as such even though it was described as . . . imperialist. The focus was on Britain and its colonies [with Moscow attempting] to do everything possible to end the British empire.

West Germany plays a major role in Soviet policy; Arkady Shevchenko rejects the Western view that the Soviet Union is in fear of the Federal Republic of Germany. Rather, Soviet decision makers regard Germany as a target of opportunity and hope to neutralize it:

Actually, there is no fear of Germany, because [Soviet leaders] understand very well that Germany is no threat to [them]. It really is an area of opportunity. They just disguise it all in propaganda. In [my] book,[5] I mentioned several cases about "how the revolutionary forces will act," their prediction on what the world will be like in 2017. . . . Much of the language I have seen [in Soviet publications], as well as reading between the lines, [views] Germany . . . [as a target for] neutralization, which is really an enthusiastic goal of the Soviets.

In the case of France, the Soviet Union, viewing the situation realistically, attempted manipulation that would encourage French withdrawal from NATO. Sejna speaks of Czechoslovak efforts to influence Gaullism.

[Khrushchev] said that we could play DeGaulle like a violin. We could exploit his strong French nationalism. He believed, in 1963 already, that the French would pull all the way out of NATO. . . . The Czechoslovak party [KSC] was given instructions to support DeGaulle in his anti-American posi-

---

[5] Arkady N. Shevchenko, *Breaking with Moscow* (New York: Alfred A. Knopf, 1985).

tions. . . . Even when DeGaulle began developing nuclear weapons for France, the Soviet leaders did not believe that these weapons would ever be used against the Soviet Union. Instead, the nuclear program was perceived as [adding] prestige for DeGaulle, to allow him to consider France an equal partner to the United States. In the operations plan [of the Czechoslovak Ministry of Defense, MNO], we never included in our calculations the possibility that French nuclear bombs would fall on Czechoslovakia or the Soviet Union.

Soviet Perceptions: The Middle East, Africa, and Latin America

In the context of Soviet perceptions of Middle Eastern developments, Galina Orionova notes the degree to which the Soviet media are permeated by an obsession with a Zionist conspiracy.

> [The Zionist conspiracy theory] permeates the Soviet press corps at both the national and the local level. They are not only interested in Israel itself. They're interested in the power of the American Jewish lobby and how it defines American foreign policy. . . . They published a large book on Jewish organizations in the U.S., how they are formed, all the names of Jewish businesses. Someone even tried to write a Ph.D. [dissertation] on Jewish capital in the U.S. But that is how they see it in the Soviet Union. It may change but I think they are really interested in the Jewish lobby and its influence on Capital Hill and how to expose its power and to liquidate it.

Orionova also explains that the IUSA [United States and Canada Institute] analyzes the situation as it pertains to *Soviet* strategy concerning the Middle East, including Israel, not merely as a function of *American* policy— the ostensible target of the Institute's operations.

Because of Soviet backing of the Arab states, the USSR worked for the defeat of the Israelis and believed this [aim] could be achieved, as Stiller points out:

> Soviet thinking was very long term. The objective was clear: get the Egyptians to the point where they could take on the Israelis and win. I saw some of the reports written by the military people, the assessments they sent back to Moscow. There was a report on how the Soviet advisers were training the Egyptians so that they would be sufficiently skilled, sophisticated and technically proficient. The question was always the same, however: when will they be ready to blast Israel, to wipe it out. This was to be accomplished by 1973.

Soviet and East European analysis concerning African developments underwent shifts, as Tadeusz Kucharski relates:

Africa would be in chaos [if established frontiers were changed]. Most tribal territories cross state borders. It would be a devastating mess to redraw all the frontiers of Africa. For this practical purpose we were instructed to support the units already existing in Africa, with the exception of Somalia, where it was hoped to play off one country against another. In Nigeria, during the Biafran secession, the Ibos' aspirations were opposed because they were clearly supported by the West.[6] Therefore, there was an all-out effort within the bloc to keep Nigeria whole and not to allow Biafra to become a separate state based on tribal principles. There was no policy to create tribal units in Africa. It was to be left as it had been by the colonial powers. However, the Solidarity Committees were designed as a continuation of the decolonization process in Africa, but not out of sincere support for African aspirations. It was Moscow's intention to cripple the Western powers by depriving them of their colonies and of sources of raw materials. . . . All the aspirations of African countries were used only to promote Soviet objectives. . . .

Also, it was hoped to influence as many African countries as possible to follow the socialist path. This was the case in Ghana and other countries where the Soviet Union tried to influence their development. It was realized that to have a long-term impact, financial and material assistance was required. Moscow was unwilling to provide such assistance to African countries. During this period, many Africans became disillusioned about Soviet material help. As a result the focus of Soviet policy in Africa changed from aiding developing countries to aiding those who were not yet independent. For this purpose they chose pro-Marxist movements to promote their policy. This led to the Solidarity Committees' long-term support for those liberation movements I mentioned. Most of them gained power. . . . ZAPU[7] lost, but now it is hoped that SWAPO and the ANC will win. South Africa is the most important playground for the Soviet Union in Africa. It is only a question of time until the ANC's chances of success will be tested.

The Soviet leaders and their regional allies, Miguel Bolaños-Hunter notes, have a flexible timetable in Central America:

[T]he strategy is set, but the timing is flexible. It is hard for [Soviet leaders and their regional allies] or for anybody to set the time, but the strategy is very much long term in all directions. The Salvadoran situation was the main one but that doesn't mean other areas were neglected. For example, in the Costa Rican case, they were training people and providing them with weapons since 1980. The Sandinistas were also developing the hard line among the unions in Costa Rica . . . and on some of the plantations also. They were cultivating and directing their agents and in a more violent way. Although the time is not specifically set, they are looking for results soon. . . . Subversion is a double-edged sword for them. If they do it right, they will get

---

[6] Actually, only by France.
[7] Zimbabwe African Peoples Union.

pressure off themselves by having some more allies around, but they can also attract attention if the Americans or somebody else comes in and attacks them. El Salvador has been a test case for them. They are now able to say, "Let's go ahead, let's unleash the dog."

Bolaños-Hunter believes that the USSR and its regional allies anticipate a certain sequence of events in Central America:

In their realistic appraisal, Guatemala is going to blow up like Salvador. One day the guerrillas will appear in large numbers and with weapons. The political situation is very unstable, so it will be similar to Salvador. Costa Rica is more of a feeling ground now. It takes more time and they are using different methods. They are trying to destabilize the country by setting the unions against the government by increasing demands on the government. What they are trying to do is to force a confrontation to provoke repression that has never existed in Costa Rica. Repression directed against the workers would give an excuse for armed groups to appear "in defense of the people."

Right now, the Costa Ricans have more weapons than men. If the Sandinistas just created [a] guerrilla group and it appeared in the mountains, it would be counterproductive because the people in Costa Rica would reject them. The Costa Ricans have a civil defense force made up of volunteers. They have people to take the weapons and they know the United States would provide them with aid. The Sandinistas know it wouldn't work if they did it like that. They must first find the "contradictions" and bring them to a level of violence.

Rurarz presents testimony concerning Soviet and East European analysis of the developing regions as a whole:

In the discussions which we had in *Zvezda dva*,[8] the developing countries were believed to be a decisive factor in the future. They were seen to be anti-Western, especially anti-American, and prone to all kinds of crises. It was believed that they would be a constant headache for the West, which could be exploited. I remember that we were discussing this question just at the moment when Somoza was about to be overthrown. Nicaragua was very much on the agenda, and the Soviets said, "This is only the beginning!" . . . Even if Third World countries are not very pro-Soviet, they still are much more anti-Western or anti-American than anti-Communist or anti-Soviet, and this plays into Soviet hands.

Mexico was very seriously discussed in this context. It is believed in Moscow that Mexico is a reservoir of revolution. One Soviet official told me that the Germans were ahead of their time when they tried to incite Mexico to war against the United States in 1916; at that time, he said, Mexico had

---

[8] A Warsaw Pact think tank of which Zdzislaw Rurarz was a member.

a population of only 15 million, whereas the United States had 105 million, a ratio of one to seven. Now, he said, the rate is less than one to three, and it will continue to go down. Half of Mexico was taken by the United States, he continued, and many Mexicans and other Hispanics are now living in the United States. When I arrived in Japan I paid a visit to a Mexican ambassador, and I was astonished that he repeated almost exactly the same song and dance.

Soviet and East European Views of Other States under Communist Leadership

With few exceptions, Galina Orionova says, the USSR has viewed the PRC negatively, especially once Mao Tse-tung died, and Moscow felt that the PRC had missed its chance to return to the fold. Sejna stresses errors in the Soviet appraisal of Chinese developments:

> The Soviet Union underestimated the strength of the anti-Soviet group in China. [Soviet leaders] thought that when Mao died there would be a return to pro-Soviet policies, but, of course, they were completely wrong. [At the same time], the Soviet leadership thought that the Chinese leadership was united and did not perceive a split at the top. What happened to Lin Piao and others came as a major surprise to them. They thought that the way to build leverage was to recruit lower officials. . . .

Hus revealed a general tendency on the part of the Soviet Union to treat high-handedly the views of Eastern Europeans in formulating foreign policy:

> Gromyko liked to handle major issues, and this had resulted in poor relations with the East Europeans. He would come to a conference, present the Soviet line, and not elaborate. He treated East European foreign ministers as if they were children. His attitude of not paying much attention to Eastern Europe helped lead to events such as those in 1968. Now Gorbachev has reversed this policy. Previously, there was not a problem over management; there was no management. Gromyko did not care about Eastern Europe; he is an Americanist. To him, relations with the United States were the most important part of Soviet foreign policy. Also relations with Eastern Europe are mainly handled by the CPSU Central Committee. As a result, the Foreign Ministry often viewed Eastern Europe [simply as fellow] communists, and so did not think that they were important in determining foreign policy.
>
> For example, when the Soviet negotiators walked out of the talks in Geneva in 1983, it backfired tremendously in Hungary and East Germany. Honecker had wanted to go to West Germany. They did not consider that this [Soviet] policy might put strains on relations with Eastern Europe, but it did. Gromyko was not good at keeping in mind the interests of the Eastern

Europeans in determining Soviet policy with the United States. This was his greatest fault. Nowadays, Gorbachev is careful to get East European agreement ahead of time, so that if a policy backfires the East Europeans will share some of the responsibility.

Of course, the way the U.S. perceives Eastern Europe and reacts to events in the area concerns the Soviet Union and affects its analysis of the region. Kucharski provides an example from 1968:

> [Because the U.S. was involved in Vietnam,] it was taken for granted that nothing would happen [that is, NATO would not intervene in Czechoslovakia]. The [invasion of Czechoslovakia] was to be based on surprise and everything was to be resolved in a few days. To the [Soviet] planners it was inconceivable that the U.S. army could be used effectively in that situation. Bloc forces would already be in place. The U.S. could not bring enough forces to bear.

Rurarz points out that, once Lyndon Johnson publicly supported Romania, after the invasion of Czechoslovakia, the Soviet leaders hesitated to follow up by invading Romania in order to put an end to the anomalous state of affairs between Moscow and Bucharest. He says further that few if any personalities in the USSR take the U.S. stand on Eastern Europe seriously.

As far as East European perceptions are concerned, Michael Checinski states:

> Polish personalities are in a very difficult position. They are Poles, they think that Poland is under a sort of occupation and they think that they have no other way to act. They don't trust the West. They say that the West betrayed Poland more than the Soviet Union. They don't like the Russians, they don't trust the Russians, but they don't trust the Germans. They fear the Germans. They have to act in the best interests of their country.

In general, the interviewees felt that East European leaders have the wrong perception of the West. Jiri Pelikan states:

> I would say that the leaders of Eastern Europe are really not well informed about what is going on in the Western . . . world as such.

Moreover, Hus believes that East European leaders do not think their region is important to the West:

> The perception in East Europe is that the United States does not believe that East Europe is too important.

Soviet Institutes

Soviet institutes dealing with international affairs existed even in Stalin's period, but have proliferated since then. IMEiMO, the Institute of America and Canada, the Institute of Oriental Studies, the Africa Institute, the Latin America Institute, and others are highly publicized. What role do they play in providing analysis for decision makers? Voslensky deals generically with the institutes:

> [T]he Soviet policy on research and academic institutions [provides more than a mere] ideologized foreign policy extension. There are people of real intellect there, not only party *apparatchiks* and KGB [personnel]. These are [genuine] researchers. . . . The Soviet institutes are . . . much larger [than American institutes]. IMEiMO has six hundred employees. The IOS [Institute of Oriental Studies] and the Africa Institute have over one thousand each, including [support] staff. [Consequently, because of overstaffing], they are not very productive.

Orionova provides background concerning the formation of various institutes of the Soviet Academy of Sciences:

> The Soviet [Union] expanded . . . into . . . new parts of the world and faced many new problems. The realization that it was in fact a global power first came in the 1960s; before that it did not view itself as a [truly] global power, despite its expansion up to that time. This is why the institutes were needed. Furthermore, it is a question of prestige in the Soviet Union to be a professor or a doctor or to be member of an academic society [so that the creation of institutes helped to create prestigious openings]. In addition, after they got Cuba, they needed a Latin America Institute (ILA) for further expansion and direction. After they became involved in Africa, they needed an Institute of Africa (IA). In China, they were persuaded by 1966–67 that the split was not just a fairy tale. They needed [an institute] to deal with [that]. And when the time came around, they recognized the need for an IUSA and Arbatov was clever enough to sense it.

She also notes some problems with the system:

> The problem with all these institutes is, and it was one of the reasons for my defection, that the [members] are confined to a very specific area of study. I first encountered a global outlook in the West. In [the Soviet Union, one does not encounter] this global outlook. One is a specialist in a particular subject. . . . [One finds] people absolutely uninterested and unaware of what is happening outside their particular area, who cannot put the whole puzzle together. The only people in my institute who dealt with problems on a global scale were Zhurkin[9] and [Genrikh] Trofimenko, because they covered

---

[9] Vitaly Zhurkin was deputy director of IUSA.

all the work of all the departments. But on a lower level, there was a complete lack [of personnel] except for some very ambitious people like Kisilev who would try to do it because he is a great Russian nationalist (if he is still alive), and he thinks in terms of covering the world. . . . People dealing with foreign relations in the Soviet Union [are concerned] with the foreign relations of their particular country [of study], not with the foreign policy of the Soviet Union.

Turning to specific institutes, Michael Voslensky was in the first group of researchers to join IMEiMO; indeed, he was part of the nucleus which helped to start the institute in 1956. He states:

IMEiMO was established in 1956, and has been important since that time. Until 1956, there was no institute of political science, no research institute on international relations and world economy.[10] So this was an objective necessity. The idea for the establishment of IMEiMO appeared in 1954 or 1955. When I left to go to the WPC[11] in 1953, there was no discussion of establishing such an institute, [but then there came] a decision of the CPSU Central Committee that the institute should be established. By July, 1955, it was clear that such an institute would appear. The others began to appear later. The IOS was expanded from an Oriental [language and area studies center] to a political institute; the earlier having been a purely scientific institute. . . . The staff's idea that it could have input into the policy-making process proved to be futile. The institutes are there [primarily] for propaganda—propaganda in the form of scientific studies for home consumption; propaganda abroad, in our context, for the [Western] scientists who visit the institute. There were conferences of institutes on international relations and foreign policy which were started in the early 1960s, and continue until now. These include Chatham House.

The staff wrote papers for the Central Committee's perusal, Michael Voslensky says, but the ideas were very rarely, if ever, used except by CPSU Central Committee members to write their own papers. He adds that such papers were always written in a set form, because of the type of information: TASS releases, special bulletins, and internal personal channels to people in the KGB, GRU, or embassies.

Shevchenko presents IMEiMO as playing an active role:

[B]efore the creation and organization of Arbatov's institute, IMEiMO handled some of the functions now performed by Arbatov's institute. Inozemtsev's[12] personal stature was also a big factor. But IMEiMO, like Arbatov's institute, has a very close connection with the International

---

[10] The Institute of World Economics and World Politics, IMEiMO's predecessor, was dissolved in 1947, when E. Varga, its leading personality, came under heavy criticism.

[11] World Peace Congress.

[12] Nikolai N. Inozemtsev, former director of IMEiMO; full member of the Soviet Academy of Sciences; chairman of the Scientific Research Council on Peace and Disarmament.

Department, and they do work on what are called "special contacts." Indirectly there was involvement in the decision-making process because they [wrote] papers for the International Department, editing the papers, submitting analytical kinds of papers prepared by the International Department, and so on. So there was some involvement.

In 1963 and 1964, Shevchenko states, there was a discussion over the discovery that "military dictators are a progressive class." This took place under the direction of the CPSU Central Committee's International Department.

Shevchenko goes on to say that qualified personnel from IMEiMO would occasionally be called in to advise the ID on specific projects, and that IMEiMO, therefore, does have a role in shaping Soviet perceptions of the outside world.

Voslensky discusses the areas covered by IMEiMO's work:

> I did not have an impression that the institute was occupied very much by the problems of the Third World. Of course, since the institute had such a globalist character, they had to pay some attention to it. But the main problems were, first of all, the theoretical problems of world capitalism; and, second, the West. That's why different institutes researching the Third World were created afterwards; on America also, but not on Europe. There is no institute of European research, because IMEiMO is practically the European institute.

Another important entity to which repeated reference has been made already is the Institute of the United States and Canada, under Georgy A. Arbatov's directorship, founded in 1968. This is the main think tank for North American studies; most of the best Americanologists in the Soviet Union work, or at one time worked there. Hus explains why it was necessary to form the institute:

> When the institute was set up, the Soviet Union was facing several problems. There was talk of economic reform, trouble with China, and the problem of Czechoslovakia. At that time they realized that they needed a better understanding of the number one class enemy. [That enemy] was supposed to be in decline, yet, despite Vietnam, the United States was economically sound. The Soviet Union needed to understand what was happening. Also, as summits came up, the need to know about the United States continued to increase.

Orionova relates some of the early history of the IUSA:

> IUSA was organized in 1968—some say in December 1967, but the official date was February or March of 1968. Arbatov was actually in a rather difficult position. He had carried through on his idea that there should be a separate body in Moscow to study the U.S. but this idea was not popular in

academic circles. This meant Arbatov's first problem was a shortage of labor. People from places like IMEiMO were quite happy where they were and did not know quite what to think about the new IUSA. In addition, for a year or eighteen months, IUSA did not belong to the Soviet Academy of Sciences but to the Central Committee (CC). . . . It was under the International Department (ID).

Arbatov came out of the ID with his idea but without any people. He started building IUSA not with academics—there were few American specialists in the Soviet Union at that time—but with the Ministry of Foreign Affairs (MFA) staff and journalists. I think this was a very clever idea. Arbatov was also very serious about postgraduates because they were to become the nucleus of his new institute. It was later calculated that the average age of IUSA staff was thirty-two to thirty-five years old.

For the first three to four years, IUSA had a very low political profile but then one [began] to see people such as Kosygin's grandchild or someone married to an important figure. These people all had good connections.

Orionova goes on to comment that the IUSA developed into something more than was expected, given the relative lack of Soviet influence in the United States at the time:

As far as IUSA and the propaganda in which it is involved is concerned, they were indeed planning to make contacts with Americans, but it was a very small institute [then] and they never imagined what shape it would take or to what dimensions it would grow. It may have been in Arbatov's mind, but he never shared it with us. [Americans preferred visiting well-established institutions]. Arbatov, until 1974–1975, did not have the reputation he has now. . . . The initial plan was more to gather information about what was going on inside the U.S. than to propagate Soviet ideas.

The question was how to structure the institute, what should it do, what [was] going on in the U.S., what directions [were] being taken in the U.S. [Arbatov] was trying to establish a sort of RAND Corporation which would work for the government. Suddenly, the institute started to grow and to attract children from very nice Russian backgrounds when trips abroad became available in 1969. The institute then became more famous than any other establishment in Soviet academia. Some laugh or sneer at it saying that it doesn't do any work, it just does propaganda. But this propaganda function arose as a result of the success of the institute among Americans.

Stanislav Levchenko stresses both the analytical and the propagandistic functions of the institute:

First of all, the domestic purpose of Arbatov's institute is the analysis and collection of information. There are a few hundred people there. The KGB relies heavily upon the institute for this purpose. Another area is active cultural propaganda, which is not quite active measures; it is psychological warfare.

They are trying to disarm American academicians—not just any academicians, but American academicians who are prominent enough to be in touch with either a Democratic or Republican administration, who have a strong voice in public organizations, or who are writing books which will become popular. In this sense, it is classic active measures.

Hus places heavier emphasis on the propagandistic than the analytical work of the various institutes:

The main role of the institutes is really propaganda. They cannot compete with the Foreign Ministry, which has diplomats stationed abroad, in providing timely information to the policy makers. Most of the people in the institutes depend on secondary sources for their information in doing analytical work.

Levchenko addresses the question of the influence of the institute's staff on American academicians:

They would love to establish contact with every American academic, but are not able to do so. There are too many, so what they are trying to do is to influence the key people in the [American] academic world. Not just because they are in the academic world, but because prominent people in the [American] academic world usually have access to politicians, either a senator, a representative, or someone in the National Security Council. It is quite possible that they will never contact such people, but it is also possible that they may adopt something they heard from the academics.

One should be cautious criticizing people. For instance, put yourself in the position of a prominent American scholar, who is not a specialist in the Soviet Union. When Arbatov, who [comes to the U.S.] every year, . . . confides that there are doves and hawks in the Soviet Union, it is believable. It was picked up right away and believed. I do not want to exaggerate his position, but Arbatov is one of the few extremely effective emissaries of the Soviet establishment in overt and semi-overt measures. He is an example of high efficiency . . . it is an unusual institute. It is wrong to say that half of it is KGB. It is not half, but the KGB presence there is undoubtedly massive. One of Arbatov's deputies is KGB. It does not mean they do not trust him; they do. They just want him to be up-to-date when he goes abroad.

Levchenko adds that the institutes work with Western socialist and communist parties within the institutes' area of specialization, and also with Western conservative organizations:

They are trying to improve relations with the Socialist International. Through people like Arbatov they are establishing personal contacts with conservatives in France. They are also running the friendship societies. The intensity of their work is quite high. They also work long hours and frequently weekends. Sometimes the chief of section is a dictator, like Kovalenko. He will wake you up in the middle of the night and do whatever he wants to. One wonders why people continue to work there.

Hus notes a change in the Soviet attitude toward the United States after the IUSA was founded, and refers to resulting confusion in the ranks of analysts in communist countries:

The United States was seen as the strongest, most dangerous opponent. The events of 1968 [in Czechoslovakia] were presented mostly as a CIA operation. At the same time [Soviet analysts] would say that the United States was in decline and decaying. The student demonstrations in the U.S. in 1968 were put into this framework. They wanted the United States to appear as a strong [adversary, trying to subvert communism], but they also had—in accordance with Lenin's doctrine—to present the United States as being in a constant decline. I could not figure out what they wanted us to believe. They could not make up their minds in this respect. The Soviet perceptions of the United States were incredibly simple until Arbatov founded his institute. They taught as if nothing had changed in the United States since Lenin's time. They ignored the United States' ability to solve its own problems through the democratic system. We were told, for example, that the president was actually pre-selected at a meeting of the top monopolies' representatives, and that all campaign speeches were a charade. . . . In 1974, it was Arbatov's institute which contributed greatly to an understanding of the United States. Under Arbatov people became much more specialized in their studies of the United States.

A. Piatigorsky relates his experience at the Institute for Oriental Studies:

In the early 1960s, I went on working at the Institute of Oriental Studies. Not everything was bad, even though they published a lot of trash. I was very prosperous, not in terms of promotion, but in reputation and whatnot. Somewhere around 1965 there was a change. In retrospect, it was not a drastic change, but it was definitely for the worse. The very atmosphere of the institute changed. Not so much its external or global orientation, but in its internal matters. It was directly related to the coming to power of our new deputy director, a Sinologist, Sontsev. . . . It coincided with the first trials of Sinyavsky and Y. Daniel . . . and the second group of trials of the first dissidents. It was the beginning of the dissident movement. Some of the institute members signed the petition in favor of those dissidents. I was among those who signed. It was extremely unreasonable behavior, but I was not a serious dissident—just a very shy, cowardly, law-abiding Russian Jew.

Now I cannot see how I signed these petitions, which was a bit much at that time, even for the extremely liberal Institute of Oriental Studies. In that particular case, the whole machine worked very slowly. . . . Nobody was

dismissed, to my knowledge. At the level of political discussion in our institute, they tried to present the [Sino-Soviet rift] as if there were a drastic
change on the Chinese part, a very Russian attitude. "We gave you so much,
and you suddenly betrayed us." [If it was formulated in this manner, then no
Soviet official would be demoted for the China debacle since no one in the
USSR could be held responsible for a rift caused allegedly by the Chinese.]

The Soviet evaluation of the situation in the People's Republic of China
shifted frequently. Piatigorsky speaks of prevailing attitudes while he worked
at the Institute for Oriental Studies (IOS):

Even at that time, critique was permitted only on a certain level and within
certain limits, never to be transgressed. In as tactful a way as possible—
because one man told me personally that all his articles had suffered terribly
under the censorship, all his anti-Maoist articles—Mao was never totally dismissed from the Soviet ideological vocabulary. Mao remained Mao, in spite
of all the petty gripes in the Soviet Union and exaggerations of the Cultural
Revolution. From the beginning of the Cultural Revolution, the money
started pouring into the Chinese departments. A new institute was organized,
and they started courting the members of our institute. Tikvinsky became its
director. That was at the beginning. I do not know if he is still there or if he
died. All of us immediately felt that it was a new era, a new age, in Sinology.

The IOS was reformed. Piatigorsky explains:

[The IOS was reconstituted] under Gafurov,[13] who was also not an Orien-
talist. He was the former first secretary of the party Central Committee of
Tadzhikistan. I knew him. He was, well, not bad, but certainly an Oriental
despot. The institute was not an institute, it was his estate; it belonged to
him. He took this and that and what he wanted. This was his opinion. That's
why it was clear that the institute would no longer exist under him as a purely
academic, Oriental institute. It became a political institute, more and more
political.
    . . . Originally, this Institute of Oriental Studies of the Academy of
Sciences was an institute where these Orientalists wrote about different countries—history, the linguistics, anthropology, and certainly not about politics.
And then Gafurov came. He did not understand why [political work should
be omitted]. So he began with his "party line" as he used to say. That has
continued to the present day.

Piatigorsky concludes with the statement that the IOS deals with Asia as
a whole, while the Far Eastern Institute deals with China only.

---

[13] Bobodzhan G. Gafurov, former director of the IOS, former first secretary, CC of Tajikistan
CP; deceased.

Orionova notes problems in creating an appropriate infrastructure for the study of the Middle East:

> I can give you an example of how the base of knowledge is built. [Let us] look at the Middle East, for instance, which became a real problem for the Soviet Union the second time they broke relations with Israel in 1967. Still, the Middle East was not seriously studied anywhere in Moscow. One would have thought that it should become the target in 1967 for the Institute of Oriental Studies or certainly for IMEiMO, which in this case would have been more appropriate. In actuality the whole thing started much later and the Middle East section of the institute was only organized, though not officially, in 1970–1972. It began with the initiation of American-style game simulations which were very popular at the institute. [The IOS staff] started doing different sorts of war games [concerning] the Middle East only in 1970–1971 and brought in specialists like [Georgy] Mirsky from IMEiMO. Kisilev appeared at that time and they did those sorts of simulation exercises. I don't remember if Avakov[14] participated at this time; but I do remember Mirsky because he's an important personality, and I think a very good specialist.

Finally, Voslensky discusses the African Studies Institute:

> [Ivan] Potekhin was indeed an Africanist, the first—and the last until now—Africanist to be the director of the Africa Institute. Under Potekhin the institute was indeed a scientific and not a political institute. It's quite correct that all these [African] frontiers were artificial [as Potekhin stressed when he backed revision of these boundaries]. Soon after his death, Solodovnikov came, then Anatoly Gromyko.[15]

Institutes in Other Communist Countries

Other communist countries also have institutes which deal with various non-Soviet bloc countries or regions of the world. Cuba, Poland, and even Ethiopia have such centers.

Benemelis mentions an institute for African studies in Cuba:

> In 1979, I was approached by a colonel of Cuban intelligence to set up an Africa Institute. I did not want to get involved because, for a long time, I was trying to decide what to do with my life. One cannot refuse a lot of things; one has to be very careful. . . .[The colonel] was ambassador in Brazzaville. He said, "This will be a very important institute. Africa is very important for

---

[14] Georgy Mirsky and R. Avakov, specialists on Egyptian affairs at IMEiMO.
[15] Anatoly A. Gromyko, son of Andrey A. Gromyko, Director of the African Institute.

us. We need qualified people, and we know you wrote several books and have a lot of experience. You have not been out of touch with Africa. We want you."

. . . [Requests for information] always [came to] the DGI[16] or the Americas Department, even though Castro might ask the MFA [Ministry of Foreign Affairs] first, unless the person involved was close to Castro, like Osmany Cienfuegos. Osmany would ask me through the MFA for a report on the Nigerian economy in the next five years. I would answer him directly. The machinery in charge of making these studies was the MFA. Now the Americas Department or the Department of Foreign Relations of the Central Committee puts [material] together, using information from the MFA, *Prensa Latina,* the embassies and certain intelligence information. Their analysis is better than any other foreign affairs agency in Cuba.

Kucharski refers to a foreign relations center in Poland:

There is an Institute of International Affairs in Poland. It is a scientific institution, but it has an ideological inclination. It . . . deals scientifically with problems including the Third World, Africa, liberation and development. However, in order to publish something [it is] subject to normal censorship. Therefore, the [publications] more or less present the party line.

Kucharski indicates that practitioners and implementors of policy were rarely invited to speak at the institute because the institutes deal with theory, not practical applications.

Goshu Wolde speaks of the establishment of an ideological institute in Ethiopia—with the assistance of the Soviet Union. The USSR even sent instructors to the institute at first, but by the time the former foreign minister left, Ethiopian cadres were in charge and fully responsible for it.

International Institutes

Two Soviet-led international institutes, or think tanks, were created for coordination of sensitive topics among communist countries. Zdzislaw Rurarz was a participant in both institutes, and thus serves as a primary source concerning their activities:

[I]n the years 1977 to 1979, I was a member of two Soviet-led think tanks— *Zvezda Dva,* which means "Star Two," and *Moment Dva,* or "Moment Two"—through which the Soviets, East Europeans, Cubans, and Mongolians would meet five to six times a year in different capitals. Romania, however, was excluded, and the Romanians were not aware of the meetings.

---

[16]DGI, Cuba's General Directorate of Security.

The [institutes] were personally coordinated by Konstantin Rusakov,[17] one of the CPSU secretaries, although he did not attend the meetings. . . . As to *Zvezda Dva,* it dealt with social, political, and economic problems, whereas *Moment Dva* dealt exclusively with military problems, such as disarmament. . . . [F]rankly speaking, at that time we were discussing how to finish off the West. . . . [P]ractically all [in these groups] were representing military intelligence, or KGB and [their] equivalents. General Milshtein,[18] who was once one of the top directors of GRU, was there, along with many others who, like him, would speak but never disclose their names. They were probably on active service, not under cover or anything like that.

Oversight over Institutes

According to Arkady Shevchenko, the CPSU Central Committee's International Department [ID] and the KGB both oversee the IUSA, Arbatov's institute. The KGB studies prospective guests of the institute to determine the best approach to use, while the ID helps establish a guest list and determines the direction of the studies. The deputy director of the institute, Orionova points out, is Radomir G. Bogdanov, KGB colonel, First Chief Directorate. It is important, Shevchenko reminds us, to realize that the KGB has individuals who are good writers and leading professionals in their fields. Arbatov's institute was created partly in order to deal with Western personalities who may not be very sympathetic to the Soviet cause. Institute activities frequently overlap with the work of press, security, and diplomatic organs.

Personnel

Who staffs the various institutes? What kinds of specialists are needed for the various tasks? Piatigorsky focuses on the KGB role:

> We had a secret section at that time and a political section. Secret not in the sense of the KGB—that is, KGB observing members of our institute—but secret in the sense of . . . secret information [for use by] the Central Committee, the Foreign Office, and other parts of the [Soviet] bureaucracy. We had . . . a political or international policy section. The general impression was that they were doing nothing, because they did not have real influence. All of the political work was produced by the director and his personal clique.
>
> Each [division] head was a director's man in one way or other. Then we had the foreign section, dealing more with KGB matters, which was connected with foreign visitors from abroad and Soviet visitors abroad. Do not

---

[17] Konstantin V. Rusakov, former director of the CPSU Central Committee Department for Liaison with Communist and Workers' Parties of Socialist Countries, former aide to Leonid Brezhnev, former secretary of the CPSU Central Committee.

[18] Lt. Gen. M.A. Milshtein, former head of the Academy of the Soviet General Staff.

confuse these two sections. One dealt with international policy, the other with purely personnel KGB-type affairs. The foreign section's function was to suprevise all transactions involving foreign scholars visiting our institute or any other place connected directly or indirectly with our institute. Also, those Soviet scholars who were going to visit any foreign country. They were given advice and instructions—purely a KGB function.

How are these specialists hired? Levchenko elaborates:

In the university, the students had learned to accept the system from their childhood. Except for several careerists, the majority of the students looked at the political seminars (where we spent four hours a week for six years) as a tax which they have to pay for their careers. An effort was made in lectures on Marxism-Leninism and modern political history to indoctrinate us in the Soviet approach and Soviet national interests in foreign policy. One just had to accept the ideology, without thinking about it deeply, and learn to live with it. By the time the graduate goes to work, he has already started to take certain points for granted.

At research institutions, people became more upset than those in practical work. They had expected that it would be more flexible to work for a research institute, but when they got there, they not only had to accept [Soviet] doctrine, but they also had to utilize it and to work out a better understanding for the sake of the CPSU Central Committee. That is why one-third of the staff of the six research institutions in the Academy of Sciences, where social research is done, practically belongs to the International Department of the Central Committee. Meanwhile, all those people who had wanted to specialize in ancient history and other areas not related to contemporary issues are [forced] to do practical [contemporary] work.

Those who work for the KGB or the CPSU Central Committee [CC] tend to stay in their positions at the institutes no matter how incompetent or unqualified they may be. Piatigorsky elaborates:

In [one leading official's] case, there is no question that he had been KGB. He was one of the worst men I have ever seen in my life—an absolutely professional traitor, and a terrible anti-Zionist. [On the other hand, while] Gafurov's political position was at its lowest ebb, he still preserved a lot of old connections. The institute was his own estate and manor. One sees how the feudal picture comes back again and again. Under Soviet conditions, it was much better than soulless party bureaucracy, because it was more personal. Gafurov employed a lot of very stupid, ungifted people, but at the same time he employed a lot of talented people. . . . Remember that at that time we needed not only bright people, but industrious people. At the beginning, it was a good proportion. A lot of people worked very hard. There was an outburst of enthusiasm for Oriental studies.

A. Piatigorsky was able to work in the Institute of Oriental Studies because he was interested in southern India and had an academic background suitable for concentration on the area. The age structure of researchers in his institute was unique. He explains:

> Our institute was regarded as an asylum for senile diplomats and intelligence service officers who became too old for active service or had failed in their duties.

Hus explains where younger replacements come from and he compares Soviet and Czechoslovak hiring practices with regard to the foreign policy apparatus:

> [The people at Arbatov's institute] were a mixed group. Some were not very impressive. Many of them got to the institute through their relatives. Those who were more impressive got there through hard work. In the Soviet foreign policy apparatus, a great number of mediocre people are receiving important positions. Unlike Czechoslovakia, however, the door is still kept open for the very brightest people. In Czechoslovakia it is totally controlled by the elite. There, bright people with no family connections have no chance of getting such positions.

Galina Orionova, too, has some insight on the background of the newest workers:

> Regarding bright students—there are some very bright young people who get into the University and graduate, but then they face a choice about where to go. And because everything in Moscow is too overstaffed, many go to the provinces and disappear. The IUSA and all other first-rate academic institutes are overstaffed.

Ideology and its Effect on Analysis

In recent years, the role of ideology in the Soviet system has come to be questioned, as Western analysts review events in the USSR and other communist states. Is ideology really dead in the communist world, or does it play a significant role in Soviet analysis of world affairs?[19] Responses to this important question varied and no clear picture emerged. Levchenko speaks of the cynicism with which ideology is widely viewed in the USSR:

> Do[es anyone] think that the vast majority of civilians and officers take [ideology] seriously? In Japan, I remember one counselor in the Soviet embassy who was an exceptionally bright person. He was the author of

---

[19] For an original approach to this topic, see Vaclav Havel, "The Power of the Powerless," in Vaclav Havel et al., *The Power of the Powerless: Citizens Against the State in Central-Eastern Europe* (Armonk, NY: M.E. Sharpe, Inc., 1985), pp. 23–96.

several books, which is highly unusual for his position. He was involved in some friendly ideological confrontations with the Japanese. Those confrontations were just an intellectual game for him. He extracted pleasure from them, because he managed to turn everything around and to prove that black is white. It was a challenge. Hence, there is at least one type of person who is bright and is desperately looking for a kind of psychological outlet.

Another type of person is . . . also very capable, but . . . performs his duties just for the sake of his career. When he thinks that he has to spend a certain number of hours doing a job, then he does it; but if for some reason he feels that it is not absolutely necessary, then he will not. That is a very cynical approach. The embassy staff in general does not spend too much time in the library.

Does ideology have a genuine role in Soviet affairs?

I am not saying that ideology plays no role. . . . It does play a role. I do not think that the members of the Soviet Politburo are absolutely cynical. . . . [T]here are people [who are simply survivors and do what is expected]. . . . However, in the future career of a Soviet MFA officer, a Foreign Trade Ministry officer, a KGB officer, or a GRU officer, ideology is important because it continues the process of brainwashing, which began with childhood.

Of course, ideology poses concrete problems. Hus explains:

Gorbachev has begun to depend upon the Americanists. However, [while he was] ambassador, Dobrynin [had to pretend] that imperialism is dying. Not until he was promoted to the Central Committee [could] he really say what is happening. . . . However, in reports for the government, one must still follow the parameters set by ideology. When I joined the [Czechoslovak] Foreign Ministry in 1971, everything that was written about Soviet relations with the United States had to begin with criticism of the United States and a compliment for the Soviet Union and communism. Then the author could go on and say what he wanted to say. With ideology weakening, the officers are losing their sense of what is acceptable. The parameters are becoming wider.

Piatigorsky found other problems:

I think that [the] very branch of traditional historical materialism and its [effect on] national politics is extremely ambiguous and has always been in Soviet ideology. It is extremely difficult to ascertain to what extent the situation now is progressive or reactionary. . . . [The concept that the U.S. is in the third stage of the general crisis of capitalism] was extremely popular in the late 1960s. Ul'yanovsky was one of those who [supported] that proposition. He published quite a few articles not only in scholarly journals and magazines, but also in *Literaturnya Gazeta* and some other newspapers. It was part and parcel of the official ideology, no doubt about that.

At the popular level, ideology, in fact, is replaced by myth, as Piatigorsky explains:

> [The Soviet population cherishes myths] concerning how the people in the West live. This structure is very simple. There are three patterns in the world: Soviet, German and American. In the USSR we do not work, and we are not paid. . . . In Germany, they work well and are paid well. In the United States, it is a paradise. They do not work, but they are paid very well. This is popular Soviet mythology.

Goshu Wolde, former Ethiopian foreign minister, points to the fundamental problem of the ideologically based society:

> There was a time at one of the meetings of the foreign affairs committee when I said that if scientific socialism is a science, as some suggest in Ethiopia, then this is what Gorbachev is doing: science always has to take into account the facts of life. For the last sixty-odd years the Soviet system had operated in a certain manner and now, late in the 1980s, it suddenly has dawned on the Soviet leadership that it is not functioning properly. Is it for us in Ethiopia to continue to work and operate for another seventy or eighty years and then discover that the system does not work and dismantle it again? This was considered heretical and anti-Soviet. I was not anti-Soviet, but the system simply did not work. And when a system does not work, it is high time for a country which is experimenting with that system to try to correct it.
>
> In Ethiopia, even the creation of economic benefits—if the system were successful, and it isn't—[would] not outweigh the political conditions, the freedom and independence that the Soviet system really lacks.

In Wolde's opinion, the one major stumbling block to reform in systems of the Soviet type is that any change that fundamentally contradicts ideology would indicate that the party itself was wrong. This would be tantamount to questioning the legitimacy of the system as a whole. Is the answer, therefore, to allow gradual, marginal changes only? The interviewees respond in different ways, beginning with Checinski:

> [To take Gorbachev as an example, his is not really] a deviation from Soviet policy. . . . He is addressing Soviet domestic problems. *Glasnost* is just an addition to that. It is not central to the real problem. The real problem is the Soviet economy. They can't compete against Western technology, etc. So they try to find an answer. It is not a new answer. . . . You have to look at acts not at words. Words in the Soviet Union are nothing. . . . However, the dynamic is such that [Gorbachev] could lose control of East Europe. . . .

Stefan Svirdlev, a former Bulgarian intelligence (DS) officer, asserts that a major change in ideological assumptions is taking place:

[In accordance with ideological precepts,] it has always been pointed out that in the case of a new world war, it would be the end of capitalism. This has changed with Gorbachev, who has said we will live together or die together.

Jan Sejna, on the other hand, states:

When I defected, . . . I [was] asked, "General, do you think communism has changed in the last decade?" And I said, "No, what has changed is the tactics." "You are wrong," [my questioner] said, "communism has changed." "Look," I answered, "I was a member of the Central Committee and first secretary of the party at the Ministry of Defense, and I didn't know that communism has changed. How can you know that?"

Strategic Precepts and Perceptions

The Soviet Union operates globally in accordance with certain strategic precepts. Responses on this issue, however, failed to produce a clear picture. Stanislav Levchenko addresses the aims of Soviet global strategy:

One [strategic goal] is destabilization, [another is] the undermining of the credibility of Western governments, [which can work] because of the lack of [Western] counteraction. The primary interest of the Soviet Union outside the two blocs is to be feared and respected, not to be loved.

Arkady Shevchenko, introduces certain caveats:

There [is not] really a strategic plan, that is prepared and proclaimed by the Central Committee, [although we may refer to] a global strategy which exists in their minds. However, I can tell you that when there is a change of administration involving a change in the party, there can be quite a division over strategy. But, in general, I would say there is more consistency in the strategy process in the Soviet Union.

It is possible to discuss the ultimate objectives of the majority [of CPSU leaders]. Gorbachev now will decide about long-range strategy for the next twenty years, meaning the way that they will reconcile global objectives with domestic objectives. . . . [TASS cited one of his statements] which indicated his global strategy and his view of the dialectic. He mentioned that we have different systems, and he specifically makes references about "who will win," and how "we have our philosophy and you have your philosophy," and so on. But he goes on to mention that "we have time, we should not be in a hurry". . . . [T]here is also a shift in Gorbachev's opinion about the correlation of forces . . . back to the idea that the global correlation of forces will depend upon the performance of the Soviet Union . . . i.e., that the future of the Soviet system depends on how they resolve the domestic situation, and the social and economic problems.

Shevchenko goes on to say:

> [Soviet leaders] would like to split the Europeans and the United States. They
> . . . test the strength of the governments. They would like to make friends
> and [at the same time to undertake] provocative [operations] . . . even the
> use of terrorism, even directly [but] carefully so it can't be "located." But Gor-
> bachev himself . . . [does not] want to have things like that. . . . A lot of these
> terrorist actions don't bring [a favorable] result at all . . . and they can actu-
> ally be against the interest of the Soviet Union.

Galina Orionova speaks of the concept of détente as it was viewed at her
institute:

> As far as the institute was, and I'm sure still is, concerned, they are pro-détente
> because it is their bread and butter. That is why no one thought about détente
> in very specific terms but rather vaguely and abstractly as [a] possibility of
> a broader improvement in Soviet-American relations. . . . They looked at it
> as some sort of process which could be expanded and explored.

Already Shevchenko points out that, even in a closed society, policy does
not have to be monolithic:

> The people who implement [policy] become prisoners of a certain philosophy
> and outlook, of certain views. And there have always been quite a lot of
> factions and quite a lot of different attitudes.

For a non-Soviet communist approach, Juan Benemelis describes how
Africa fits into the general strategy, as viewed by the Cubans:

> They did not name specific countries during training; they listed the condi-
> tions to look for. We analyzed country by country. The Cubans emphasized
> factors which the Soviet Union did not. The Soviet Union was [much] too
> influenced by the views of European communist parties concerning Africa in
> the 1960s. Their policies always ran through communist organizations.
> Castro and the Chinese were using [other] organizations for their purposes.
>   The Cubans stressed that if there is a dedicated group, there is a founda-
> tion for revolution and for a future socialist state. It was definitely a vanguard
> philosophy. The Cubans did not understand their own revolution. They
> thought it was an agrarian revolution, which was not true. This pattern was
> transplanted to Africa. Because it was a rural continent, it was ideal for us.
> We were aware from the beginning of the existence of all these political
> organizations in Africa. We thought we could transform them into Marxists.
> . . . You had to beat the U.S. with the instrument of violence wherever and
> whenever possible; and Africa was a good place, underestimated by the
> American political establishment.

Shifting Priorities of Soviet Foreign Policy

Soviet historians and analysts have always paid particular attention to the concept of periodicity in Soviet history—a concept that plays a significant role in Marxist-Leninist ideology. Stanislav Levchenko addresses this question, adding, however, the element of personality, which plays only a minor role in Marxism:

> Basic Soviet policies can change, but it depends on what period of . . . Soviet history we are talking about, and who is in charge: Khrushchev [and his policy of "peaceful coexistence"], Brezhnev and détente, Andropov, Chernenko (who hardly had time to establish himself in office), or Gorbachev.

To 1945—Preparing for the Postwar World

During the latter stages of World War II, Soviet leaders were preparing for a postwar world which would be dominated by a new set of antagonists. Peter Deriabin notes when Soviet policy shifted:

> I arrived at the [SMERSH] school in April of 1944. Those who knew German continued to study it and a few studied English, but there was not too much interest in English at that time. Within two or three weeks this changed however; it was then announced that Germany was essentially defeated and that we had to turn our attention to the Western countries: Great Britain and the U.S. The war lasted another year and the Germans were still the enemy, but lectures were given about the imperialist forces and how Europe and the USSR would get along after the war. Even in the SMERSH school there was a feeling that the world would be peaceful after the war, and the USSR, Britain and the U.S. would organize trade and things like that. France was not mentioned much because it was a defeated country.
>
> By late 1944 or early 1945, the theme of our political training changed. The line became that the imperialist forces still wanted to destroy the Soviet Union and that we had to be prepared. We had to ensure that revolution occurred in the East European countries so that friendly regimes were established there. Our main task was to root out the bourgeois elements in East Europe, Western Ukraine, Byelorussia, Latvia, Lithuania, Estonia (and even Finland was included at that time). The goal was to have the proletariat-peasant working class gain power so that there would be a union of friendly states surrounding the Soviet Union.

This task was left to the members of Deriabin's SMERSH class who did not stay in Moscow for further, more specialized, training. He explains their methods:

> They went to existing partisan units to organize the leadership and enroll the right kind of Poles, Czechs, etc. These groups were already operating;

allegedly they had mushroomed out of the local population, but the task of SMERSH was to ensure the right kind of leadership was in place to fight for the "rebirth" of a new Poland, Czechoslovakia, etc.

Stalin's Last Years

The period from 1945 to 1953, Stalin's last years, witnessed the creation of a Soviet satellite region in East Europe, and, at least initially, the rise of powerful communist parties in Western Europe. Voslensky describes the Soviet approach to the new situation:

> In . . . France and Italy, there were representatives of the *Sovinformburo*. . . . [They were the equivalent] of *Novosti* [personnel now]. We sent all our articles to them by telex, and they tried to put them in their press. Those were cold war times and the main enemy, then as today, was American imperialism. The designation of the USA as the main adversary is constant. This started in 1947 after the declaration of the Truman Doctrine. Before that the main adversary had been Germany and fascism. It [was] stated quite clearly in the framework of Cominform. [Andrey] Zhdanov said it, as did [Mikhail] Sluslov.

Deriabin, from the viewpoint of an operative of the Soviet intelligence service, stresses that, despite the new focus of Soviet policy, Germany still was treated as a special case, extending even to the Soviet zone of occupation:

> I joined the Austro-German Department [of Soviet Security] in 1952 and in the following years the feeling was that in spite of the fact that we had thousands of agents in East Germany and reliable leadership—although Stalin did not like [Walter] Ulbricht for some reason—Germany was still our . . . enemy. [Our] policy was to recruit Germans and use them for our ends. There was no talk of independence or of reconciliation with West Germany.

However, Deriabin intimates that an alternative option for underground operations in Central Europe was also being prepared:

> In 1952 an important order went into effect preparing a deep cover apparatus in Germany and Austria. The possibility of the end of the Soviet occupation must have been considered and orders were issued to develop a large network of agents to leave in place if Soviet forces would ever leave. The MGB[20] worked very hard to implement this order. East German nationals were recruited and given the proper documentation, and [relocated] to Austria. Austrians were put into Berlin to acquire the Berlin accent, and [were] then to be sent to West Germany as Soviet agents. Some would arrive illegally in West Germany and claim to be from Dresden. Because Dresden was damaged

---

[20] MGB, Soviet Ministry of State Security (subsequently named KGB).

so heavily in the war, the records were destroyed and there was no way to check the background of our agents.

Another aspect of this operation was the recruitment of prisoners of war (POWs) that had not yet been repatriated. Many of them were recruited, but with the knowledge that attrition would be very high. Thirty percent would turn themselves in, another thirty percent would be discovered; but even if only ten percent were successful, that would be enough to be effective. Even the POWs who did not keep [in] contact after going to the West had still signed a paper pledging to cooperate with Soviet authorities.

Gregory integrates the Middle East into the picture of Soviet strategy during Stalin's last years:

In 1947, we were informed that Stalin was thinking carefully about the oil regions in the Middle East, including Iran. We felt that if we could establish strong influence in Iran, we could use that as a foothold in the region. At the same time, however, Stalin was claiming the Bosphorus, the Dardanelles, Kars, Ardahan . . . [the latter two are provinces in Turkey ceded by Lenin].

We had a plan: destroy the [existing] society and replace it with one we liked and through this we would get control of the oil. It was an attempt to gain control of a resource that would give us power against the West. This was a long-term strategy, [particularly after we broke] relations with Israel [in 1953] and were on better terms with the Arab countries. . . .

We knew that Mossadeq was ousted with American aid. Our response to the American success was to try harder to win a victory somewhere else; we could not surrender the field because that would have been a sign of weakness.

The Initial Khrushchev Period

Two interviewees express the view that, if Soviet objectives during the Cuban missile crisis are understood adequately, the outcome was not an unmitigated Soviet defeat. Rurarz states:

Mostly, at first, the reaction was that the USSR had lost that conflict. Later, however, when I started to study certain things, I had the impression that it was the United States that had lost, removing Jupiter and Thor missiles from Turkey, [and other places]. Besides, the United States actually recognized the existence of a Soviet sphere of influence in the Caribbean. I was much less interested in Cuba than I was in the scrapping of those [U.S.] missiles which could hit Soviet territory. Of course, they were replaced by submarine-launched ballistic missiles and the Pershings, but their importance was not exactly the same. Many of us felt extremely uneasy when we realized that it was actually the United States which had lost. But that impression was shared only by the people in the [Polish] embassy [in Washington, D.C.] who had some understanding of military affairs; the rest continued to believe that it was a Soviet defeat.

Vladimir Kostov sees events in a similar light. He accepts, to some extent, as does Shevchenko, the party claim that Khrushchev achieved his political goal—ensuring that Castro would remain in power:

I have never underestimated this [American] guarantee [to Cuba]. I remember very well how much importance it had. Actually, the humiliation was softened very much by the Americans, because it was so soon after the Bay of Pigs. . . . If you look at the whole episode overall, in a historical perspective, I don't think it was such a big defeat for Khrushchev. Rather, it was a victory, because what has come of the Soviet commitment no to deploy missiles with nuclear warheads in Cuba? Nothing. They have nuclear-powered subs which don't need refueling, and it's not necessary for the Soviet navy to come to Cuba to play tennis. Essentially, the strategic value of the Cuban deal has almost entirely lost its significance because of the changes in technology. What has remained is an American commitment.

The Change in Soviet Strategic Posture

The strategic posture of the Soviet Union in the 1960s began to change. Jan Sejna explains:

[Boris] Ponomarev . . . came to Prague and Warsaw in 1965 . . . [after] . . . Soviet strategy [changed] in 1963–1965 from defense to offense not just [in] military terms, but the Soviet Union turned completely to strategic initiative. The idea that capitalism is lost forever fits with the strategic initiative. All these things led to an increase in training because in the beginning, as Marxism says, revolution must go from the masses down and from the street up.

I think Khrushchev in the beginning, tried to present [a] major deception, the peaceful coexistence policy, a major strategic deception stating that he is different and communism is different. . . . Later on, in the Brezhnev years, they said it was not realistic because capitalism and imperialism [remained unchanged, whether the USSR changed its] image or not. . . . This is why [the post-Khrushchev Soviet leaders] decided to put through the so-called strategic initiative, sabotage and other things, while Khrushchev went more, for example in 1959 and 1960, for espionage [and] for stealing as much technology as possible.

Brezhnev decided that Khrushchev's initial approach was ineffective. Sejna says that the [Czechoslovak] Defense Council approved the decision to proceed more aggressively in the active measures department. Sejna also notes the importance of local wars:

Khrushchev said that . . . [an] ideal policy would be if behind every diplomat stood a strong marshal. Brezhnev turned that around, believing that what was important was that behind every marshal stood a diplomat. [A significant] use of military power was to support local wars. Until 1963, they did not accept the [concept] of local wars, whereas after that they did.

It was only beginning to work for them in Vietnam, so the doctrine had to adjust. In a sense, the change—from Khrushchev's emphasis on diplomats or deception first and more caution with the military, to Brezhnev's stress on military power ahead of diplomacy—seems to reflect a change in the Soviet view of the correlation of forces. By the end of the 1970s, the Soviets felt that they could be more intimidating than at the end of the 1950s.

. . . [T]he Kremlin came to the conclusion that local wars need not escalate to nuclear war. For example, they decided that it might be possible to occupy Austria without triggering global war. Interestingly, they also said [overtly] that the military forces were to play a major role in the struggle for peace and socialism. Not the working class, and not the party, but the military forces.

The Third World became more important as the transition proceeded. Stanislav Levchenko refers to another change in policy:

The most serious change was in the 1960s, when [the Soviet leaders] realized the futility of trying to bring national liberation movements [to power] and, eventually, to have quasi-socialist countries in the Third World. However, they still could influence the newly developed countries and so they put together the "non-capitalist road" definition. This only means that it is somewhere in between capitalism and socialism politically and socially. They found many supporters of this theory . . . particularly in the Asian countries. This increased the social and political layers the Soviet Union had to provide support for. That was a dramatic change, because they had given up hope in establishing quasi-socialist regimes.

The Soviet leaders became more pragmatic than . . . before. They support regimes which have demonstrated domestic stability and which do not have any other way out than to support the main points of Soviet policy. . . . Soviet support is granted not out of political interest, but out of military or paramilitary interest. Countries whose governments support the Soviet Union politically are less valuable than those with strong military capabilities. If such a country is militarily strong, it can create a threat to neighboring countries. Then the Soviet Union can use this country for political or even military blackmail. Since 1960, the Soviet Union almost totally ceased to provide non-military aid to Third World countries. Before this they provided aid with education. . . . Since the 1960s, the Soviet position has become quite cynical and pragmatic. It does not play games, such as the signing of hundreds of millions of dollars for the construction of the Aswan dam, or other types of agricultural or economic aid.

Levchencko continues to describe the object of Soviet Third World policy as helping anti-Western groups to seize, consolidate, and stay in power, with further Soviet assistance thereafter. Soviet policy in general is to provide military aid to such entities—for example, in Ethiopia. Gregory provides additional information on these aspects of Soviet policy:

> In the early 1960s, Khrushchev scaled down Soviet spending on Africa. In 1958–1960, the Soviet government spent billions in pure grants—gift money that did not produce results. The heads of African states were pleased to get this money with no obligations, of course. Soviet policy changed and began to demand results. State relations came first. They wanted to limit Western influence and persuade the African states that socialism was more suitable for them. The pledge to create strong military forces was very important; we told them that, in time, they could fight neo-imperialism with our help. Liberation movements were present in Rhodesia, Mozambique, Angola, Namibia and South Africa. We sent arms to Tanzania that were provided expressly for the liberation movements in southern Africa. They were light arms for guerrillas, not tanks of course. The Soviets spent a lot of money on these arms. The goal was to have Africa in Soviet hands from Cairo to Mozambique. But Kenya was a difficult country. Soviet influence in Egypt, Sudan and Uganda was strong. Zambia was a mixed case. We tried to increase our influence but the Chinese made it difficult. They built the railway from Lusaka to Dar es Salaam. One of my tasks was to see how many Chinese were involved and I visited many of the East African countries by car for this purpose.

According to Gregory, in the 1960s Soviet diplomats and intelligence officers portrayed the PRC to their Western contacts as being purportedly a more immediate adversary of the Soviet Union than was the U.S.

> *Gregory:* One of my tasks was to give [the Americans] the official [Soviet] line: that we were two great countries and the Chinese were insulting us and trying to humiliate us, that in spite of the problems in U.S.-Soviet relations it would be better to work together because the main enemy was the PRC. I would refer to U.S.-Soviet ties in World War II, the PRC's nuclear program, Chinese nationalism, etc. I tried to persuade [Americans] that the PRC was becoming a more important opponent. Another issue I raised was the amount of money sent to the PRC from expatriates in Indonesia, the U.S., and so on.

> *Q:* What was the response from the Americans?

> *Gregory:* They did not dismiss my arguments as nonsense because they saw how many Chinese were in Tanganyika and Zanzibar. They never admitted that they saw the PRC as a real threat but I fulfilled my task of getting the Soviet view to them.

Voslensky details Khrushchev's policies toward the Third World as attributable to Khrushchev's recognition that the region constituted an important asset to the West. Therefore, numerous institutes and front groups were established during this time, and the development of Soviet ties with selected Third World countries continued in Brezhnev's era. Voslensky goes on to say:

It was a process of decolonization. It was clear [what] the Soviet reaction should be, and indeed was: . . . There was more interest in development in the Third World; an attempt to play an important part in this development began, it is clear. Lumumba University was created [in the late 1950s], and the institutes [of the Soviet Academy of Sciences were founded].

After Brezhnev took power, Yuri Andropov, former Soviet ambassador to Hungary (when the Red Army suppressed the Hungarian revolution), became head of the KGB. This development had an important impact on the way in which "national liberation movements" were handled. According to Stiller, some changes had been made even before Andropov officially became the KGB chief:

I think it's significant that a major shake-up occurred in the KGB at that time. I don't know whether it was caused by Andropov coming, or by Nosenko's defection; I do think it was much broader than just the defection. I still hold the view that Andropov took effective control of the KGB in 1965 or so, and that's when the changes started to occur. . . . I think Andropov and the KGB were put in charge of overhauling the whole system, gearing it up to handle, in a clandestine way, the communication needs of any country in the world that had a potential national liberation movement, group, or personality.

There are two important things that happen in this period. First [was] the great expansion in language programs. Second [was] the emergence of ID [personnel] in Soviet Embassies. In view of Andropov's background in partisan work, this all fits together.

Détente

With Brezhnev's increasing control of the centers of Soviet power, the West increasingly came to use the elusive term détente. Détente triggered SALT I and II, but did not extend to Latin America and other areas of regional conflict. Hus explains what détente (actually peaceful coexistence in Soviet parlance) meant in Soviet bloc operational terms:

Before 1974, some Eastern bloc diplomats did not look at détente as another phase in the conflict. There was a division over views [regarding] the United States. To some the United States was changing. They forgot about the power struggle and about Lenin. These people were pragmatists. They thought the time of antagonism was over. . . . It was known for sure that détente was the first phase in achieving Soviet supremacy. Before détente the Soviet Union was behind the United States. With détente parity was achieved. Then the Soviet Union began to build up, as the United States declined.

Détente was seen as a useful period of tranquillity before Soviet ascendancy. It was not part of an official doctrine; however it did fit in with what I had learned about the West in Moscow. To the Soviet leadership it appeared as if history was working as Lenin and Marx had predicted. Détente meant that the United States and the Soviet Union were on an equal level, but [one] from which the Soviet Union was growing in strength and the United States was declining. Watergate and the Carter years appeared to prove this.

One must also remember that détente was useful for both sides for other reasons. The United States had been concerned about Vietnam, and the Soviet Union about China and Czechoslovakia.

(In the Soviet encyclopedia, the index entry for détente has a note referring the reader to peaceful coexistence, which was defined in Khrushchev's 1961 CPSU program as, "a specific form of class struggle . . . [which] facilitates the struggle of the peoples of colonial and dependent countries for their liberation—quite different from the Western definition. This definition caused occasional embarrassment for Soviet representatives and was dropped subsequently from the CPSU program.)

Presidents Nixon and Carter worked with Brezhnev on the Strategic Arms Limitation Treaties. According to the accepted American attitude, the SALT process was one of education. Through negotiation, the U.S. would teach the Soviet Union the objective realities of contemporary nuclear parity. However, Soviet strategists apparently viewed the process differently, as illustrated in these remarks by Shevchenko:

> The whole SALT process was in itself, to a certain degree, a deception, because SALT I permitted the Soviet Union to go ahead in many ways without actually violating SALT. Brezhnev was right, but Grechko didn't understand it properly. [Marshal] Grechko didn't realize what they could achieve with that, and they did achieve it, because they succeeded in convincing the United States that . . . all else could be based [on SALT]. In reality it's a fact that, if we assess the whole process throughout the seventies and early eighties, we can come to only one conclusion. . . . In 1972, the Soviet Union was very much behind in practically all weapons systems. . . . By 1982, there was real parity. In '72, there was parity only on paper. And this was a great achievement, through the machinery of SALT. . . .
>
> [I]f we talk about strategic deception, there are two goals of SALT. One, which is tactical, which even placed some limitations on the Soviets, and the other goal is strategic deception. . . . In the 1950s to 1960s, and even in the early '70s, the top Soviet military leadership was dominated by people who never learned about the sophistication of the balance of power and strategic thinking, etc. They still had a very primitive understanding [or arms control]. . . .
>
> But the more sophisticated people saw that [the USSR] also had to have some restraint, to act within some limitations of the balance. But they also saw other things. They saw that they could achieve more or less what they wanted, in the early 1970s. In those areas where they saw the Soviet Union was behind the United States, particularly in submarines and in sub-based missiles, SALT didn't have any constraints.

Anatoly Fedoseyev suggests that neither SALT I nor SALT II was perceived by the Soviet military and scientific community as having imposed serious limitations on the military buildup:

> I was not aware of [real] limitations [on the Soviet military buildup] at that time. And to the best of my understanding all colleagues of mine, without exception, never felt any limitations of this kind which they proposed or developed. SALT I and SALT II are agreements between a wolf and a sheep. The stupid sheep is always at fault. . . . SALT I had no effect on our business. . . . Not only did we continue to develop the ABM, but . . . research on other horizons, such as lasers and antisatellite weapons, continued.

In the 1970s, the Third World became a target of priority for Soviet planners. Soviet objectives were to be achieved, if possible, through the utilization of surrogates, rather than by means of direct Soviet intervention. Benemelis discusses the role of one of these surrogates in Cuba:

> There was a turning point for Cuban foreign policy in 1972. Cuban policy changed from a strategic point of view to a geostrategic view, even though Cuba [itself] has no inherent geostrategic interests. Cuba assumed the Soviet geostrategic principles. Our foreign policy had three dimensions: Cuba was involved in East-West issues, it was an underdeveloped country because of its location and population (North-South issues), and because of its strange relationship to the USSR (not a member of the Warsaw Pact), Cuba is non-aligned. One will not find this fluidity in any other Soviet bloc country. It is an asset which Cuba has and the Soviet Union uses.
>
> That is why Castro moved from one dimension to another. It is not a change in outlook; he is simply taking advantage of Cuba's position to move from a North-South issue, such as the debt, to a Third World problem, such as nonalignment, to an East-West issue. It is a tactical change which the Soviet Union also uses. Castro is using the debt to show Gorbachev that he can work with North-South problems. Gorbachev cannot do that, but Castro can.
>
> Why is 1972 a turning point? This was when the Cuban military entered the foreign arena. . . . There were many factors: including Castro's position, Cuba's position, what was going on inside Cuba, Castro's view of the USSR, and what was going on in the U.S. It was very complex. Both sides benefited from the change. Castro knew he had to do it to repay the Soviet Union, to maintain his leverage, and to placate his allies in the Soviet government. He was convinced that the USSR would surpass the U.S. strategically, clearly, and forever. That was his second mistake. His first mistake was believing Khrushchev's claims that the USSR had reached parity with the U.S. He swallowed the Soviet view twice. He saw how the Soviet assistance had transformed the Cuban army in only two years from a [mass] apparatus to a highly trained and specialized organization. This was finished by 1972. It had started in 1968.

Eden Pastora Gomez, a former commander of Sandinista forces in Nicaragua, stresses the shift of Cuban operations in the 1970s from Latin America to the African continent, as a result of a reevaluation of strategic priorities:

> It is well known that the Cubans helped the Sandinista front, the FSLN, but in '69 there came a change in policy when . . . political thinkers . . . decided that revolution wasn't possible in Latin America, and they started to advise . . . that [Cuba] should look to the African continent and to go to Africa and promote revolution there. At that point, in 1969 and 1970, Cuba suspended its training camps and its economic assistance to the revolutionaries in Latin America and [instead of armed revolutionary struggle, Cuba] started a *diplomatic* offensive in Latin America.
>
> [As a result], between that period and 1977, they achieved diplomatic advances in Latin America, while they [also carried out military operations in] Africa.

Military Contingency Planning: Warsaw Pact/NATO

Testimony concerning Soviet military contingency plans, although dating back to previous periods, may be still of more than historic interest. Two of the witnesses—Gen. Jan Sejna (Czechoslovakia) and Zdzislaw Rurarz (Poland)—had access to some of the Warsaw Pact plans. The plans make certain revealing assumptions concerning Western forces. Soviet strategic planners concern themselves not only with weapons and technology, but also with morale, determination and manpower, according to Rurarz:

> It is believed [by Warsaw Pact leaders] that the firepower of NATO would be [significantly] reduced because of the [variety of] munitions systems, [and because] the soldiers are undertrained. The *Bundeswehr,* unlike American [military forces], is trained only locally, where there is not enough room to learn to fight effectively. . . . Officially, of course, the [Polish] government exaggerates NATO's plans, just to intimidate the people and to justify the war effort. But I've seen the training manuals of the Western armies, and I was surprised to see how much spare time the soldier has. Polish soldiers are kept busy from five in the morning to eleven [at night], with no time even to write a letter! I think the same is true of the Soviets. Those [soldiers] are in a system that tries to turn them into animals who would kill their own parents.

Rurarz goes on to say that the Warsaw Pact forces could engage the first line of NATO defenses with as little as three-and-a-half-hours warning, using the Third Guards Shock Army in the Magdeburg area of East Germany. The absence of nuclear weapons in the arsenal of the *Bundeswehr* makes the possibility of German surrender to Soviet forces in the event of slow American retaliation to a surgical nuclear strike appear realistic to the pact leaders. The likelihood that the Germans could function as an army with the threat of unanswerable nuclear annihilation hanging over their heads is slim, at best. Given all these factors, Rurarz believes that the Soviet leaders must have been tempted to exploit their military advantages on the battlefield; however:

> Maybe they have information that leads them to believe they can "Finlandize" West Germany, or that they can gain Europe or the Persian Gulf without a war.

Such plans, according to Rurarz, are not just sitting on a shelf to be perused at leisure by Polish and other pact generals. They would take only hours to initiate.

On the other hand, the events in Poland in 1981 pointed to a deficiency in Soviet strategy, and briefly left the Warsaw Pact forces weakened, had there been an offensive against NATO:

> [I]t was believed [in Polish military intelligence] that by 1981 the Soviets would complete the preparatory stage for a possible blitzkrieg in Europe following the "Shield '81" maneuvers. Then came the turmoil in Poland which wrecked the opportunity. . . . The Soviets could possibly have launched their *blitzkrieg* without the active participation of the Polish army, but to do so they would have [had] to bring more of their own divisions closer to East Germany, which would not [have] escape[d] the attention of the West. . . . [T]he fifteen Polish divisions are of critical importance for the Soviet blitzkrieg against NATO.

Sejna points to caveats that were reflected in statements by Soviet planners:

> [E]ven in Marshal Grechko's 1975 book, there is a hint that the war may not be terminated within a week, although the outcome will be decided by then. . . . The most crucial period is the beginning of the war; . . . it is then that the whole thing will be decided. . . . Of course, he mentions that we must do everything not to have a nuclear war, that we must therefore have weapons that will replace nuclear weapons in effectiveness. That is a call for biological and chemical weapons.

Sejna believes, moreover, that some shifts toward less sanguine expectations in Soviet military thought could be detected toward the end of the 1970s.

It is an open question to what extent such concepts, perceptions, and contingency plans have been overtaken by new politico-military thinking in the USSR during the last few years; this question may not be answered conclusively for some time.

Epilogue

I t may be argued that a less opportune moment for oral history work
on the Soviet Union would be difficult to find than the present time,
when obsolescence seems to be threatening all of the phenomena that
Sovietologists have come to view as constants. The study of the USSR has
been beset always by the methodological problems and risks that are attendant on analysis of closed societies. These difficulties have intensified during
the last few years, not only because of the attempted changes in the structure
of the Soviet polity and society, but, paradoxically, also as a result of the
flood of Soviet media revelations that often are mutually contradictory and
add to, rather than detract from, the problems of deciphering the meaning of
Soviet developments.

However, current efforts at innovation have yet to make their impact, let
alone become irreversible, and strenuous resistance by the Soviet *apparat* to
any substantive modification demonstrates the glacial nature of systemic
change. This book attempts to expand the repository of data available to the
Sovietological community, some of which may be primarily of historical interest, but most of which remain relevant for analysts of the contemporary
Soviet scene. To go beyond that by trying to project the implications of such
data for the future of the Soviet system leaves one vulnerable to Adam
Michnik's harsh dictum that such attempts are "a job for a prophet or a
swindler."

Persons Mentioned

Abakumov, Victor S. Former Soviet minister of state security; deceased.

Adzhubey, Aleksei I. Khrushchev's son-in-law; Chief editor of *Izvestia,* 1959–1964; removed from the Central Committee and all other official positions after Khrushchev's fall in 1964.

Agayants, Ivan I. Former general of the KGB; former head of the Disinformation Service; deceased.

Aleksandrov-Agentov, Andrei M. Assistant to CC CPSU General Secretary L.I. Brezhnev.

Allende, Salvador. Former president of Chile, overthrown by General Augusto Pinochet; deceased.

Alves, Nito. Leader of a Soviet-backed coup against the Neto government in Angola.

Aman, M. Former Ethiopian general; executed in 1977.

Andropov, Yury V. Former general secretary, CC CPSU; chairman, USSR Committee for State Security (KGB); deceased.

Arbatov, Georgy A. Director of the Soviet Institute for the Study of the USA and Canada; member of the CC CPSU; member of the Soviet Committee for the Defense of Peace.

Avakov, A. Member of the Soviet Institute of World Economics and International Relations [IMEiMO].

Bajanov, Boris. Stalin's former secretary; defected in January 1928; deceased.

Beria, Lavrenty P. Former member of the Politburo of the CPSU; chief of the Soviet Security Services; minister of the Interior; Marshal of the USSR; executed after Stalin's death.

Bierut, Boleslaw. Former president of Poland; first secretary of the Polish Communist Party; Polish prime minister; deceased.

Bil'ak, Vasil. Former secretary of the CC of the Communist Party of Czechoslovakia (KSC); former Politburo member.

Blatov, Anatoli I. Former assistant to CC CPSU General Secretary L.I. Brezhnev.

Borge, Tomas. Member of the National Directorate of the FSLN (Sandinista National Liberation Front); minister of the Interior, Nicaragua.

Bovin, Alexander Ye. Former member of the Central Auditing Commission of the CC CPSU.

Brezhnev, Leonid I. Former general secretary of the CC CPSU; former chairman of the Presidium of the Supreme Soviet; marshal of the Soviet Union; deceased.

Brutents, Karen N. Deputy chief of the CC CPSU International Department.

Bukharin, Nikolay I. Bolshevik leader, close to Lenin; executed during the purges of the 1930s.

Bulganin, Nikolay A. Former chairman, USSR Council of Ministers (CoM); former member of the Politburo of the CC CPSU; former Soviet minister of defense; former marshal of the USSR.

Castro, Raul. Cuban Minister of Defense; brother of Fidel.

Ceaucescu, Nicole. Current leader of Romania.

Cepicka, Alexej. Former Czechoslovak minister of defense; son-in-law of Klement Gottwald.

Cerna, Lenin. Member of the Prolonged Popular War faction of the Nicaraguan Sandinistas; described by Bolaños-Hunter as liaison between the KGB and DGI.

Chebrikov, Viktor M. Member of the Politburo of the CC CPSU; former chairman of the Committee for State Security; secretary of the CPSU; chairman of the CC CPSU Legal Commission.

Chernayev, Anatoly S. Personal assistant to Gorbachev and head of his private chancery; former deputy chief of the International Department, CC CPSU.

Chernenko, Konstantin U. Former general secretary of the CC CPSU; former chief of the General Department of the CC CPSU; deceased.

Chervenkov, Vulko. Former leader of the Bulgarian Communist Party; symbol of Stalinism; purged by Todor Zhivkov, the current Bulgarian leader.

Chervonenko, Stepan V. Member of the CC CPSU; former chief of the Cadres Abroad Department; former ambassador to Prague; catalyst of the 1968 Warsaw Pact invasion of Czechoslovakia.

Chicherin, Georgy V. A member of a distinguished aristocratic Russian family, originally a Menshevik; former peoples commissar for foreign affairs under Lenin and during the initial period of Stalin's rule; deceased.

Chnoupek, Bohuslav. Member of the CC, Communist Party of Czechoslovakia; former Czechoslovak minister of foreign affairs.

Daniloff, Nicholas. American journalist; arrested in Moscow in August of 1986; released without a trial in September of the same year.

Dobrynin, Anatoly F. Former Soviet ambassador in Washington, D.C.: former chief of the International Department CC CPSU; now in the foreign policy *apparat* of the USSR.

Dubcek, Alexander. Former first secretary of the Czechoslovak Communist Party (KSC); replaced by Gustav Husak in April, 1969 and purged from the party.

Falin, Valentin M. Member of the CC CPSU; chairman of the International Department; former chairman of the Novosti Press Agency.

Fierlinger, Zdenek. Former Czechoslovak ambassador to Moscow; former Social Democratic Leader; later joined the KSC; deceased.

Fojtik, Jan. Member of the Presidium of the KSC; chairman of the new Ideological Commission, CC KSC; deputy of the Chamber of Nations of the Czechoslovak Federal Assembly.

Gafurov, Bobodzhan G. Former first secretary of the CC of the Tadzkikistan CP; former director of the Institute of Oriental Studies.

Gierek, Edward. Former leader of the Polish Communist Party (PZPR); his fall in 1980 was followed by the emergence of the Solidarity movement.

Gomulka, Wladyslaw. Former general secretary of the PZPR; deceased.

Gorbachev, Mikhail. Current general secretary of the CC CPSU; chairman of the Presidium of the Supreme Soviet; chairman of the State Defense Council and commander-in-chief.

Gorshkov, Sergey G. Former USSR first deputy minister of defense and commander-in-chief, USSR naval forces; member of the CC CPSU.

Grechko, Andrey A. Former Soviet minister of defense; former member of the Politburo; deceased.

Grechko, Georgy M. Deputy chairman of the Soviet Committee for the Defense of Peace.

Grishin, Viktor V. Former member of the Politburo of the CC CPSU; former Moscow party chief.

Gromyko, Andrey A. Former member of the Politburo, CC CPSU; former chairman of the Presidium of the Supreme Soviet; former Soviet minister of foreign affairs.

Gromyko, Anatoly A. Son of Andrey A. Gromyko; director of the African Institute, Soviet Academy of Sciences.

Habash, George. Head of the Popular Front for the Liberation of Palestine.

Hall, Gus. Chairman of the Communist Party of the USA (CP USA).

Hendrych, Jiri. Former secretary of the CC KSC; deceased.

Honecker, Erich. Current leader of the ruling Communist Party (SED) in the German Democratic Republic.

Husak, Gustav. Former general secretary of the CC KSC; currently president of Czechoslovakia.

Inozemtsev, Nikolai N. Former director of IMEiMO; member of the Soviet Academy of Sciences; chairman of the Scientific Research Council on Peace and Disarmament.

Ismail, Abdul Fatah. First secretary of the ruling party of South Yemen.

Israelyan, Viktor L. Former Soviet U.S. representative; member of the Kollegium of the Soviet Ministry of Foreign Affairs.

Jablonski, Henryk. Former chairman of the Polish Council of State; former minister of higher education.

Jankovcova, Ludmila. Former minister of the Czechoslovak government; responsible for consumer goods during the 1950s and 1960s.

Jaroszewicz, Alfred. Former Polish premier; former Politburo member.

Jaruzelski, Wojciech. General secretary of the Polish United Workers Party (PUWP/PZPR); general of the Polish armed forces; chairman of the Polish Defense Council.

Kaganovich, Lazar M. Former first deputy chairman, USSR CoM; former member of the Politburo, CC CPSU; removed from the CPSU in 1957.

Kania, Stanislaw. Briefly leader of the Polish Communist Party (PZPR); replaced by Gen. Wojciech Jaruzelski.

Khrushchev, Nikita S. Former first secretary of the CC CPSU; former chairman, Soviet Council of Ministers; deceased.

Kirilenko, Andrey P. Former secretary of the CC CPSU; former member of the Politburo.

Kisiliev, Tikhon Y. Former candidate member of the Politburo of the CC CPSU; former first secretary of the Byelorussian Communist Party.

Kliszko, Zenon. Chief of Cadres Department of the Polish United Workers Party; one-time supporter of Gomulka.

Koldunov, Aleksandr I. Former Soviet commander of PVO (anti-air defense forces); marshal of the Soviet Union.

Komplektov, Viktor G. Member of the Central Auditing Commission, CC CPSU; deputy minister of foreign affairs.

Korniyenko, Georgy M. Soviet first deputy minister of foreign affairs.

Kosygin, Aleksey N. Former chairman of the USSR CoM; former member of the Politburo, CC CPSU; deceased.

Kovalenko, Ivan I. Former deputy chief of the International Deparment, CC CPSU.

Krivitsky, Walter. Former senior Soviet intelligence officer; defected to the West in 1937; deceased.

Kruglov, Sergey N. Former head of MVD; played a role in the arrest of Lavrenty Beria in 1953; deceased.

Kulikov, Viktor G. Former commander-in-chief, Warsaw Pact forces; member of CC CPSU; marshal of the Soviet Union.

Kunaev, Dinmukhamed A. Former first secretary of CC, Kazakh CP; former member of Politburo, CC CPSU.

Kuznetsov Aleksey A. Former secretary of the CC CPSU; contested control of Soviet security forces with Beria; shot during the purge of the Leningrad party apparatus.

Ligachev, Yegor K. Member of the Politburo and secretary of the CC CPSU; chairman of the Agriculture Commission of the CC.

Lin Piao. Former minister of defense of the People's Republic of China; member of the Standing Commission of the Politburo; deceased.

Litvinov, Viktor A. Deputy chairman of the State Commission for Foreign Economic Relations.

Lomsky, Bohumir. Former Czechoslovak defense minister.

Macek, Jaroslav. Member of the secretariat of the Czechoslovak general secretary; member of the Central Committee of the Communist Party of Czechoslovakia, KSC.

Malenkov, Georgy M. Former chairman, USSR Council of Ministers; briefly first party secretary of the CC CPSU; Politburo member; deceased.

Malik, Yakov A. Former Soviet deputy minister of foreign affairs; former permanent representative to the U.N.

Malinovsky, Rodion Y. Former marshal of the Soviet Union; USSR minister of defense; commander-in-chief, Far East Troops; deceased.

Mariam, Mengistu H. Leader of the Ethiopian armed forces; current leader of Ethiopia.

Medvedev, Vadim A. Member of the Politburo, and secretary, CC CPSU; chairman of the Ideological Commission, CC CPSU.

Merkulov, Vsevolod N. Former head of NKGB; former Soviet minister of state control; shot in 1953.

Mikoyan, Anstas I. Former chairman of the Presidium of the USSR Supreme Soviet and Politburo member; deceased.

Mirsky, Georgy. Senior analyst at the Institute of World Economics and International Relations (IMEiMO) of the USSR Academy of Sciences.

Moczar, Mieczyslaw. Former Polish minister of internal affairs; former member of the Politburo, PUWP; former leader of the Partisans (veterans of the Polish Communist Party's wartime military organization).

Molotov, Vyacheslav M. Stalin's foreign minister; former chairman of the Presidium of the USSR Council of Ministers; former Politburo member; one of the architects of the Stalin-Hitler Pact of August 1939; deceased.

Neto, Angostinho. Leader of Angola's ruling party (MPLA).

Nosenko, Igor. A Soviet defector who claimed to have had access to the KGB file on Lee Harvey Oswald.

Novotny, Antonin. Former first secretary of the KSC and president of the Czechoslovak Republic; deceased.

Nowak, Zenon. Former member of the Politburo of the Polish Workers Party; former Polish deputy premier; former head of the Natolin faction.

Ochab, Edward. Former first secretary, CC PUWP; former head of the Polish Council of State.

Ogarkov, Nikolay V. Former Soviet chief of staff; marshal of the Soviet Union; currently commander-in-chief, Western Theater of Operations.

Olszewski, Kazimierz. Former Polish vice premier; former Minister of foreign trade and maritime economy; former Polish ambassador to Moscow.

Panyushkin, Aleksandr S. Former chief of the Department of Cadres Abroad (DCA), CC CPSU; former Soviet ambassador to the PRC.

Panyushkin, Valery P. Deputy chief of the Soviet Ministry of Foreign Trade.

Pineiro Losada, Manuel. Former head of Cuban intelligence; chief of the Americas Department of the Cuban Communist Party's Central Committee.

Podgorny, Nikolay V. Former member of the Politburo; former secretary of the CC CPSU; former chairman of the Presidium of the USSR Supreme Soviet.

Polyanskiy, Dmitriy S. Former member of the Soviet Politburo; former USSR ambassador to Japan.

Ponomarev, Boris N. Former secretary, CC CPSU; former candidate member of Politburo; former chief, International Department.

Popkov, Pyotr S. Former leader, Leningrad CPSU; executed in 1949 for alleged participation in the Leningrad Affair.

Poskrebyshev, Aleksander N. Former chief of Stalin's personal secretariat; deceased.

Potekhin, Ivan. Founder of the Africa Institute (IA) of the USSR Academy of Sciences.

Risquet, Jorge. Member of the Cuban Politburo.

Rodinov, Mikhail I. Former chairman of the RSFSR Council of Ministers; purged in the Leningrad Affair.

Rokossovsky, Konstantin K. Former Polish minister of defense; marshal of the Soviet Union; released from Gulag to become a commander of Soviet forces to repel the German invasion.

Romanov, Grigory V. Former secretary, CC CPSU; former member of the Politburo, CC CPSU; former Leningrad leader of the CPSU.

Rusakov, Konstantin V. Former secretary, CC CPSU; former chief of the Department for Liaison with Communist and Workers' Parties of Socialist Countries, CC CPSU.

Ryzhkov, Nikolay I. Member of the Politburo of the CC CPSU; chairman of the Soviet Council of Ministers.

Savinkin, Nikolay I. Member of the Central Committee; former chief of the Department of Administrative Organs, CC CPSU.

Semyonov, Vladimir S. Former Soviet deputy foreign minister and Soviet ambassador to the Federal Republic of Germany.

Serov, Ivan A. Former chairman of the KGB and former chief of Soviet military intelligence (GRU); deceased.

Shcherbakov, A.S. Former chief of the Main Political Administration of the armed forces; deceased.

Shcherbitsky, Vladimir V. First secretary, CC Ukrainian CP; member of Politburo CC CPSU.

Shevardnadze, Eduard A. Soviet foreign minister and member of the Politburo CPSU.

Siroky, Viliam. Prime minister in pre–1968 Czechoslovakia; deceased.

Smirnov, Leonid V. Former deputy chairman, USSR Council of Ministers; former chairman, USSR Military-Industrial Commission; member CC CPSU.

Solodovnikov, Vasily G. Deputy chairman of the Presidium of the Soviet Committee for Solidarity with Asian and African Countries.

Solomentsev, Mikhail S. Former chairman, Party Control Commission, CC CPSU; former member of the Politburo, CC CPSU.

Spychalski, Marian. Former marshal of the Polish army; former member of the Politburo of the Polish Communist Party; deceased.

Strougal, Lubomir. Former Czechoslovak prime minister and member of the Politburo, KSC; former minister of the interior.

Suslov, Mikhail A. Former member of Soviet Politburo and secretary, CC CPSU; deceased.

Svoboda, Josef. Former chief of the personal secretariat of the Czechoslovak Communist leader, Antonin Novotny; former member of the Central Committee.

Tikhonov, Nikolay A. Former chairman, USSR Council of Ministers; former member, Politburo, CC CPSU.

Trofimenko, Genrikh. Senior analyst of the United States of America and Canada Institute of the USSR Academy of Sciences.

Ulbricht, Walter. Former party chief of East Germany; deceased.

Ustinov, Dmitry F. Former USSR minister of defense; former member, Politburo, CC CPSU; marshal of the Soviet Union; deceased.

Vishinsky, Andrey Ya. Former general prosecutor of the USSR during the 1930s purges; later he became minister of foreign affairs and chief Soviet delegate to the U.N.; deceased.

Vlasik, Nikolay. Soviet general, one of Stalin's chief bodyguards; deceased.

Voroshilov, Klimenty E. Former marshal of the USSR; former member of the Politburo, CC CPSU; chairman of the Presidium of the Supreme Soviet, USSR; deceased.

Vorotnikov, Vitaly I. Member, Politburo, CC CPSU; currently chairman, Presidium, Supreme Soviet, RSFSR; former chairman, RSFSR Council of Ministers.

Voznesensky, Nikolay A. Former Politburo member, executed in 1950 for alleged part in the Leningrad affair.

Yakovlev, Aleksandr N. Member of the Politburo, and secretary, CC CPSU; chairman, International Commission, CC CPSU.

Yakubovsky, Ivan I. Former Soviet marshal and commander-in-chief of the Warsaw Pact forces; deceased.

Yepishev, A.A. Former chief of the Main Political Administration of the Soviet armed forces; deceased.

Yeltsin, Boris. Former candidate member of the Politburo; CC CPSU; former head of the Moscow party *apparat.*

Yugov, Anton. Former Bulgarian prime minister; former minister of the interior.

Zagladin, Vadim V. Member of the CC CPSU; former first deputy chief of the International Department, CC CPSU.

Zamyatin, Leonid M. Former chief, International Information Department, CC CPSU: member, CC CPSU.

Zhdanov, Andrey A. Former member of the Politburo, CC CPSU; former CPSU chief in Leningrad; considered Stalin's heir apparent after World War II; deceased.

Zhivkov, Todor. Former chief of the Bulgarian Communist Party.

Zhukov, Georgy K. Marshal of the Soviet Union and a leader of the Red Army during World War II; former Soviet defense minister; deceased.

Zhurkin, Vitaly V. Deputy director of IUSA; deputy chairman Soviet Committee for the Defense of Peace.

Index

About the Editors

Uri Ra'anan is a University Professor and director of the Institute for the Study of Conflict, Ideology and Policy at Boston University. He is also a fellow of the Russian Research Center at Harvard University. Prior to his arrival at Boston University, he taught at the Fletcher School of Law and Diplomacy at Tufts University; at the Massachusetts Institute of Technology; at Columbia University; and at City University of New York. He has authored, edited, and contributed a score of books, primarily on Soviet Affairs, including *The USSR: Today and Tomorrow*.

Igor Lukes is an associate professor at Boston University's Department of International Relations, concentrating on the Soviet Union, Eastern Europe, and United States/Soviet relations. He is also a fellow of the Russian Research Center at Harvard University. A contributing editor of *Guerrilla Warfare and Counterinsurgency,* Lukes has also published in the areas of Soviet decision making, ideology, and current developments in Eastern Europe.